THE PageMaker® COMPANION

THE PageMaker® COMPANION

PC Version 3.0 Edition

Dow Jones•Irwin
Desktop Publishing Library

Craig Danuloff &
Deke McClelland

Publishing Resources Inc.

Dow Jones-Irwin
Homewood, IL 60430

Library of Congress Cataloging-in-Publication Data

McClelland, Deke, 1962–
The PageMaker companion.

Available also in 3.0 PC ed.; order of author's names reversed on PC ed.
Includes index.
1. Desktop publishing. 2. PageMaker (Computer program) I. Danuloff, Craig, 1963– . II. Title.
Z286.D47M376 1989 686.2'2 88–33550
ISBN 1–55623–189–X

Printed in the United States of America.

3 4 5 6 7 8 9 0 ML 6 5 4 3 2 1 0

The PageMaker Companion

is also available in a Macintosh Version 3.0 Edition

Table of Contents

CHAPTER 2: *Installing PageMaker* (cont.)

CHAPTER 5: *Working in the Publication Window* (cont.)

CHAPTER 6: *Creating a Simple Newsletter* 177

CHAPTER 6: *Creating a Simple Newsletter* (cont.)

CHAPTER 7: *Creating and Adding Text* 233

CHAPTER 8: *Editing Text in PageMaker* 277

CHAPTER 8: *Editing Text in PageMaker* (Cont.)

CHAPTER 9: *Using Style Sheets in PageMaker* 313

CHAPTER 11: *Creating an Intermediate Flyer* (cont.)

CHAPTER 12: *Using Color in PageMaker* 437

CHAPTER 13: *Printing Publications* 453

CHAPTER 13: *Printing Publications* (cont.)

CHAPTER 14: *Creating an Advanced Catalog* 503

Glossary G-1

Index X-1

Another Book?

and how it can help you...

So you've just bought Aldus PageMaker. Or maybe you recently upgraded to version 3.0. You've browsed the Aldus User's Guide, spent some time working in the application, but still don't feel that you are mastering PageMaker as quickly as you could. And now you are trying to decide if a book can help you gain the knowledge and productivity you desire.

There are two kinds of books about PageMaker:

- **Tutorial-based books**. These teach PageMaker by walking you through the creation of a few different kinds of documents. They succeed in providing you with some hands-on experience using PageMaker, but often they lack a broad scope in the intricacies of PageMaker. Once you have gone through the exercises, it is difficult to later find the discussion of a particular topic.

Tutorials can provide absolute beginners with a good introduction to the basic abilities of PageMaker, but it is difficult for these books to provide the range of experience necessary for the intermediate or advanced user. They also are not particularly helpful when you need to solve a problem in your own work, or answer a specific question.

- **Reference-based books**. These books use a traditional approach, presenting chapter-by-chapter explanations of the commands and abilities of PageMaker. At their worst, these book are no more than rehashes of the *Page-Maker User Manual*.

  Reference books are best suited to helping with problem-solving, since their topical break-downs usually make it easy to quickly locate information relevant to any problem. They often suffer, however, from the piecemeal way in which they present information. In practice PageMaker is used dynamically, with any number of commands and features affecting the way in which you work at any specific moment. Reference books are most useful when you want to expand your understanding of one particular aspect of PageMaker at a time.

This book, *The PageMaker Companion*, combines the best of both of these approaches. We provide all of the technical details and conceptual discussions that you need when trying to use and understand a specific PageMaker feature *and* sample projects that tie all the technical details together and help you move from one level of expertise to the next.

The PageMaker Companion includes:

- **Eleven reference chapters**. In these we examine every menu command, dialog box, and feature available in PageMaker. For each, we present the basic technical details *and* offer specific tips, tricks, and techniques that will solve your PageMaker problems and increase your PageMaker productivity. The underlying concepts are explained so you can apply this information to your particular situation.

- **Three hands-on projects**. In these you learn by experience—the creation of a newsletter, a coupon-flyer, and a catalog are chronicled. In the process, we use and discuss virtually every command and feature PageMaker provides. These projects describe both how publications are produced, and why we chose to do them using the methods described. Whether you are a PageMaker beginner, intermediate, or expert, following along with these projects will teach you something new about using PageMaker.

How *you* should use this book

The best way to use this book depends on how well you already know PageMaker and what your specific goals are in using PageMaker. We realize that, in most cases, you will not read this book cover to cover. Instead you will read a chapter or two at a time, or even a few pages at a time, skipping around based on your interests and requirements. Fortunately, this book has been designed for this type of use.

General suggestions

Throughout the book we have purposely repeated information in order to make each discussion and explanation as clear as possible. When a complete reiteration is not possible, cross-references are provided to direct you to additional information. When you need to quickly locate a specific piece of information, use the Table of Contents, Index, chapter and section names, and chapter summaries (provided on the first page of each chapter).

You may or may not want to read this book while working in PageMaker. In general, we recommend that you experiment on-screen when learning new concepts, but read the book while away from the computer when you want to advance your understanding of a particular topic. You may even want to read sample projects while not using your computer—think through the production of the project to compare our methods with those you might have used. By doing this "detail reading" away from the computer, you challenge yourself to understand the concepts and technical details without relying on the visual familiarity of the on-screen environment. Also, this helps you to get past any bad habits or incorrect assumptions that you may have developed. Of course, after you have studied a section of new material, you will want to experiment on-screen with your new knowledge to solidify it.

The most important recommendation we can give concerning the use of this book, or any computer book or manual, is to reread it often. As you progress in your experience and understanding of PageMaker, the point of reference from which you read will change. As you progress, you are able to understand more and more of the details included in our discussions. Comments that meant nothing on a previous reading suddenly make sense, and you learn a faster or easier way to perform some task or discover possibilities that you didn't previously realize. This is how "power users" earn their wings—by slowly accumulating understandings, tips, and tricks.

Even after three years of almost daily use of PageMaker, we learned many features, functions, and tactics while preparing this book. Many were documented in the *PageMaker User Manual*, but although we have read it often, for one reason or another we missed some details on earlier reading. Do not think "I understand that dialog box," and then skip the section covering it. The weakest link in the chain of your knowledge always exists, and once you understand the basics, you need to work on understanding the details.

Finally, do not hesitate to read the *PageMaker User Manual* and *PageMaker Reference*. These manuals are well prepared, very informative, and offer another description of most of the topics presented in this book. Often their discussions are less complete than those that we present, but if you are having trouble understanding a specific topic, a fresh approach may prove helpful.

Tips and Hot Tips

In order to place particular emphasis on items that we thought particularly useful or obscure, throughout the book certain paragraphs are identified as "Tips" or "Hot Tips" by the placement of icons in the margins. The difference between "Tips" and "Hot Tips" has to do primarily with their obscurity. "Tips" are probably common knowledge among more experienced PageMaker users, but unknown to beginners or infrequent users. "Hot Tips" are expert-only knowledge, items that you could miss even with years of PageMaker experience. In fact, many of the "Hot Tips" represent discoveries we made while preparing this book.

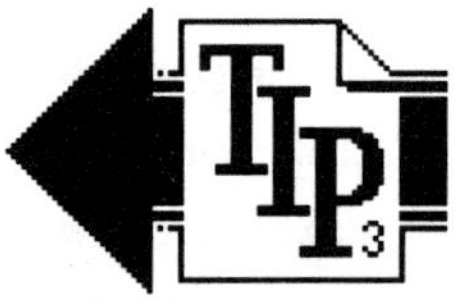

The "Tips" and "Hot Tips" icons that appear in the margins througout this book.

Specific usage strategies

There are three broad starting points from which you may be reading this book: as a beginner, as an intermediate, or as an expert. To help you sort through the information and use this book and your time most effectively, we offer the following suggestions.

- **Beginners**. Read each chapter in order. If you would like, skip Chapter 9, *Using Style Sheets in PageMaker*; Chapter 12, *Using Color in PageMaker*; and our third sample project in Chapter 14, *Creating an Advanced Catalog*. You probably won't need these advanced topics immediately.

Do not hesitate to just skim through any sections that seem too difficult. The first time through, you might want to read the reference chapters without following along on-screen. Be sure, however, to complete the first two sample projects: Chapter 6, *Creating a Simple Newsletter* and 11, *Creating and Intermediate Flyer*.

After you've had have a few hours' experience working on your own publications, reread the chapters. Many more concepts will make sense at this time. In general, don't worry about the details so much, just try to get an idea of what PageMaker can do. You can always look up the specific commands that you need. Whenever you feel unsure of something, try to look it up in the Table of Contents or the Index.

Later, when you have had sufficient practice with the basics, read Chapter 9, *Using Style Sheets in PageMaker*, and Chapter 12, *Using Color in PageMaker*, and complete the sample project in Chapter 14, *Creating an Advanced Catalog*.

- **Intermediates** As in racquetball, mediocrity comes easiy in PageMaker. The problem with this is that you tend to become set in your ways, including both the bad habits and the good ones. Intermediates can probably skip Chapter 2, *Installing PageMaker,* and the last two-thirds of Chapter 3, *Terms, Tools, and Menus.* You should not, however, skip chapters 4 and 5, *A Brief Tour of PageMaker* and *Working in the Publication Window*. These discuss relative basic PageMaker tasks; however, because these tasks are so commonly used, anything you learn about them will save you considerable time and trouble when using PageMaker. Highlight information that you want to remember, so you can later reaccess it quickly without having to reread entire chapters.

Each of the remaining chapters should be read thoroughly. Highlight new information so that you can quickly locate it later. Especially check out the tips and hot tips—these are the real time-savers. The sample project in Chapter 7, *Creating a Simple Newsletter,* is probably too easy to bother with, but do complete the projects in chapter 11 and 14, *Creating an intermediate Flyer* and, *Creating an Advanced Catalog*.

After a month or so, reread all the chapters, focusing on the items that you highlighted earlier. Of course, you are encouraged to look up any specific topic as it is needed in the course of your own document production.

- **Experts**. Even very experienced PageMaker users will probably find lots of new information in *The PageMaker Companion*. Pay particular attention to the parts of the application that you generally don't use or don't understand completely—try to learn about those. Topics such as replacing text and graphics, hyphenations, letter and word spacing, style sheets, and specific printing techniques are common areas of weakness even among full-time "PageMakers."

You can probably skip Chapter 2, *Installing PageMaker* and the last two-thirds of Chapter 3, *Terms, Tools, and Menus*, and the sample project in Chapter 6, *Creating a Simple Newsletter,* without missing any new information. The rest of the book, however, should be read thoroughly. You should highlight new information as you read it, so it will be easy to locate later. Chapter 7, *Creating and Adding Text*; 8, *Editing Text in PageMaker*; 9, *Using Style Sheets in PageMaker*; 10, *Using Graphics in PageMaker*; and 13, *Printing Publications,* will probably contain the most "expert level" information.

Chapter summaries

The PageMaker Companion consist of fourteen chapters plus an index and glossary. The following listing provides a brief synopsis of each chapter.

- **Chapter 1: The Publication Cycle**.We look at the entire process of document production so that we can put into perspective the part that PageMaker plays. Included in our examination are the personnel requirements, time requirements, and economic considerations of using PageMaker.
- **Chapter 2: Installing PageMaker**. We begin by discussing the hardware and software environment needed to use PageMaker. We then give complete instructions for installing PageMaker

on your hard drive. Finally we discuss the optimal placement of PageMaker files, tips for using PageMaker over a network, and methods that allow you to continue to use PageMaker versions 1.0 and 1.0a.

- **Chapter 3: Terms, Tools, and Menus**. We first define the terminology used throughout this book, including basic Macintosh terms that are often ambiguous. We then look at each menu command available in PageMaker, briefly noting its function. The tools in the toolbox are then discussed, and finally a comprehensive listing of all available keyboard equivalent commands is provided.

- **Chapter 4: A Brief Tour of PageMaker**. The purpose of this chapter is to introduce the most fundamental PageMaker operations. We discuss launching PageMaker, opening PageMaker files, the publication window, default settings, saving files, closing files, and quitting the PageMaker application.

- **Chapter 5: Working in the Publication Window**. This chapter is also devoted to fundamentals, focusing on basic interactions performed in the publication window: changing view size, working with rulers, the creation and manipulation of column and ruler guides, and a complete discussion of text and graphic objects as used in PageMaker.

- **Chapter 6: Creating a Simple Newsletter**. This

chapter presents our first sample project. By documenting the step-by-step creation of a newsletter, which you are encouraged to follow along and create, we present another introduction to the fundamental concepts of creating documents in PageMaker.

- **Chapter 7: Creating and Adding Text**. This chapter is the first of three that cover the subject of text in PageMaker. Here we focus on the available methods of getting text into our PageMaker publications—entering text directly into PageMaker, importing text from word-processors, and bringing text into PageMaker via the Windows Clipboard.

- **Chapter 8: Editing Text**. This chapter discusses PageMaker's many text-editing features. We learn how to format text, including both character and paragraph formatting, how to work with tabs and indents, and how to use PageMaker's hyphenation features. Finally, this chapter looks at PageMaker's ability to export text back into word-processing format.

- **Chapter 9: Using Style Sheets**. This chapter is a complete reference to the use of style sheets in PageMaker. We introduce the ways that style sheets can be defined, look at how they are used, and examine the process of editing and exporting style sheets as well.

- **Chapter 10: Using Graphics**. This chapter first examines the types of graphics that can be used in PageMaker, then looks at the various methods of importing these graphics for use in publications. We then examine PageMaker's own graphic-creation tools. We also learn how to wrap text around graphic objects.

- **Chapter 11: Creating an Intermediate Flyer**. Our second sample project, this chapter covers an intermediate-level publication, again presenting a step-by-step discussion designed for you to follow along. This time we explain more detailed techniques for working with text and graphics, including the use of tabs and hyphenation.

- **Chapter 12: Using Color in PageMaker**. This chapter covers PageMaker's ability to define and assign colors to text and graphic objects in any publication. We look at the process of defining colors, sharing colors between publications, and the actual application of colors. A discussion of how our color documents can be printed completes this chapter.

- **Chapter 13: Printing Publications**. This chapter takes a detailed look at the process of preparing Windows for printing and of printing your PageMaker publications on PostScript and PCL printers, including all options presented in the printing-related dialog boxes. We examine specialized printing techniques such as those required by oversized or color documents, and look at how you can "print to disk."

- **Chapter 14: Creating an Advanced Catalog**. In our last sample project, you are invited to follow along as we create a catalog containing a wide variety of text and graphics. Our focus is on the use of style sheets, advanced text formatting, and issues important when working in longer documents.

CHAPTER 1

The Publication Cycle

In this chapter we examine:

- *The rationale behind desktop publishing*
- *Why PageMaker is useful in this environment*
- *How PageMaker works with other applications*

Before we begin discussing the use of PageMaker, we'll first take a brief look at why we want to use PageMaker and how it fits with other aspects of the document production cycle. PageMaker is known as "page composition software." It provides us with the ability to electronically integrate text and graphics on the pages of publications in ways not possible with traditional word-processing or graphic software. This power makes PageMaker an important tool for businesses of all sizes.

Using PageMaker it is possible to create professional-quality documents, including:

- Newsletters
- Flyers
- Reports
- Proposals
- Periodicals
- Catalogs
- Sales literature
- Business letters
- Statements
- Owner's manuals
- Overheads
- Posters
- Certificates
- Labels
- Cover letters
- Business forms
- Brochures
- Business plans
- Books
- Newspapers
- Price lists
- Advertisements
- Contracts
- Directories
- Product documentation
- Calendars
- Menus
- Resumés
- Envelopes
- and many others.

PageMaker has achieved its respected position in the desktop publishing market, despite intense competition, because it is a well conceived program that is both powerful and easy to use. In the three years since its introduction, Aldus Corporation has substantially upgraded and improved the PageMaker software application, as well as associated support programs including PageMaker Classroom and advanced technical support.

Desktop page creation

The process of creating documents is a potentially long and complex one, in which PageMaker has only one, albeit important, function. Before a document can be produced in PageMaker, you must first determine its purpose, design, and content. After a document is layed out in PageMaker, it must then be edited, revised, and reproduced. Each of these tasks requires the time and talents of any number of people, and the additional use of word-processing and graphic software applications. In total this process is often called *the publication cycle*.

For most publications that will be created with PageMaker, the publication cycle includes:

- **Identifying your needs**. Before beginning any other aspect of the publication cycle, you must decide why the publication is needed by specifically defining your purpose. Who is your intended audience? How do you intend to capture your audience's interest? Where does your audience presently get information that will be covered by your publication? Is there an existing publication with which you will be required to compete? Or perhaps you are competing with audio or video media. How will your publication differ from existing material? Will these differences appeal to your intended audience? Only after you have determined the answers to these basic questions can you then specify the parameters that will define the creation and appearance of your printed pages.

- **Specifying your financial and organizational parameters**. Once it is known why you want to produce a document, you must then determine the basic parameters for its creation. When do you need it? How much money can be spent producing it, including writers, artists, and distribution costs? How much manpower do you have to assist in the production? Are there any distribution requirements, such as size, weight, or format? Who specifically are your target readers? Do you require a mailiing list? These and other related questions will help you to isolate your resources. It is useful to determine what you have, what you don't have but must get, and what you don't have and must do without. Knowing your parameters helps you to determine how you may best focus limited resources to create a professional-quality publication.

- **Determining content and format**. Once you have determined how your publication will get to its audience, you must specify what your audience will get from the publication. What do your readers want to know that you can tell them? What general information must you convey and what information should you avoid? How much information should be presented in writing, and how much should be presented visually, in the form of figures? Does your publication require a name, and if so, how should it be presented? Do you intend for your publication to last a long time, or to be read once and thrown away? How can you demonstrate this using content and format?

- **Delegate responsibilities**. Many experts agree that desktop publishing's main advantage doubles as its primary drawback—namely, its ease of use. It is far too tempting to try to do everything, from determining story requirements to writing the copy, from publication design to art direction and graphic development, from layout to editing to printing to scheduling commercial duplication. The fact is, it is rarely an efficient use of your time to single-handedly create a publication from beginning to end. Your publicatiuon also suffers the disadvantage of only one visual and textual perspective—your own. All publications, regardless of what tools are used in their creation, benefit from the combined energy of several talented professionals. This is why it is necessary to determine a publication staff: who will write, who will edit, who will design, who will execute graphics, who will layout, who will revise, who will print, who will distribute, and who will oversee the entire process? It is not essential that you assign only one person to a task, and a single person may assume more than one task. The key is to delegate specific responsibilities to specific people, reducing confusion and increasing personal efficiency.

- **Writing the "body copy**." This is the first step in the actual creation of a document. PageMaker, though powerful, is not suited to the creation of large bodies of text. Text will not automatically pour onto pages as you write, you are not permitted to see pages and pages of text at the same time, nor does PageMaker provide a spell-checker, thesaurus, and so on. It is always best, when writing a story over one page long, to create the majority of your text in a wordprocessor such as MICROSOFT WORD, WORDPERFECT, or WINDOWS WRITE. These applications provide numerous specific featured designed exclusively to aid in the writing and text editing process. Text originating from a mainframe computer, a Macintosh or almost any other personal computer system, or an OCR scanning device can also be imported into PageMaker.

  Once a story has been written, spell-checked, and copy-edited, it is then permissible to pour it into PageMaker. Additions, deletions, or corrections may easily be made in PageMaker, and if a story needs major renovations, it can be exported back into a wordprocessor. Most wordprocessors also allow you to format text—assigning a font, type size, leading, and so on.

Some allow you to specify these text attributes in the form of style sheets. In most cases, formatting and style sheet names are retained in PageMaker once the text is poured, so that there is absolutely no visual or informational loss between copy writer and publication coordinator.

- **Creating or obtaining graphic elements**. PageMaker is even less suited to the creation of graphics than it is to creating large amounts of text. However, there are a wide variety of specialized graphics applications that allow you to create both ornamental and technical illustrations. These graphics may then be exported in one of four formats—paint, PICT, EPS, or TIFF—to be used in PageMaker. In fact, PageMaker's main purpose is to easily combine text with graphics in a restriction-free, electronic environment. Graphics applications which PageMaker supports include PC PAINT, PC PAINTBRUSH, PUBLISHER'S PAINTBRUSH, WINDOWS PAINT, MACPAINT, AUTOCAD, MICROGRAFX IN*A*VISION, WINDOWS DRAW!, ZENOGRAPHICS' MIRAGE, LOTUS 1-2-3, SYMPHONY, ADOBE ILLUSTRATOR, ALDUS FREEHAND, and many more.

- **Designing the publication**. Before beginning to create any publication, you should have a good idea of how it is going to look when your textual and graphic elements are combined. Be aware of the amount of information that you need to fit in your publication, the size of which may be limited by reproduction and distribution costs. The design of any document you create is as important to its effectiveness as the contents, and certainly there are many professionals who would argue that it is more so. A great layout can gloss over a weak content, or make a weak content seem strong. But like it or not, the best of contents will inevitably get lost in a bad presentation. Call it a sign of the times or whatever you want, design will almost always overshadow the written word, so it important that the two work together and in the same direction.

There are several places you can learn more about publication design, and you should consider it as important as learning to use PageMaker itself. *The Aldus Guide to Basic Design* and *Looking Good in Print,* both by Roger C. Parker, provide introductory lessons in electronic page design, and *Desktop Publishing Type and Graphics, A Comprehensive Handbook* acts as a catalog to visual design possibilities. We also recommend design classes, available through many desktop publishing instructional institutions, seminars, and community colleges.

Another good way to learn good design technique is to copy from existing publications. Find similar documentation that you admire and notice how they format their text, how they set their columns, where they use headlines, how they produce their graphics, which text/graphic relationships work and which do not.

After emulating these techniques, you can decide which elements of design you want to incorporate into your own work, as well as designing new techniques yourself.

- **Print proof copies**. PageMaker is designed specifically to create camera-ready printed pages. This is why it is so essential to proof your work using a dot-matrix printer or, preferably, a laser printer. A printed page is a much more accurate representation of your PageMaker document than its on-screen representation, and much more portable, so that they can be reviewed and commented on by many people before any final prints are made. Proofs are also useful for last-minute editing, confirming layout and design, and checking the quality of any graphic elements.

- **Print final camera-ready pages**. Final master prints can be output to laser printers or, preferably, to professional-quality imagesetting devices. This book, for example, was printed at 1270 dots-per-inch using a Linotronic 100 imagesetter. Although imagesetters range in price between $30,000 and $100,000, many national desktop publishing service bureaus offer this service on a per-page basis. The difference in quality is almost always worth the price.

- **Commercial reproduction and distribution**. The final step is to create reproductions of your publication. PageMaker is capable of outputting black and white composite originals, spot color separations, or four-color process separations.

> Incidentally, it is not adviseable to print many copies of a single publication using a laser printer. Instead, we recommend printing only one original per page of your publication. Then reproduce these pages through a commercial printer, either through photocopying or professional-quality offset printing, depending on your publication's budget.

While the level of formality with which each of these stages is executed varies dramatically depending on the kind of publication you create, each stage will almost certainly be a part of your publication cycle. In some cases, one person will execute one of these phases in a single day, or even a few hours. In other cases, many people will be involved and the process will take longer. Nonetheless, it is always important that the operation be completed in order and on time, avoiding wasted effort and money.

Installing PageMaker

In this chapter we examine:

- *PageMaker's hardware and software requirements*
- *How to install PageMaker on your hard disk*
- *Configuring MicroSoft Windows*

PageMaker 3.0 for the PC ships either on five 1.2-megabyte 5.25-inch or on nine 720-Kbyte 3.5-inch disks. Before you can use PageMaker, you must configure your computer system appropriately, install Microsoft Windows (if it isn't currently installed), and install the PageMaker application itself. This chapter will help you to determine if your computer is ready to run PageMaker, look at how you can optimize your system to improve PageMaker's performance, and detail the installation of both Windows and PageMaker.

System requirements and recommendations

In order to run PageMaker 3.0, you must have Microsoft Windows version 2.0 or Windows/386 (a **run-time** version of Windows 2.0 is included with PageMaker). Your system must run DOS version 3.1 (or higher), have at least 640 Kbytes (k) of memory, and your hardware must be fully compatible with these versions of DOS and Windows. Although Page-Maker 3.0 will run on an original IBM PC with the 8088 processor, it will run so slowly as to be useless. Furthermore, you must have a hard-disk drive with at least 3.5 megabytes of free space after Microsoft Windows is installed, or 4.5 megabytes of free space if Windows isn't installed, and you intend to install the run-time version included with PageMaker. These are the *minimum* requirements. PageMaker 3.0 will not work with less.

Exceeding these minimum requirements in one or more categories can provide considerable advantages when using PageMaker. This section reviews each component of a PC publishing system, discussing how each can improve Page-Maker's performance.

The computer

The particular PC model on which you run PageMaker has an obvious effect on the operation of the software: a computer that uses an 80386 processor will be faster than an IBM AT or AT-compatible (which uses an 80286 processor), which in turn will be faster than a IBM PC (which uses an 8088 or 8086 processor). In addition to the processor, the *clock speed* of your computer also has an important effect on PageMaker's performance. The 8088 processor has a clock speed of 4 Mhz; the 80286 processor in the AT has a speed of 10MHZ TO 20 Mhz, depending on the model; and 80386 processors have a clock speed between 16 Mhz and 25 Mhz. The higher the clock speed, the better the computer's performance.

Because PageMaker (and all applications running under WINDOWS) are such complex programs, a faster processor makes a big difference. Use the fastest 80286 computer available,or, better yet, an 80386 computer. Based on prevailing performance standards, many people find PageMaker's performance on AT-class computers barely acceptable. If you must use PageMaker on AT-class computer, you should seriously consider the extended memory options discussed later in this chapter.

Random access memory

As mentioned earlier, PageMaker 3.0 requires 640k of memory—the maximum amount of RAM that can be made available to standard application software in DOS. If you are unsure of how much memory is available on your computer, use the MEMORY.EXE program provided with your PageMaker 3.0 application. This program will tell you how much memory is installed in your computer, and how much is currently available (some memory is used by DOS and other memory-resident programs and device drivers that you might be using). If this program indicates that less than 640k of conventional memory is installed in your computer, you must have additional memory installed in order to run PageMaker. If MEMORY.EXE indicates that 640k is installed, but less than 550k of memory is free, PageMaker may not be able to operate; in this case, you must restart your computer using fewer memory-resident programs or device drivers.

When at least 550k of memory is available you will be able to launch Windows and PageMaker. Unfortunately, neither Microsoft Windows nor PageMaker 3.0 fit into only 640k of memory, so portions of each are continually **swapped** in and out of memory from your hard disk as needed. Since the process of swapping program sections from the hard disk slows PageMaker greatly, less swapping will improve PageMaker's performance.

The best way to minimize disk swapping is to make as much memory as possible available to Windows and PageMaker. This can be done by removing unnecessary memory-consumers before launching PageMaker (as discussed earlier) or by adding more memory to your computer.

Two different kinds of extra memory can be added to your computer—expanded memory and extended memory. **Expanded memory** is a direct extension to the 640k of memory installed in your computer, allowing more and larger portions of your programs to remain in memory. Adding one or more megabytes of expanded memory will significantly improve PageMaker's performance.

PageMaker can only use expanded memory boards that follow LIM 4.0, a specification developed by Lotus, Intel, and Microsoft. If you use an 80286 computer, you must install the AST RAMpage or a comparable expanded memory board. On a 80386 computer, Windows /386 automatically treats any additional memory (even if it is not installed on expanded memory boards) as expanded memory.

Extended memory is any memory after the first 640k that is not installed on special LIM boards (or in a computer using Windows /386). Extended memory can be used only for special purposes, such as disk caching or for RAM disks. **Disk caching** stores information most recently loaded from the hard drive in RAM, so that if it is required again, it can be read from the cache rather than from the hard disk. Since information can be loaded from RAM two to four times faster than from disk, PageMaker will run noticeably faster with extending memory to allow disk caching. If only a small amount of extended memory is available (64–512k), or if you already have more than one megabyte of expanded memory, disk caching is an excellent method of improving performance.

Either expanded or extended memory can be used with **RAM Disk**. software. A RAM disk acts exactly like a floppy or hard drive, except that RAM memory is used instead of magnetic disks. Again, because RAM can be accessed two to four times faster than any disk, hard or floppy, performance is improved. A RAM disk requires one megabyte or more in order to be useful. It also requires special preparation and can lose its data in the event of a system crash. While RAM disks do provide excellent performance benefits, we recommend their use only when large amounts of extended or expanded memory is available and you are already using expanded memory and disk caching.

Hard drive size

When deciding on the size hard drive you will need to run PageMaker on your PC, it is important to be aware of the amount of space required by Windows, PageMaker, and the files you will put together as a publication. PageMaker itself requires two megabytes of hard-disk space, not including Help files, templates, and tutorial files. The complete package, including run-time Windows, requires 5.5 megabytes. The files that you create when using PageMaker will vary in size, but are generally larger than the files created with word-processors or most graphics applications.

The chart in Figure 2.01 shows the average file size of several types of publications.

2-page newsletter, no graphics	*60k*
6-page brochure, no graphics	*70k*
10-page technical paper, few graphics	*400k*
20-page book chapter (like this chapter)	*320k*
1-page flyer with two EPS graphics	*70k*
12-page technical manual, draw graphics	*90k*
50-page book chapter (such as Chapter 6)	*600k*
6-page catalog	*200k*

Figure 2.01: *Examples of file sizes.*

If you multiply these sizes by the number of publications you produce in a month, or by the number you will be updating regularly (and therefore want to keep on your hard drive), you can see how fast the megabytes get filled up. In addition, you will often have more than one version of a publication on your hard drive. Finally, remember that when you import text and graphics from other applications into your publication, PageMaker uses copies of those files. For example, if you import a 50k text file, PageMaker makes a copy of it and uses the copy in the publication. The original file remains on the hard disk, unchanged. Together, the original and the copy use 100k of disk space. Figure 2.02 displays the files—such as text, graphics, and backup—along their filename suffixes, that are used during the creation of a typical publication in PageMaker 3.0.

NEWSLETTER.PM3	*PageMaker publication*
ARTICLE1.WP	*Word Perfect text file*
ARTICLE2.WP	*Word Perfect text file*
ARTICLE3.DOC	*Microsoft Word text file*
CHART.DOC	*Multimate file*
GRAPHIC1.PCX	*PC Paintbrush paint graphic*
GRAPHIC2.EPS	*Encapsulated PostScript graphic*

Figure 2.02: *Files associated with the creation of a typical PageMaker document.*

Printers

Since PageMaker runs in the Windows operating environment, PageMaker publications can be printed on any printer supported by Windows. Microsoft Windows supports many printers, including dot-matrix models. However, dot-matrix printers lack the resolution, precision, and clarity of laser printers; dot-matrix output is useful only for rough drafts of your PageMaker publication. Most PageMaker users print their publications on laser printers equipped with a PostScript interpreter, such as one of the Apple LaserWriter series, or on PCL printers such as the Hewlett-Packard LaserJet series. Figure 2.03 lists the laser printers for which printer drivers are included on the Drivers disk that accompanies PageMaker 3.0.

PostScript Printers:

AST PS-R4081	*IBM Personal Pageprinter*
Agfa P400PS	*Linotronic 100/300/500*
Apple LaserWriter	*NEC SilentWriter LC-890*
Apple LaserWriter Plus	*QMS-PS 800, 800A, 800+*
Dataproducts LZR 2665	*TI OmniLaser*
Digital LN03R ScriptPrinter	*Varityper VT-600*
Digital LPS Print Server 40	*Wang LCS15-DSK*

PCL Printers:

Hewlett-Packard LaserJet	*Kyocera F-1010 Laser*
HP LaserJet Plus	*Apricot Laser*
HP LaserJet 500 Plus	*Quadram QuadLaser 1*
HP LaserJet Series II	*Tandy LP-1000*
HP LaserJet 2000	*Okidata LaserLine 6*
Epson GQ-3500	*Tegra Genesis*

Figure 2.03: *Printer drivers supplied with PageMaker.*

The most important difference between PostScript printers and PCL printers has to do with the capabilities of these printers to print type and graphics. PostScript printers can be used only with PostScript type faces, but can print these type faces in any type size that you can specify. PostScript printers can always print any amount of graphics on a single page. PCL printers work with bit-mapped fonts, which are usually available only in specific point sizes. Depending upon the amount of memory in the PCL printer, it may or may not be able to print full-page graphics.

The data transfer rate between the PC and the printer is another important factor. Different types of connections, also called ports, transfer data at different speeds. According to Aldus, the transfer times required to send 2.5 megabytes of data to a printer using these methods are; RS-232—39 minutes; Parallel—14 minutes; AppleTalk—less than 5 minutes; Printer-specific adaptor—less than 3 minutes. You may have more than one type of port in your computer, and you should select the fastest method available to you. If you are using a PostScript printer, you might consider buying an AppleTalk card for your PC—even if you do not use AppleTalk for any other purpose. These cost only about $250, and will increase your printing speed considerably.

Monitors

Three attributes of computer display systems are worth considering when using PageMaker: size, resolution, and color. While standard PC displays are approximately 8inches by 11 inches, larger displays up to 24 inches square are now available. Large-screen monitors have become popular because they increase the size of the display, thus reducing the amount of on-screen movement required while composing pages. Less movement will save you considerable time and effort in the page-layout process. These displays help you to get a much better sense of your publication on-screen, and in most cases provide better resolution than their smaller counterparts.

The higher the resolution of your display, the sharper the images you will see on-screen. This is especially important when working in PageMaker where the characters on the screen must match as closely as possible the printed type. Resolution is normally controlled by the display adaptor that is used. There are several classes of display adaptors, each with their own general resolution ranges, as shown in Figure 2.4. Generally, you will want to use an EGA or VGA display adaptor when using PageMaker. Before purchasing any display adaptor, be certain that it is compatible with Microsoft Windows.

CGA—640 pixels horizontal × 200 pixels vertical
EGA— 640 pixels horizontal × 350 pixels vertical
VGA—640 pixels horizontal × 480 pixels vertical

Figure 2.04: *Display adaptor categories and their resolutions.*

CGA graphics cards were developed in the early 1980s along with the original IBM PCs, and are nearly obsolete because of their low vertical resolution. EGA and VGA cards provide on-screen displays that are much easier to read, particularly if you will be working on the screen for more than a couple hours. However, EGA and VGA cards require high-resolution monitors and cannot be used with an older IBM color monitor. Be sure to match the display card with the appropriate monitor.

Color displays are common among PageMaker users, primarily because most graphic display adaptors that are compatible with Windows are color adaptors. The need to show colors on-screen is only a secondary concern—regardless of whether your display is in color on in black and white, PageMaker's color capabilities allow you to specify the color of elements and then create color separations while printing.

Microsoft Windows

Microsoft Windows is an graphics-based operating environment that offers a mouse pointer, pull-down menus, and the ability to show multiple windows on-screen simultaneously. Different windows can be used to perform different tasks, including running Windows-compatible applications, such as word-processors or graphics packages, or performing DOS file maintenance. Applications that run in the Windows environment benefit from Windows' easy-to-use interface and the fact that multiple programs can be run at once.

Microsoft Windows is an application program that is started before any applications that run inside the Windows environment are started. Of the several available versions of Windows—from version 1.03 to Windows/386—PageMaker 3.0 is compatible with Windows 2.0, 2.03, or Windows/386. If you do not already own one of these versions, you can use the run-time version of Windows 2.0 that is included with the PageMaker 3.0 application.

The run-time version of Windows is a stripped-down version of full Windows, providing only the essential services required to use PageMaker. While the regular versions of Windows allow you to perform a variety of DOS tasks and operate other Windows-compatible application programs, run-time Windows can be used only with PageMaker 3.0.

If you do not use any other Windows-compatible software applications, run-time Windows will suit your needs perfectly. If, however, you wish to use more than one Windows-compatible application, you should purchase a complete version of Windows and use it in place of the run-time version included with PageMaker 3.0.

Installing PageMaker

Once you have the proper hardware configuration to run PageMaker, you are ready to install the application on your hard drive. First, check the amount of free space on your hard drive. You must have at least 2 megabytes to install the minimum configuration, which is the PageMaker program and its required files. Installing the PageMaker application, its tutorial and newsletter files, and the run-time version of Windows requires 4.5 megabytes of free space. If you have already installed Windows, you need 3.5 megabytes of free space.

These are the steps for installing PageMaker 3.0:

- Remove the old version of Windows from your hard drive.
- Remove or update PageMaker version 1.0 if it is on your hard drive.
- Install Windows 2.0, Windows/386, or the run-time version, if it is not already installed.
- Install PageMaker 3.0.
- Install screen fonts and printer drivers.

Windows 1.0 and PageMaker 1.0

If you have been using PageMaker 1.0 and Windows 1.0 (either the full version or the run-time version included with PageMaker 1.0), it will be necessary to erase Windows and either erase or update your PageMaker 1.0 application. Publication files created with PageMaker 1.0 can be used with version 3.0, so in most cases there is no need to keep version 1.0.

To begin the removal process, move all the publication files that you have created out of the PageMaker 1.0 directory so that they are not deleted along with the Windows and PageMaker files. If you added any screen fonts to Windows 1.0, they must be converted and reinstalled into your new version of Windows.

Copy the screen fonts into another directory or onto a floppy disk. Windows comes with five generic fonts, Helvetica (HELVB), Times Roman (TMSRB), Courier (COURB), Script (SCRIPT), and Modern (MODERN). Additional screen fonts can be identified by their unusual file names, such as POB_____.FON, which is the Palatino Bold screen font. Later, when the new version of Windows is installed, you will copy these screen fonts back to the Windows directory and update them.

To delete all Windows 1.0 files, simply type DEL C:\WINDOWS*.* (assuming WINDOWS is the name of your Windows directory), press the RETURN key, and then press Y to confirm the deletion). To delete all PageMaker 1.0 files, type DEL C:\PM*.* and press the RETURN key (and then press Y to confirm the deletion). If you want to keep using PageMaker 1.0, delete only the Windows 1.0 files, and run the CONVFONT.BAT file as described in the following section,

Converting Screen Fonts. In any case, be sure that Windows 1.0 has been deleted. It is very important that you do not have two copies of Windows on your hard drive—even in separate directories.

1.2 Mbyte, 5.25 inch disks:

PageMaker disks:	*Install/Program/Dictionary*
	Drivers/Filters/Templates
	Getting Started
run-time Windows disks:	
	Setup/Build/Displays
	Utilities/Fonts

720 Kbyte, 3.5 inch disks:

PageMaker disks:	*Install*
	Program/Dictionary
	Drivers/Filters
	Templates
	Getting Started
Run-time Windows disks:	
	Setup/Build
	Displays
	Utilities
	Fonts

Figure 2.05: *The PageMaker disks and their contents.*

Installing Windows 2.0

If you have not already installed Windows 2.0, now is the time to do so. If you have the full version of Windows 2.0, install it as described in the accompanying documentation, and go on to the next section of this chapter, *Installing PageMaker 3.0*. If you plan to use the Run-Time version of Windows 2.0 included with your PageMaker application, insert the WINDOWS SETUP/BUILD/FONTS disk in drive A.

At the DOS prompt, type A:, press the ENTER key, then type SETUP and press ENTER. This begins the Windows installation program. After a few instructions, a screen appears asking you to name the directory into which Windows will be installed. The default directory name is \PM. This is generally an acceptable name, unless you already have PageMaker 1.0 files installed in an existing \PM directory, in which case you may want to change the directory name to \PM3.

```
SETUP PROGRAM for Microsoft Windows 2.0 - Runtime Version


Setup prepares Runtime Windows to run on your computer.

To run Setup you need to know the following:

  * what kind of pointing device (mouse) you have, if any
  * what kind of graphics adapter (display) you have
  * what kind of printer(s) you have, if any
  * which port your printer is connected to

To set up Runtime Windows properly, you should complete the Setup program.
You can leave the Setup process by pressing CONTROL+X (press and hold
the CONTROL key, and press the X key). Please keep in mind that Setup will
not be completed and Runtime Windows will not be installed on your computer.

        WHEN YOU'RE READY TO                              PRESS

        Continue Setup                                    ENTER
        Exit without completing Setup                 CONTROL+X
```

Figure 2.06: *The Windows Installation Setup screen, the first screen you encounter when installing windows.*

As the installation continues you will be asked to insert different disks needed by the installation program. You will also be asked to identify your computer, keyboard, display adaptor, fonts, and mouse type. It is very important that you accurately respond to these requests, or Windows and PageMaker may not operate properly. You will then be asked to install printer drivers. Respond by installing printer drivers for each type of printer on which you intend to print documents. You may wish to install a PostScript printer driver, even if you do not have a PostScript printer, so that you will be able to prepare documents for output at a service bureau that uses PostScript printers. When Windows is installed, you will be asked if you want to install PageMaker. Press C to start the PageMaker INSTALL program.

```
                  PAGEMAKER INSTALLATION MAIN MENU

To select one or more options, use the arrow keys to highlight the
option(s), then press ENTER.  To deselect an option, move the cursor
to the highlighted option, then press ENTER again.

When you have selected your options, press F1 to start the installation
process.  To quit, use the arrow keys to highlight QUIT, press ENTER,
then press F1 to exit.

                  ►INSTALL PAGEMAKER 3.0
                   INSTALL IMPORT/EXPORT FILTERS
                   COPY PAGEMAKER GETTING STARTED FILES
                   COPY PAGEMAKER TEMPLATE FILES
                   INSTALL ALL OPTIONS LISTED ABOVE
                   QUIT
```

Figure 2.07: *PageMaker installation main menu.*

Installing PageMaker 3.0

Once Windows has been installed on your hard drive, you are ready to install PageMaker 3.0. If you already have the full version of Windows 2.0 or Windows /386 installed, you can begin the PageMaker 3.0 installation by inserting the INSTALL/PROGRAM/DICTIONARY DISK into your A: drive and entering A: INSTALL (Return).

As the install program begins, you will be asked to name the directory into which the PageMaker 3.0 files will be copied,and then for the name of the Windows directory. If you did not delete PageMaker 1.0, you may wish to change the default \PM directory to \PM3 so that your PageMaker 1.0 files are not overwritten.

The PAGEMAKER INSTALLATION MAIN MENU dialog shown in Figure 2.07, will now appear, offering a choice of five possible installation options. Use the arrow keys to move up and down this menu, pressing the RETURN key to highlight each option you would like installed.

The five installation options are:

- INSTALL PAGEMAKER This option installs the PageMaker 3.0 application (PM.EXE) in the \PM directory (unless you specify otherwise), along with the hyphenation dictionaries (PMUSRAM.DCT and PMUSDISK.DCT), screen fonts (PMFONTA.FNT, PMFONTB.FNT, or PMFONTE.FNT, depending on your monitor), and the PageMaker help file (PM.HLP).
- INSTALL IMPORT/EXPORT FILTERS. PageMaker can automatically read in files from many popular wordprocessors and graphic programs.

For many other programs, you must specifically install an Import/Export Filter in order to use those files with PageMaker. Selecting this option allows you to view the list of available Import/Export filters, and install any of them into your PageMaker application, if necessary.

- COPY PAGEMAKER GETTING STARTED FILES. This option copies to your hard drive the sample files that are used in the PageMaker tutorial. The tutorial text is included in the *Getting Started* manual supplied with PageMaker. If you do not intend to use this tutorial, these files do not need to be installed.

- COPY PAGEMAKER TEMPLATE FILES. This option copies the 20 PageMaker Templates to your hard drive, to a sub-directory called TEMPLATE in the PM directory. You can use these templates as starting points for your own newsletters, calendars, spec sheets, and price lists.

- INSTALL ALL OPTIONS LISTED ABOVE. This option executes the installation of each of the above listed options.

After selecting your installation options, press the F1 key. The INSTALL program now checks your hard drive to confirm that you have enough free space for the installation options you have selected. You will be informed if adequate free space is not available, and then prompted to either quit the installation process (so that you can create more free space on your hard drive) or return to the PAGEMAKER INSTALLATION MAIN MENU dialog, where you can reduce the number of files you have selected for installation.

If enough free space is available to accommodate all the options you have selected, PageMaker begins the installation process. As the installation continues you will be prompted for specific disks needed by the installation program, and the progress of the installation will be documented on-screen.

You will then be informed that several modifications must be made to your CONFIG.SYS and AUTOEXEC.BAT files, and asked if you would like the installation program to make these modifications for you. Unless you are familiar with modifying these files and wish to manually make these changes, we recommend that you allow the installation program to make them for you. When the installation has been completed, the PAGEMAKER INSTALLATION MAIN MENU will return. Move the pointer to the last option, press ENTER, and press the F1 key. This will return you to the DOS prompt.

Files and your hard drive

After installing run-time Windows and PageMaker you will have a directory on your hard drive which contains all of your PageMaker-related files and run-time Windows files. Unless you changed the default setting, this directory is named \PM. If you are using a full version of Windows you will also have a directory containing your Windows files, which is named \Windows unless you specified differently.

The \PM directory, and its sub-directories, contain all of the PageMaker-related files and run-time Windows files that you have installed. The \Windows directory includes all of your Windows related files. During operation, PageMaker and Windows will need access to these files, so both directories have been added to the PATH command in your AUTOEXEC.BAT file. You may move any of these files to other locations on your hard disk, but if you do so it will be necessary to modify your PATH command so that all files can be accessed at any time.

If you do choose to rearrange your files, keep these suggestions in mind:

- The PMUSDISK.DCT and PMUSRAM.DCT files should remain in the same directory as the PM.EXE file. If these files are not available when PageMaker loads, an Alert dialog, shown in Figure 2.08, will inform you that they are missing, and you will be unable to use PageMaker's automatic-hyphenation feature.

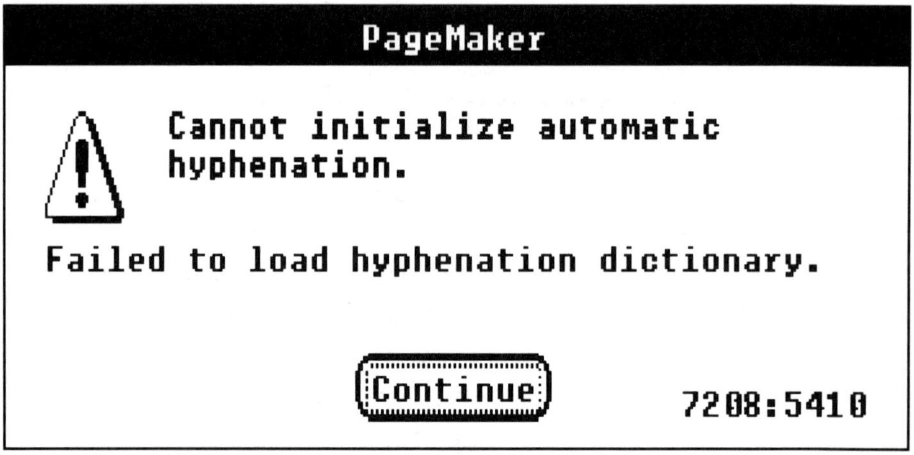

Figure 2.08: *The Alert dialog that appears when the hyphenation files are missing.*

- The PMUSUSER.TXT file, the user hyphenation dictionary, should also stay in the same directory as PM.EXE. If this file is not available when PageMaker loads, an Alert box appears notifying you that PageMaker "cannot read supplementary user dictionary." This Alert box will continue to appear each time PageMaker is loaded until you add the PMUSUSER.TXT file from your original PageMaker disk (just copy it into place normally), or create an empty text file called PMUSUSER.TXT (this can be done in any word-processor).
- The PM.CNF, the PageMaker default settings file, should remain in the \PM directory. This file is not installed during the PageMaker installation, but is automatically created the first time you run PageMaker. The default settings file is updated whenever you change an application default, as explained in Chapter 4, *A Brief Tour of PageMaker*. If this file is deleted, PageMaker reverts to its factory-set default settings.

Publication files created by PageMaker will be placed in the same directory as the PM.EXE application by default, but you can store them in any directory. As a rule it is not a good idea to keep publication files in the \PM directory because the directory listing will be very long. Instead, you should create another directory, perhaps called \PMFILES, and store your publication files there.

Post-installation preparations

After Windows and PageMaker have been installed, there are a few additional changes to make before using PageMaker. Many of these are procedures that you might have to repeat as your hardware or software configurations change. These include the installation or removal of screen fonts and printer drivers, the setting of printer connections, and the configuration of your mouse.

Installing additional fonts

One of the many benefits of Windows is that it is able to display on-screen representations of any typeface for which a **screen font** has been installed. The Windows installation process installs only a few basic fonts, which it selects based upon the printers and font sets that you specify in the installation options. In order to use see additional fonts on-screen, additional screen fonts must be installed.

Before we look at the process of installing screen fonts, a few words about how fonts work are in order. In Windows, four components are used to select, display, and print fonts:

- **Font Names**. All available font names appear in the font selection dialog box of any particular Windows application. The original set of font names included are those included in the printer drivers that have been installed, although additional font names may be added by installing fonts purchased separately. Each font name corresponds to either a font metric file or a screen font file, and to a printer font file.

- **Font Metric Files**. If a screen font is not available for a particular font name then Windows substitutes one of it's "generic" screen fonts on the display but uses information from the font metric file to determine character widths and other technical information.

- **Screen fonts**. Screen fonts contain bit-mapped drawings of each character in a font, which are used to display the font on-screen. Screen fonts also include all of the technical information about fonts found in font metric files. Windows includes five "generic" screen fonts (Helvetica, Times Roman, Courier, Modern, and Script), which it uses to represent fonts which do not have corresponding screen fonts.

- **Printer fonts**. Printer fonts contain the actual information used by the printer to draw each character of the font. Printer fonts are sometimes loaded into the printer manually, either by inserting a font cartridge or by downloading a printer font file, or they may be automatically sent to the printer whenever needed by a printing document.

Depending upon the printers that you have installed, you will probably have four to ten font names available after installing Windows, some of which correspond to the generic screen fonts, and some of which rely on font metric files for technical information but use the generic fonts for display purposes. For instance, if the Apple LaserWriter Plus printer is installed, the Palatino type family is an option in PageMaker—the printer will print Palatino characters, but the letters on the screen will be generic Roman fonts that only approximate Palatino. By adding additional fonts, you can either supply true screen fonts to font names that where using generic screen fonts, or you can add entirely new font names along with their screen and printer fonts.

For PostScript printers, the most popular fonts are available from Adobe Systems Inc., and Bitstream. For PCL printers such as the Hewlett Packard LaserJet series, which are the most common in the PC world, a wide variety of fonts are available from many different companies. Font packages usually include installation programs specifically designed for Windows which adds both the font names, screen fonts, and printer fonts.

If you do not have an installation program for your windows-compatible fonts, you may be able to use the ADD FONTS... command from the SETUP menu on the Windows Control Panel to add the font names and screen fonts. You will have to add the printer fonts according to the instructions included with your fonts. The Windows Control Panel also provides a REMOVE FONTS... command that can be used to remove any font names and screen that have been installed in your Windows application.

Adding or removing printer drivers

During the original installation of Windows, printer drivers were installed into your Windows application for the printers you specified at that time. If you later change printers, or want to prepare documents that will be printed on a different printer, you must install additional printer drivers for these new printers. There is no limit to the number of printer drivers that you may install in Windows.

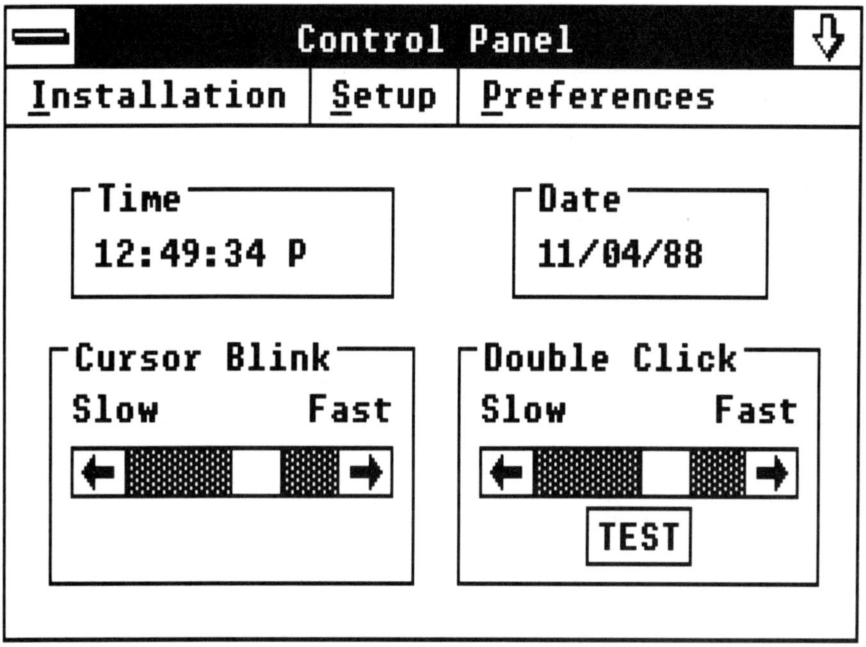

Figure 2.09: *The Windows control panel.*

To add new printer drivers, choose the CONTROL PANEL option from the Windows SYSTEM menu, as shown in Figure 2.09 Now choose the ADD NEW PRINTER...command from the INSTALLATION menu. Insert the DRIVERS floppy disk in your A: drive, then enter a: in the option box, and click the OK button. Windows will now display a list of printer drivers available for installation. Select the printer driver you want to add and then click the ADD button. Use the PostScript driver if you use any of the PostScript printers listed earlier in Figure 2.03, and the PCL/LaserJet driver for the PCL printers listed in the same figure. You will then be asked to enter the path which specifies the directory where you want to install the new printer drivers. In most cases you should add these new drivers to the same directory which holds all of your other Windows files, either \PM or \Windows.

Specifying printer connections

When you have finished adding printer drivers, or wish to change the setup for existing printer drivers, choose the CONNECTIONS... command from the SETUP menu. This will bring up the dialog box shown in Figure 2.10, where you may specify which printer port each installed printer will use. Each printer may be assigned to only one port, and each port to only one printer. Whenever you physically change the connections of your printers and printer ports, you will have to return to this dialog and reconfigure these options.

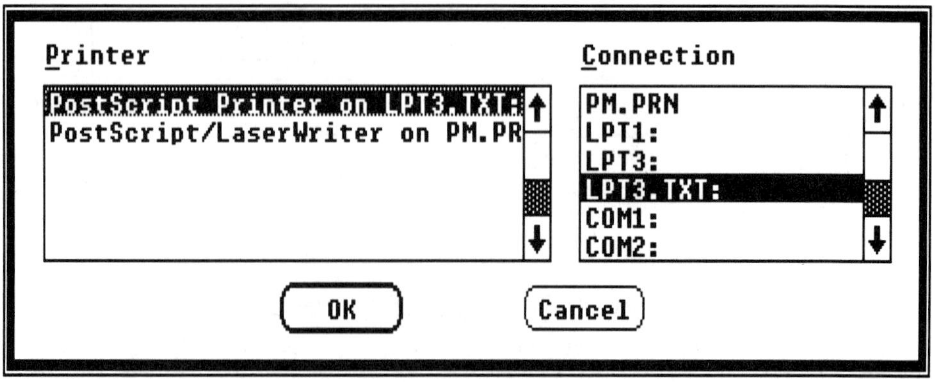

Figure 2.10: *Windows control panel Connections dialog box.*

The CONTROL PANEL CONNECTIONS dialog box contains a "Port" option, listing three types of printer ports—LPT, COM, and EPT. Nearly all dot-matrix and conventional impact printers use the LPT, or parallel, ports. Laser printers, such as the Apple Laser-Writer and the Hewlett-Packard LaserJet, use the COM ports, and the IBM Personal PagePrinter uses the EPT port. Check your printer documentation to determine which kind of port it requires. If you have a dot-matrix printer connected to your computer, you can use any one of the three LPT ports, but we recommend you use LPT 1, since this is the default port for most applications

To specify your connections, click on a printer type in the left box, and click on the port it is connected to in the right box. If you have two printers connected to your computer—or example, a dot-matrix printer and an Apple LaserWriter—make sure that each printer is assigned to a different port.

If you are using a laser printer, you also will need to configure the serial port using the COMMUNICATIONS... command on the Windows Control Panel (Figure 2.09) See your printer documentation to determine how the serial port should be set. When you have finished, click the OK button.

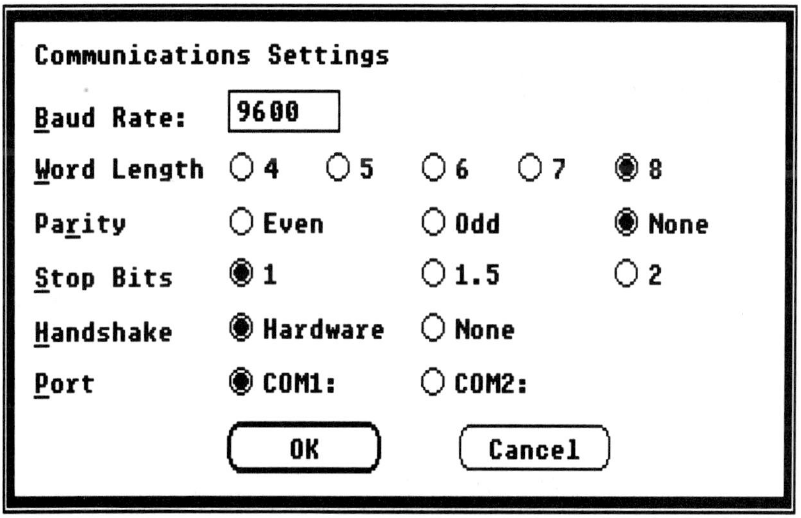

Figure 2.11: *The Windows Communications dialog box with standard laser printer settings.*

Configuring your mouse

The mouse connected to your PC may have two or three buttons. In Windows, one of these buttons is known as the **primary mouse button**, and the others are known as the **secondary mouse button(s)**. By default, the left-most button is the primary mouse button and the buttons to the right are secondary buttons. This is done using the MOUSE... command in the PREFERENCES menu on the Windows Control Panel.

In the MOUSE PREFERENCES dialog box you can also set the time between double clicks on the mouse. If you work quickly in PageMaker, a long delay settings can be irritating because it may register two separate double-clicks as one. Alternatively, if you are learning to use a mouse, you may appreciate the longer delay.

The WIN.INI file

In order to keep track of all of the user-selectable options used by Windows and by Windows applications such as PageMaker, Windows keeps a text file called WIN.INI in the same directory as the Windows applications. When loading, Windows reads the WIN.INI file and uses the settings it finds there. PageMaker also reads WIN.INI when it is launched, reading the PageMaker settings.

The information contained in the WIN.INI file includes;

- Whether the Windows Spooler is turned on or off
- Which printer drivers are installed, and which ports they are connected to.

- Which fonts are installed
- Printer communication settings
- Which PageMaker import and export filters are installed
- The locations of specific files needed by Windows or PageMaker

Many of the settings kept in the WIN.INI file are set by the Windows and PageMaker installation programs, and others are set by the Windows Control Panel. However, it is possible to directly modify the WIN.INI file using any text editor. This allows you to quickly change a variety of settings, and to make changes to the WIN.INI file that are not possible using any other means.

Below we have reprinted a typical WIN.INI file. Throughout the listing we have added comments describing modifications that you might want to make to the WIN. INI file. To make these changes, open the WIN.INI file in a text editor such as Windows Notepad (on the Windows SYSTEM menu) or Windows Write. Make the changes and then save the WIN.INI file as a text-only document. Be vary careful when making changes to the WIN.INI file— incorrect changes could prevent a document from printing or even prevent an application from running. You might want to make a copy of your original WIN.INI file, rename it WIN.OLD, and keep it in a safe place.

```
[windows]
; The "spooler" entry enables and disables the Spooler. Setting
; this entry to "yes" enables the Spooler; setting it to "no"
; disables the Spooler.
spooler=yes
```

The "spooler" option is used to turn the Windows Spooler on or off. Set this line to "Spooler=no" if you do not want the spooler to be used when launching Windows.

```
DoubleClickSpeed=500
CursorBlinkRate=550
; In the MS-DOS Executive, the View menu's Program command displays
; those files which have an extension specified by the "programs"
; entry. You may want to add the "pif" extension to this list.
programs=com exe bat
; The "NullPort" entry determines the text used to denote that a
; peripheral device ( i.e. a printer ) is not connected to a port.
; In the Control Panel, see the Set menu's Connections command.
NullPort=None
; The "load" entry determines what applications should be loaded
; as an icon when you start Windows.
load=
; The "run" entry determines which applications will run when Windows
; is started. Specify an application name or a file with one of the
; file extensions listed in the [extensions] section. The former simply
; runs the application; the latter not only runs the application, but
; also loads the specified file into the application.
run=
device=PostScript Printer,PSCRIPT,LPT3:
```

The "device" option specifies the default output device.

```
DeviceNotSelectedTimeout=15
TransmissionRetryTimeout=45
beep=no

[extensions]
cal=calendar.exe ^.cal
crd=cardfile.exe ^.crd
trm=terminal.exe ^.trm
txt=notepad.exe ^.txt
ini=notepad.exe ^.ini
msp=paint.exe ^.msp
wri=write.exe ^.wri
PM3=PM.EXE ^.PM3
PT3=PM.EXE ^.PT3
xls=excel.exe ^.xls
xlc=excel.exe ^.xlc
xlw=excel.exe ^.xlw
xlm=excel.exe ^.xlm
```

```
[colors]

[pif]
swapdisk=?
swapsize=0
assign.com=1
attrib.exe=32
backup.com=128
backup.exe=128
chkdsk.com=64
chkdsk.exe=64
command.com=32
comp.com=64
diskcomp.com=128
diskcomp.exe=128
diskcopy.com=128
diskcopy.exe=128
edlin.com=64
find.exe=64
format.com=64
format.exe=64
join.exe=20
mode.com=1
mode.exe=1
more.com=64
print.com=1
print.exe=1
recover.com=64
recover.exe=64
restore.com=128
sort.exe=64
subst.exe=20
win.com=1

[intl]
dialog=yes

[ports]
; A line with [filename].PRN followed by an equal sign causes
; [filename] to appear in the Control Panel's Connections dialog.
; A printer connected to [filename] directs its output into this file.
LPT1:=
LPT2:=
LPT3:=
COM1:=9600,n,8,1
COM2:=9600,n,8,1
EPT:=
AppleTalk=
PrintMe.PRN=
```

The [ports] section lists each of the available ports, which appear in the CONNECTIONS dialog box in the Windows Control Panel. The COM ports are configured here as to their speed, parity, number of data bits, and number of stop bits. We have added a new line, "PrintMe.PRN=", which allows us to print a file to disk. This is used primarily with PostScript, to save a PostScript version of your file to disk so that it can be transmitted to a service bureau for output. This process is described more fully in Chapter 13, *Printing Publications.*

```
[fonts]
Helv 8,10,12,14,18,24 (Set #3)=HELVB
Courier 8,10,12 (Set #3)=COURB
Tms Rmn 8,10,12,14,18,24 (Set #3)=TMSRB
Roman (Set #1)=ROMAN
Script (Set #1)=SCRIPT
Modern (Set #1)=MODERN
Palatino-Roman=POR_____
Palatino-Italic=POI_____
Palatino-Bold=POB_____
Palatino-BoldItalic=POBI____
```

The [fonts] section lists each of the fonts currently loaded into Windows. The first six fonts are the Windows default fonts. Each of these lists the font name and available point sizes. In this WIN.INI file, the PostScript Palatino font family has also been added.

```
[PageMaker]
Defaults=C:\PMCLASS\PM.CNF
```

The "Defaults" option specifies the directory in which the the PM.CNF file resides. The PM.CNF file holds the PageMaker default information. You may want to change this if you use PageMaker on a network, as discussed later in this chapter.

```
User Dictionary=\PM\PMUSUSER.TXT
[wingrab]
display=5
filemask=C:\pmc

[devices]
PostScript Printer=PSCRIPT,LPT3:
```

The [devices] section lists the printers currently installed and the ports to which they are currently connected. These settings can be changed directly or modified using the Windows Control Panel as described earlier in this chapter.

```
[PostScript,LPT3]
device=Apple LaserWriter Plus
resolution=300
orientation=0
papersource=1
paper0=Letter
paper1=Letter
paper2=Letter

[PostScript,PM.PRN]
device=Apple LaserWriter Plus
resolution=300
orientation=0
papersource=1
paper0=Letter
paper1=Letter
paper2=Letter
```

These sections list the current configuration settings for any printers that you have currently installed. The settings in these configurations are changed using the CONNECTIONS... and COMMUNICATIONS... commands in the Windows Control Panel.

PageMaker on a network

PageMaker 3.0 can be run over most networks, including Novell Netware, 3+, AppleShare, and Tops, as a single-launch application. (Single-launch applications permit only one user at a time.) Using PageMaker over a network will inhibit performance significantly, and if possible, we recommend installing PageMaker on the hard disk of each workstation that will be using it rather than on the network. Networks are best suited to the sharing of data files (including PageMaker publications) and printers.

If you choose to install PageMaker on a network, all PageMaker files except the PMUSUSER.TXT and the defaults file may be placed in write-protected volumes or folders. Microsoft Windows cannot be run over a network and must be installed on each computer that will be using PageMaker. If you want to use your customized default settings each time you use PageMaker, you must keep a private defaults file (PM.CNF) on your computer in the \PM directory. Use the Windows NotePad (on the WINDOWS CONTROL menu in PageMaker) to add the following line to the WIN.INI Windows file, just below the word, [PageMaker], as in the sample WIN.INI file shown in the preceding section.

Defaults=C:\PM\PM.CNF

User Dictionary=\PM\PMUSUSER.TXT

Using PageMaker 1.0 or 1.0a

Now that you have installed PageMaker 3.0, you will probably be using it to create all your new publications. And, since PageMaker 3.0 can open any existing publication that was created in PageMaker 1.0 or 1.0a, you will probably edit most of your existing publications in version 3.0. You may, however, have some documents that you wish to continue editing in version 1.0, and perhaps even some documents that you want to continue to create in version 1.0

In order to do this, you must reconfigure your version 1.0 files so that they use Windows 2.0 (or the run-time version of Windows 2.0 included with PageMaker 3.0). There are three steps in this process:

- All files from your previous version of Windows must be removed.
- Your PageMaker 1.0 files must be moved into another subdirectory *or* when installing PageMaker 3.0 you must change the default directory to something other than /PM. Set your PATH command in your AUTOEXEC.BAT file so that it includes both the directory where your PageMaker 3.0 application is stored and the directory where your PageMaker 1.0 application is stored.
- The screen fonts included along with PageMaker 1.0 must be updated so that they can be used with Windows 2.0. This is done using a utility called CONVFONT which is included along with PageMaker 3.0.

Re-installing PageMaker 3.0

If your PageMaker 3.0 application is damaged or removed from your hard disk, re-run the installation program as described in this chapter. If you change your display adaptor, mouse, or keyboard, you will need to re-install Windows, and PageMaker will adapt to the changes. You can add additional printers or fonts, as described above, without re-installing PageMaker.

Terms, Tools, & Menus

In this chapter we examine:

- *Basic PC and PageMaker terminology.*
- *PageMaker's menus and tools.*
- *Keyboard equivalents.*

Aldus PageMaker on the PC relies on Microsoft Windows for its *user interface*. This means that your proficiency in PageMaker depends on your ability to use the mouse and keyboard to interact with menus, tools, and dialog boxes. In this chapter, we introduce these most basic aspects of working with PageMaker. We will discuss each PageMaker menu command and tool and summarize many of the associated dialog boxes.

After reading this chapter, you should have an understanding of the range of PageMaker's capabilities. More experienced users may find this information sufficient to allow them to begin their own experiments with PageMaker. Less experienced users may find these summaries a bit overwhelming. In either case, remember that this is only a brief tour; the remainder of this book will provide all the details required to master the range of possibilities suggested in this chapter.

Before touring the menus and tools, however, we will take a moment to define the terms used throughout this book in describing the PageMaker/ Microsoft Windows interface. Ambiguous terms such as *select*, *choose*, *options*, and *commands* are defined to lay the foundation on which this book will build in describing the use of PageMaker. Because most of these terms are not universally defined, we recommend that even experienced PC users review this section before going on to the other chapters of the book.

We will assume that you know how to perform a few functions required for the fundamental operation of your PC. These include turning on your computer, inserting a disk, and copying files. You must also be familiar with the meaning of the terms mouse, monitor, window, icon, cursor, and desktop. If you are unfamiliar with these functions or terms, please consult your DOS operations manual.

Basic terminology

The terms defined below are ones with which you are probably familiar in a general sense. The concepts will be used often throughout this book and while these terms may have alternative definitions elsewhere, these are the meanings that we will use in this book. Words and phrases in *italics* are vocabulary words, but are not included in our glossary, since their meanings pertain more to the operation of Windows than to the operation of PageMaker. Words and phrases in **bold type** are included in the glossary at the end of this book.

Mouse operations

A mouse may have one, two, or three buttons. As described in Chapter 2, *Installing PageMaker*, unless you specify differently using the Windows Control Panel, the left mouse button is the primary mouse button, and the right mouse button is the secondary mouse button. PageMaker uses both the primary and the secondary mouse buttons. Whenever we talk about mouse operations in this book, use of the primary mouse button is implied. Any uses of the secondary mouse button will be specifically noted.

To *click* the mouse is to press the mouse button and immediately release. To *drag* is to press and hold down the mouse button, move your mouse to a new location, and release. To *double-click* is to press and release the mouse button twice in rapid succession.

Menus

To *choose* a command is to pick it from a group of related items. A command is chosen from a **pull-down menu** by dragging the mouse pointer down the menu choices until the command you wish to choose is *highlighted*, and then releasing the mouse button. On color monitors, highlighted commands appear in a different color than the menu itself, on monochrome monitors, highlighted commands are displayed in reverse video, with the characters and the background inverted from their normal shading.

Three basic kinds of commands are available in PageMaker's menus:

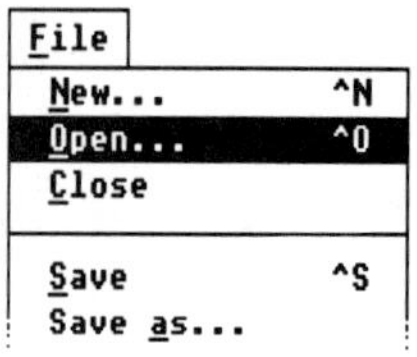

- **Commands followed by an ellipsis**. When a menu command name is followed by an ellipsis (...), a *dialog box* will appear when the command is chosen. This dialog box will request information before executing the command.

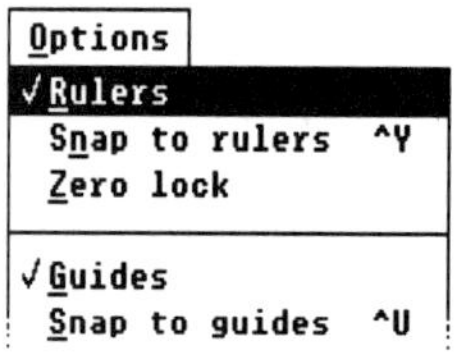

- **Toggling Command Options**. These commands are options that turn on and off a particular PageMaker function. In some cases, these commands display a check mark (✓) in front of the command name when the feature is turned on. In other cases, the name of the command itself changes to reflect the effect that choosing the command will have.

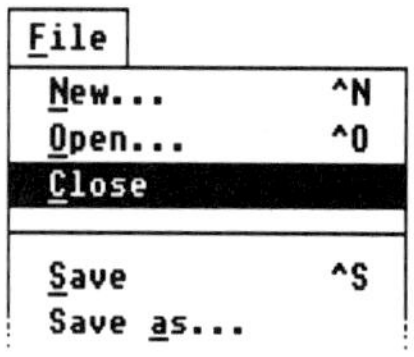

- **Executing Commands**. Commands that do not fall into one of the above categories simply execute as soon as they are chosen.

Many menu commands may be chosen either from the keyboard or by using the mouse. Key sequences that choose menu commands are called *keyboard equivalents*. In Windows three forms of keyboard equivalents are available—those that use the ALT key, those that use the CTRL key, and those that use the function keys (F1-F10).

ALT keyboard equivalents are marked in Windows by letters underlined in menu titles, menu commands, or dialog box options and are accessed by pressing the appropriate key. To use an ALT keyboard equivalent to choose a menu command, you must first use the ALT key equivalent to select the menu containing the command that you wish to choose, and then press the key for the specific command that you wish to execute. For example, to select the GUIDES command from the OPTIONS menu, press ALT-O and then press G.

CTRL key equivalents access menu commands directly, making it unnecessary to first choose any menu key equivalent. CTRL key equivalents are much faster than ALT key equivalents. Whenever a CTRL keyboard equivalent for a command is available, it is listed to the right of the command in its menu.

Function key equivalents are similar to CTRL key equivalents, and are also listed next to all commands for which they are available.

Throughout this book we list keyboard equivalents in parenthesis after menu commands are discussed.

Dialog boxes and options

A *dialog box* can present information to you, request information from you, or both. In most cases, dialog boxes appear in response to a command that you have chosen or an action you have taken. When dialog boxes request information, they do so by presenting you with options.

Three kinds of *options* are found in dialog boxes:

- **Radio buttons**. To present a group of options from which you may select only one, small round buttons are used before the option names. These are called radio buttons. To *select* a radio button option, click on the round button itself or on the name of the option following the button. Only one radio button option in a set may be selected at a time: selecting one will deselect any other. The radio buttons in a set are usually close together. Several sets of radio buttons may appear in a single dialog box, but only one from each set may be selected at any one time. A filled radio button indicates that an option is selected, and empty button indicates that it is deselected.

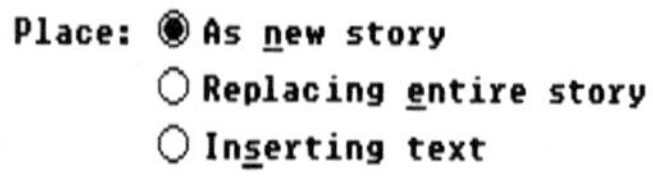

- **Check boxes**. To present a group of options from which you may select any number, small square buttons are used before the option names. These are called *check boxes*. To *select* or *deselect* a check box, click on the square before the option name or directly on the option name itself. If that option was previously deselected, it will become selected; if it was selected, it will become deselected. More than one check box in a set may be selected or deselected. An 5 is displayed in a check box to show that an option is selected, and an empty box means that option is deselected.

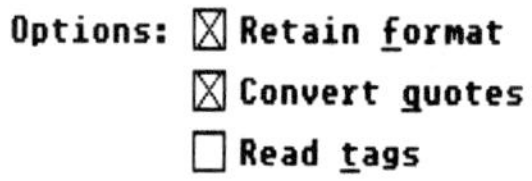

- **Option boxes**. Options for which you must enter data are called *option boxes*. Most option boxes contain default data when the dialog box first appears. When this default data is selected (highlighted with white characters on a black background) you can enter new values from the keyboard and the default data will be re-

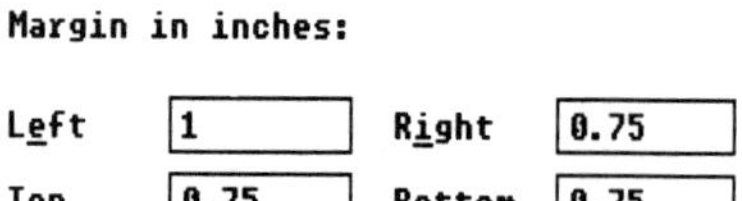

placed. To *select* a value in an option box in order to change it, double-click on a newly entered value or drag the cursor over the current value.

If there are several options in a particular dialog box, you can move to the next option by pressing the TAB key. You can also tab to a button. Pressing the TAB key highlights the next option or button by drawing a dotted box around it. When a button is highlighted, pressing the RETURN key executes the button.

Buttons in dialog boxes are used much like commands are used in menus. Some buttons bring up additional dialog boxes (when followed by an ellipsis), and others execute commands. The most common buttons are the OK and CANCEL buttons, which both close the current dialog box, saving the changes made or reverting to the original settings, respectively. Several buttons found in PageMaker are shown in the margin. Buttons are invoked either by clicking on them with the mouse button or by pressing the TAB key until they are highlighted, and then pressing the RETURN key.

Dialog boxes that do not request information are known as **Alert dialog boxes**, since their purpose is to alert you of some fact. Some Alert boxes warn you of the consequences of the action you are about to take and allow you to abort that action. Other Alert boxes inform you of some event that has already happened, allowing you only to acknowledge that you have been told.

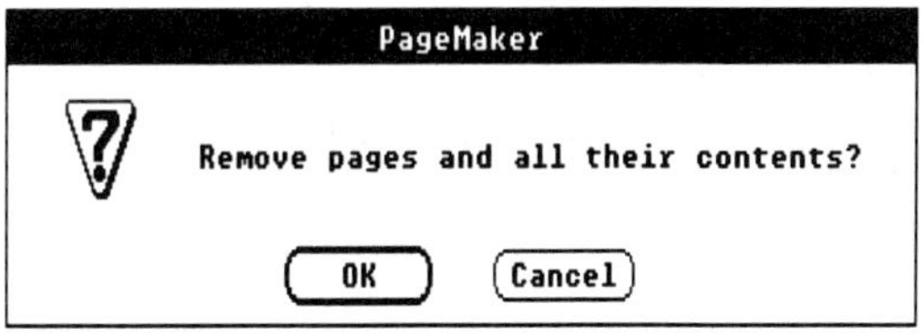

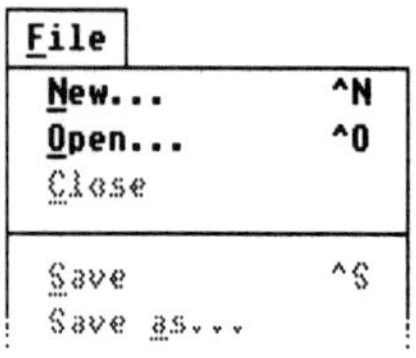

You may discover that an option, command, or menu is *dimmed* (appearing gray or faded), which means that it has no effect on the current situation. Dimmed items cannot be chosen or selected.

Typographic conventions in this text

We occasionally tell you to press a key while performing a mouse operation. Such keys are listed in small caps (SHIFT, TAB, ALT, CTRL, etc.). Menus, commands, buttons, and dialog box names are also printed in small caps to set them apart from text. The names of options inside dialog boxes are shown in quotation marks. The names of files that appear on your disk, or of other software applications, are printed in all capitals (MSPAINT.EXE, PMUSUSER.TXT).

Miscellaneous terms

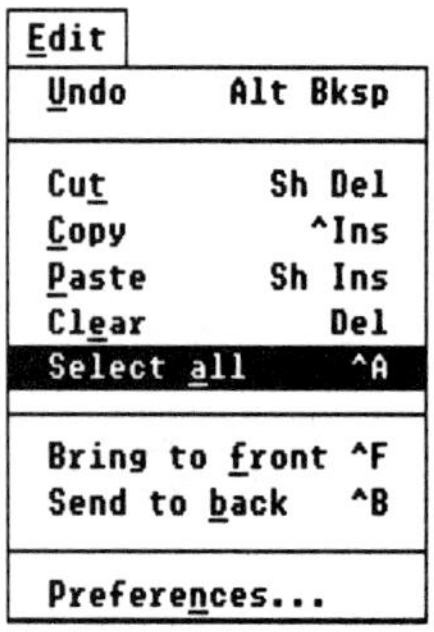

A **publication** is any PageMaker file, and is sometimes called a document. A **story** is an entire text file in PageMaker, including all the text in all the text blocks that the text threads through. A text document may be placed into PageMaker from a word-processor, or it typed directly into PageMaker. You can determine which text is part of a particular story by placing the text insertion point anywhere in the story and choosing the SELECT ALL command (CTRL-A) from the EDIT menu—all text in the story will become selected, including all text blocks on every page in the publication that includes any portion of the story.

TechTile: Flash!

By: Joan Clickrite

Every day, all of us at TechTile Industries produce a wide variety of printed materials—letters, memos, overheads, reports, and more. How those business communications look says something about TechTile Industries.

To make all the company's materials look their best, TechTile Industries has always used state-of-the-art technology for business communications. Over the years, we have moved from manual to electric typewriters, then to centralized word-processing centers. During the past three years, every office worker—from clerical to manager—has been given the option of equipping his or her desk with a personal computer and various software packages for word-processing, spreadsheets, graphics, and electronic mail.

Now, TechTile Industries advances beyond letter-quality word-processing to typeset-quality desktop publishing. Every employee can use personal computers to create more effective printed communications on the job.

Halfbright Wins Scholarship!

Bill Jones, CEO of TechTile Industries

Figure 3.01: *All text from a single story can be selected even though it flows through several text blocks.*

The PageMaker menus

In addition to the Windows Control menu commands, PageMaker 3.0 uses seven pull-down menus to present its 61 commands. In this section we will briefly review these menus and commands in order to understand the basic purpose of each. Later in this book we will take a very detailed look at each command, expanding on the simple description provided below. If an CTRL keyboard equivalent exists for a menu command, it is listed in parentheses following the command name. If an ALT keyboard equivalent exists for a menu or command, it is underlined in the menu or command name.

The Windows Control menu

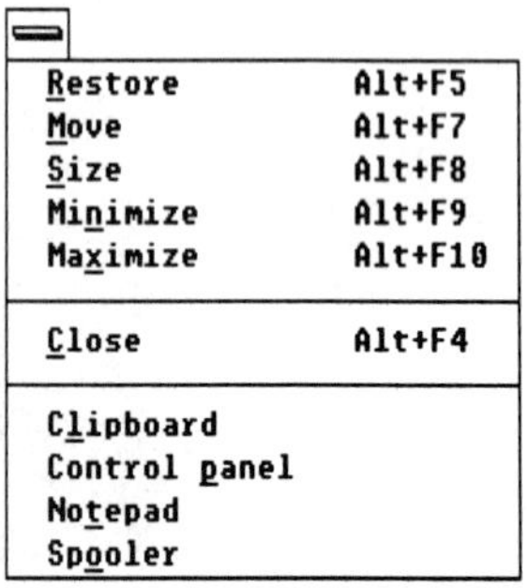

The WINDOWS CONTROL menu lists the commands that control the current window and provides access to the Clipboard, Spooler, and Control Panel. See your Windows documentation for more information on the Clipboard, Spooler, and Control Panel.

RESTORE (ALT-F5) Restores a window to its original size.

MOVE (ALT-F7) allows you to move a window around the desktop. In PageMaker you can also move windows by simply placing the mouse pointer on the window's title bar, dragging the window to where you want it, and releasing the mouse button.

SIZE (ALT-F8) allows you to change the size of a window. In PageMaker, you can also resize a window by pointing to the corner of the window you want to resize and pressing the mouse button, dragging the corner of the window to the size you want, and then releasing the mouse button.

MINIMIZE (ALT-F9) shrinks the selected window to an icon at the bottom of the screen while keeping the application or file in memory. You can also click on the down arrow at the upper right corner of the window. Use this feature to keep the screen free of several layers of windows. If you are finished with an application or file, use the CLOSE command to remove it from RAM memory.

MAXIMIZE (ALT-F10) enlarges the selected window to cover the entire screen, including the icon area that usually appears at the bottom of the screen. You can also use the up arrow in the upper right corner. Use this feature when you want to use the entire screen to view your publication.

Close (Alt-F4) closes the selected window. Use this command to close an application or utility when you have finished using it.

Clipboard shows a window containing the contents of the Windows Clipboard. Clipboard contents are usually the result of the last Cut or Copy command, but may be leftover copy from some application that was open before PageMaker was opened. The Cut, Copy, and Paste commands may be used while the Clipboard window is open., but the Clipboard window will disappear behind the now-active publication window. To view both windows simultaneously, adjust the size of the publication window until you can see the Clipboard window. To close the Clipboard, use the Close command in the Windows Control menu.

Control Panel opens the Windows Control Panel application. This is used to to install or remove fonts and printers, change the screen colors and mouse settings, and a variety of other Windows environmental parameters. The Control Panel is dimmed whenever a publication is open in PageMaker.

Notepad opens the Windows Notepad application. The Notepad is a small text editor that you can use to create, edit, and print text files.

Spooler opens the Windows Spooler application. The Spooler is used to reduce the amount of time that your computer is busy while printing documents. When the spooler is turned on, printed documents go into the spooler, which then handles all interface with your printer, making your computer available for use while the printing continues.

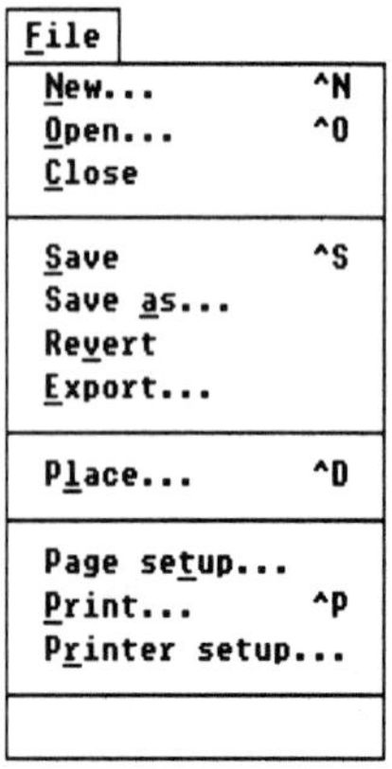

The File menu

As in most Windows applications, the PageMaker File menu controls broad document-level activities including the opening, closing, printing, and saving of documents. Additionally, the File menu controls the importation of text and graphic images and the export of text files.

New... (Ctrl-N) brings up the Page setup dialog box, where you define the attributes of the new publication or template. Clicking the OK button in the dialog box creates the new publication and displays the new publication window on-screen. The New... command is dimmed whenever a publication is already open in PageMaker.

Open... (Ctrl-O) brings up the Open publication dialog box in which you may locate and select any existing PageMaker publication file or template to open. The Open... command is dimmed whenever a publication is already open in PageMaker.

Close closes the open publication or template document, but does not quit the PageMaker application. If you have made changes to the file being closed but have not saved these changes, the Save changes before closing? dialog box appears, prompting you to either save changes, discard changes, or abort the file closure. Choosing the Close command when a file is untitled brings up the Save as dialog box, which prompts you to name and save the file. The Close command is dimmed when no publication or template document is open.

Save (Ctrl-S) updates the disk file of the publication or template document to include all changes made since the last version was saved. Choosing the Save command for an untitled document brings up the Save as dialog box, which prompts you to specify a filename and location before the file is saved. The SAVE command is dimmed when no changes have been made since the last time your publication was saved.

SAVE AS... brings up the SAVE AS dialog box, which prompts you to name and save the document, select the location to which the document will be saved, and choose whether the document will be saved as a publication or as a template. Saving documents via the SAVE AS... command reduces the size of the file and leaves the previously saved version of the file available. If you try to save a document using the name of an existing file, an Alert dialog box will appear asking you to confirm the replacement of the existing file with the document you are saving.

REVERT discards all changes made to the publication or template and restores the file as it was last saved using either the SAVE or SAVE AS... command. Choosing the REVERT command brings up an Alert dialog box that prompts you to confirm or abort the reversion. Pressing the SHIFT key while choosing the REVERT command discards only those changes made since the last mini-save, instead of the last SAVE or SAVE AS.... Once the REVERT command has been selected and confirmed, you can not undo it. The REVERT command is dimmed when no changes have been made to the current publication.

EXPORT... brings up the EXPORT DOCUMENT dialog box, which allows you to save the currently selected text or story to a separate disk file. Exported files can be saved in text-only format or in the format of several popular word-processors, depending on which export filters you have installed. The EXPORT... command is dimmed if no text is selected or if the insertion point is not set in a text block.

Place... (Ctrl-D) brings up the Place document dialog box, in which you select a text or graphic file to be imported into PageMaker. Text documents, word-processed documents, paint-type graphics files, draw-type graphics files, encapsulated PostScript (EPS) files, and Tag Image File Format (TIFF) files can all be placed in a publication.

Page setup... brings up the Page setup dialog box, which contains various options for the electronic page on which a publication is created. This is the same dialog box that appears when you choose the New command. If no document is currently open, a change in the settings of the Page setup options will change the default values used for any new documents created at a later date.

Print... (Ctrl-P) brings up the Print dialog box, in which you specify printing options and initiate printing.

Printer Setup... brings up the Printer setup dialog box, which allows you to select among the currently available printers and specify options for the selected printer.

Exit exits the PageMaker application, closes the publication window if it is open, and returns you to the MS-DOS Executive if you have the full version of Windows, or to the DOS prompt if you are using run-time Windows. If you choose the Exit command before you have saved the most recent changes made to your publication, the Save changes dialog box appears, prompting you to save or discard the changes. If you are working on an untitled publication when you select the Exit command, the Save as dialog will appear, prompting you to name and save the document.

The Edit menu

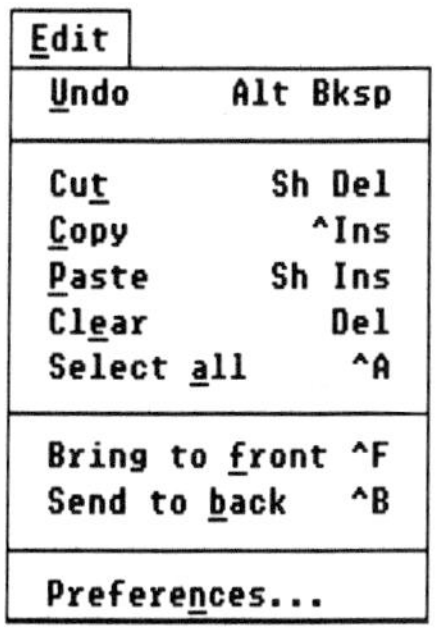

Some of the commands in the Edit menu are standard Edit menu commands in all Windows applications. These commands control the manipulation of selected elements, as well as the Windows Clipboard. Additionally, the Edit menu is the home of PageMaker's Preferences command.

Undo reverses the effect of the last action, returning the file to its exact state prior to the last action. Not all actions can be undone: the Undo command will read "Cannot undo" and will be dimmed if the last action cannot be reversed. If the action can be reversed, the Undo command will name the action eligible for reversal. Immediately after one action has been undone, but before another action is done, the Undo command becomes a Redo command, allowing you to undo the undo or, equivalently, to redo the original action.

Cut (Shift-Del) deletes the selected text, elements, or text and elements from your document, placing them on the Windows Clipboard. The effect of this command is identical to the operation of the Cut command in other Windows software. If no text or element is selected, the Cut command is dimmed.

Copy (Ctrl-Ins) makes a copy of the selected text, elements, or text and elements from your document, and places them on the Windows Clipboard..The effect of this command is identical to the operation of the Copy command in other Windows software. If no text or element is selected, the Copy command is dimmed.

Paste (Shift Ins) places a copy of the Windows Clipboard contents into your document. These elements are selected after being pasted into the document so that you can easily adjust their position. A copy of the pasted text or graphic objects remains on the Clipboard so it may be pasted again. If the Clipboard is empty, the PASTE command is dimmed.

CLEAR (DELETE-) deletes the selected text, elements, or text and elements from your document without placing them on the Clipboard. If no text or element is selected, the CLEAR command is dimmed.

SELECT ALL (CTRL-A) selects all objects in the current publication window *or* all the text in the current story. If the text tool is positioned within a story, the entire story is selected. If the text tool is not positioned within a story—that is, if any tool other than the text tool is selected or if the text tool is positioned on a empty portion of the page—all text and graphic objects on the page(s) are selected, along with all text blocks and graphic objects on the pasteboard.

BRING TO FRONT (CTRL-F) moves the selected element(s) to the top of the **stacking order** that PageMaker uses for layering elements. Moving a text block or graphic element automatically brings it to the front.

SEND TO BACK (CTRL-B) moves the selected element(s) to the bottom of the stacking order that PageMaker uses for layering elements.

PREFERENCES... brings up the PREFERENCES dialog box. The options in this dialog control the units of measure used in the rulers and in all the dialog boxes, the position of ruler and column guides in the stacking order, the point size at which text is **greeked** during display, and the point size at which vector fonts are substituted for screen fonts. If no document is currently open, a change in the settings of the PREFERENCES options will change the default values used for any new documents created at a later date.

The Options menu

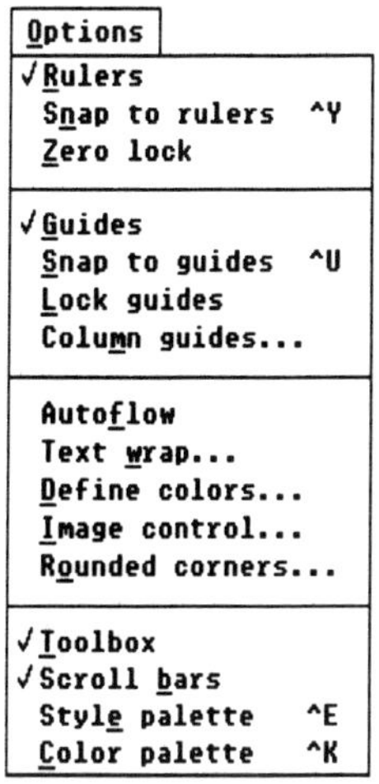

The Options menu contains a variety of commands, most of which are unique to PageMaker.

Rulers toggles on and off the display of the rulers along the top and left edges of the publication window. A check mark (✓) shown next to the command indicates that it is currently selected (rulers are displayed); choosing it at this time will deselect it (rulers become hidden). Rulers use the measurement system specified in the Preferences dialog box. If no document is currently open, a change in Rulers command will change the default values used for any new documents created at a later date.

Snap to rulers (Ctrl-Y) automatically repositions any text or graphic elements so that they align with the vertical and horizontal tick marks of the rulers. A check mark (✓) before the command indicates that it is currently selected (elements snap to ticks); choosing it at this time will deselect it (elements will not snap to ticks when moved). If no document is currently open, a change in Snap to rulers command will change the default values used for any new documents created at a later date.

Zero lock locks the zero point of the rulers so that the intersecting lines in the upper left corner of the publication window become unselectable and immovable. A check mark (✓) showing before the command indicates that it is currently selected (zero point is locked); choosing it at this time will deselect it (zero point becomes unlocked). If no document is currently open, a change in Zero lock command will change the default values used for any new documents created at a later date.

Guides displays all non-printing column, ruler, and margin guides that have been created for the pages in the publication window. A check mark (✓) before the command indicates that it is currently selected (guides are displayed); choosing it at this time will deselect it (guides become hidden). If no document is currently open, a change in Guides command will change the default values used for any new documents created at a later date.

Snap to guides gives all column, ruler, and margin guides a magnetic pull on the pointer, text blocks, and graphic elements. A check mark (✓) before the command indicates that it is currently selected (elements snap to guides); choosing it at this time will deselect it (elements will not snap to guides when moved). If no document is currently open, a change in Snap to guides command will change the default values used for any new documents created at a later date.

Lock Guides (Ctrl-U) locks all the column and ruler guides and prohibits the creation of new guides. A check mark (✓) before the command indicates that it is currently selected (guides are locked); choosing it at this time will deselect it (guides become unlocked). The Lock guides command is dimmed when the Guides command is not turned on.

Column guides... brings up the Column guides dialog, in which you define or edit the number of columns and the space between them for the current page(s). The column guides... command is dimmed when the Guides command is not turned on. If no document is currently open, a change in the settings of the Column guides options will change the default values used for any new documents created at a later date.

Autoflow activates the automatic text flow feature used when placing text. The actual flow method used is determined by the use of the mouse and various key commands while the text is being poured into the document. A check mark (✓) before the command indicates that it is currently selected (autoflow is activated); choosing it at this time will deselect it (autoflow becomes deactivated). If no publication is open, changing the Autoflow command will change the default setting for any new documents.

Text wrap... brings up the Text wrap dialog box. This dialog allows you to specify how text will fit around the currently selected graphic(s). Text can be set to flow over the graphic, wrap the graphic rectangularly, or wrap the graphic according to some customized shape. If no document is currently open, a change in the settings of the Text Wrap options will change the default values used for any new documents created at a later date.

Define colors... brings up the Define colors dialog box, in which spot colors can be added, edited, or deleted. If no publication is open, changing the Define colors...command will change the default setting for any new documents.

Image control... brings up the Image Control dialog box, in which you may manipulate the appearance of a currently selected graphic (either a paint-type graphics file or a scanned image). Controls include lightness and contrast of images, line screens, and and gray levels for gray-scale images. The Image control... command is dimmed unless a paint-type graphic or a TIFF image is selected.

Rounded corners... brings up the Rounded corners dialog box, which presents six alternative corners for rectangles and squares drawn in PageMaker. Selecting a rounded corner when no rectangle or square is selected will alter the default used for any new rectangle or square created thereafter. If no document is currently open, a change in ROUNDED CORNERS option will change the default value used for any new documents created at a later date.

TOOLBOX toggles the display of the Toolbox window (palette) on-screen. The Toolbox can be moved and closed just like any other window. A check mark (✓) before the command indicates that it is currently selected (Toolbox is displayed); choosing it while the check mark is displayed will deselect it (Toolbox is hidden). If no document is currently open, a change in TOOLBOX command will change the default display used for any new documents created at a later date.

SCROLL BARS toggles the display of the scroll bars on the right and lower edges of the publication window. You may wish to hide the scroll bars to provide additional space on the screen for the display of your publication. A check mark (✓) before the command indicates that it is currently selected (scroll bars are displayed); choosing it while the check mark is displayed will deselect it (scroll bars will be hidden). If no document is currently open, a change in SCROLL BARS command will change the default display used for any new documents created at a later date.

STYLE PALETTE (CTRL-E) toggles on and off the display of the Styles window (palette), which lists the names of all currently defined PageMaker text styles. The Styles palette can be moved and sized using the mouse pointer. A check mark (✓) before the command indicates that it is currently selected (Styles palette window is on the screen); choosing it while the check mark is displayed will deselect it (Styles palette window becomes hidden). If no document is currently open, a change in STYLE PALETTE command will change the default display used for any new documents.

Color Palette (Ctrl-K) toggles on and off the display of the Colors window (palette), which lists the names of all currently defined PageMaker colors. The Colors palette can be moved and sized as a window using the mouse pointer. A check mark (✓) before the command indicates that it is currently selected (Colors palette is displayed); choosing it while the check mark is displayed will deselect it (Colors palette will disappear). If no document is currently open, a change in Color palette command will change the default display used for any new documents.

The Page menu

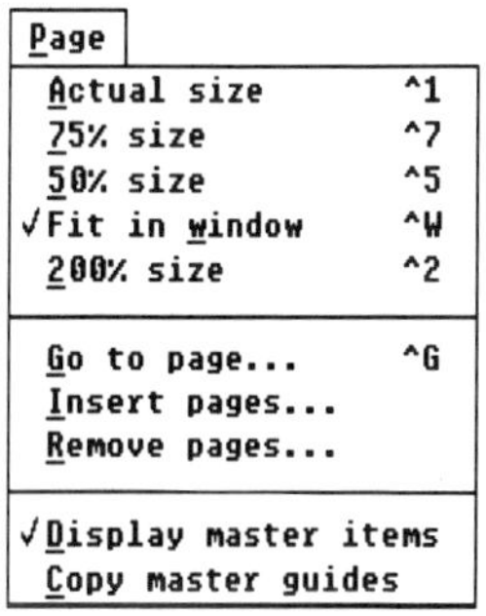

The Page menu contains commands that affect the view size used to display the currently selected page(s), the number of pages in the document, which page(s) are currently selected, and the use of items from the master page(s).

Actual size (Ctrl-1) changes the display in the publication window to a full-size representation of the current page(s). PageMaker centers the display based on the items centered in the previous view size. Choosing the Actual size command when it is already selected will refresh the video display. A check mark (✓) before the command indicates that it is selected. You can also click the secondary mouse button to see the publication at actual size.

75% size (Ctrl-7) changes the display in the publication window to 75% of its actual size. PageMaker centers the display based on the items centered in the previous view size. Choosing the 75% size command when it is already selected will refresh the video display. A check mark (✓) before the command indicates that it is selected.

50% SIZE (CTRL-5) shows the publication at 50% of its actual size. PageMaker centers the display based on the items centered in the previous view size. Choosing the 50% size command when it is already selected will refresh the video display. A check mark (✓) before the command indicates that it is selected.

FIT IN WINDOW (CTRL-W) changes the display in the publication window so that all of the currently selected page(s) is displayed. The actual reduction required for this display depends on the size and resolution of your monitor. Choosing the FIT IN WINDOW command when it is already selected will refresh the video display. A check mark (✓) before the command indicates that it is selected. Holding down the SHIFT key while selecting this command changes the display to include all of the selected page(s) plus the entire pasteboard.

200% SIZE (CTRL-2) changes the display in the publication window to 200% of its actual size. PageMaker centers the display based on the items centered in the previous view. Choosing the 200% size command when it is already selected will refresh the video display. A check mark (✓) before the command indicates that it is selected.

GO TO PAGE... (CTRL-G) brings up the GO TO PAGE dialog, in which you may enter any page number in the document or select the left or right master page. The display then changes to the selected page.

INSERT PAGES... brings up the INSERT PAGES dialog box, in which you may specify any number of pages to be added to the current document. New pages may be placed before or after the current page or between the current pages (if you are working on facing pages).

Remove pages... brings up the Remove pages dialog box, in which you may remove any number of pages from the current document. Pages to be removed are specified by page number. Removing a page deletes the contents of the page and removes the page icon from the bottom of the screen. All remaining pages in the publication are renumbered appropriately.

Display Master items toggles on and off the display of all text and graphics from the appropriate master page on the current page. For example, if this command is on (indicated by a check mark, ✓), a border placed on the right master page appears on the current page (if it is a right-hand page); if this command is deselected (unchecked), the border is not displayed. Master items will print only if they are displayed.

Copy master guides sets the column guides and ruler guides on the current page(s)exactly as they appear on the corresponding master page. If the guides on the current page are set exactly as those on the master page(s), this command is dimmed. Any customized guides set on the current page are removed when this command is chosen.

The Type menu

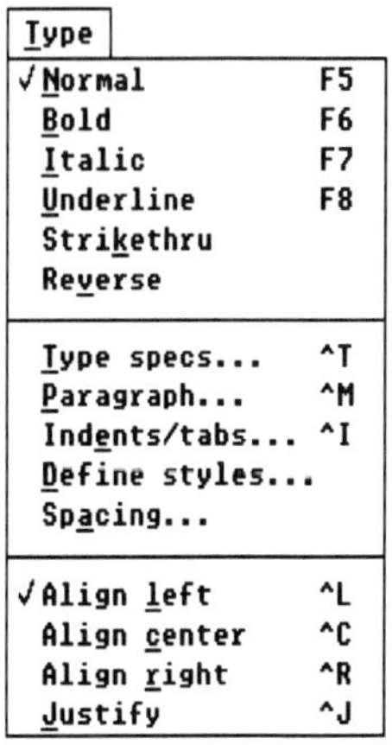

The Type menu contains commands used to edit and alter text in PageMaker. Any changes made using commands in the type menu, if made when no text is selected, become the defaults used when creating new text blocks. Any changes made when no publication window is open become application defaults and will apply to all new publications created at a later date.

Normal (F5) changes the style of the selected text to the plain style, deselecting Bold, Italic, Underline, and Strikethru for the selected text. A check mark (✓) means the selected text is plain.

Bold (F6) changes the style of the selected text to bold. A check mark (✓) means the selected text is in this style.

Italic (F7) changes the style of the selected text to italic. A check mark (✓) means the selected text is in this style.

Underline (F8) underlines the selected text. A check mark (✓) means the selected text is in this style.

Strikethru draws a line through the selected text. A check mark (✓) means the selected text is in this style.

Reverse changes the color of the text to the paper color, defined by the Define Colors command. If you choose the command while reversed text is selected, the color of the text is changed to black again. A check mark (✓) means the selected text is in this style.

Type Specs... (Ctrl-T) brings up the Type specifications dialog box, where you may alter the type face, type size, leading, type style, case, and position of the currently selected text.

Paragraph... (Ctrl-M) brings up the Paragraph specifications dialog box, where you may specify the hyphenation, pair kerning, alignment, indents, and spacing of the currently selected paragraph(s).

Indents/tabs... (Ctrl-I) brings up the Indents/Tabs dialog box, in which you may specify the left and right margins, first-line indent, and tab settings for the current paragraph(s).

Define styles... brings up the Define styles dialog, which allows you to create a new style sheet, edit or remove the existing style sheet, or import a style sheet from another publication or template.

Spacing... brings up the Spacing attributes dialog, which allows you to set the word spacing, letter spacing, hyphenation zone, calculation of auto leading, and leading method for the currently selected text or story.

Align left (Ctrl-L) aligns the selected paragraphs to the left margin of the text block. A check (✓) mark indicates that the selected paragraph is aligned to the left margin.

Align center (Ctrl-C) centers each line of the selected paragraphs between the left and right margins of the text block. A check (✓) mark indicates that the selected paragraph is centered.

Align right (Ctrl-R) aligns the selected paragraphs to the right margin of the text block. A check (✓) mark indicates that the selected paragraph is aligned to the right margin.

Justify (Ctrl-J) stretches or compresses the text in each line of the selected paragraphs so that both the left and right margins are flush to the edges of the defined text block area. A check (✓) mark indicates that the selected paragraph is justified.

The Lines menu

The Lines menu contains the various line weights and styles that may be applied to any graphic element created with a line or shape tool from the toolbox, along with the option to reverse the line's color or shading. Graphics can have only one style or line weight. If only one graphic element is selected, the check (✓) appears next to the line weight or style name of the graphic. If more than one graphic element is selected, a check mark will appear only if all selected elements use the same line weight or style.

Selecting a line weight or style when a line or shape tool is not selected will alter the default, and the weight or style will be applied to all new lines or shapes created thereafter. If no document is currently open, a change in LINES menu will change the default value used for any new documents.

The Shades menu

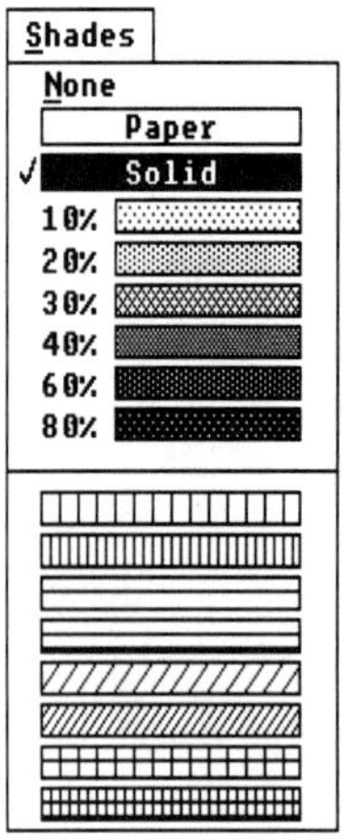

The SHADES menu contains the various shades and patterns that may be used to fill any graphic element created with the shape tools from the toolbox. Only one shade or pattern may be selected for each graphic element. If only one graphic is selected, the check (✓) appears next to the name of the shade or pattern that is applied to the graphic. If more than one graphic element is chosen, a check mark will appear only if all selected elements use the same shade or pattern.

Selecting a shade or pattern when a shape tool is not selected will alter the default, and the shade or pattern will be applied to all new lines or shapes created thereafter. If no document is currently open, a change in LINES menu will change the default value used for any new documents created at a later date.

The Help menu

The HELP menu appears at the far right of the menu bar, and lists two commands.

INDEX ...(F1) brings up a dialog box with a list of topics for which help is available. Double-clicking on a particular topic brings another list of specific tasks, and double-clicking on the particular task will display a screen of text explaining that task. Click the CANCEL button to return to your publication.

ABOUT PAGEMAKER...shows the copyright notices for PageMaker as well as the version number and the release date of the PageMaker version you are using.

The PageMaker toolbox

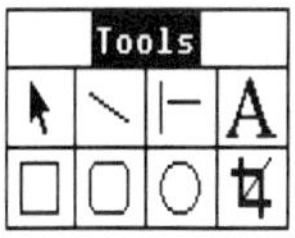

The tools from PageMaker's toolbox are used to initiate a variety of actions. Any tool is selected by clicking on its icon in the toolbox palette. The toolbox itself can be repositioned anywhere within the publication window by **dragging** its title bar, and it can be closed by choosing the TOOLBOX command from the OPTIONS menu so that the check mark (✓) disappears. Once closed, the toolbox can be re-displayed by choosing the same command, and the check mark will reappear.

The **arrow tool** is used to select text and graphic objects, move the column and ruler guides, operate the scroll bars, turn pages, and choose commands from the menus. The arrow tool appears automatically whenever the cursor is positioned over the menu bar, page icons, scroll bars, the Style or Color palettes, or the toolbox itself.

The **diagonal-line tool** is used to to create a line between any two points on the current page(s) or pasteboard. The line will be created with the weight or style currently set in the Lines menu and can be changed by selecting another weight or style from that menu while the line is selected.

The **perpendicular-line tool** is used to create vertical and horizontal lines, as well as lines at 45° angles, on the current page(s) or pasteboard. The line will will be created with the weight or style currently set in the Lines menu and can be changed by selecting another weight or style from that menu while the line is selected.

The **text tool** is used to create a new text block, to set the insertion point in an existing text block, or to select text in an existing text block.

The **square-corner** or **rectangle tool** is used to create a rectangle with square corners. Holding down the SHIFT key while creating a rectangle will constrain the rectangle to a square. The corners of any shape created with the Square-corner tool can be adjusted using the Rounded corners... command on the Edit menu. The new shape will consist of lines of the weight and style specified in the Lines menu and filled with the shade specified in the Shades menu. Either the line or shade can be changed by selecting from the appropriate menu while the shape is selected .

The **rounded-corner tool** is used to create a rectangle with rounded corners as set in the Rounded corners dialog box. Holding down the SHIFT key while creating a new rectangle will constrain the rectangle to a square. The corners of any rectangle created with the Rounded corner tool can be adjusted using the Rounded corners... command in the Options menu. The rectangle will consist of a line of the weight and style specified in the Lines menu and will be filled with the shade specified in the SHADES menu. Either the line or shade can be changed by selecting from the appropriate menu while the shape is selected.

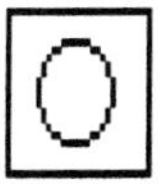

The **ellipse tool** is used to create an oval. Holding down the SHIFT key while creating a rectangle will force the shape to be a circle. The oval will consist of a line of the weight and style specified in the LINES menu and will be filled with the shade specified in the SHADES menu. Either the line or shade can be changed by selecting from the appropriate menu while the shape is selected.

The **cropping tool** is used to crop an imported graphic, uncrop a cropped graphic, or position the remainder of a cropped graphic within the graphic frame.

The keyboard

Although most interaction with PageMaker is done with the mouse, a number of commands, functions, and operations can also be executed using the keyboard. Commands which are executable via the keyboard are known as keyboard equivalents. PageMaker offers two kinds of keyboard equivalents for menu commands, plus a variety of keyboard equivalents for other functions.

The first type of keyboard equivalent for menu commands rely primarily on the CTRL key, and execute the commands directly. The second type of keyboard equivalent for menu commands uses the ALT key, and requires one keyboard equivalent to select the appropriate menu and another to execute the desired command. All keyboard equivalents of all types are listed on the following pages.

Menu command	*ALT equiv*	*CTRL equiv*
File menu	ALT-F	
New...	N	CTRL-N
Open...	O	CTRL-O
Close	C	
Save	S	CTRL-S
Save as...	A	
Revert	V	
Export...	E	
Place...	L	CTRL-D
Page setup...	T	
Print...	P	CTRL-P
Printer setup...	R	
Exit	X	
Edit menu	ALT-E	
Undo	U	
Cut	T	SHIFT-DELETE
Copy	C	CTRL-INSERT
Paste	P	SHIFT-INSERT
Clear	E	DELETE
Select all	A	CTRL-A
Bring to front	F	CTRL-F
Send to back	B	CTRL-B
Preferences...	N	
Options menu	ALT-O	
Rulers	R	
Snap to rulers	N	CTRL-Y
Zero lock	Z	
Guides	G	
Snap to guides	S	CTRL-U
Lock guides	L	
Column guides...	M	
Autoflow	F	
Text wrap...	W	
Define colors...	D	
Image control...	I	
Rounded corners...	O	
Toolbox	T	
Scroll bars	B	
Style palette	E	CTRL-E
Color palette	C	CTRL-K

Menu command	*ALT equiv*	*CTRL equiv*
Page menu	ALT-P	
Actual size	A	CTRL-1
75% size	7	CTRL-7
50% size	5	CTRL-5
Fit in window	W	CTRL-W
200% size	2	CTRL-2
Go to page...	G	CTRL-G
Insert pages...	I	
Remove pages...	R	
Display master items	D	
Copy master guides	C	
Type menu	ALT-T	
Normal	N	F5
Bold	B	F6
Italic	I	F7
Underline	U	F8
Strikethru	K	
Reverse	V	
Type specs...	T	CTRL-T
Paragraph...	P	CTRL-M
Indents/tabs...	E	CTRL-I
Define styles...	D	
Spacing...	A	
Align left	L	CTRL-L
Align center	C	CTRL-C
Align right	R	CTRL-R
Justify	J	CTRL-J
Lines menu	ALT-L	
None	N	
Hairline	H	
Reverse	R	
Shades menu	ALT-S	
None	N	
Help menu	ALT-H	
Index	I	
About PageMaker...	A	

Selecting tools

Arrow tool	SHIFT-F1
Diagonal-line tool	SHIFT-F2
Perpendicular-line tool	SHIFT-F3
Text tool	SHIFT-F4
Square-corner tool	SHIFT-F5
Rounded-corner tool	SHIFT-F6
Ellipse tool	SHIFT-F7
Cropping tool	SHIFT-F8

Moving about in the publication window

grabber hand	ALT-drag
vertical or horizontal grabber hand	SHIFT-ALT-drag

View sizes

from any to "actual"	2nd mouse button click
from "actual" to "fit-in-window"	2nd mouse button click
from any to 200%	SHIFT-2nd mouse button click
from 200% to "actual"	SHIFT-2nd mouse button click
from any to entire pasteboard	SHIFT-choose FIT IN WINDOW

Moving the insertion point

by one character	←(left), →(right)
to beginning of current or next word	CTRL-←(left), CTRL-→(right)
to beginning of current or next line of type	HOME (current), END (next)
by one line	↑(up), ↓(down),
to beginning of current or next sentence	CTRL-HOME (current), CTRL-END (next)
to beginning of current or next paragraph	CTRL-↑(current), CTRL-↓(next)
by a screen within the current text block	PAGE UP (up), PAGE DOWN (down)
to beginning or end of current story	CTRL-PAGE UP (beginning), CTRL-PAGE DOWN (end)

Moving between pages

to next page	CTRL-TAB
to previous page	SHIFT-CTRL-TAB

Text flow

from auto to manual	CTRL key
from manual to auto	CTRL key
from auto to semi-auto	SHIFT key
from manual to semi-auto	SHIFT key
interrupt autoflow	click mouse button

Kerning

delete space (1/48 of size)	CTRL-DELETE
add space (1/48 of size)	SHIFT-CTRL-DELETE

Type style

normal	F5
bold	F6
italic	F7
underline	F8

Type size

one point smaller	F3
one point larger	F4
next smaller size	F9
next larger size	F10

Type alignment

flush left	CTRL-L
flush right	CTRL-R
centered	CTRL-C
fully justified	CTRL-J

Special characters (not shown on keyboard)

	ANSI	Roman 8
register mark ®	CTRL-SHIFT-R	same
copyright mark ©	CTRL-SHIFT-C	same
cent symbol ¢	ALT-0-162	ALT-0-191
pound symbol £	ALT-0-163	ALT-0-187
yen symbol ¥	ALT-0-165	ALT-0-18
bullet ▪	CTRL-SHIFT-8	ALT-0-242
left double quote "	CTRL-SHIFT-[	same
right double quote "	CTRL-SHIFT-]	same
left single quote '	CTRL-[	same
right single quote '	CTRL-]	same
down question ¿	ALT-0-191	n/a
down exclamation ¡	ALT-0-161	n/a
plus or minus ±	ALT-0-177	n/a
one-quarter symbol ¼	ALT-0-188	ALT-0-247
one-half symbol ½	ALT-0-189	ALT-0-248
three-quarter symbol ¾	ALT-0-190	ALT-0-245
degree symbol °	ALT-0-176	n/a
en dash –	CTRL-=	same
em dash —	CTRL-SHIFT-=	same
thin space	CTRL-SHIFT-T	same
en space	CTRL-SHIFT-N	same
em space	CTRL-SHIFT-M	same
optional hyphen	CTRL--	same
page number character	CTRL-SHIFT-3	same

Note: Many, but not all, PCL printers use the Roman 8 character set rather than the ANSI character set used by PostScript printers and Windows. Check your printer manual to find which it uses.

A Brief Tour of PageMaker

In this chapter we examine:

- *Opening PageMaker and creating a new document*
- *The publication window*
- *Saving your pages and quitting the application*

Now that we have defined the terms we will use to discuss PageMaker, and have taken a look at the tools and menus PageMaker offers, we can start using PageMaker. This chapter examines the most fundamental PageMaker tasks, and introduces a few more basic concepts that we will use repeatedly throughout our PageMaker experience. Even though these topics do not directly relate to the manipulation of text and graphics, they are essential to your successful use of PageMaker.

Starting PageMaker

To begin using PageMaker, you must launch the PageMaker application. PageMaker can be launched by executing a DOS command at the C: prompt, or from the MS-DOS EXECUTIVE if you are using a full version of Windows.

To launch PageMaker when using the run-time version of Windows, enter PM at the C: prompt, and press the ENTER key. Entering PM *filename* will launch PageMaker and load the PageMaker publication named in *filename*. Anytime you are launching PageMaker from a DOS prompt, you will have to be in the sub-directory where PageMaker was installed if you did not modify your PATH statement as described in Chapter 2, *Installing PageMaker*. If you are also loading a PageMaker publication, you must either specify the full path name where the publication resides or choose a publication which resides in a directory that is included in your PATH statement.

To launch PageMaker when using a full version of Windows, enter WIN PM at the C: prompt, and then press the ENTER key. Entering WIN PM *filename* will launch PageMaker and load the PageMaker publication named in *filename*. In either case, the rules described above regarding directories and paths apply.

From the MS-DOS EXECUTIVE, you can also launch PageMaker by double-clicking on the PM.EXE file, which is located in the sub-directory where you installed PageMaker. Double-clicking on the name of any PageMaker publication listed in the MS-DOS EXECUTIVE will both launch PageMaker and load the selected publication.

As PageMaker loads, Alert dialog boxes will appear if the application is unable to locate any of the files needed to run PageMaker (such as the hyphenation dictionary files) or if enough memory or disk space is not available. In some cases, you can use PageMaker without correcting the problem. In other cases you cannot use PageMaker until the problem is corrected. If you encounter one of these problems, check the installation and setup as described in Chapter 2, *Installing PageMaker*.

Once PageMaker has successfully loaded, the copyright window and menu bar appear. The copyright window, shown in Figure 4.01, is provided as an introduction to the software, verifying that you are running the PageMaker application.

Figure 4.01: *The PageMaker copyright screen.*

When the software is finished loading, click anywhere on the screen and the copyright window will disappear. Now you are ready to begin using PageMaker. At this point there are no open windows on the desktop (unless you are using another Windows application), as shown in Figure 4.02, and most of PageMaker's menu commands are dimmed.

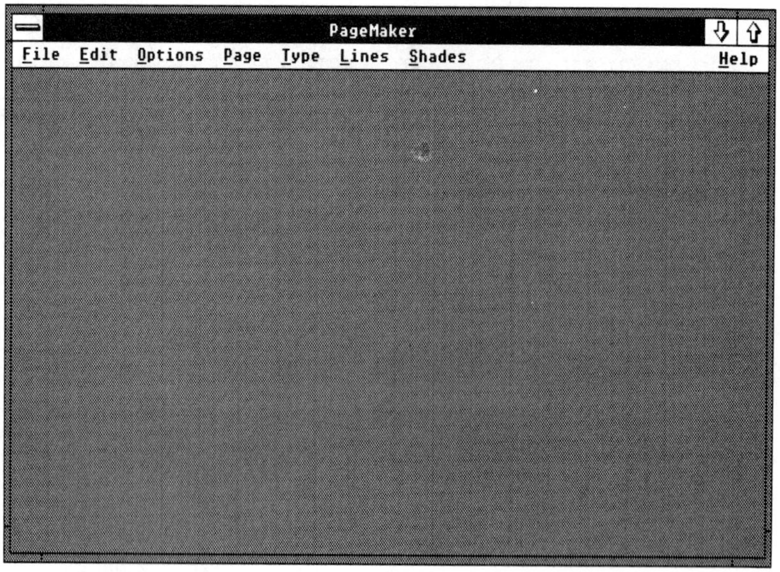

Figure 4.02: *The PageMaker desktop with no files open.*

You may choose one of four possible actions:

- Create a new PageMaker publication or template document.
- Open an existing PageMaker publication or template document.
- Alter PageMaker's application default settings.
- Quit PageMaker and return to the MS-DOS EXECUTIVE, or to DOS.

The first two actions, creating a new publication and opening existing publications, are discussed in the next sections of this chapter, and the last action, quitting PageMaker, is discussed at the end of this chapter. Altering PageMaker defaults and exiting PageMaker are discussed at the end of this chapter.

Creating a new publication

A new PageMaker publication is created by choosing the NEW... command from the FILE menu (CTRL-N), and specifying the attributes of the new publication in the PAGE SETUP dialog box (see Figure 4.03). Since PageMaker can work with only one publication at a time, the NEW... command is dimmed whenever a publication is already open. In this case you must close the open publication (using the CLOSE command from the FILE menu or the close box in the publication window) before creating a new publication.

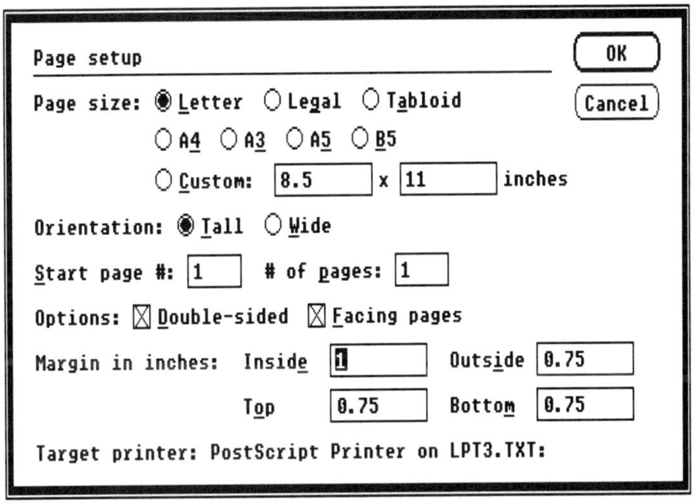

Figure 4.03: *The Page setup dialog box.*

The PAGE SETUP dialog box, which appears when the NEW... command is chosen, controls several important attributes of your publication:

- The size and orientation of each page in your document.

- The number of pages that make up your document and the page number of the first page.
- Whether the pages will be prepared as a double-sided document and whether facing pages will be viewed simultaneously on-screen.
- The size of the top, bottom, inside, and outside margins.

When the OK button in the PAGE SETUP dialog box is clicked, PageMaker creates a new publication based on the specifications set in this dialog box. If the CANCEL button is clicked, you are returned to the PageMaker desktop, and no new publication is created.

The remainder of this section takes a detailed look at each option in the PAGE SETUP dialog box. Later in this chapter, we will revisit this dialog box and discuss changes that can be made to the options once a publication has been created.

Page size and orientation

The first option in the PAGE SETUP dialog specifies the size of every page in the publication. The dimensions specified for the "Page size" are those of the on-screen electronic pages that PageMaker displays to represent your publication.

Eight "Page size" options are available, seven of which represent commonly used page sizes (the dimensions of these are listed in Figure 4.04). An eighth option, "Custom," is used to specify the dimensions of any non-standard page size. "Custom" page sizes may be defined as any size up to 17 inches by 22 inches (or, equivalently, 102 picas by 132 picas). Values entered in the option boxes for the width and height of a "Custom" page are accurate to 1/100 inch (or 0.06 pica).

In most cases, you will select the predefined page size which matches the paper size on which you will be printing your publication. It is not necessary, however, that your on-screen electronic pages equal any of the paper sizes available in the printer on which you will print your publication—you can use an electronic page that is larger or smaller than the paper sizes available in your printer. In these cases, however, special printing techniques must be used to output these pages (see Chapter 14, *Printing Publications*).

If you are creating a document that requires a custom page size you can either select the "Custom" option and specify your page or select the next largest predefined page size and use larger margins to define your custom page size. Neither technique is necessarily better than the other, although by using custom page sizes you make it more difficult to accidentally position elements beyond the usable area of any page.

- *"Letter" defines a U.S. letter-size page, 8.5 × 11 inches*
- *"Legal" defines a U.S. legal-size page, 8.5 × 14 inches*
- *"Tabloid" defines a page 11 × 17 inches*
- *"A4" defines a page 210 × 297 mm (8.26 × 11.69")*
- *"A3" defines a page 297 × 420 mm (11.69 × 16.53")*
- *"A5" defines a page 148 × 210 mm (5.82 × 8.26")*
- *"B5" defines a page 176 × 250 mm (6.92 × 9.84")*

Figure 4.04: *Dimensions of the seven standard page sizes in inches and millimeters.*

The "Orientation" option determines whether your electronic pages will be positioned as taller than wide or wider than tall when displayed. Figure 4.05 demonstrates the "Tall" vs "Wide" orientation for a "Letter"-sized page. In some other applications, the "Tall" orientation is known as "Portrait" and the "Wide" orientation is called "Landscape."

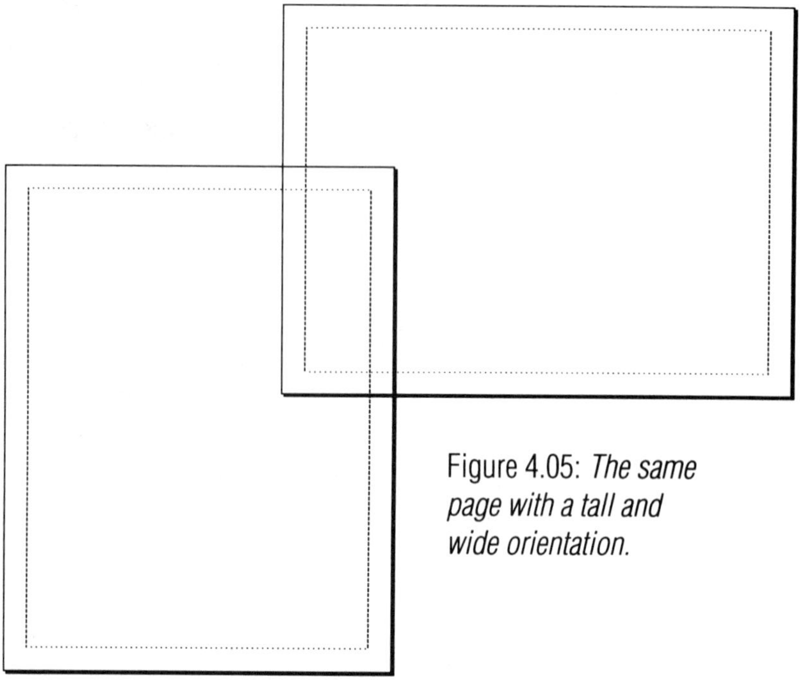

Figure 4.05: *The same page with a tall and wide orientation.*

Page numbers and the number of pages

The "Start page #" option determines the page number given to the first page in the publication. This number is used to identify the page on the page icon and is also used by PageMaker's automatic page-numbering feature. Each page after the first is automatically numbered sequentially. PageMaker can accept a starting page number as high as 9999; however, since this is also the highest page number that

PageMaker can assign to any page, a document with 9999 as the "Start page #" could contain only one page. Practically, the highest usable starting page number is (9999 – the number of pages in the publication). Attempting to use a "Start page #" that would require a page number higher than 9999 will cause an Alert dialog box to appear, as shown in Figure 4.06.

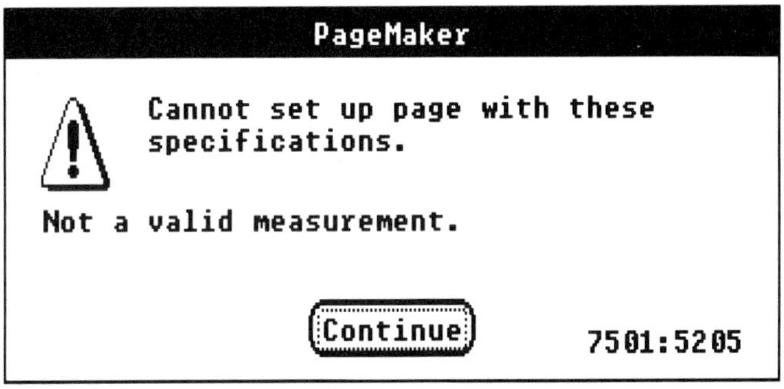

Figure 4.06: *The Alert dialog box indicating that an invalid number is entered in either the "Start page #" or "# of pages" options.*

The "# of pages" option specifies the number of pages in the new publication. The maximum number of pages in any single PageMaker publication is 128, and the minimum is 0 (although such a publication would have only master pages, which cannot be printed). Additional pages can be added to a publication at any time, so you do not need to specify extra pages "just in case."

Publications that require more than 128 pages must be created using several PageMaker documents. In general, it is a good practice to break long publications into several smaller PageMaker documents before they reach PageMaker's 128 page limit.

While it is difficult to make general statements, we recommend breaking most longer publications into documents of approximately 30 to 60 pages. At these lengths, file size and performance should be acceptable unless a document contains a large number of imported graphics. You can always add pages to any publication at any time, and PageMaker's autoflow feature automatically adds them as needed. No problems should arise if you underestimate page requirements when first creating a new publication—it is probably better to err with too few pages rather than too many because blank pages in a publication affect the file size of the document, wasting disk space and slowing down operation while they remain unused.

Creating larger publications as a series of smaller PageMaker documents has many benefits:

- **Manageability**. Documents can easily fit onto floppy disks when they are smaller, making it easy to transport them and back them up.
- **Speed**. Documents can be opened, closed, and saved more quickly if they are reasonably sized.
- **Safety**. Fewer pages will be affected by file loss, damage, or internal corruption, should it occur.
- **Logic**. Smaller documents represent logical subdivisions of the publication, such as chapters or sections. This allows running heads or footers containing the chapter or section name to be placed on publication master pages, which is not possible in a single PageMaker document that contains several logical sections.

Setting up double-sided documents

The "Double-sided" option is used when creating documents that will be reproduced on both sides of the paper—it does not make PageMaker *print* double-sided documents. When the "Double-sided" option is selected, PageMaker presents two master pages instead of one, allowing unique master page items such as running heads, footers, and graphics to be added to left and right pages. It also positions the "inside" and "outside" page margins appropriately on left and right pages.

If you are creating a publication that will be reproduced as double-sided but will not have any distinguishing differences between right and left pages, *it is not necessary for your document to be defined as double-sided*. The only advantage in doing so is that you can use the "Facing pages" option. The possible disadvantage is that you may have to create two identical master pages—requiring additional effort and perhaps the chance of introducing small errors.

The page icons that represent pages in the current publication identify right and left pages by the bent corner at the top outer corner of each page, as shown in Figure 4.07.

Figure 4.07: *Page icons for a double-sided document.*

In a double-sided document, every odd-numbered page in a double-sided publication will be a right-hand page, and every even-numbered page will be a left-hand page. Changing the value of the "Start page #" option to an odd value from an even one will force right pages to become left pages and left pages to become right pages. The "Inside" margin will always be on the left edge of odd pages and the right edge of even pages.

When the "Facing pages" option is selected, PageMaker displays adjacent left and right pages in the publication window. Working on facing pages is no different than working on a single page, except that PageMaker must generally use a larger reduction to display both pages at the "Fit-in-window" view size. Using the "Facing pages" option allows you to easily see the relationship between pages, although it tends to slow down the speed of screen refreshes because more information is being displayed.

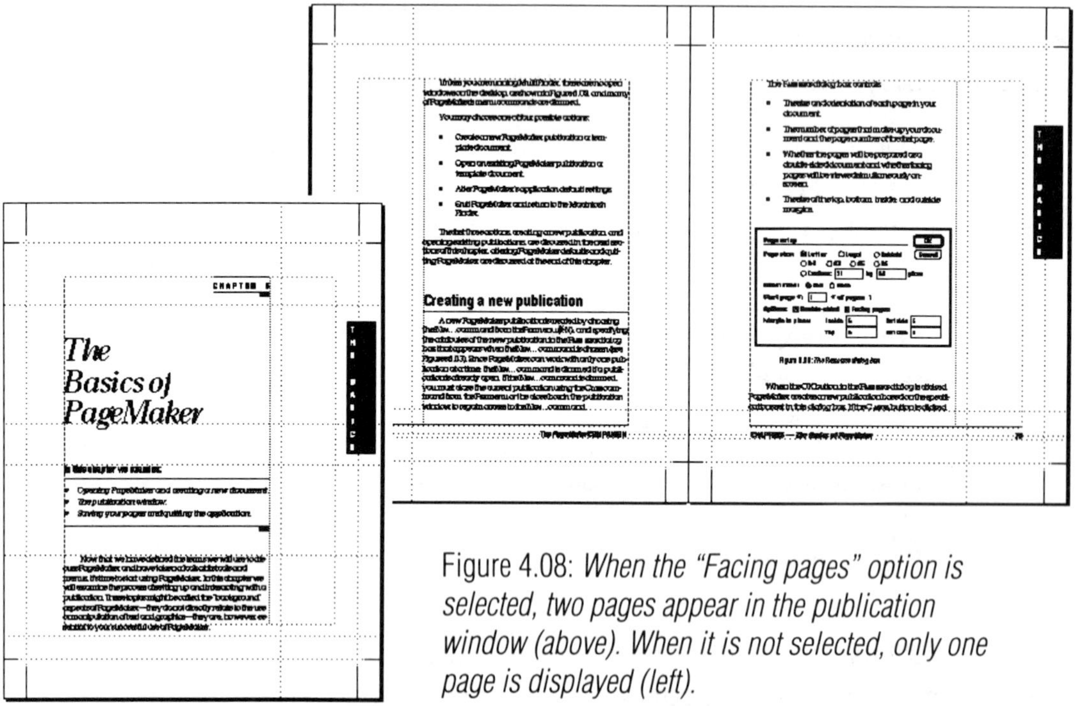

Figure 4.08: *When the "Facing pages" option is selected, two pages appear in the publication window (above). When it is not selected, only one page is displayed (left).*

As we will see later in this chapter, the "Facing pages" option can be toggled on and off while you are working on your publication. This allows you to enjoy the speed benefits of viewing single pages while doing the bulk of your layout work, and the visual benefits of facing pages when adding the finishing touches to your publication.

Margins

The "Margin in______" option comprises four option boxes: "Inside," "Outside," "Top," and "Bottom" (the "Inside" and "Outside" options will become the "Left" and "Right" options when working on single-sided publications).

The values entered in these option boxes represent the distance from the edges of the electronic page to the margin lines that PageMaker automatically adds to each page of a publication. Values for these options are entered in the current **unit of measure**, which is specified in the PREFERENCES dialog box. To override the current unit of measure, use the one-character abbreviation for the unit of measure you wish to specify (*i* for inch, *p* for pica, *c* for Cicero, *m* for millimeter—these are described later in this chapter in the *Preference dialog box* section).

In most cases, the area within your margins will contain the body copy or primary elements of each page of your publication. You do not, however, have to put every element on your pages within the margins. It is possible to position, display, and print elements outside of any margin boundary. For example, master page items such as running heads, footers, and page numbers, are commonly positioned outside the defined margin boundaries, as shown in Figure 4.09.

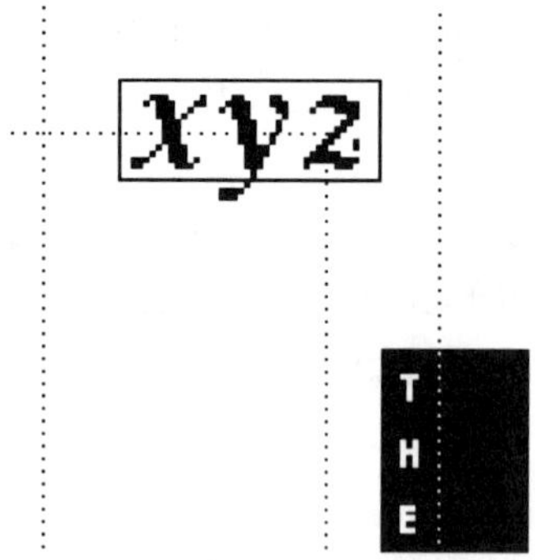

Figure 4.09: *Margins are self-imposed recommendations that help guide the placement of text and graphic objects. Any object may, however, exceed the margins of any page.*

Once you are satisfied with the settings in the PAGE SETUP dialog, click the OK button or press the RETURN or ENTER key on your keyboard. PageMaker will now create the new document you have specified, and PageMaker's publication window will appear, showing the first page of your new document.

The publication window

The overall screen display presented when a document is open is called the *publication window*. Assuming that the application defaults have not been changed, your publication window includes:

- **The PageMaker menu bar**. This bar contains seven primary menu-bar titles, each representing a group of PageMaker commands that can be displayed by selecting the menu-bar title.

- **A window for your publication**. This will be named "Untitled" until you save and name your document, at which time the document name is displayed in the title bar. One or two pages of your document are visible in this window, depending on the currently selected page, whether you defined your document as "Double-sided," and whether the "Facing pages" option was selected. The margins of each page are marked with dotted rectangles. After you begin working on your document, the page will display all the text and graphics you add, as well as column and guide lines.

- **Two rulers**, one at the left edge of the publication window and one across the top of the publication window. The rulers are displayed by choosing the RULERS command from the OPTIONS menu, and use the standard of measure currently selected in the PREFERENCES dialog box. A small dotted line on each ruler marks the current location of the cursor as it moves in the window. The zero point of the rulers is fully adjustable, as described in Chapter 5, *Working in the Publication Window*.

- **The Toolbox**, containing PageMaker's eight tools. The tool currently selected is highlighted, and the cursor will display the icon of the selected tool when positioned anywhere over the publication. A tool is selected by clicking on its icon with the selection arrow that appears any time the cursor is positioned over the toolbox. The toolbox can be opened, moved, and closed, just like any other window.

- **Page icons for the Master page icons** (labeled L and R) **and regular page icons** (labeled with their page numbers). If your screen is not large enough to show all the regular page icons, arrows for scrolling the page icons will appear before the first page icon and after the last page icon. The icon of the page currently displayed is highlighted, and you may move to another page by clicking on its page icon.

- **The pasteboard**, which is the area in the publication window surrounding the displayed pages. This pasteboard can be used to store text and graphic elements that are temporarily not being used on the displayed pages.

- **Scroll bars for the publication window**. These operate exactly as other Windows scroll bars: click the mouse pointer on the arrows to scroll line by line, click in the dark area of the bar to scroll the distance of about half the screen, or drag the scroll box to scroll the display as far as you want.

- **The pointer**. This appears while the arrow tool in the toolbox is selected or the cursor is positioned over the rulers, menu bar, toolbox, palettes, or scroll bars. This pointer will change depending on which tool is selected.

The publication window also includes several items common to all applications running under Windows:

- **The Windows Control menu**. This menu, brought up by selecting the horizontal bar in the upper left corner of the window, provides access to the Windows command and accessories described in Chapter 3, *Terms, Tools, & Menus.*

- **Window Size arrows** These arrows, in the upper right corner of the publication window, allow you to change the size of the publication windows.
- **Application bar**. If you are using a full version of Windows and the publication windows is not expanded to maximum size, icons for each Windows application currently running appear at the bottom of the screen.

4
Brief Tour

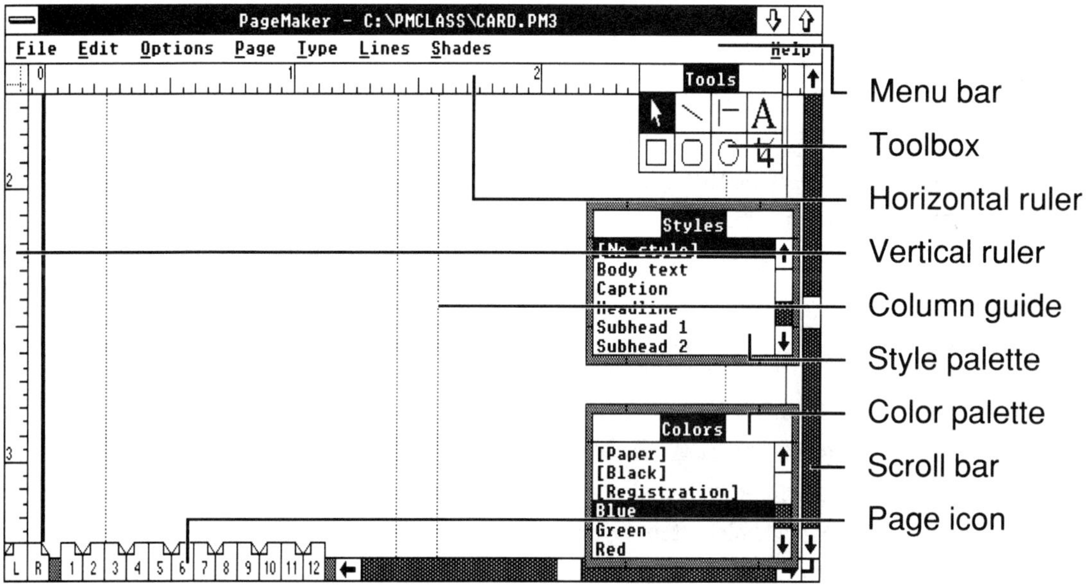

Figure 4.10: *The publication window.*

Opening an existing publication

Existing PageMaker 3.0 publications can be opened while inside the PageMaker application or directly from the MS-DOS EXECUTIVE. PageMaker 3.0 can also open files created in PageMaker 1.0 on the PC or in PageMaker 2.0 or 3.0 on the Macintosh.

Using the Open... command for 3.0 files

To open an existing PageMaker document while inside PageMaker, select the OPEN... command from the FILE menu (CTRL-O). This action brings up the OPEN dialog box shown in Figure 4.11. Next, select the filename that represents the file you wish to open from the list of files, and click the OPEN button. Alternatively, you may double-click on the filename you wish to open. When the list contains many filenames, you can quickly move to a specific section of the alphabetical listing by typing the first letter of the desired filename, and you can locate a specific file by typing the first few letters of the filename.

In addition to listing the names of available files, the scrolling list also includes the names of other available drives or directories. To look inside a sub-directory for a specific file, double-click on the name of that sub-directory, which will be surrounded by brackets: [*sub-directory name*]. To look on a different drive, double-click on the letter of the drive you wish to view (drive letters are also enclosed in brackets). To close a directory and move back up the hierarchy of directories, scroll down the list and double-click on the [..] option.

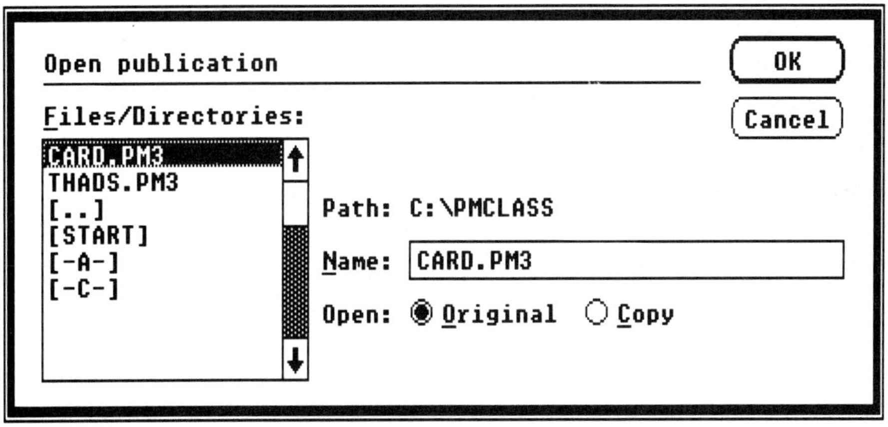

Figure 4.11: *The Open dialog box.*

Opening files from the desktop

When launching PageMaker, enter the filename of a PageMaker publication after the launching command (either PM or WIN PM, depending on your version of Windows) to open the named file as soon as PageMaker is running. Most PageMaker publications have the filename extension .PM3. PageMaker will only be able to locate your publication if it is either in the current directory or in a directory specified via the PATH command (see Chapter 2, *Installing PageMaker).*

Figure 4.12: *The PageMaker 3.0 publication icon on the Windows application bar.*

Double-clicking on the name of any PageMaker publication listed in the WINDOWS EXECUTIVE will also launch PageMaker and open the selected publication. PageMaker 3.0 publications will have the icon shown in Figure 4.12. If an Alert box with the message "File not found" appears when you double-click on a PageMaker publication, try launching the PageMaker application and then opening the file using the OPEN... command as described above.

Opening PageMaker PC 1.0 or 1.0a files

To open files created in PageMaker 1.0 or 1.0a, you must first launch the PageMaker application and then use the OPEN... command described above. As the file is opening, PageMaker converts the publication to the 3.0 format. Converted files will be untitled, so you will encounter the SAVE AS dialog box as soon as you try to save the file.

If PageMaker cannot convert the file, you may not have adequate memory and disk space available. PageMaker 1.0 files will become approximately 20% larger when converted to the 3.0 format. If the file being converted includes encapsulated PostScript (EPS) files, you might try removing the EPS files from the PageMaker document before conversion and then replacing them once the file is successfully converted.

Opening PageMaker files from the Macintosh

Using files created on the Macintosh version of PageMaker in the Windows version of PageMaker is surprisingly easy. First, if the file you wish to open was created in PageMaker version 1.2 or 2.0 on the Macintosh, use PageMaker 3.0 on the Macintosh to convert the file to 3.0 format. Next, transfer the Macintosh PageMaker 3.0 publication file to a PC disk using any available method: use a Macintosh-PC transfer program (such as MACLINK PLUS); move the file over a network connected to both Macintoshes and PCs (such as TOPS or APPLESHARE); send the file over a modem; or use an Apple PC 5.25-inch Drive or a DAYNAFILE to move a Macintosh file onto a PC disk. Finally, open the Macintosh PageMaker 3.0 publication in PageMaker PC using the OPEN... command from the FILE menu, just as described above for PageMaker PC publications.

After a file is opened

When an existing PageMaker publication is opened, the PageMaker publication window appears, as described earlier, and you are ready to work on your publication. Opened publications display as they were at the time when they were last saved, i.e. the same page is selected, view size chosen, etc. Because PageMaker allows only one open document at a time, you must close the current publication before you can open or create another.

Changing Page setup options

After you have been working on a publication, you may need to change the options specified in the PAGE SETUP dialog box when the publication was first created. This can happen for many reasons. For example, you may not be able to fit all the required information into your publication without going to a larger page size, or you may decide to reformat your publication as double-sided. By choosing the

PAGE SETUP command from the FILE menu, you can again display the PAGE SETUP dialog box, shown in Figure 4.03, and then edit the available options.

The options in the PAGE SETUP dialog box were fully introduced earlier in this chapter, but we will review them here, paying particular attention to the effect that changes to these options will have on an existing publication:

- **Page size**. Changes made to the page size will not affect any elements that have already been placed on the pages of the publication. Existing elements will remain in place, with the new page size being positioned behind them. If the new page size is smaller than the old, some objects may now appear on the pasteboard. They can, of course, be repositioned anywhere on the new pages.

- **Orientation**. As with the "Page size" option, changes to the orientation of a page will not affect existing text or graphic elements. Existing elements will remain in place, with the page being rotated behind them. Almost certainly some of the existing page elements will now be positioned on the pasteboard, but they can be repositioned anywhere on resulting page.

- **Start page #**. The starting page number can be changed to any number between 1 and 9999, so long as the highest resulting page number in the publication is not higher then 9999. If working on a double-sided publication, changing this option from an odd number to an even one, or visa-versa, will change all right-hand pages to left-hand pages, and all left-hand pages to right-hand pages. If you are working in a double-sided publication with facing pages, objects that bleed across the two pages remain attached to what were formerly the left-hand pages. In addition to renumbering the page icons at the bottom of the publication window, PageMaker will also update all page number references created with the automatic page-numbering feature.

4

Brief Tour

- **Number of pages**. This is the only option in the PAGE SETUP dialog box that cannot be edited. To add or delete pages from the publication, use the INSERT PAGES... and REMOVE PAGES... commands from the PAGE menu. This option will, however, show the current number of pages in the publication.

- **Double-sided**. The primary effect of changing the setting for the "Double-sided" option is on the margins of your pages. A double-sided publication has "Inside" and "Outside" margins instead of "Right" and "Left" margins. Depending on the current margin settings, changing this option can have an important effect on the margins displayed in your document. Also, the "Facing pages" option is available only when the "Double-sided" option is selected. If you change from a double-sided publication with facing pages to a single-sided publication, remember that objects that bleed across the two facing pages remain attached to the right-hand page, which was formerly the left-hand page.

- **Facing pages**. Deselecting the "Facing pages" option leaves objects that bled across the two pages attached to the left-hand pages only. Selecting the "Facing pages" option will force PageMaker to delete some ruler guides if any now-facing pages have a combined total of more than 40 ruler guides.
- **Margins**. Resetting any of the margins will move the margin lines on all pages of the publication without adjusting the position of any existing text or graphic objects. Objects can, of course, be manually repositioned if required.

Defaults and preferences

Most options and command settings in PageMaker are pre-set to some **default** settings before you alter them. Generally speaking, these default settings represent the most commonly used setting for each particular option and are intended to save you the time and trouble of choosing the same options over and over again. By default, for example, new publications are created on letter-sized pages, rulers and the toolbox are displayed in the publication window, text does not wrap around graphics, and lines and shapes are created with a 1-point line weight.

When default settings are not those that you use most of the time, the process of constantly changing options from one setting to another takes valuable time.

Not surprisingly, you can customize PageMaker to remember the default settings that you choose. This is true for a wide range of options that are found in dialog boxes as well as for toggle menu commands. The complete list is shown in Figure 4.13. It is possible to change default settings permanently, so that all new publications use the new defaults, or temporarily, so that they are used only for one particular publication.

Default settings that are changed permanently are called **application defaults**. These default settings are changed from the PageMaker desktop *before* a publication window is opened. Every menu command that is not dimmed can have its default settings changed. Application defaults remain set until you change them or until the PM.CNF file is deleted from your hard drive (which is a quick way to reset all application defaults to their factory settings). These defaults apply to all new publications created after they are set—they do not affect any existing publications.

Default settings that are changed within a publication apply only to that specific publication. These **publication defaults** can be changed only while a publication is open. They remain set until modified, even if the application defaults are reset or the PM.CNF file is deleted from your PageMaker directory.

Dialog box	Options
Page Setup	Page size Orientation Starting page number Number of pages Single- or double-sided pages Facing pages Margins
Preferences	Measurement system Vertical ruler Custom Guides Greek text below Stretch above Vector above
Column guides	Number of columns Space between columns
Text wrap	Wrap option Standoff in unit of measure
Rounded corners	Corner option
Type specs	Font Size Leading Case Position Type style
Paragraph	Hyphenation Pair kerning Alignment Indents Spacing
Indents/tabs	Default tabs Alignment Leader
Spacing	Word space Letter space Hyphenation zone Auto leading Leading method
Define styles	All styles

Menus	*Command options*
Options	*Snap to rulers*
	Rulers display
	Ruler zero point lock
	Lock guides
	Guides display
	Toolbox display
	Scroll bars
	Style palette display
	Color palette display
Type	*Type style*
	Alignment

Figure 4.13: *All of the dialog box options and menu commands whose defaults can be reset as either application defaults or publication defaults.*

Preferences dialog box

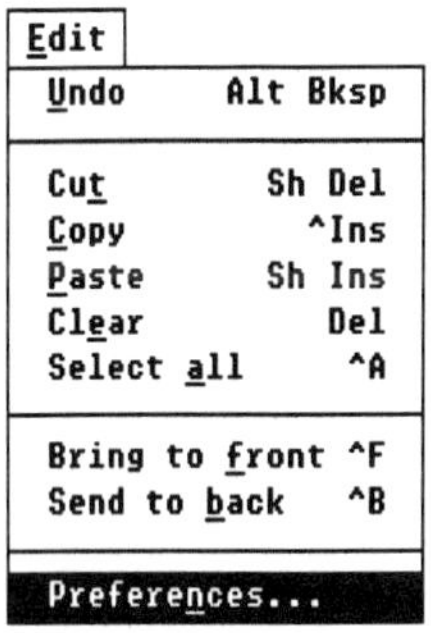

The PREFERENCES dialog box, accessed via the PREFERENCES... command in the EDIT menu, contains several options that control specific aspects of working in the publication window. As with all of the other options described above, the default settings of these options can be set for a specific publication, or as application defaults that apply to each new publication that you create. Since your preferences concerning these options will usually apply to every publication you create, it is sensible to set them as application defaults by choosing the PREFERENCES... command from the EDIT menu at the PageMaker desktop when no publication is open.

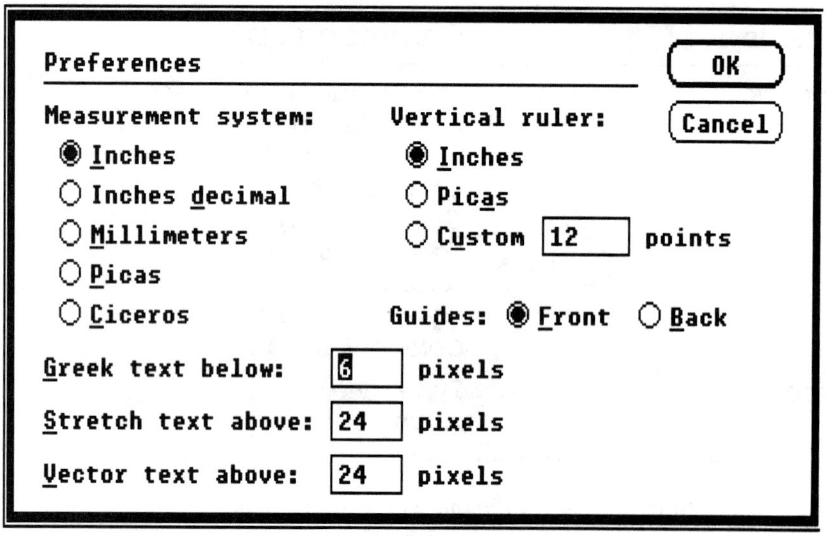

Figure 4:14: *The Preferences dialog box.*

The options available in the PREFERENCES dialog are:

- **Measurement system**. The "Measurement system" option offers a choice of five units of measure. The selected units are displayed in the rulers and used in all dialog boxes requiring measurements.

  Although it is possible to change the "Measurement system" option at any time while creating a publication, be aware that doing so might make it difficult to properly align objects. This is because the ruler tick marks in the new measurement system do not correspond to those in the previous system, and objects aligned with tick marks are more accurately positioned than objects aligned between tick marks. Therefore, objects positioned using the new measurement system will probably not line up with objects aligned with tick marks from the previous measurement system.

When entering measurements into a dialog box, you can override the selected measurement system by adding an abbreviation to the value—*i* for inch, *m* for millimeter, *p* for pica (with the points value following the *p*), or *c* for Cicero (with the points value following the *c*). For example, if the dialog asks for "Margin in inches," entering 3p6 (or 3½ picas) would specify 3 picas 6 points; entering 20m would specify 20 millimeters; and entering 8c3 would specify 8 Ciceros 3 points (or 8¼ ciceros).

- **Vertical ruler**. The "Vertical ruler" option allows you to use a different unit of measure on the vertical ruler than on the horizontal ruler. The top option is the unit of measure chosen as the the current "Measurement system" option. The second option is always "Picas." The third option, "Custom," allows you to specify a vertical ruler divided by any number of points.

  By using the "Custom" option and specifying the points of leading in the body copy of your publication, it is easier to accurately position text blocks—especially when trying to align adjacent columns. Using the SNAP TO RULERS command provides additional assistance.

- **Guides**. Selecting the "Front" option sets the guides at the top of the stacking order on any particular page, making it easy to select them for repositioning. Selecting the "Back" option sets the guides at the bottom of the stacking order, making it difficult to select them inadvertently when trying to reposition graphics or text blocks.

Holding down the CTRL key while selecting an object makes it impossible to select the guides.

- **Greek text below**. This option controls the type size at which PageMaker no longer displays characters on the screen, replacing the characters of the text with thin gray bars (see Figure 4.15). The size is specified in the number of pixels that would stack vertically to display a capital letter of the type. This, of course, depends on both type size and the current view size. For example, when 6-point type is displayed at the "fit-in-window" view size, the height of its characters is less than 6 pixels; when displayed at 200%, the height of its characters is more than 6 pixels.

The benefit of greeking text is speed. PageMaker is able to display the thin gray bars much faster than it can draw each character. Since characters smaller than 6 pixels are probably illegible on your screen, it is usually better to forgo the accurate character display in favor of a faster screen refresh.

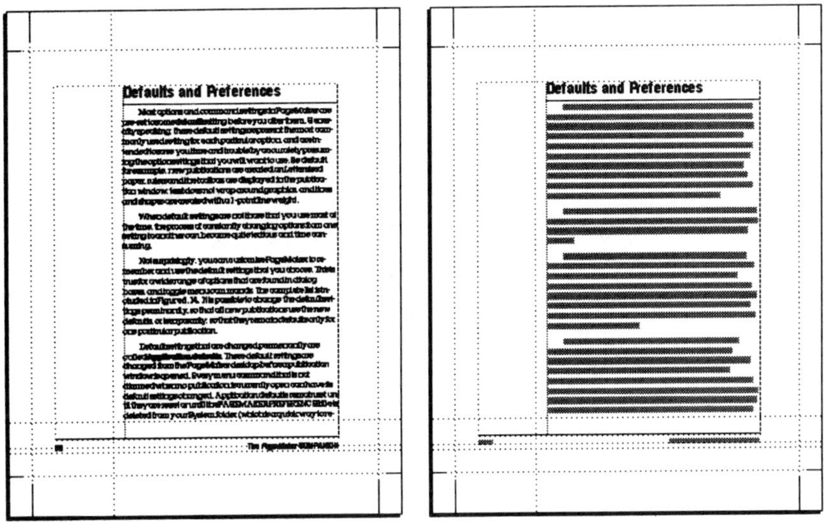

Figure 4.15: *The same page at "fit-in-window" size with standard (left) and "greeked" (right) text display.*

Saving the publication

Throughout the course of creating your publication, we strongly recommended that you frequently save your work to disk by choosing the SAVE (CTRL-S) or SAVE AS... commands from the FILE menu. This is important because even though PageMaker does use a form of automatic saving to protect you from disaster, it is not foolproof. If your computer crashes, or if there is a power failure, you will probably lose all the work that you have done since your publication was last saved.

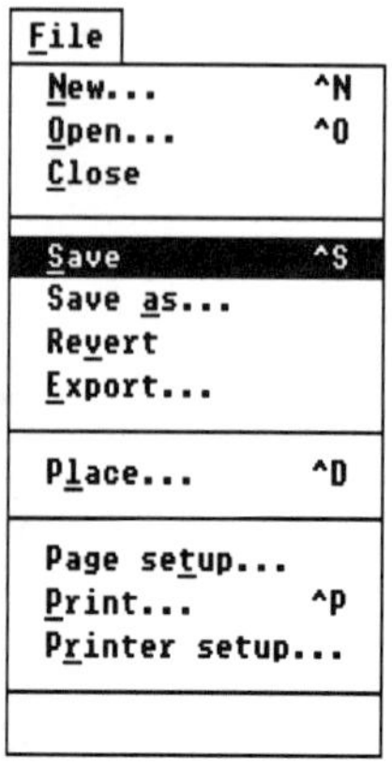

There are two ways to save a publication:

- **The Save command** (CTRL-S): If the current publication has been previously saved and named, the Save command updates the disk version of the file to reflect the current contents of the file and the preference settings. If the document is untitled, the Save command invokes the Save as... command described below. It is possible to receive a "Disk Full" error message during the save operation, in which case the Save as... command must be used to change the drive or volume on which the publication is to be saved.

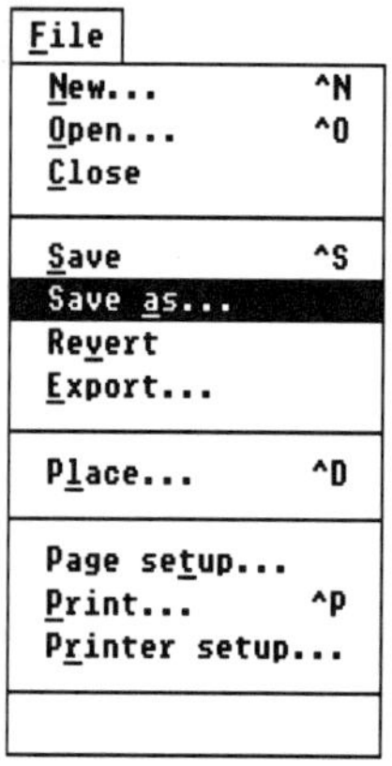

- **The Save as...command.** Use the Save as... command to determine the drive, filename, and file type of a document before it is saved. Choosing the Save as... command from the File menu brings up the Save publication as dialog box, shown in Figure 4.16.

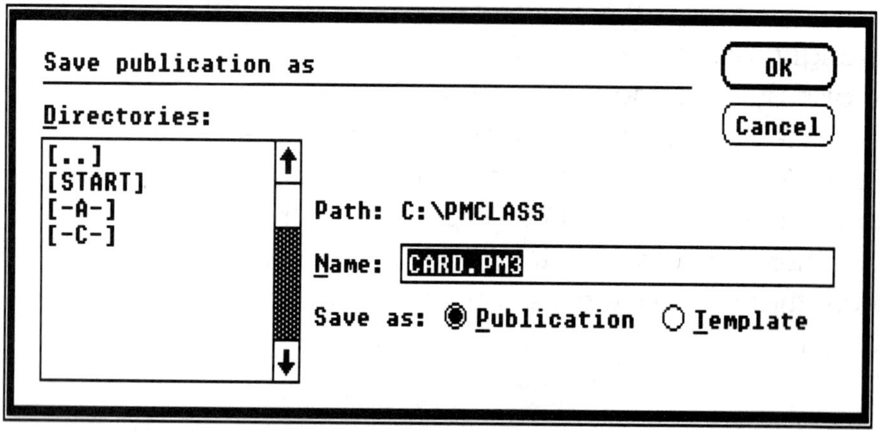

Figure 4.16: *The Save publication as dialog box.*

4

Brief Tour

This dialog box is used to name your publication and specify the drive and directory to which the file will be saved. If your publication already has a name, the current filename appears in the "Name" option box next to the list of files. If your document is untitled, the "Name" option box will be empty. Enter or edit the filename as you wish, using up to eight characters. Unless you enter a different filename extension when naming your file, PageMaker 3.0 files are automatically given the filename extension.PM3.

The location to which your file will be saved is specified using the scrolling file listing, which lists available drives and sub-directories, and the "Path" option line, which lists the current location setting. To select another drive, double-click on the drive name in the scrolling list. To enter a sub-directory, double-click on the sub-directory name in the scrolling list. To move out of a sub-directory and into the next higher directory, double-click on the [...] in the scrolling list. Clicking the secondary mouse button on the slash character (/) in the "Path" option line will bring up a dialog box allowing you to specify any available drive and directory and make that the current destination.

The SAVE AS dialog box also includes the "Save as" option, which determines whether your publication will be saved as a normal PageMaker publication document or as a template document. Template documents are usually used as master documents for additional publications, and automatically choose the "Copy" option in the OPEN PUBLICATION dialog box when they are opened.

When you have selected the filename, location, and file type, click the OK button, or press the RETURN key to save your file. You may also click the CANCEL button in the SAVE PUBLICATION AS dialog to return to the publication window without saving the file. If you try to save a publication with the same name as an existing publication (in the same drive and directory), PageMaker will present the REPLACE EXISTING dialog box, shown in Figure 4.17, asking you to confirm that you wish to replace the existing file. Click YES to save over the existing file, or NO to return to the SAVE PUBLICATION AS dialog box, where you may change the filename or destination of the saved file.

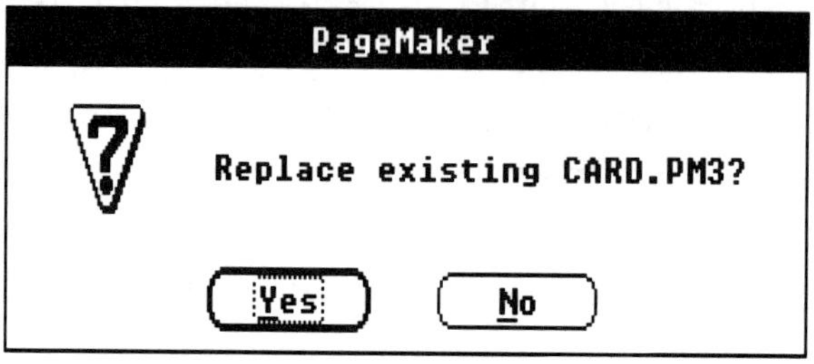

Figure 4.17: *The Replace existing dialog box.*

If the disk or volume that you have selected does not have enough room for the file being saved, the CANNOT SAVE AS dialog box appears, as shown in Figure 4.18. Clicking the CONTINUE button returns you to the SAVE AS dialog box so that you may select another drive and try again.

Figure 4.18: *The Cannot save as dialog appears when you try to save a publication or template to a disk or volume without adequate space available.*

When to use Save as...

Saving different versions of a publication has two main benefits. The first is security—by having multiple versions of your publication in more than one location, your chances of losing a lot of work due to file corruption or other mishap is drastically reduced. Second, files saved using the SAVE AS... command are often significantly smaller than those saved with the SAVE command. Depending on the contents of the file, executing a SAVE AS... command can reduce the size of the file by 20% to 50%. This savings occurs because Page-Maker purges all deleted graphics and discards temporary data that has built up during the document production process.

PageMaker's mini-save

During your work in PageMaker, any time you move to another page, change the page setup, insert or delete a page, or click the icon of the current page, PageMaker performs a **mini-save** of your document. The information from this mini-save is stored in a special temporary file on your disk—your current working file is not updated. PageMaker uses the information from the mini-save to minimize the amount of work lost in the event of a crash.

In most cases when you re-open a PageMaker file after you have crashed while in PageMaker, you will find that your publication still has the changes that were made to it *after* it was last saved—these are the result of the mini-saves PageMaker had done before the crash. If you want to discard these mini-save changes and return your file to its state as of your last formal save, choose the REVERT... command from the FILE menu.

While working on a publication you can return to the last mini-save, discarding all changes made to your file since the last save, by holding down the SHIFT key and choosing the REVERT... command from the FILE menu. This provides an important "second line of defence" when you discover that you made a big mistake in a document because reverting to the last mini-save can often undo the mistake while preserving the rest of your work since the last formal save. The regular REVERT command would erase all the changes (A complete discussion of the REVERT...command is included in Chapter 5, *Working in the Publication Window.)*

Although the mini-save is a tremendous feature of PageMaker, and it will probably save you some effort at one time or another, do not let awareness of the mini-save discourage you from executing the SAVE or SAVE AS... commands often. Mini-saves should be considered only a safety net of last resort.

Finishing with PageMaker

When you have finished working in a publication you can close the publication window, at which time you may open a different publication, create a new publication, or quit PageMaker altogether.

Closing the publication

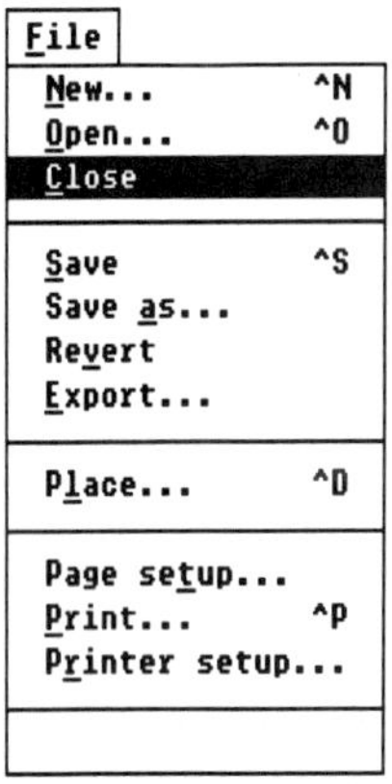

To close your current publication, choose the CLOSE command from the FILE menu, or choose the close command in the Windows Control menu in the upper left corner. If you have made any changes to your document or to its display in the publication window, a SAVE CHANGES? dialog box will appear, as shown in Figure 4.19, asking you if you would like to save your publication before closing it. Clicking the YES button will perform a SAVE operation (or a SAVE AS... if the file is untitled) and then close the file; clicking the NO button will close the file without saving the changes; and clicking the CANCEL button will return you to the publication window without saving or closing the file. Cancelling is useful if you want to perform a SAVE AS... operation in order to change the name or location of the file, or if you would like to continue working on the publication.

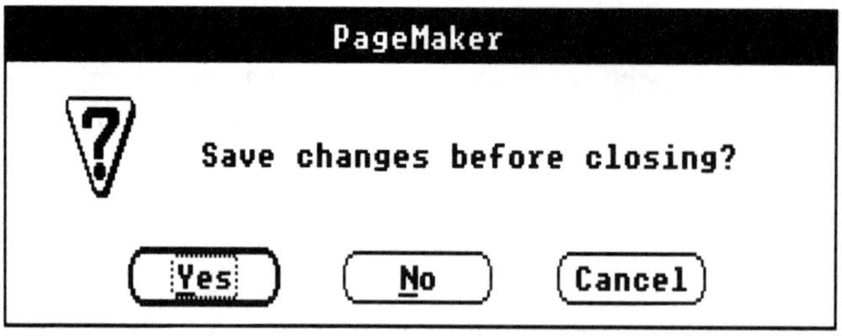

Figure 4.19: *The Save changes? dialog box.*

Once your publication is closed, you see the PageMaker desktop, where only the PageMaker menu bar appears. At this point your options are the same as they were when you first launched PageMaker: you can create a new PageMaker publication, open an existing PageMaker publication, alter PageMaker's application default settings, or quit PageMaker and return to the MS-DOS EXECUTIVE or to the DOS prompt.

Creating a new publication, opening existing publications, and changing PageMaker's defaults were discussed in the preceding sections of this chapter. Quitting PageMaker is discussed below.

Quitting PageMaker

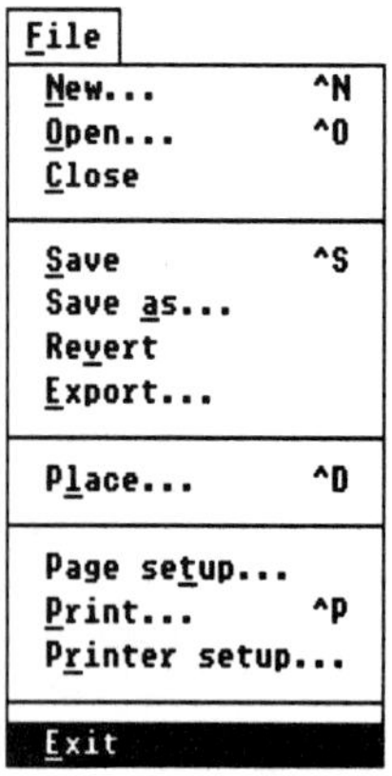

When you have finished your work in the PageMaker application, choose the EXIT command from the FILE menu to close the current publication (if one is open) and return to the MS-DOS EXECUTIVE if you have the full version of Windows installed, or to return to the DOS prompt if you are using the run-time Windows supplied with PageMaker. Double-clicking on the WINDOWS CONTROL Menu has the same effect as choosing the EXIT command.

Like the CLOSE command, the EXIT command prompts the appearance of a SAVE CHANGES? dialog box, as shown in Figure 4.19, and you will be asked if you want to save any of the changes you have made to the publication since your last save operation. Clicking the YES button will perform a SAVE operation (or a SAVE AS... if the file is untitled), close the file, and then close the application; clicking the NO button will close the file and the application without saving the changes; and clicking the CANCEL button will return you to the publication window without saving or closing the file. If no publication window is open, or if you have not changed anything in the publication since the last save operation, you will not need to verify the EXIT command.

Working in the Publication Window

In this chapter we examine:

- *Working with master pages*
- *Using column guides and ruler guides*
- *Fixing mistakes: the Revert and Undo commands*

One of the many reasons that PageMaker has proven to be so popular is that it has automated the design and production process without changing the basic nature of the process itself. Working in PageMaker is familiar and intuitive even to those who have never formally created documents. In this chapter we examine the specifics of our interaction with PageMaker, learning how to adjust the display of our work on the screen, use the various rulers and guides to help format our layouts, and work with objects—the text and graphic building blocks we use to create documents.

Manipulating the display

The PageMaker publication window, as described in *Chapter 4, A Brief Tour of PageMaker*, displays one or two pages of the current publication. In this section you will learn how, while working on your publication, to specify the magnification or reduction at which you want to view a page, and if only part of a page shows on the screen, how to choose which part you want to see.

View sizes

When a new publication is first created, the pages that appear in the publication window are reduced so that they fit in the space available on your display. This reduced view is one of seven **view sizes** available in PageMaker.

Each view size provides a different level of magnification of the pages in the publication window. High magnifications provide great detail, but allow only small portions of a page to be displayed on your screen. Reduced views allow us to look at an entire page or set of pages at one time, but provide very little detail. By repeatedly changing view sizes, we can accurately edit the text and graphic details of our publications and still maintain the overall design consistency and quality afforded by "the big picture."

PageMaker's seven view sizes are:

- **Super fit in window**: This little-known view displays the entire pasteboard on the screen along with the current page(s) of the publication. It is accessed by holding down the SHIFT key while selecting the FIT-IN-WINDOW command from the VIEW menu. This view size is useful only when manipulating elements that are located on the pasteboard outside the portion of the pasteboard displayed in the "fit-in-window" view size.

- **Fit in window**: This view reduces the currently selected pages so that they are entirely visible within the publication window, along with some of the pasteboard. This is the view that is displayed when a new publication is created. The keyboard equivalent for this command is CTRL-W.

  The actual percentage of reduction used by the "Fit in window" view size depends on the size of the monitor that you are using. For example, on a 12" monitor, the reduction percentage would be much greater, and the resulting view much smaller, than it would be on a 24" monitor. This view size is used primarily to get a "big picture" look at the layout of the publication. It is also used when placing or making broad changes to text or graphic elements.

- **50% Size**: This view displays the publication at 50% of its actual size and is used primarily to see larger sections of the publication than are possible at "75%," "Actual," or "200%" view size. The keyboard equivalent for this command is CTRL-5.

- **75% Size**: This view displays the publication at 75% of its actual size, and is used primarily to see larger sections of the publication than are possible at "Actual" or "200%" view size. The keyboard equivalent for this command is CTRL-7.

- **Actual Size**: The "Actual size" view displays the publication on the screen at exactly the size it was specified in the PAGE SETUP dialog box. "Actual Size" is used for most text and graphic editing. The keyboard equivalent for this command is CTRL-1. Clicking the secondary mouse button will also change the view to Actual size, as will holding down the CTRL and ALT keys while clicking the primary mouse button.

- **200% Size**: This view size is an enlargement twice the actual size of the publication. Only a small portion of a page is visible at the "200%" view size, which is used primarily for text editing and precision placement of text and graphics. The keyboard equivalent for this command is CTRL-2. You can change from the "Actual size" view" to this view by holding down the SHIFT key and clicking the secondary mouse button, or by holding down the SHIFT, CTRL and ALT keys while clicking the primary mouse button.

- **400%**: Another little-known view, the 400% view, which displays the publication at four times its actual size. This view is available only by pressing the SHIFT key while choosing the 200% command from the PAGE menu. At this view size, it is extremely easy to accurately position objects or edit text that is set in very small point sizes.

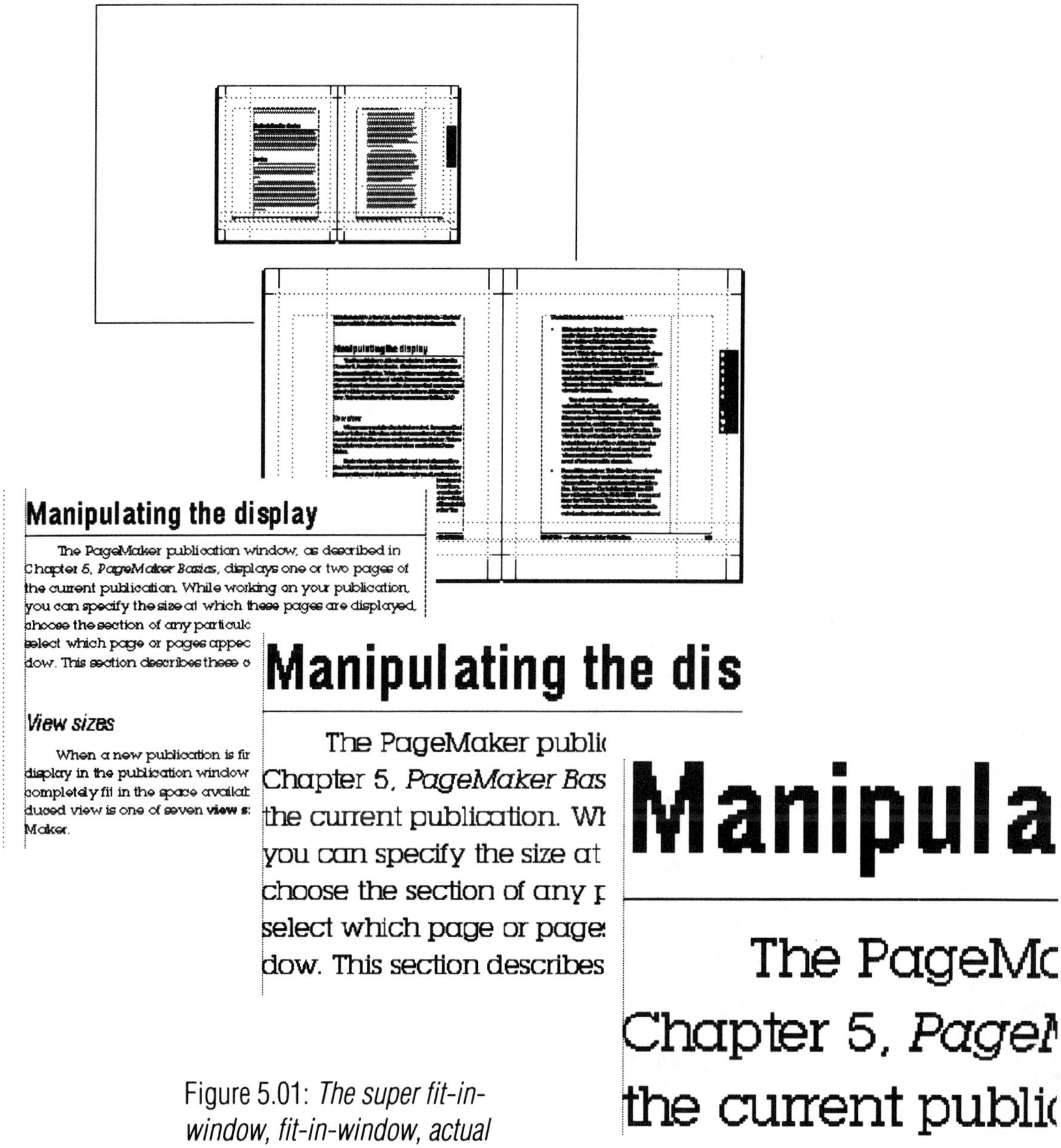

Figure 5.01: *The super fit-in-window, fit-in-window, actual size, 200% size, and 400% views.*

to "Actual size" from any view: CTRL-1

Point the cursor to the part of the page that you want centered in the magnified view and click the secondary mouse button; or press CNTL-ALT, point the cursor to the part of the page that you want centered in the magnified view, and click the primary mouse button.

to "Actual size" from "200%": CTRL-1

Point the cursor to the part of the page that you want centered in the magnified view, press the SHIFT key, and click the secondary mouse button; or press CNTL-ALT -SHIFT, point the cursor to the part of the page that you want centered in the magnified view, and click the primary mouse button.

to "Fit-in-window" from "Actual size": CTRL-W

Point the cursor to the part of the page that you want centered in the magnified view and click the secondary mouse button; or press CNTL-ALT, point the cursor to the part of the page that you want centered in the magnified view, and click the primary mouse button.

to "200%" from "Actual size": CTRL-2

Point the cursor to the part of the page that you want centered in the magnified view, press the SHIFT key, and click the secondary mouse button; or press CNTL-ALT -SHIFT, point the cursor to the part of the page that you want centered in the magnified view, and click the primary mouse button.

Figure 5.02: *Methods of changing view sizes.*

There are three ways to change the view size: you can select the view desired from the VIEW menu, you can use a keyboard equivalent for the menu choices, or you can use a combination of keys and mouse buttons. Using the commands from the VIEW menu will center the new view of the page based on what is centered in the current view. By using the keyboard/mouse shortcuts, you can determine what will be centered on the screen in the new view by pointing the the mouse arrow at this location before changing the view size. Figure 5.02 lists the alternative methods for changing view sizes.

Scrolling the display

Since most view sizes only show a portion of the current page(s) on the screen, it is also important to know how to move the page around on the screen. This can be done using the horizontal or vertical scroll bars, using the grabber hand, or using the CTRL-mouse click methods of changing the view size.

- **The Scroll bars**. As with all Windows scroll bars, you can reposition the displayed area vertically or horizontally using the scroll bars on the right and bottom edges of the publication window. If the scroll bars are not visible, choose the SCROLL BARS command from the OPTIONS menu.

  The scroll bars can be used in two ways: you can drag the white box in the scroll bar to the part of the page, relative to the entire pasteboard, that you want to see; or you can click in the gray area of the scroll bar to move the page about halfway across the screen.

- **The grabber hand**. The grabber hand is a special cursor icon that is accessed by holding down the ALT key while pressing and holding down the mouse button. When the grabber hand is activated, moving the mouse will move publication displayed in the publication window the same direction and distance as the mouse. This is an excellent way to make fine adjustments in the display and is generally preferred to the scroll bars, which are better suited to more dramatic changes in the display.

Holding down the SHIFT key while using the grabber hand constrains the display movement to horizontal or vertical movement only, depending on the first direction moved with the mouse. The grabber hand icon disappears as soon as the ALT key is released, returning the cursor to its previous form.

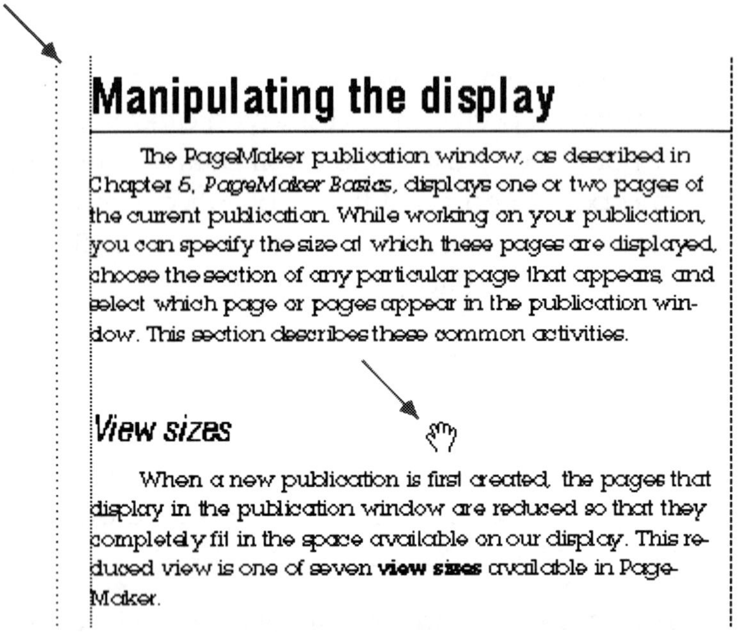

Figure 5.03: *The grabber hand in action.*

- **Keyboard/mouse button view changes**. As described in the previous section, when changing view sizes by clicking the secondary mouse button, or with certain keys and the primary or secondary mouse button, you are able to pinpoint the exact object that will be centered on the screen. When working at actual size, 200%, or 400%, you can very quickly zoom out to fit-in-window, locate the element that you want centered in your display, and then zoom in on it. This can be faster then using either the scroll bars or the grabber hand when working in magnified views.

5 Publication Window

Turning the page

As we've seen, PageMaker's publication window displays only one page (or two pages if the "facing pages" option is selected) of our publication at any time. The highlighted page icon at the bottom of the screen indicates which page is currently displayed in the publication window.

There are three ways to move to another page:

- **Click on the appropriate page icon at the bottom of the publication window**. The maximum number of page icons that fit along the bottom of the display depends on the size of your monitor. If they cannot all fit, left and right arrows appear before the first and after the last page icon. It may be necessary to scroll these icons to locate the page that you need. This is done by clicking on the left or right arrow.

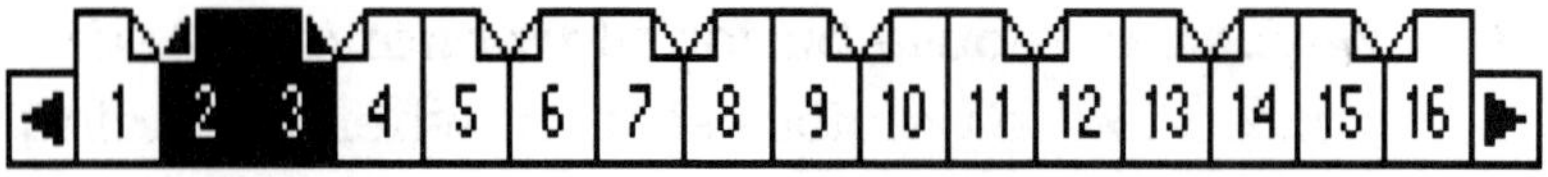

Figure 5.04: *Page icons are used to select the page or pages to display. Left and right scroll arrows appear when all page icons cannot fit on the screen.*

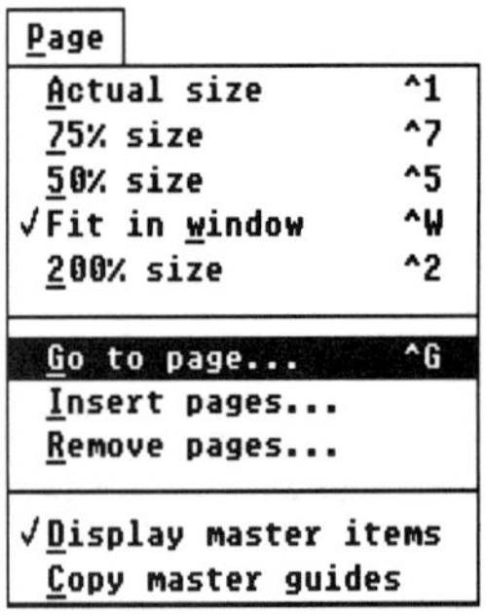

- **Press the ALT-TAB keys to turn a page forward, or ALT-SHIFT-TAB to turn a page backwards**. These keyboard combinations will move by one page if the "facing pages"option is not selected, or to the next set of facing pages if it is. These combinations are usually the fastest method of moving to the next or previous page or set of pages.

- **Choose the Go TO PAGE... command from the PAGE menu**. This command brings up the Go TO PAGE dialog shown in Figure 5.05. Enter the page number in the option box and click the OK button. The effect of this action is exactly the same as selecting a page icon, as described above. If you enter an unavailable page number, the Alert dialog shown in Figure 5.06 will appear. Clicking the CANCEL button in the Go TO PAGE dialog will return you to the currently displayed page.

After applying one of the above methods for turning pages, the watch cursor will appear momentarily while PageMaker reads information about the new pages from your disk and executes a mini-save. The new page will then appear on the screen at the same view size and screen position as when last saved or viewed.

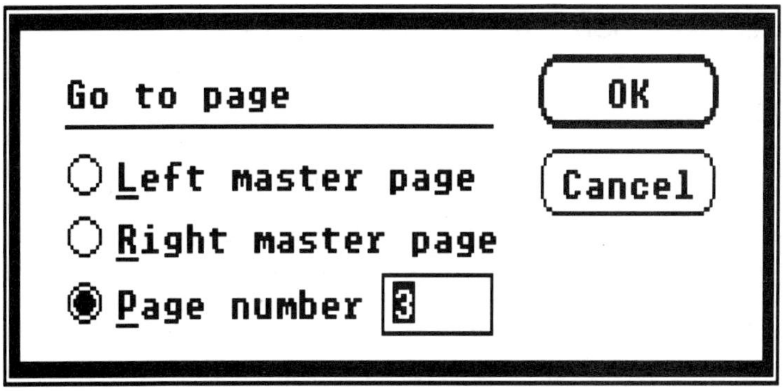

Figure 5.05: *The Go to page dialog box.*

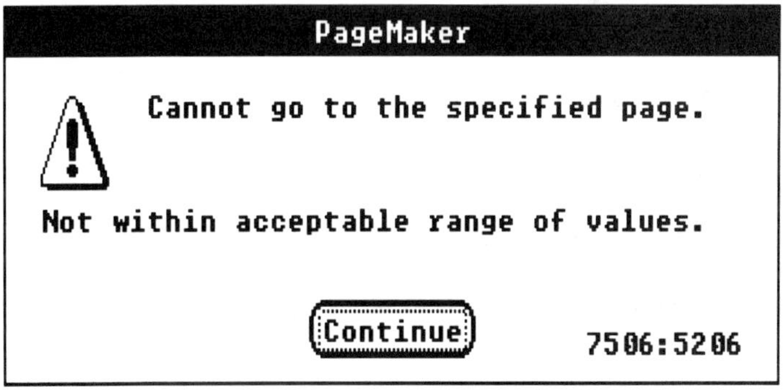

Figure 5.06: *The Alert box that appears when you enter invalid page numbers in the Go to page dialog box.*

Adding pages

While creating a publication you may often find that you need more pages than currently exist in the file. As long as the current publication has less than 128 pages, you can easily add any number of additional pages using the INSERT PAGES command from the PAGE menu. As we shall see, pages are inserted before, after, or between the currently selected

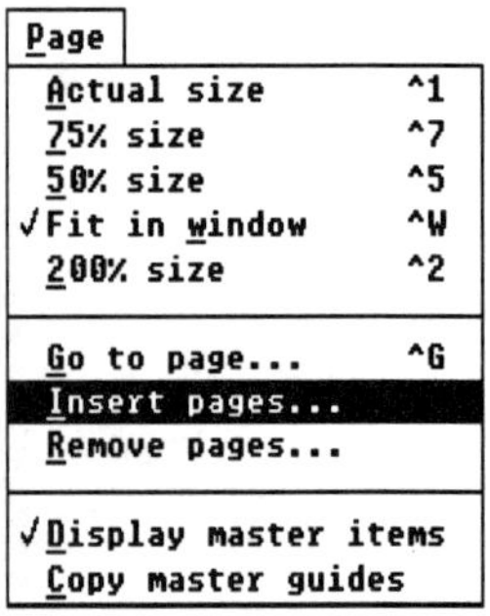

pages, so you should turn to the appropriate page in the existing publication before choosing the Insert pages... command.

Once chosen, the Insert pages dialog will appear, as shown in Figure 5.07. Here you may specify the number of pages that you wish to add, and where you want them to be placed relative to the currently selected publication page(s).

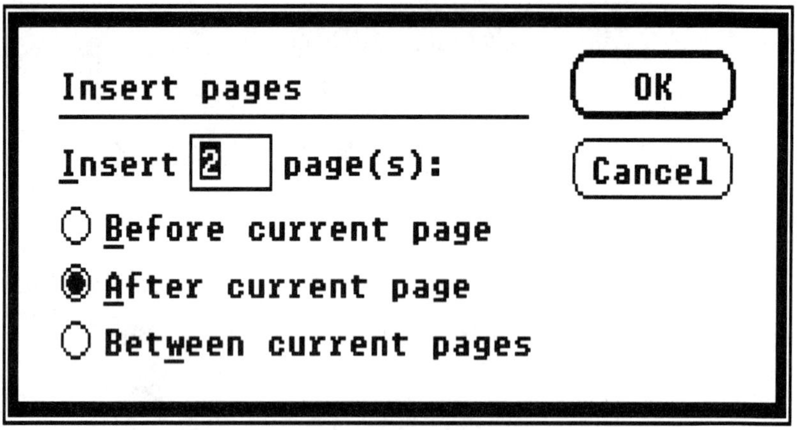

Figure 5.07: *The Insert pages dialog box.*

Click the OK button after making these selections to insert the pages. If you try to add too many pages, forcing the publication to exceed 128 pages, an Alert dialog will appear, and you will have to modify your request. Clicking the Cancel button in the Insert pages dialog will return you to the current page(s) without adding any pages.

The pages you have inserted—either before, after, or between the selected pages—will have no effect on the items already positioned on any existing pages. For example, if threaded text blocks (described in Chapter 7, *Adding and*

Creating Text in PageMaker) link pages 8 and 9, and you have inserted two pages between pages 8 and 9, the threaded text will remain in place, now flowing from page 8 to page 11. All following pages in the publication are renumbered as soon as the new pages are inserted. New pages always display all master page items and guides.

Pages are automatically inserted in your publication when placing text using the "Automatic text flow" option. If the automatically flowing text reaches the end of the last page in the publication PageMaker automatically inserts pages, one or two at a time, and the text flow continues until either all of the text is placed or the 128 page publication limit is reached. The process of automatic text flow is described more fully in Chapter 7, *Adding and Creating Text in PageMaker*).

Removing pages

Occasionally, you will want to remove certain pages from your publications. Removing a page deletes it, along with all items on that page. If you want to save any elements on a page before you delete it, move those elements to the pasteboard prior to choosing the REMOVE PAGES... command. Elements on the pasteboard are not affected by page removal.

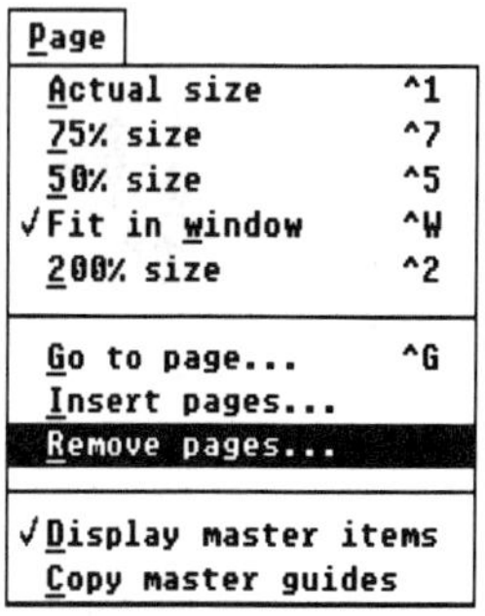

The REMOVE PAGES... command in the PAGE menu is used remove pages. When this command is chosen, the REMOVE PAGES dialog appears, as shown in Figure 5.08. Here you may specify the range of page numbers to be deleted. When this dialog box appears, PageMaker assumes that you want to delete the currently selected page(s). Any legitimate page range may be specified, even one including every page in the publication. An Alert dialog will appear if you specify nonexistent pages for removal. Click the OK button or press the RETURN or ENTER key after selecting the page(s) you want to remove

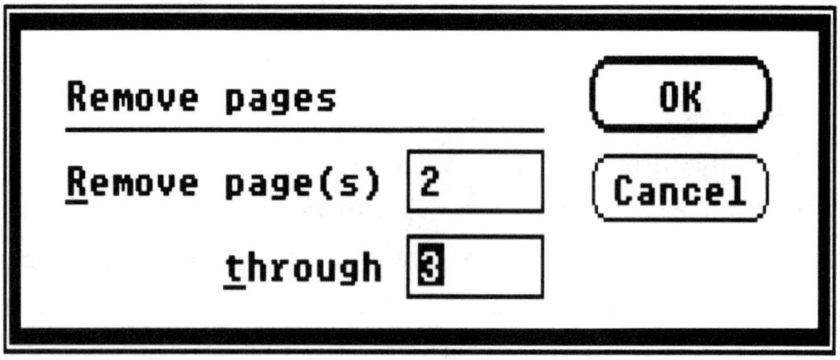

Figure 5.08: *The Remove pages dialog box.*

Before PageMaker deletes a specified pages, an Alert box (see Figure 5.09) warns you that you cannot undo the removal of a page; You may either cancel the removal or click the OK button to delete the page(s). All following publication pages will be renumbered after the deletion. Note that deleting an odd number of pages in a double-sided publication will cause the pages following the deleted pages to switch from being left pages to right pages, and vice versa.

You can undo the removal of pages using the UNDO command from the EDIT menu, but you must do so immediately after the removal. Later, you can regain deleted pages by using the REVERT command, or the "revert to mini-save" option described at the end of this chapter.

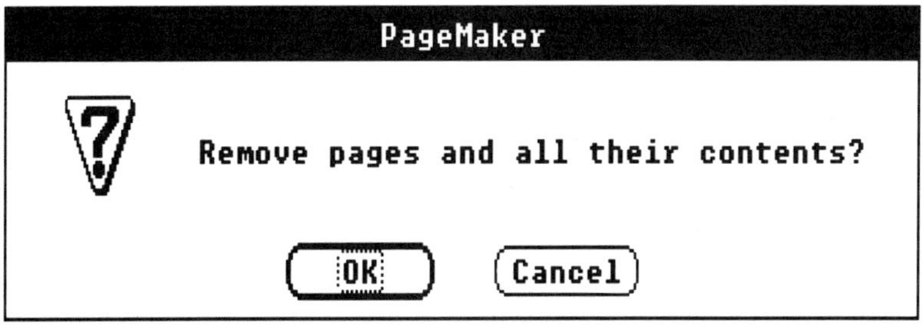

Figure 5.09: *The Alert box which displays before pages are deleted.*

Working with master pages

Each PageMaker publication begins with one or two master pages, represented by the L (Left master page) and R (Right master page) icons in the lower left corner of the publication window. Single-sided publications, which are made up only of right pages, have only a right master page. Publications that have the "Double-sided" option selected in the PAGE SETUP dialog have both left and right master pages.

Master pages hold text, graphics, and column and ruler guides that repeat on some or all of the publication pages in a document. By definition, anything that you add to a master page automatically appears on every corresponding (left or right) page in the document. Positioning these items on master pages, rather than on each individual page, avoids the potential for error associated with retyping or repositioning elements, and also minimizes file size.

There are several common uses for master pages:

- **Headers**. Master pages often carry running heads or footers, including rules, chapter and book titles, and page numbers.
- **Design grids**. Design grids are often set up on master pages, including column guides and horizontal and vertical ruler guides.
- **Repeating elements**. Page borders and common graphic elements, such as company logos, are often put on master pages for flyers, handouts, or transparencies.

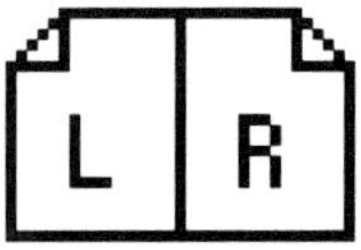

To work on a master page, simply select the master page icon in the publication window. Master pages look and act exactly like all other pages of a publication, except that they cannot be printed. Text can either be created on the master page by using the text tool, or imported by using the PLACE... command. Graphics can also be created on the master page by using one of PageMaker's graphic tools or imported as Paint-type, PICT, EPS, or TIFF graphic files using the PLACE... command. Once positioned on the master page, both text and graphics can be edited in the same manner as on publication pages.

Page numbering

Automatic page numbering can be established for any document by entering the automatic page-numbering character into a text block on the master page(s). The automatic page-numbering character can be set alone in a text block or as part of a text block containing other text. To begin, select the text tool from the toolbox, position it as desired, and click the mouse to create a new text block. Enter any text that you wish to appear before the page number itself, such as the word "Page". Now press CTRL+SHIFT+3, and a zero (0) will appear as shown in the examples in Figure 5.10. You can then continue to enter additional text in the text block, if desired. The page number character can only be created while working on master pages—pressing CTRL+SHIFT+3 on a normal publication page will have no effect.

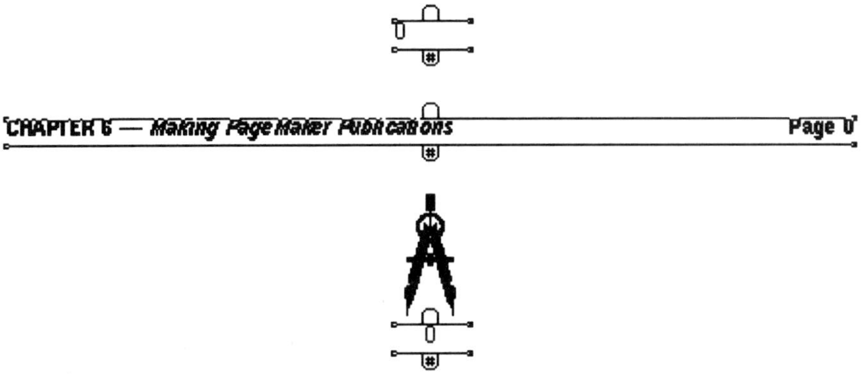

Figure 5.10: *Three sample page numbers as set on a master page. The first is set alone in a text block, the second is set with other text in the block, and the third is centered under a graphic.*

This zero (0) will be replaced by the actual page number when it appears on any real page in the publication. Even though the page-number character is only a single digit, page numbers of up to four digits will appear on the publication pages, depending on the starting page number of your publication. Be sure to account for the number of digits that might make up the various page numbers when positioning and justifying them. For example, in the third sample in Figure 5.10, the page number is centered in a text block using centered alignment, and then positioned under a graphic. This method insures that the page numbers will be centered regardless of how many digits they contain (in contrast to the manual positioning of a text block which has not been formatted with centered alignment).

Master page elements on publication pages

Once elements have been added to the master page(s) they will appear on the corresponding publication pages and will print on these pages exactly as if they had been added to each page. On the publication pages, master page elements cannot be selected—they are inaccessible, as if already printed on the paper.

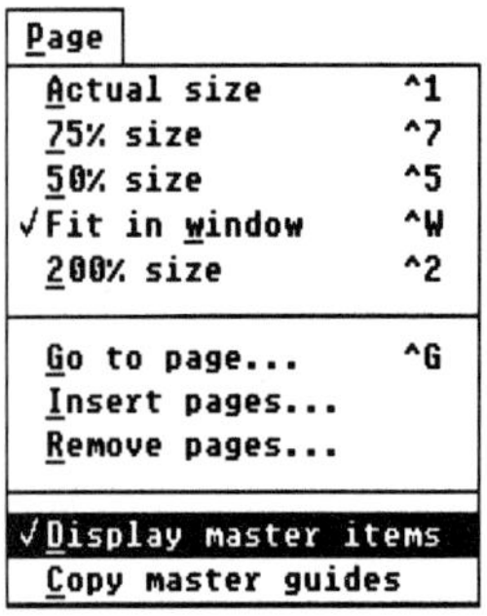

It is impossible to move, delete, or edit *individual* master page elements while working on a publication page; however, it is possible to remove *all* the master page elements on a publication page. Once removed, they will neither appear on the screen nor print. To remove master page elements choose the DISPLAY MASTER ITEMS command in the PAGE menu, which toggles on and off the display of master page elements. A check mark (✔) is displayed next to the DISPLAY MASTER ITEMS command when the master items are displayed and is removed when they are not displayed. This is often used to suppress running footers and page numbers on the first page of a chapter or section.

In many cases, you will wish to display only some of the elements from the master page. Since PageMaker provides only all-or-nothing control over master page elements, many users have found a simple technique that allows them to selectively delete master page elements.

To "remove" selected master page elements, place a PageMaker-created graphic shape on top of the master page element to be hidden, filling the shape with the shade "Paper" and giving the shape a line weight of "None." This creates an opaque mask that covers the master page element so that it will not display or print. Other elements can be placed on top of the covering shape, as long as they are above the opaque mask in the stacking order. An example of this is shown in Figure 5.11

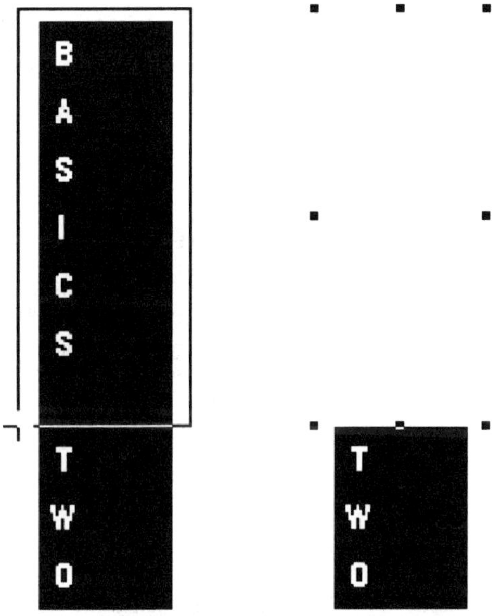

Figure 5.11: *Creating a shape with a "None" line and "Paper" shade allows you to selectively mask master page elements on any page of your publication.*

Guidelines and the master page

Master pages can hold text and graphics, as we have seen, and they are frequently used to set up a design grid that is used on most or all pages of the publication. This grid is made up of column guides and ruler guides that are used in the placement and positioning of text and graphics. These guide lines are placed on the master pages and appear on corresponding publication pages, just like text and graphic master page elements. Unlike text and graphic elements, however, guide lines from the master pages may be repositioned or even deleted on each individual publication page. Moving guides on a publication page does not affect those guides on the master pages or on any other page. Manipulating guides on the master pages, however, immediately changes those guides as they appear on every publication page on which the guide lines have not been customized.

The details of working with column guides and ruler guides on publication pages are included in the next section of this chapter.

Printing master pages

It is not possible to print master pages, but printing a blank publication page with the DISPLAY MASTER ITEMS command selected has the effect of printing only the elements of the master page.

Guidelines and rulers

Earlier, we described PageMaker as a program used primarily for the precise positioning of text and graphics on a page. In this section we describe three important tools that PageMaker provides to help you achieve this goal: column guides, ruler guides, and rulers themselves.

Column guides

Column guides serve as the left and right margins for blocks of text that are added to a page. They may also be used to position or align graphics. PageMaker provides control over the number and placement of column guides on any page. Since the number of columns per page is usually consistent throughout a publication, column guides are often placed on master pages, although their position can be modified on any particular publication page.

When a publication is first created, PageMaker automatically assigns at least one column guide to the master pages and to every publication page. When additional pages are added, they have the same number of column guides as does the associated master page.

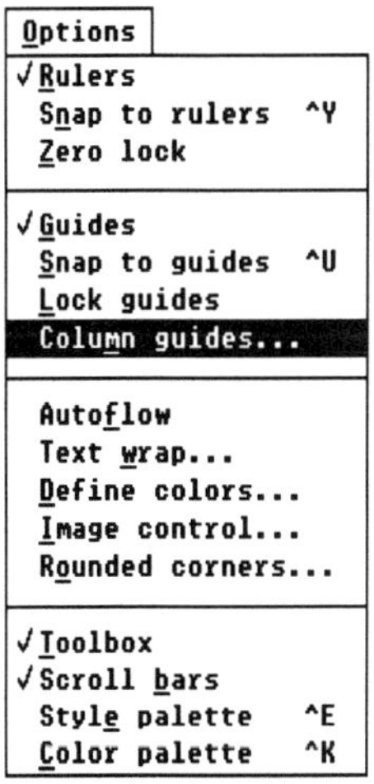

To add column guides to any page (including a master page), or to alter existing column guides, select the COLUMN GUIDES... command from the OPTIONS menu. The COLUMN GUIDES dialog box, shown in Figure 5.12, will appear. The COLUMN GUIDES command will be dimmed when the GUIDES command is deselected (and the guides will be hidden).

The "Number of columns" and "Space between" options will display the current specifications for the page. If you have customized the column guides, the word "Custom" will appear in the "Number of columns" option box. A page may have up to 20 columns (which must be at least ⅙-inch wide), and the space between columns may be any value between zero and the width of the margins minus ⅙ inch for each column. Any value entered for the "Space between columns" is ignored if only one column is defined.

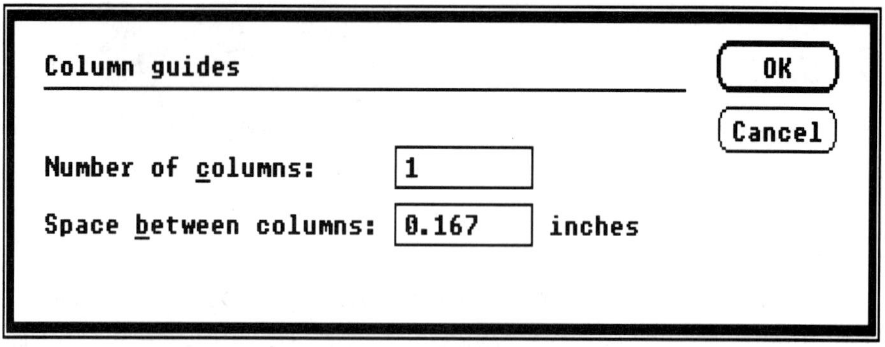

Figure 5.12: *The Column guides dialog box as it appears for single sided publications.*

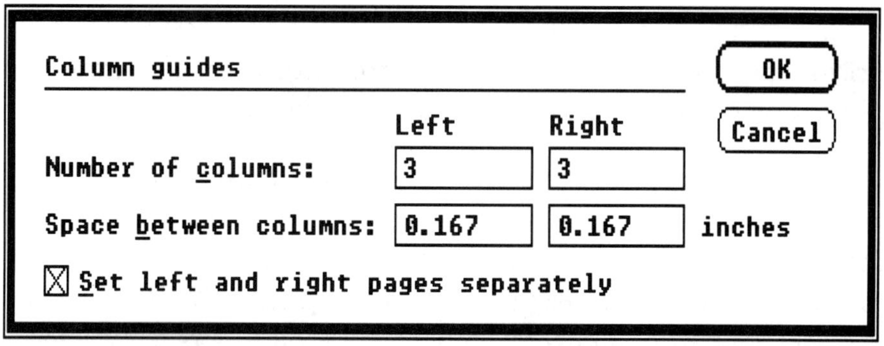

Figure 5.13: *The Column guides dialog box as it appears for double-sided publications when the Set left and right separately option is selected.*

If the "Facing pages" option is being used, PageMaker assumes that you wish to set identical column guides for both pages. If you want to enter unique column guide specifications for the left and right pages, select the "Left and Right separate" option, and the COLUMN GUIDES dialog will then display separate option boxes for the left and right pages, as shown in Figure 5.13.

When the OK button is clicked, PageMaker calculates the width of each column and then draws the column guides on the page. Column guides are represented by dotted vertical lines as shown in Figure 5.14. Since the leftmost and rightmost column guides are placed directly on top of the margin guides, they appear as darker lines.

Figure 5.14: *A page with three columns defined.*

Columns created by the COLUMN GUIDES dialog box are always equally spaced between the left and right page margins. However, once the column guides have been created, they can be manually repositioned so that they are not equally spaced. Like other PageMaker elements, column guides can be dragged to new positions at any time.

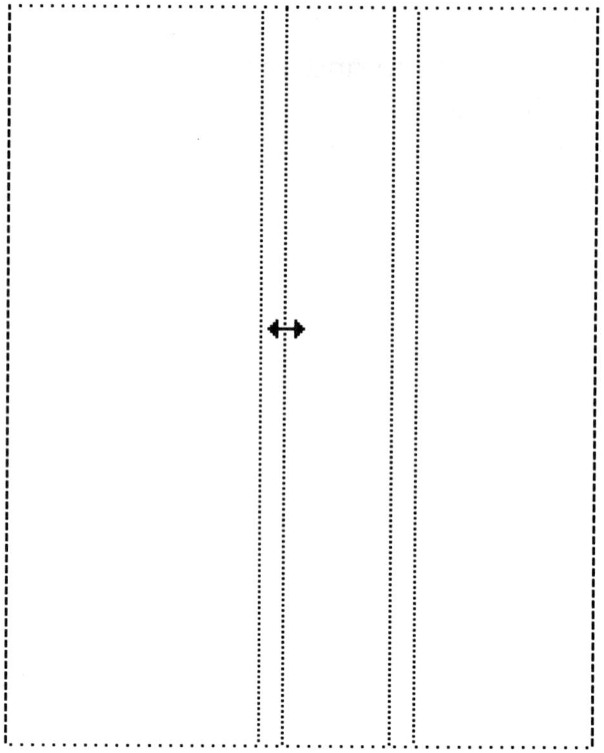

Figure 5.15: *Moving one of the column guides by dragging it with the arrow cursor.*

To reposition a column guide, press and hold the mouse button while positioning the arrow tool on the column guide. The cursor will become a double-sided arrow when you have successfully selected the column guide and will remain a double-sided arrow as long as you hold the mouse button down. Now move the column guide to where you want it. Use the small dotted lines that track the location of the cursor on the rulers to help position the column guides. Column guides can be positioned not less than one pica (1/6 inch) from another column guide.

Rulers

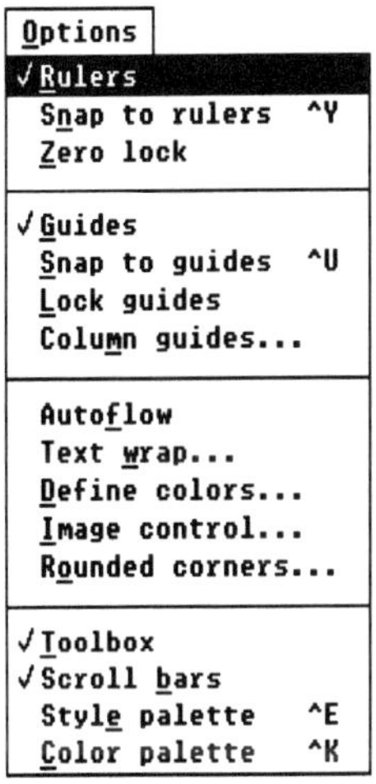

PageMaker provides vertical and a horizontal on-screen rulers to help you accurately place text and graphics. The rulers are displayed or hidden by using the RULERS command on the OPTIONS menu. When the RULERS command has a check mark (✔) in front of it, the rulers are displayed; choosing the RULERS command again will hide the rulers.

Each ruler has *tick marks* that divide the ruler into subunits of the unit of measure specified in the PREFERENCES dialog box. The "Measurement system" option specifies the units used in the horizontal ruler, while the "Vertical ruler" option specifies the units used in the vertical ruler. The vertical ruler can be set in the same unit of measure as the horizontal ruler, or in picas or points. A complete discussion of this option is included in Chapter 4, *A Brief Tour of PageMaker*.

The amount of space between two tick marks depends on the size and resolution of your monitor, the current view size of the publication, and the unit of measure. The enlarged or reduced along with the publication view size, as illustrated in Figure 5.16.

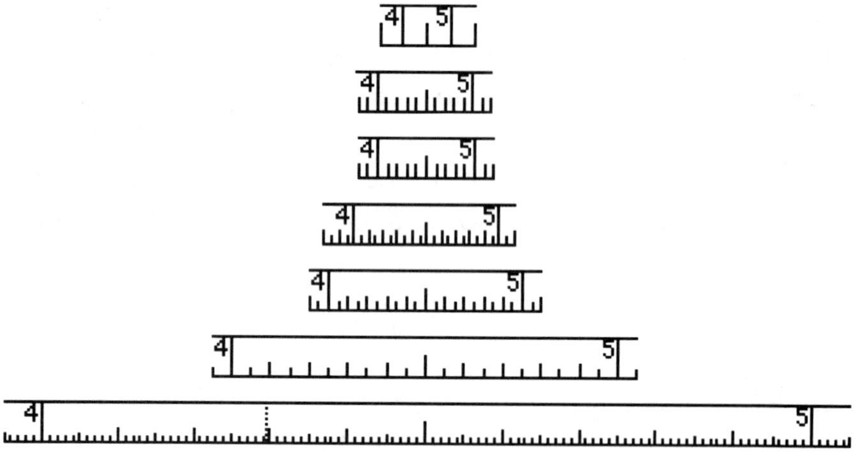

Figure 5.16: *Ruler tick marks change with the view sizes. The decimal inch ruler is shown above (top to bottom) "Super-fit-in-window" size, "Fit-in-window" size, 50% size, 75% size, "Actual" size, 200% size, and 400% size. Note that the "Fit-in-window" size and 50% size are similar due to the size of the monitor.*

The space represented by the distance between tick marks at the various view sizes in the various units of measure is listed in Figure 5.17.

	Inches	Decimal	Millimeters	Picas
Fit in window	1/8"	0.1"	5.0 mm	1 pica
50% size	1/8"	0.1"	5.0 mm	6 points
75% size	1/16"	0.05"	1.0 mm	3 points
Actual size	1/32"	0.05"	1.0 mm	3 points
200% size	1/32"	0.05"	0.5 mm	1 point

Figure 5.17: *Units of measure used in the rulers at the various view sizes in the available units of measure.*

Any time that the rulers are displayed, the position of the cursor is tracked on the rulers by small dotted lines. These lines make it easier to accurately position elements and therefore reduce the need for column and ruler guides. Theoretically, elements that are precisely aligned to tick marks in the rulers are accurate to 1/4440 inch (or 0.0002 inch, 0.001 mm, or 0.016 point). Items aligned between two tick marks on the ruler are less accurately positioned. In reality, the precision of your printer, which depends on both its resolution and physical condition, determines the accuracy of such exacting specifications.

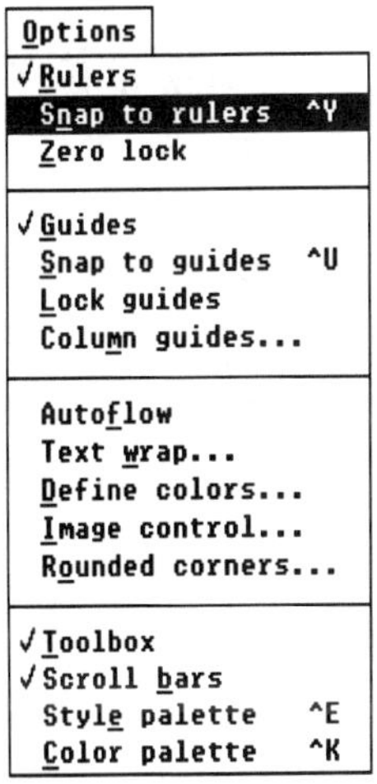

To help you position objects so that they are precisely aligned with a ruler tick mark, PageMaker provides the SNAP TO RULERS command in the OPTIONS menu. When this command is selected, indicated by a check mark (✔) in front of the command, it is impossible to position objects between ruler tick marks—the edges of the object nearest to the cursor will automatically "snap" to the nearest ruler tick marks, vertically and horizontally. Since the number of tick marks varies with the current view size, you can place objects more precisely by enlarging the view size.

To turn on the SNAP TO RULERS command, simply choose the SNAP TO RULERS command (CTRL-Y) in the OPTIONS menu. The SNAP TO RULERS command will display a check mark (✔) in front of it as long as it is selected. To turn off the SNAP TO RULERS command so you can position objects freely, choose the SNAP TO RULERS command again, and the check mark before the command will disappear.

Measuring with the ruler

When using a ruler to measure a distance in real life, you typically place the zero point of the ruler at the beginning of the distance and read the measured distance from the tick marks on the ruler. Only when it is impossible to put the zero point at the beginning of the distance being measured are you forced to calculate the distance between two points by subtracting two values. For example, if the measured distance starts at 1.5 inches and ends at 4.75 inches, your measured distance is 4.75 – 1.5 = 3.25 inches.

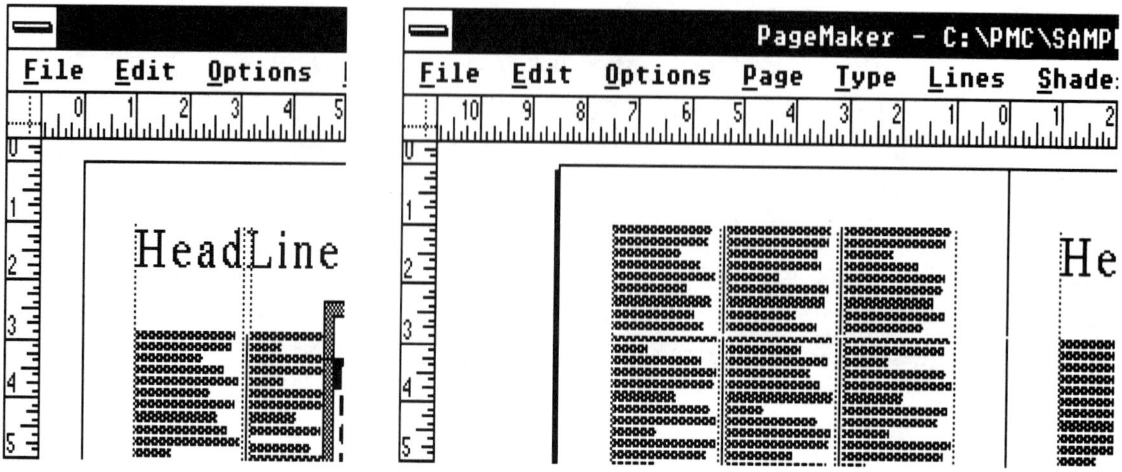

Figure 5.18: *The default zero points for single and facing page displays.*

To measure distances on PageMaker's electronic page, you use the same technique as in real life, except that instead of moving the ruler so that the zero-point is aligned with the beginning of the distance to be measured, we change the position of the zero point. For any new single-sided publication, the zero point of both the horizontal and vertical rulers is at the upper left corner of the electronic page. For double-sided publications, the zero point is located at the top of the electronic pages and centered between them. The default zero point is shown in Figure 5.18 for both a single page and a double-sided publication.

To reset the zero point, simply drag the *zero point marker* from the upper left corner of your display (in the corner between the vertical and horizontal rulers), to a point on the publication. As the zero point marker is dragged, perpendicular lines extend across the screen so that the new zero point can be aligned precisely, as shown in Figure 5.19. As soon as you release the mouse button, both rulers will be redrawn according to the new zero point.

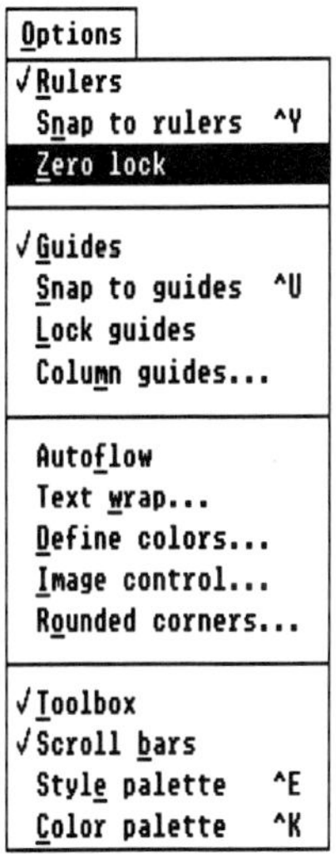

Since resetting the zero point is so easy, you can use it to measure the size of graphic elements, to accurately position text blocks, and to measure and position column and ruler guides. However, you may want to set the zero point of your ruler at a precise location from which it cannot be moved accidentally. PageMaker allows you to lock the zero point so that it cannot be moved without purposely unlocking it. To lock the zero point, simply choose the ZERO LOCK command from the OPTIONS menu. The zero point marker will disappear from the upper left corner of the display, making it impossible to select and reposition it. The ZERO LOCK command will display a check mark (✔) in front of it as long as it is selected. To unlock the zero point and make it possible to reset the zero point, choose the ZERO LOCK command again. The check mark before the command will disappear, and the zero point marker will reappear.

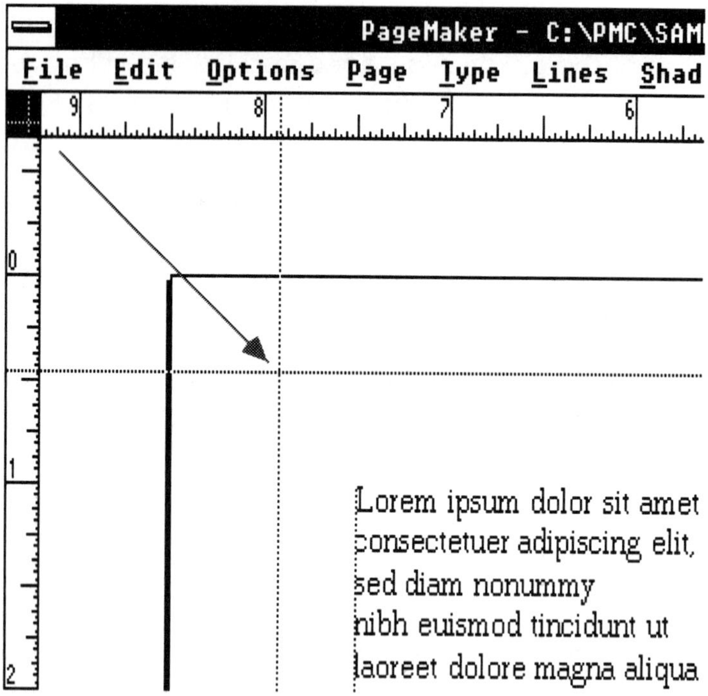

Figure 5.19: *The zero point of the rulers can be adjusted by dragging the zero point marker from the upper left corner.*

Ruler guides

As we've seen, the vertical and horizontal rulers in the publication window help us to locate any position on the screen or measure any distance. In addition to these, we can also create **ruler guide lines** to help us position and align elements. Ruler guide lines (also known as ruler guides) are non-printing dotted lines, much like column guides and margin guides, that can be put anywhere on a page as reference points for the positioning and alignment of text or graphic objects.

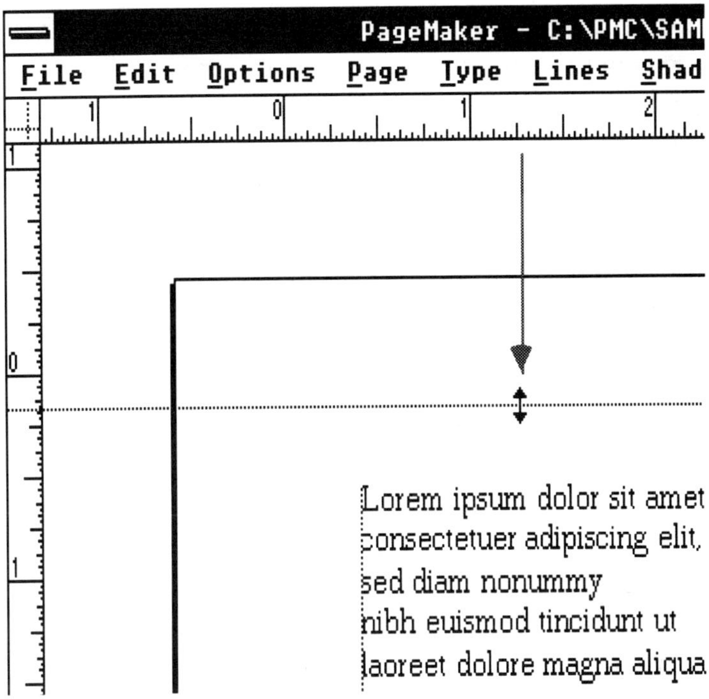

Figure 5.20: *Ruler guides are created by dragging them "out" of the rulers onto the page.*

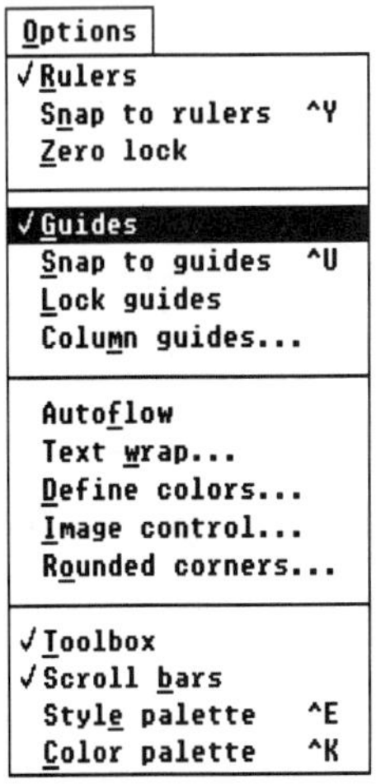

Ruler guides are created by clicking on the horizontal or vertical ruler and dragging the pointer out into the publication window, as shown in Figure 5.20. As soon as the arrow pointer leaves the ruler and enters the pasteboard, a ruler guide becomes visible. Ruler guides can be created only when the GUIDES command in the OPTIONS menu is selected, and the LOCK GUIDES command is not. You can create guides no matter what tool is selected. Up to 40 ruler guides can be created on a single page or set of facing pages, including horizontal and vertical ruler guides. Ruler guides created on the master pages, whether displayed or not on the publication page, do count in this total.

Ruler guides are most often used when you want to mark a place on the page and find it again no matter how you change the rulers. Since you may often change the zero point of the rulers while working on a publication, marking a particular position with a ruler guide saves you time when you want to position or align an element with this point. Ruler guides are especially useful on master pages where they can designate specific boundaries or positions on most or all pages.

Ruler guides can be repositioned at any time by simply dragging them to a new position. Point the arrow tool at the ruler guide and click and hold the mouse button. The arrow then becomes double-sided and can be dragged in either direction. Ruler guides cannot be selected when the LOCK GUIDES command is selected in the OPTIONS menu (indicated by a check mark (✔) in front of the command).

To remove a ruler guide simply drag it back onto the ruler and release the mouse button.

More about guides

As we mentioned earlier, column and ruler guides can be placed on master pages exactly as on publication pages. Guides placed on master pages automatically appear on the publication pages just as text and graphic elements do, but with one important difference. Text and graphic elements placed on the master pages cannot be moved or deleted on publication pages, but column and rule guides that appear on publication pages by virtue of their inclusion on master pages can be moved on or deleted from the publication pages. Changing the position of the guides on any publication page does not affect the position of the guides on the master pages or any other publication pages. Column and ruler guides from the master pages can be thought of as the starting point for guides on each of the corresponding publication pages, rather than as immovable elements.

It is possible to change the position of column and ruler guides on every page by moving them on the master pages, but you may want to return the guides to their original positions if you have moved them on a particular page. PageMaker facilitates this action with the COPY MASTER GUIDES command. Choosing this command from the PAGE menu updates all column and ruler guides on the current page so they are exactly the same as the guides on the corresponding master page. The COPY MASTER GUIDES command is dimmed if all column and ruler guides are already set exactly as they are on the corresponding master page. Immediately after choosing the COPY MASTER GUIDES command you may choose the UNDO command from the EDIT menu to return the guides to their customized positions.

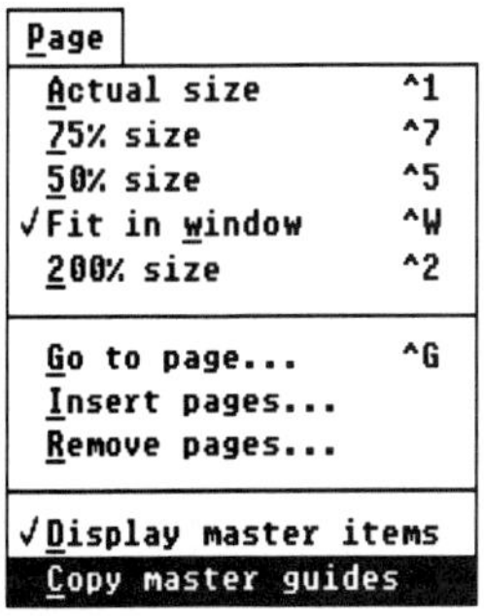

Because column guides and ruler guides can be selected and positioned just like any text or graphic element, it is possible to select and move them accidentally while trying to select other elements. Using the LOCK GUIDES command, you can make it impossible to select and move these guides. The LOCK GUIDES command from the OPTIONS menu toggles on and off this lock. A check mark (✔) appears before the command when the guides are locked.

PageMaker's column guides, ruler guides, and margin guides are normally displayed. However, these guides can be distracting when you are trying to envision the look of the publication without them. The guides can be hidden at any time by deselecting the GUIDES command in the OPTIONS

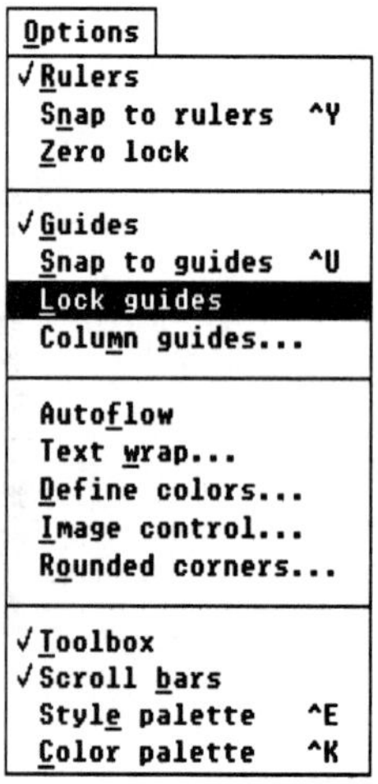

menu. This command toggles the display of the guides on and off. When the GUIDES command is deselected, the SNAP TO GUIDES, LOCK GUIDES, and COLUMN GUIDES... commands are dimmed and it is impossible to add new rulers or column guides.

The PREFERENCES dialog box, which is brought up by choosing the PREFERENCE... command in the EDIT menu, contains a "Guides" option that determines the relationship of all guides to text and graphic elements on the page (See Figure 4.14). When the "Front" option is selected, guides will be moved automatically at the top of the stacking order, and are therefore easy to select. When the "Front" option is selected, however, it is difficult to select objects positioned underneath guidelines. Holding down the ctrl key makes it impossible to select guidelines, and therefore easy to select the objects that they overlap.

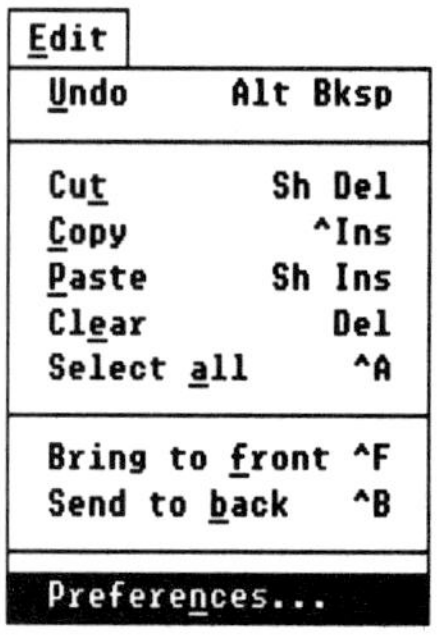

When the "Back" option is selected, guides are placed at the bottom of the stacking order, and in order to select them you will have to select them at a point at which they are not overlapped by text or graphic elements.

Guide lines do not print, whether or not they are displayed on the publication page.

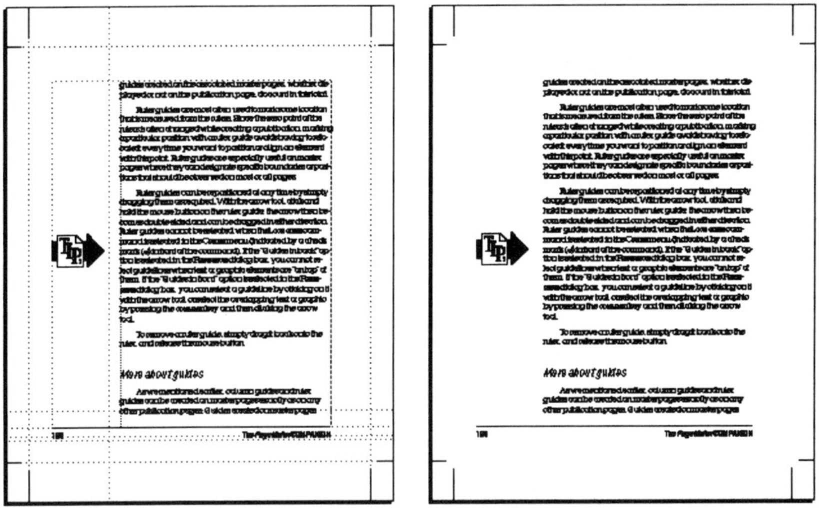

Figure 5.21: *The Guides command from the Options menu removes all column guides, ruler guides, and margin guides from the on-screen display.*

Snapping text and graphic elements to guides

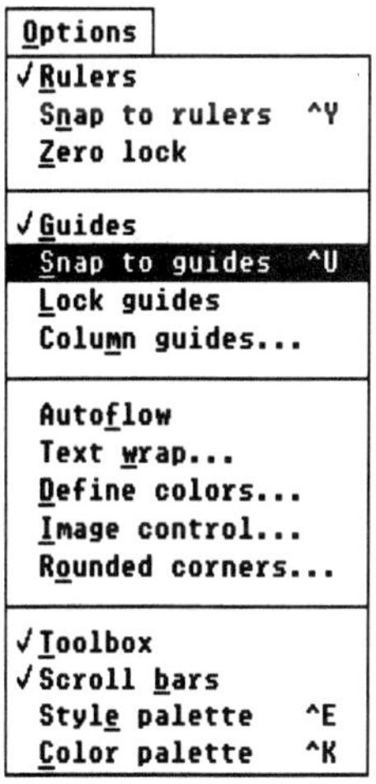

As we've seen, most column guides and ruler guides are created to help you position or align text or graphic elements on the page. Since we usually want to position an element exactly, PageMaker's column guides and ruler guides have a "magnetic" quality. This magnetism is activated by choosing the SNAP TO GUIDES command (CTRL-U) from the OPTIONS menu. The command toggles on and off the magnetic pull of the guides. When a check mark (✔) appears before the command, all guides on the page attract elements when they are very close to guides. Any element moved within two pixels of a guide will be pulled to the guide, but elements already in place will not be affected by the SNAP TO GUIDES command. This is a useful feature, saving you the trouble of trying to place elements exactly with an inexact mouse.

The magnetism of guide lines may be unwelcome in some cases. For example, you may want to position an element based on some alignment other than the existing guides, close to but not exactly aligned with one of the guides. Choosing the SNAP TO GUIDES command (CTRL-U) from the OPTIONS menu will toggle off the magnetism of the guides so that elements may be positioned very close to, but not exactly aligned with, guides on the page. A check mark will appear before the SNAP TO GUIDES command when the guides are magnetized.

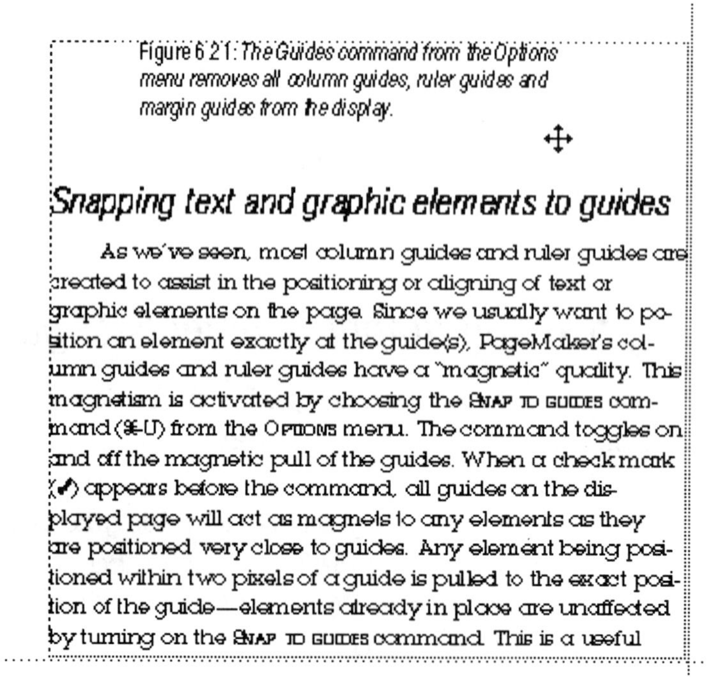

Figure 5.22: *Only with the Snap to guides command deselected is it possible to position objects close to but not even with column or ruler guides.*

Understanding objects

PageMaker publications are made up of text and graphics. Each text and graphic element is an individual object that can be manipulated on the electronic page during the process of page composition. In this section we examine the details of manipulating text and graphic objects. Topics include selecting objects, working with the stacking order (how objects are layered), and copying, moving, and deleting objects.

Object layers: the stacking order

Whenever two objects overlap in a PageMaker publication, one object is on top of the other. This is obvious because any opaque portions of the top object cover up the bottom object. If many different objects overlap, each object is above or below all other objects—no two objects are on the same layer.

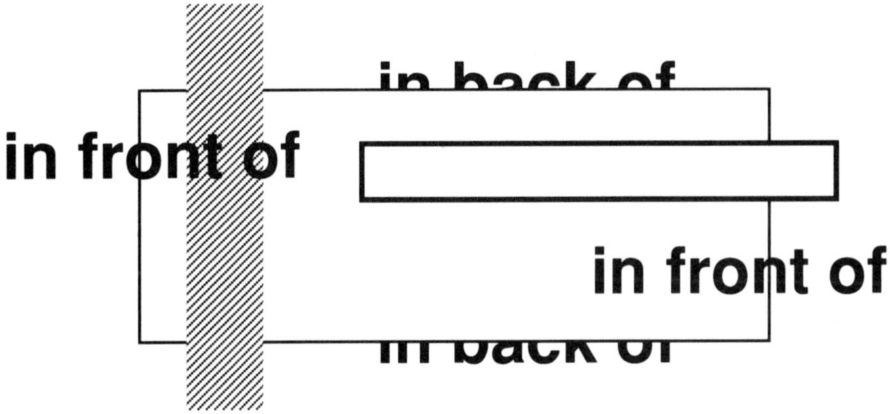

Figure 5.23: *Each text or graphic object on a page is on its own layer in the PageMaker stacking order.*

In PageMaker, the hierarchical order of objects, demonstrated by the order in which objects are drawn when the screen is refreshed and the way in which objects physically overlap, is called the **stacking order**. It is important to be aware of the stacking order because it affects the manipulation of objects, as we will discuss in the following sections.

The following principles apply to the stacking order:

- Newly created objects are placed at the top of the stack, above all other objects that already exist on the page. If an older object is moved, it is brought to the top of the stack.

- The SEND TO BACK command (CTRL-B) moves selected objects to the bottom of the stack.

- The BRING TO FRONT command (CTRL-F) moves selected objects to the top of the stack.

- When the screen is redrawn in a new view size or is refreshed in the current view size, objects are drawn in order from the bottom of the stack to the top. By watching the screen during this process, you can determine the stacking order for all objects on the page.

  Interestingly, the stacking order is also the order in which objects are added to PostScript files during printing. Occasionally, changing the on-screen stacking order of an object may correct a printing difficulty or help pinpoint a problem in the printing process.

- The stacking order of elements on the master page(s) is independent of the stacking order of elements on publication pages. Moreover, the stacking order of master page elements is, by definition, always at the bottom of the stack of all the elements on the publication page—including publication page elements that have been moved with the SEND TO BACK command.

- Column guides and ruler guides are positioned either above or below each object on a page according to the current setting of the "Guides" option in the PREFERENCES dialog box. When guides are above text and graphic objects they are easy to select and move. When they are behind all text and graphic elements on a page, you are less likely to select them by mistake when trying to select a text or graphic element. By pressing the CTRL key you make it impossible to select column guides or ruler guides, and therefore easier to select text or graphic objects.
- If you want to select an object that is underneath another, press and hold the CTRL key and then click on the stacked objects until the desired object is selected. Each mouse click selects the next lowest layer in the stacking order.

Selecting objects

The action of "selecting" an object is a fundamental skill in the Windows interface. In most Windows software, an object is selected by clicking on it with some kind of pointer tool, usually the arrow tool. Once selected, the object is highlighted or marked in some way as a visual confirmation of its selection. A selected object receives the action of various menu, dialog, mouse, and keyboard commands.

PageMaker employs these basic Windows selection concepts as well as some more advanced ones. In PageMaker, there are two levels of selection—selection of an object itself, such as a graphic or text block, and selection of text inside a text block. In this section we will discuss the selection of objects. Text selection is discussed in Chapter 8, *Editing Text in PageMaker.*

When an object is selected, **handles** become visible around the object, as shown in Figure 5.24. A selected text block shows horizontal handlebars at the top and bottom with solid rectangular handlebars at the four corners; a line shows a solid rectangle at each end; a shape is surrounded by eight solid rectangles; and an imported graphic shows a solid diamond at each corner.

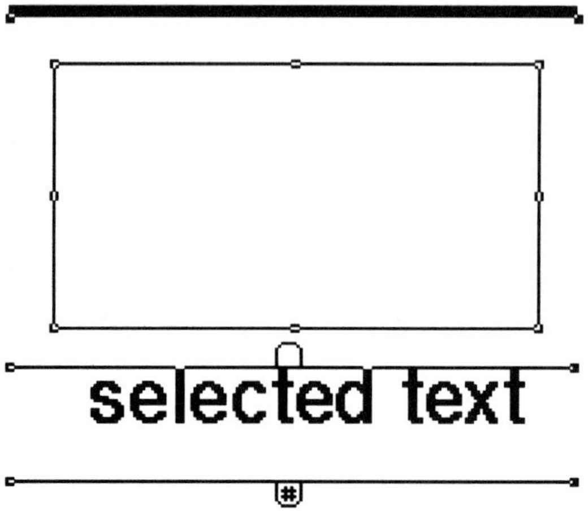

Figure 5.24: *A selected line, shape, and text block.*

Objects and groups of objects can be selected in a variety of ways:

- **Using the arrow tool**. The arrow tool can be used to select a single object, a group of objects, and objects that are partially or fully overlapped by other objects.

  To select a single object, select the arrow tool from the toolbox, and click anywhere on a text or graphic element to select the element. Graphic objects created in PageMaker, such as rectangles, with no interior shading, can only be selected by clicking on their edges. As soon as you select an object all other objects become deselected.

  To select more than one object, hold down the SHIFT key while selecting objects. This will select the new object without deselecting the previous selection—the newly selected object is instead added to the selection.

  To select objects that are completely or partially overlapped by other objects, hold down the CTRL key while clicking over the overlapped object. Each mouse click will select the object one layer lower in the stacking order. Normally, you might select the top object and then use the SEND TO BACK command in the EDIT menu to change the stacking order, but using the CTRL to select overlapped objects is a much faster method.

HOT TIP

- **Creating a marquee**. The marquee is a powerful tool for selecting objects that may be difficult to select using the arrow tool, or to quickly select a group of objects.

  A marquee is created by positioning the arrow tool on any blank space on the publication window, holding down the mouse button, and then dragging the arrow tool while keeping the mouse button depressed. As this is done, a dashed rectangle is drawn. This rectangle is called a marquee because of the way the dashed line moves around the border. All objects completely enclosed in the marquee become selected. Objects only partially contained within the marquee are not be selected.

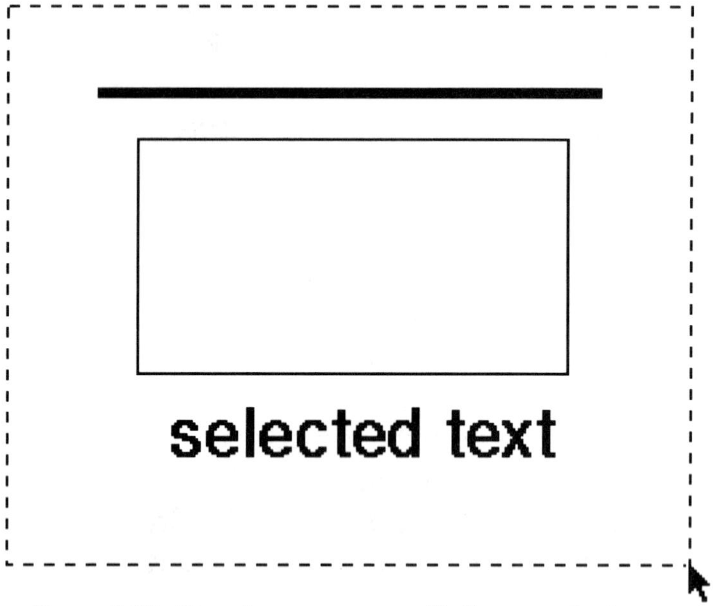

Figure 5.25: *Dragging a marquee with the arrow tool selects all objects that are completely enclosed by the marquee, but not those partially enclosed.*

It is usually easy to determine if a graphic object is entirely contained within a marquee as it is being created, but it is more difficult to tell if a text block is completely contained. This is because the handles of a text block are not displayed unless the block is already selected, and these handles often extend left and right far beyond the visible text. When using the marquee to select text blocks, be sure to create a large enough marquee to enclose the entire text block including its handlebars.

Normally, when objects are selected with a marquee, all other objects are deselected. If you hold down the SHIFT key while creating a marquee the newly selected objects will be added to the current selection

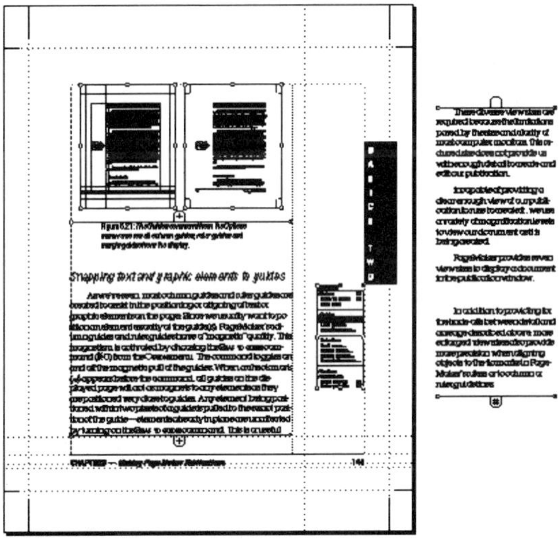

Figure 5.27: *By using the Select all command in the Edit menu, all elements on the current page and the pasteboard are selected. Master page items remain deselected.*

- **Using the Select all command**. The Select all command is a fast way to select a large number of objects. As soon as the Select all command (Ctrl-A) is chosen from the Edit menu, all objects on the currently displayed page(s) and on the surrounding pasteboard will be selected.

Deselecting objects

After one or more objects have been selected, and perhaps manipulated, you may want to deselect some or all of the selected objects. One common reason for wanting to do this is that the handles that appear while objects are selected can be quite distracting when trying to look at your publication.

To deselect an object or objects:

- **To deselect everything**. Select the arrow tool from the toolbox, position it on any blank space on the publication window, or point to the arrow tool in the toolbox, and click to deselect everything.
- **To deselect some but not all objects**. Hold down the shift key and click the arrow tool on a selected object. The object will become deselected without affecting any other selected objects. This technique, in combination with the Select all command or the marquee discussed above, makes it possible to quickly select most of the elements in an area or on a page. Create a marquee or use the Select all command to select all the objects in the area or page, then

SHIFT-click to deselect particular objects. This subtractive process is often a much faster way of selecting many objects.

Moving objects

While creating a publication in PageMaker, you will frequently need to adjust the placement of both text and graphic objects. This will occur either because your initial placement was inexact or because you have improved your design. In any case, it is easy to reposition elements. In fact, the ease with which you can move objects in a layout is one of PageMaker's greatest strengths.

Before moving an object you must first select it, as described above. There are three ways of moving objects:

- **Dragging the object into position**. With the arrow tool located anywhere on the selected object (except on one of its handles), click and hold down the mouse button and then drag the object(s) to the new position (clicking on a handle changes the *size* of an object, not its *position*). If you hold down the mouse button for a few seconds before moving the mouse you will be able to see the objects that you are repositioning while you drag them. If you move the mouse as soon as you press down the mouse button, you will see only a box outlining the selected object(s).

  Pressing the SHIFT key before or during a move will constrain the movement to either horizontal vertical movement, depending on the initial direction of the drag. This technique can be used to preserve the vertical alignment of an object while repositioning the object horizontally, or vice versa. You may also release the SHIFT key during a move to eliminate the constraint, or press the SHIFT key during an unconstrained move to add a constraint to the remainder of the move. If you inadvertently begin the move in the wrong direction, undo the move (CTRL-Z), and begin again.

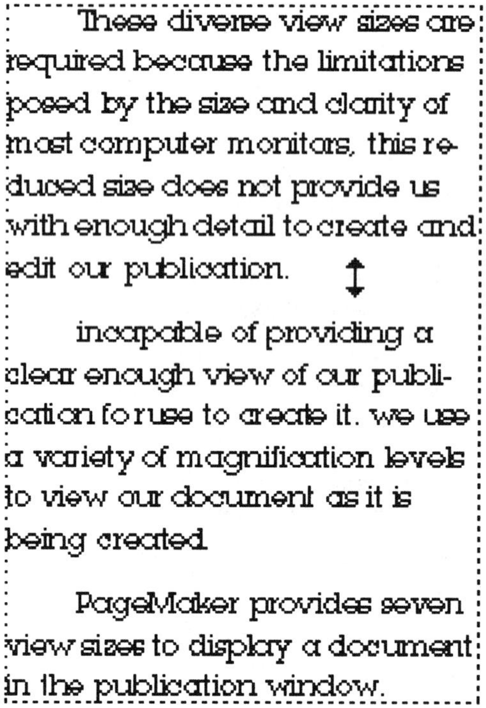

Figure 5.27: *Holding down the shift key while dragging an object constrains the move to either the horizontal or vertical axis.*

To align objects precisely, work at as large a view size as is practical. Create vertical and horizontal ruler guides to indicate the new position before you move the object, then use the SNAP TO GUIDES and SNAP TO RULERS commands in the EDIT menu as you need them. If you get the element positioned vertically, for instance, press the SHIFT key to keep this alignment while adjusting the position horizontally.

- **Cut and Paste**. To make dramatic moves, such as moving an element to another page, use the CUT and PASTE commands in the EDIT menu. After the object(s) to be moved have been selected, choose the CUT command (SHIFT-DELETE) from the EDIT menu. This will remove the objects from the current page and place them on the Clipboard. Turn the page or move the page on the screen so that the new location for the objects is visible, and then choose the PASTE command (SHIFT+INSERT) from the EDIT menu. A copy of the object is transferred from the Clipboard to the current page. You can now drag the object into position, using the techniques described above.

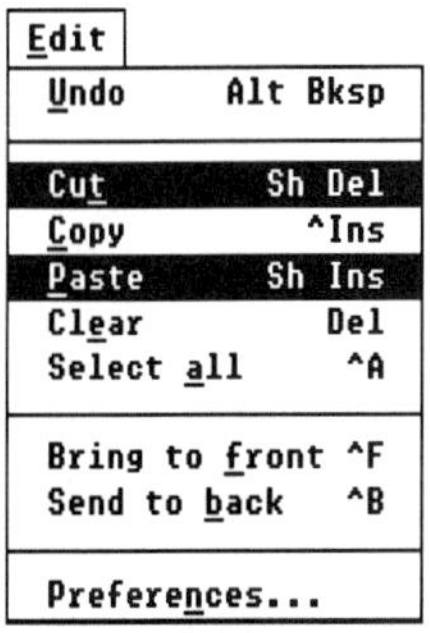

- **Dragging between pages**. To move objects between pages, drag them to the pasteboard, turn the page, then drag them onto the new page. Be sure the objects are completely on the pasteboard before turning the page; otherwise, they will remain on the original page. This method is well suited to moving large, complicated objects, which can cause system crashes when moved using the CUT and PASTE commands.

This can also be useful when you need to move an object or group of objects off one page but are not sure where they will finally be positioned. You can leave them on the pasteboard as long as you like. Once you determine where they belong, drag them off the pasteboard and into position.

Copying objects

By copying an object you can ensure consistency in your publication and avoid the effort of recreating the object. This is especially useful for any graphic object whose consistent size is important, such as a line spanning the column width or a box around photographs or illustrations.

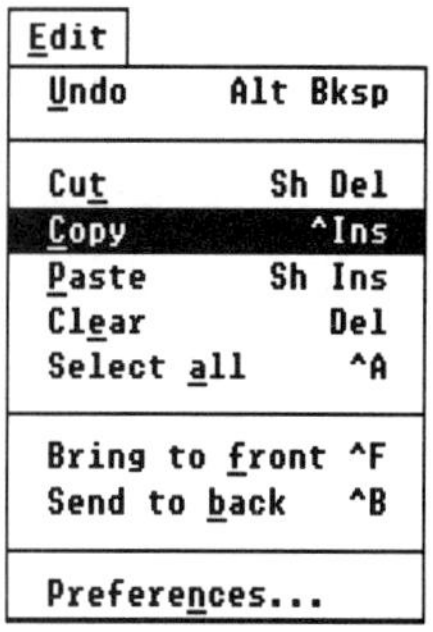

To duplicate an object or group of objects, select the object(s) and choose the Copy command (CTRL-INSERT) from the Edit menu. The Copy command will be dimmed if no object is selected. Turn the page or adjust the view if necessary and then choose the Paste command (SHIFT-INSERT) in the Edit menu. The duplicate object(s) will appear, selected, in the center of the display, and the arrow tool will be selected in the toolbox. Drag the pasted object into position.

When your publication makes frequent use of certain text or graphic objects, such as rules, photo boxes, or other ornaments, it is often a good idea to keep a copy of each on the pasteboard, as shown in Figure 5.28, copying it whenever it is needed in the publication. This saves the time and trouble of searching through the publication for the last occurrence in order to make a copy every time one is needed.

The Copy command makes a duplicate of all selected objects and places them on the Windows Clipboard. The Paste command *makes another duplicate* of the objects in the Clipboard and places the copy on the displayed page. Since the first copy remains in the Clipboard after the duplicate has been pasted, you can paste it repeatedly—until another object or group of objects is placed on the Clipboard using the Cut or Copy command. Objects remain on the Clipboard as long as your PC is turned on and you are in Windows, even after quitting the PageMaker application. Therefore, it is not necessary to paste the objects immediately after copying—you can turn the page or reposition other elements. In fact, you can choose any command except Cut or Copy without disturbing the Clipboard contents.

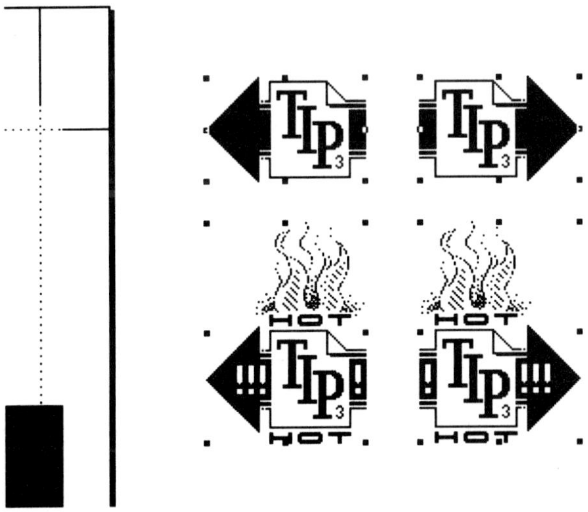

Figure 5.28: *Keep commonly used text and graphic objects on the pasteboard for easy access.*

Deleting objects

A selected object or group of objects can be deleted in three ways:

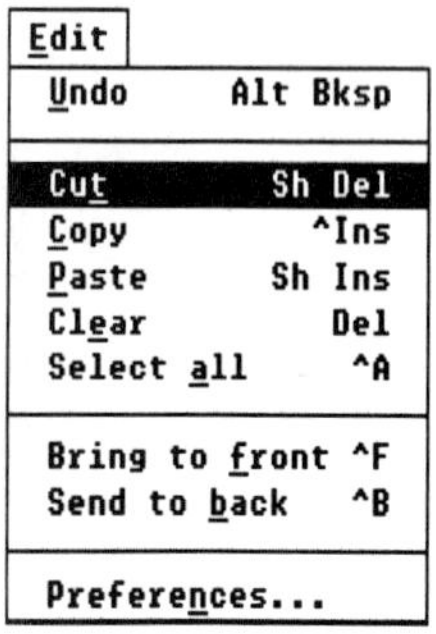

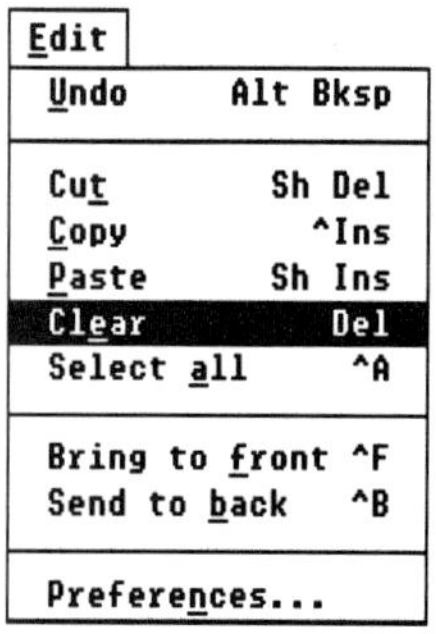

- **Choose the CUT command (SHIFT-DELETE) from the EDIT menu**. This removes the selected objects from the publication and places them on the Clipboard so that they can be pasted somewhere else. If you choose the CUT command by mistake, choose the UNDO command from the EDIT menu to restore the deleted object(s).

- **Choose the CLEAR command from the EDIT menu**. This removes the selected objects, but does not place them on the Clipboard. Use this command when you need to delete an object or group of objects but do not wish to lose the current Clipboard contents. If you choose the CLEAR command by mistake, choose the UNDO command from the EDIT menu to restore the deleted object(s).

- **Press the DEL key on your keyboard**. This is equivalent to choosing the CLEAR command. The deleted objects are *not* placed on the Windows Clipboard, but can be restored using the UNDO command from the EDIT menu. You can also use this key when you need to delete an object or group of objects but do not wish to lose the current Clipboard contents.

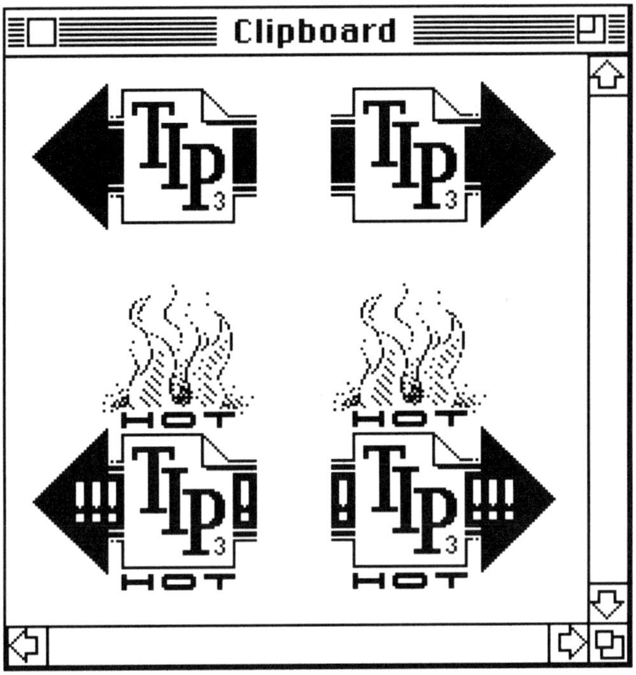

Figure 5.29: *The Clipboard can be made visible by choosing the Clipboard command from the Windows control menu.*

Undo and Revert

"I wish I hadn't done that." For all the times that you find yourself thinking these words, PageMaker provides two special commands, REVERT and UNDO. These commands reverse the last action or series of actions performed to your document.

Undo

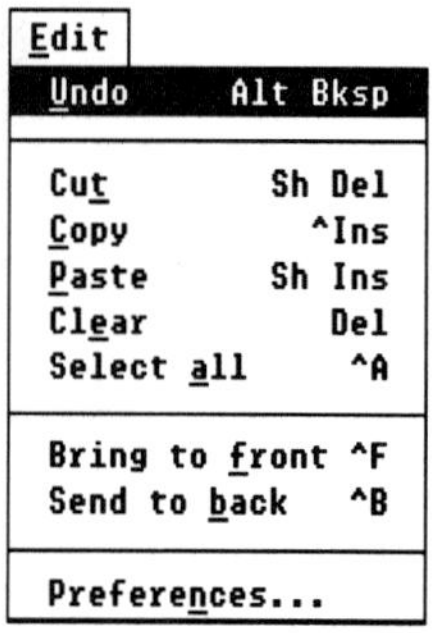

The UNDO command in the EDIT menu reverses the last action taken in your publication. Not all actions can be reversed, but most actions that affect the layout of your publication or its contents can be, including any actions that do not have a built-in opposite action.

It is possible to use the UNDO command to cancel:

- The movement of any text, graphic object, or guide line.
- The resizing of any text block or graphic.
- The cropping of any imported graphic.
- Any use of the CUT or COPY command (the PASTE command can be undone by simply deleting the pasted object(s).
- Changes made in the INSERT PAGES, REMOVE PAGES, or PAGE SETUP dialog boxes.

It is not possible to use the UNDO command to cancel:

- Any changes made using commands from the TYPE menu.
- Any changes made using the LINES or SHADES menu.
- Changes in view size or display.
- Selection or deselection of objects.
- SAVE or REVERT commands.

To use the UNDO command, simply choose it from the EDIT menu. The most important thing to remember about using the UNDO command is that you must use it *immediately* after you perform the mistaken action. Since the UNDO command can reverse only your last action, *any action taken*, however minor, after the mistaken one will make it impossible to reverse your mistaken action. For example, suppose you move some objects by dragging them with the arrow tool, and then decide that you are unhappy with their new position, and would like to return them to their original position. You must choose the UNDO command as soon as you release the mouse button after dragging the objects—if you click the mouse button or choose another tool from the toolbox, you can no longer undo the movement of the objects. The UNDO command will simply deselect the tool you have clicked on.

When the last action performed can be reversed, the UNDO command will read UNDO *ACTION*, where the word *ACTION* specifies the particular action that will be undone by selecting the command. Samples are shown in Figure 5.30. When the last action performed can not be reversed, the dimmed words, CANNOT UNDO, appear on the EDIT menu in place of the UNDO command.

Immediately after you have used the UNDO command, and your last action has been reversed, the UNDO command becomes the REDO command—allowing you to negate your use of the UNDO command. The REDO command will read REDO *ACTION*, where the word *ACTION* specifies the particular action that will be redone by selecting the command. After you choose the REDO command from the EDIT menu, the UNDO command *reappears*—it is then possible to reverse the action of REDO command.

Revert

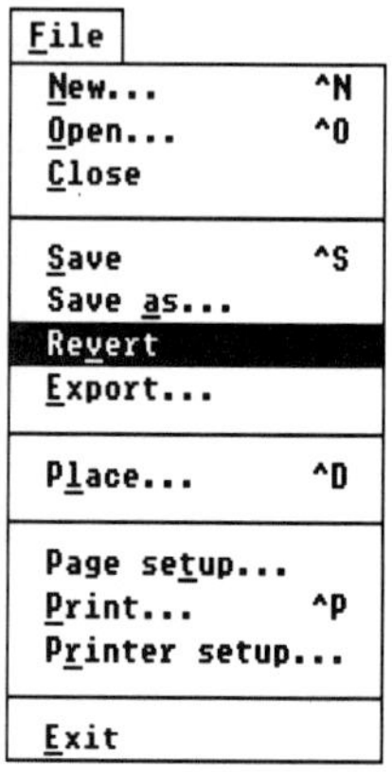

Suppose you revise your document, and after making these changes, you decide that your revisions have done more damage than benefit. Since you have performed several actions, you cannot use the Undo command to restore your original layout, and you may not even remember precisely how the document looked. But PageMaker does remember.

Using the Revert command you can return your document to its exact form as of the last execution of the Save command *or* to the last mini-save. This is useful when you have made important changes in your document that you now regret, such as deleting pages or important elements, editing text, or rearranging page elements.

Mini-saves are performed automatically whenever you turn the page in your publication, click on the current page icon, change the page setup specifications, or click OK in the Define styles dialog box. For a complete discussion of the mini-save, see Chapter 4, *A Brief Tour of PageMaker*. Information from the mini-save is kept in a temporary file on your disk so that PageMaker can access it when you use the revert command,or to recover your document in the case of a system crash. To revert to the last mini-save, hold down the shift key and choose the Revert command from the File menu. The Revert to mini-save? dialog, shown in Figure 5.30, will ask you to confirm your selection.

Once you have reverted to the the last mini-saved version of your document, you cannot return to the version of the document prior to choosing the Revert command. If you are sure that you want to revert, click the OK button; if not, click the Cancel button. If you click OK, your document will be restored to the version saved in the last mini-save. If the mini-save was executed when you turned a page, you will be returned to the page displayed prior to the mini-save.

Figure 5.30: *The Revert to mini-save? dialog box that appears after choosing the Revert command with the shift key held down.*

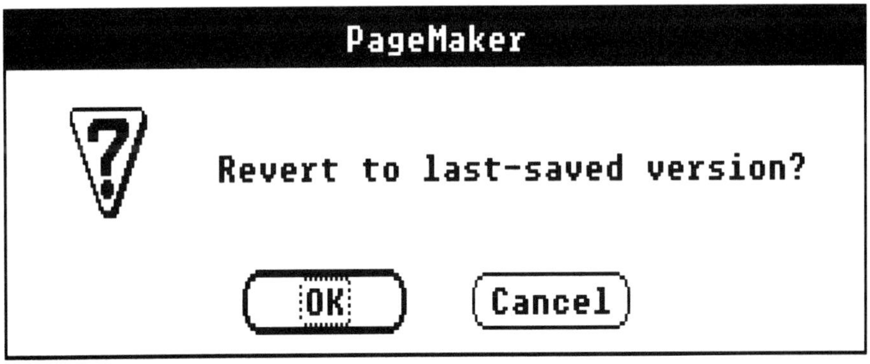

Figure 5.31: *The Revert to last saved version dialog box.*

If you want to return to an earlier version of your document than is possible using the REVERT TO MINI-SAVE command, you can now execute a regular REVERT command to return to the version saved by your last SAVE command. Choose the

REVERT command from the FILE menu (without holding down the SHIFT key). A REVERT TO LAST SAVED VERSION? dialog box will ask you to confirm your selection.

If you revert to the last-saved version, you cannot return to the version of the document now on your screen. If you are sure that you want to revert, click the OK button; if not, click the CANCEL button. If you click OK, your document will be restored to the version saved by the last SAVE command.

If you have not saved your document since opening it, the document will be returned to the version that was opened. If you are working on a new document that has never been saved and titled, the REVERT command is dimmed.

Creating a Simple Newsletter

In this chapter we examine:

- *The creation of master page elements*
- *How to establish and utilize column guides*
- *Importing and formatting text blocks*

Now that we have discussed the most fundamental aspects of using PageMaker and working in the publication window, it is time to work through our first sample project. In this book, sample projects offer another introduction to each of the features and methods discussed in the reference chapters, benefiting from the fact that each works towards a real and tangible goal.

In this first project, we will use PageMaker to create a newsletter—the quintessential PageMaker document. Through the creation of this document we will tour the abilities of PageMaker and begin to see the ways in which these abilities can be used to create virtually any kind of document. This newsletter project is the first of three sample projects presented in this book and therefore focuses on the more elementary aspects of the commands and features introduced.

The newsletter that we will create in this chapter is relatively basic. It consists of just two pages, including three short articles and a series of simple, geometric elements created inside PageMaker. You are encouraged to follow along and create the newsletter we are describing—all you will need are three one-page text files and PageMaker 3.0 itself. Don't worry that your text files don't correspond to each other or to our project. In this case, it is the construction process that is important, not the content of the finished newsletter.

Not all of the PageMaker features used in this chapter have been introduced thus far, but the introductions included in this chapter should be sufficient for your work in completing the sample project. If you are having problems with any particular topic, feel free to locate the more complete discussions included in the reference chapters.

Creating our publication

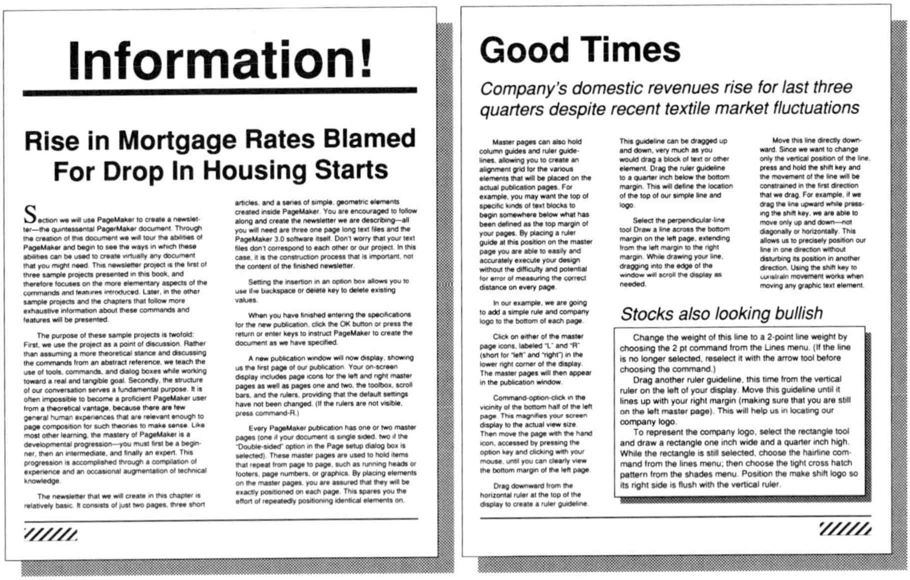

Information!

Rise in Mortgage Rates Blamed For Drop In Housing Starts

Section we will use PageMaker to create a newsletter—the quintessental PagerMaker document. Through the creation of this document we will tour the abilities of PageMaker and begin to see the ways in which these abilities can be used to create virtually any document that you might need. This newsletter project is the first of three sample projects presented in this book, and therefore focuses on the more elementary aspects of the commands and features introduced. Later, in the other sample projects and the chapters that follow more exhaustive information about these commands and features will be presented.

The purpose of these sample projects is twofold: First, we use the project as a point of discussion. Rather than assuming a more theoretical stance and discussing the commands from an abstract reference, we teach the use of tools, commands, and dialog boxes while working toward a real and tangible goal. Secondly, the structure of our conversation serves a fundamental purpose. It is often impossible to become a proficient PageMaker user from a theoretical vantage, because there are few general human experiences that are relevant enough to page composition for such theories to make sense. Like most other learning, the mastery of PageMaker is a developmental progression—you must first be a beginner, then an intermediate, and finally an expert. This progression is accomplished through a compilation of experience and an occasional augmentation of technical knowledge.

The newsletter that we will create in this chapter is relatively basic. It consists of just two pages, three short articles, and a series of simple, geometric elements created inside PageMaker. You are encouraged to follow along and create the newsletter we are describing—all you will need are three one page long text files and the PageMaker 3.0 software itself. Don't worry that your text files don't correspond to each other or our project. In this case, it is the construction process that is important, not the content of the finished newsletter.

Setting the insertion in an option box allows you to use the backspace or delete key to delete existing values.

When you have finished entering the specifications for the new publication, click the OK button or press the return or enter keys to instruct PageMaker to create the document as we have specified.

A new publication window will now display, showing us the first page of our publication. Your on-screen display includes page icons for the left and right master pages as well as pages one and two, the toolbox, scroll bars, and the rulers, providing that the default settings have not been changed. (If the rulers are not visible, press command-R.)

Every PageMaker publication has one or two master pages (one if your document is single sided, two if the "Double-sided" option in the Page setup dialog box is selected). These master pages are used to hold items that repeat from page to page, such as running heads or footers, page numbers, or graphics. By placing elements on the master pages, you are assured that they will be exactly positioned on each page. This spares you the effort of repeatedly positioning identical elements on.

Good Times

Company's domestic revenues rise for last three quarters despite recent textile market fluctuations

Master pages can also hold column guides and ruler guidelines, allowing you to create an alignment grid for the various elements that will be placed on the actual publication pages. For example, you may want the top of specific kinds of text blocks to begin somewhere below what has been defined as the top margin of your pages. By placing a ruler guide at this position on the master page you are able to easily and accurately execute your design without the difficulty and potential for error of measuring the correct distance on every page.

In our example, we are going to add a simple rule and company logo to the bottom of each page.

Click on either of the master page icons, labeled "L" and "R" (short for "left" and "right") in the lower right corner of the display. The master pages will then appear in the publication window.

Command-option-click in the vicinity of the bottom half of the left page. This magnifies your screen display to the actual view size. Then move the page with the hand icon, accessed by pressing the option key and clicking with your mouse, until you can clearly view the bottom margin of the left page.

Drag downward from the horizontal ruler at the top of the display to create a ruler guideline. This guideline can be dragged up and down, very much as you would drag a block of text or other element. Drag the ruler guideline to a quarter inch below the bottom margin. This will define the location of the top of our simple line and logo.

Select the perpendicular-line tool Draw a line across the bottom margin on the left page, extending from the left margin to the right margin. While drawing your line, dragging into the edge of the window will scroll the display as needed.

Move this line directly downward. Since we want to change only the vertical position of the line, press and hold the shift key and the movement of the line will be constrained in the first direction that we drag. For example, if we drag the line upward while pressing the shift key, we are able to move only up and down—not diagonally or horizontally. This allows us to precisely position our line in one direction without disturbing its position in another direction. Using the shift key to constrain movement works when moving any graphic text element.

Stocks also looking bullish

Change the weight of this line to a 2-point line weight by choosing the 2 pt command from the Lines menu. (If the line is no longer selected, reselect it with the arrow tool before choosing the command.)

Drag another ruler guideline, this time from the vertical ruler on the left of your display. Move this guideline until it lines up with your right margin (making sure that you are still on the left master page). This will help us in locating our company logo.

To represent the company logo, select the rectangle tool and draw a rectangle one inch wide and a quarter inch high. While the rectangle is still selected, choose the hairline command from the lines menu; then choose the tight cross hatch pattern from the shades menu. Position the make shift logo so its right side is flush with the vertical ruler.

Figure 6.01: *This chapter describes how to create the simple, two-page newsletter shown above.*

1 To begin creating our publication, we must first launch the PageMaker application. There are several ways to launch PageMaker:

- Type WIN PM at the DOS prompt if you have installed the full version of Microsoft Windows.
- At the MS-DOS EXECUTIVE in the full version of Microsoft Windows, double-click on the file, PM.EXE, in the PageMaker directory, usually called PM.

- If you are using the run-time version of Windows supplied with PageMaker, go the the PM directory and type PM and press ENTER.

Click your mouse button anywhere on your display to dispense with the copyright screen.

2 Before we begin our publication, we need to tell PageMaker what kind of printer we are using. Since one of PageMaker's greatest strengths is its ability to show the publication on-screen as it will appear when printed, it is important that PageMaker know the capabilities of your printer. Choose the PRINTER SETUP... command from the FILE menu. When the PRINTER SETUP dialog appears, select a printer from the "Target printer" listing, which displays the names of all of the printers that are currently connected to your computer. Then, click on the SETUP button to bring up the POSTSCRIPT PRINTER or HP/PCL PRINTER dialog box. In the list of printers at the bottom of the dialog, select the brand name printer that matches the printer you selected in the PRINTER SETUP dialog.

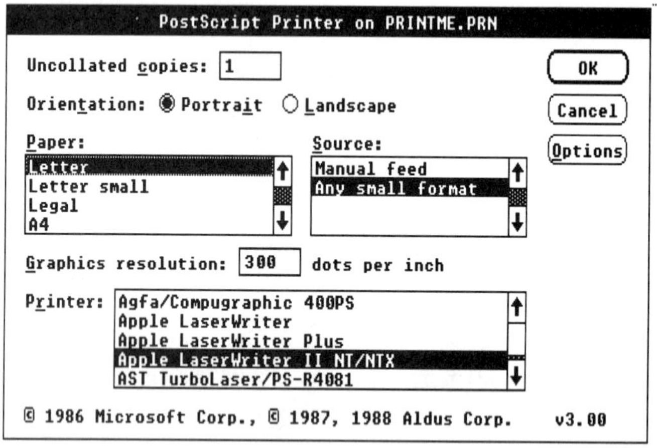

Figure 6.02: *The PostScript Printer dialog box.*

Generally, you also want to check to make sure the "Orientation" and "Paper" options are set properly in this dialog. For this sample project, we will be using tall, or "Portrait," pages on 8 ½-by-11-inch, or "Letter," paper. These options are probably already set correctly in your dialog box.

If you have a PCL printer or HP LaserJet, your dialog box will look slightly different, as shown in Figure 6.03. This dialog allows you to install additional font cartridges, if necessary. Select your font cartridges from the list at the bottom right of the dialog box to tell PageMaker which fonts you are adding. In this project we will be using the Helvetica family in 10, 24, 36, and 72 point sizes. We will also use Times 36 point, but if you don't have the Times family in your printer, use another. If you don't have Times and Helvetica, the publication on your screen may look slightly different than the screens in the figures below. Don't worry. The process of choosing font families and sizes is more important than the particular type families you use.

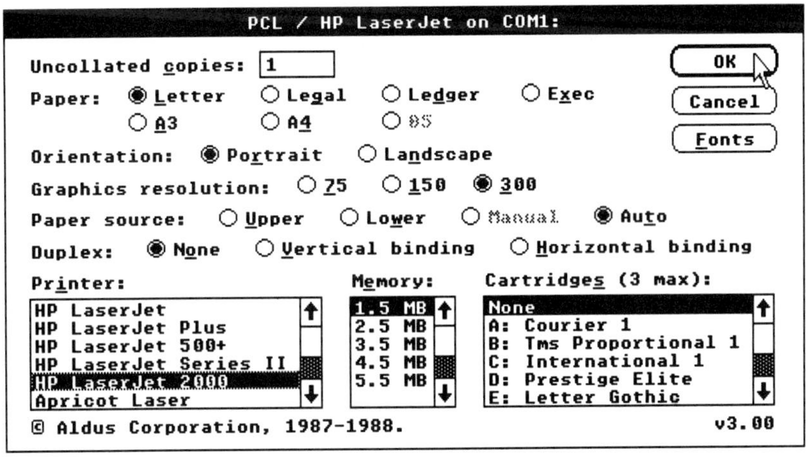

Figure 6.03: *The HP/PCL LaserJet dialog box.*

When you have selected a printer model and any appropriate options, click the OK button. This returns you to the PRINTER SETUP dialog box. Click the OK button in this dialog as well.

3 Choose the NEW... command from the FILE menu, or press CTRL-N, bringing up the PAGE SETUP dialog box, in which we may enter specifications for many global attributes of our document. Set the options should as follows:

Page size: Letter

Orientation: Tall

Start page #: 1

# of pages: 2

Double-sided: selected

Facing pages: selected

Margin in inches: Inside—0.5, Top—1, Outside—0.5, and Bottom—1.

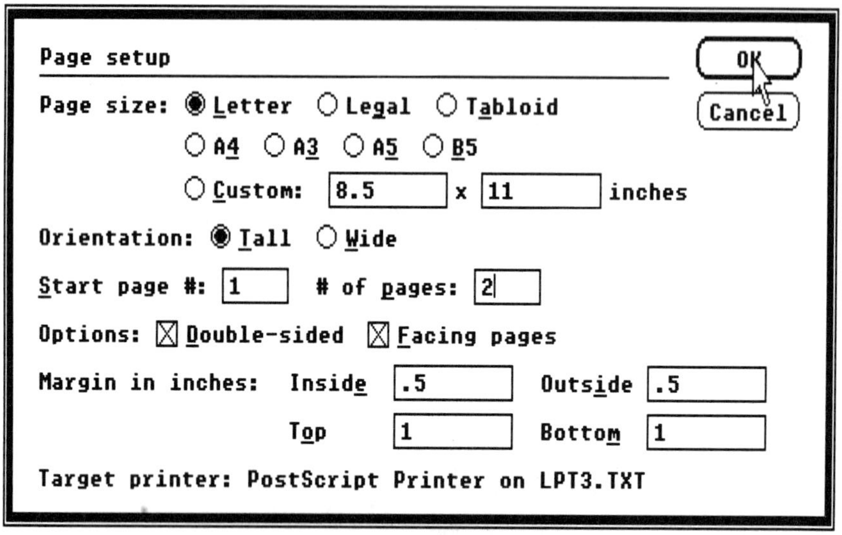

Figure 6.04: *The Page setup dialog box containing our newsletter specifications.*

(Note: Throughout this project, we will use inches as the unit of measurement. If you are not currently using inches, choose the PREFERENCES... command in the EDIT menu and select "Inches" as the current "Measurement system.")

Tips for working in dialog boxes:

- When selecting or deselecting radio button or check box options, you can click either inside the circle or square *or* on the option name next to the button or box.

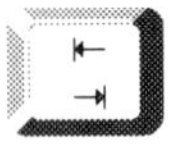

- Press the TAB key to move to the next option box, selecting the current value. Once selected, entering a new value will replace the selected value. You may also use the TAB key to move to the next check box or button. Press SHIFT-TAB to move to previous options or buttons.

- Double-clicking on the value in an option box will also select it so that it may be overwritten.

- Setting the insertion in an option box allows you to use the DEL key to delete existing values.

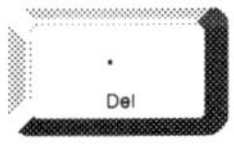

When you have finished entering the specifications for the new publication, click the OK button to instruct PageMaker to create the document we have specified.

A new publication window will now appear, showing us the first page of our publication. The on-screen display includes page icons for the left and right master pages as well as pages 1 and 2, the toolbox, scroll bars, and the rulers. Your display may be different if the default settings have been changed. (If the rulers are not visible, choose the RULERS command from the OPTIONS menu.)

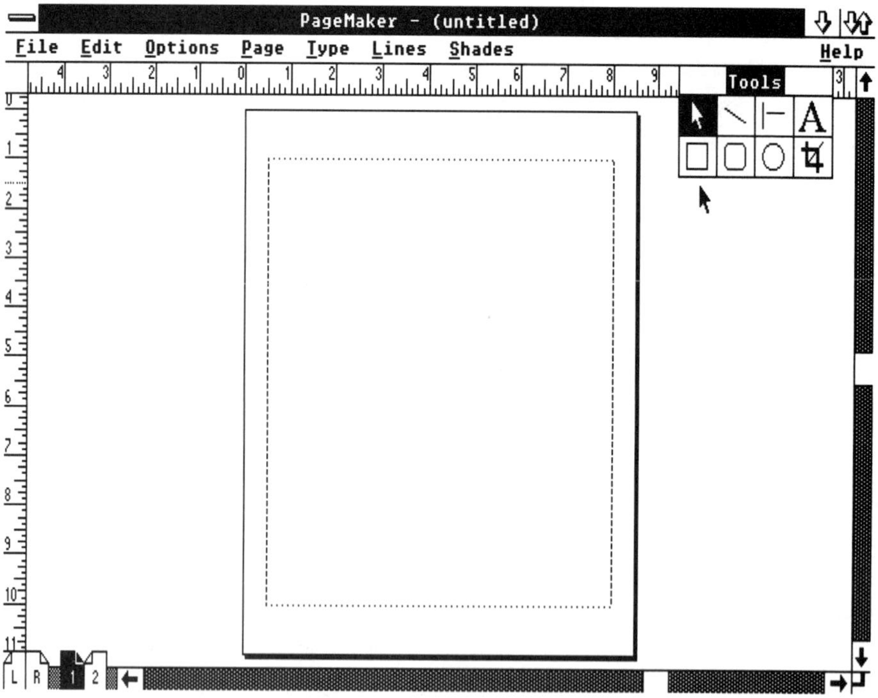

Figure 6.05: *The new publication window according to our page specifications.*

Preparing the master pages

Every PageMaker publication has one or two master pages (one if your document is single-sided, two if the "Double-sided" option in the PAGE SETUP dialog box is selected). These master pages are used to hold items that repeat from page to page, such as running heads or footers, page numbers, or graphics. By placing repeating elements on the master pages, you ensure that they will be exactly positioned on each page. This procedure saves you the effort of repeatedly positioning identical elements from page to page.

Master pages can also hold column guides and ruler guides, allowing you to create an alignment grid for the various elements that will be placed on the actual publication pages. For example, you may want the top of specific kinds of text blocks to begin somewhere below what has been defined as the top margin of your pages. By placing a ruler guide at this position on the master page you are able to easily and accurately execute your design without the difficulty and potential for error of measuring the correct distance on every page.

The left master page

In our newsletter, we are going to add a simple rule and company logo to the bottom of each page:

4 Click on either of the master page icons, labeled "L" and "R" (for "left" and "right") in the lower right corner of the display. The master pages will then appear in the publication window.

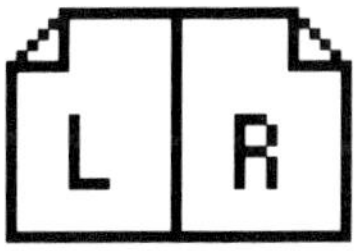

5 Click the secondary mouse button. This magnifies your screen display to the "Actual" view size. Then move the page with the hand icon, accessed by pressing the ALT key, pressing your main mouse button, and dragging the page upward until you can clearly see the bottom margin of the left page.

6 Drag downward from the horizontal ruler at the top of the display to create a ruler guide. This guide can be dragged up and down, very much as you would drag a block of text or other element. Drag the ruler guide until it is one-quarter inch below the bottom margin. This will define the location of the top of our simple line and logo.

7 Select the perpendicular-line tool. Draw a line across the bottom margin on the left page, extending from the left margin to the right margin. While drawing your line, drag the pointer into the edge of the window to scroll the right side of the page into view.

8 Move this line directly downward using the arrow tool. Since we want to change only the vertical position of the line, press and hold the SHIFT key to constrain the movement of the line to either the vertical or horizontal axis, depending on which direction we first drag the line. For example, if we drag the line upward while pressing the SHIFT key, we are able to move only up and down—not diagonally or horizontally. This allows us to precisely position our line in one direction without disturbing its position in another direction. Using the SHIFT key to constrain movement works when moving any graphic or text element in PageMaker. While holding down the SHIFT key, move the line downward until the line snaps to the ruler guide.

9 Change the weight of this line to a 2-point line weight by choosing the 2 PT command from the LINES menu. (If the line is no longer selected, reselect it with the arrow tool before choosing the command.)

10 Drag another ruler guide, this time from the vertical ruler on the left of your display. Move this guideline until it lines up with your right margin (making sure that you are still on the left master page). This will help us in locating our company logo.

11 To represent the company logo, select the rectangle tool and draw a rectangle one inch wide and one-quarter inch high. While the rectangle is still selected, choose HAIRLINE from the LINES menu; then choose the tight cross hatch pattern from the SHADES menu. Position the make-shift logo so its right side is flush with the vertical ruler guide we just created and one-eighth inch below the 2-point rule that runs across the bottom of the page.

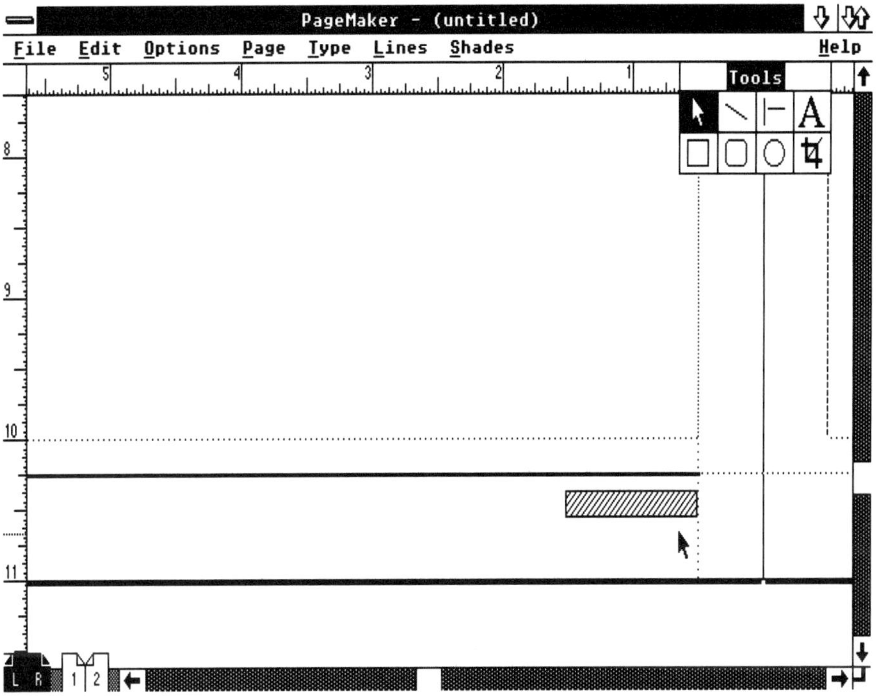

Figure 6.06: *The left master page containing the elements we have created thus far.*

The right master page

12 We now need to make a mirror image of our line and logo for the right master page. First, select both elements. You may do this by dragging a rectangular marquee around the line and logo with the arrow tool. Or you may click on the line and then shift-click on the logo. After both elements are selected, choose the COPY command from the EDIT menu, or

6 Simple Newsletter

press CTRL-INSERT. This puts a copy of both items into the Windows Clipboard, to be used later at our convenience.

13 Scroll over to the right master page using the scroll bars or the hand tool (accessed by pressing the ALT key and dragging).

14 Notice that our horizontal ruler guide is on this page, too. Horizontal guides always show up on both pages of a facing page spread. However, we are missing our vertical ruler guide. So drag a guide from the vertical ruler, aligning it with the left margin of the right master page.

15 Choose the PASTE command from the EDIT menu, or press SHIFT-INSERT. This produces a copy of our simple line and company logo in the center of your display. We will position these elements slightly differently on the right master page than we did on the left master page.

16 When you paste one or more elements, they are selected immediately after they appear on your screen so they may be easily positioned. Taking care not to deselect the line and logo, drag at either element until the 2-point line snaps with the horizontal ruler guide. Also, the left side of the line should be flush with the vertical guide.

17 Deselect both elements by clicking on a blank area of your display. Then scroll to the right, if necessary, and select our new copy of the company logo. For our purpose, we want the logo to be on the left side of the right master page, a mirror image of the left master page. While constraining your drag by pressing the SHIFT key, move the logo until its left side is flush with the vertical ruler guide.

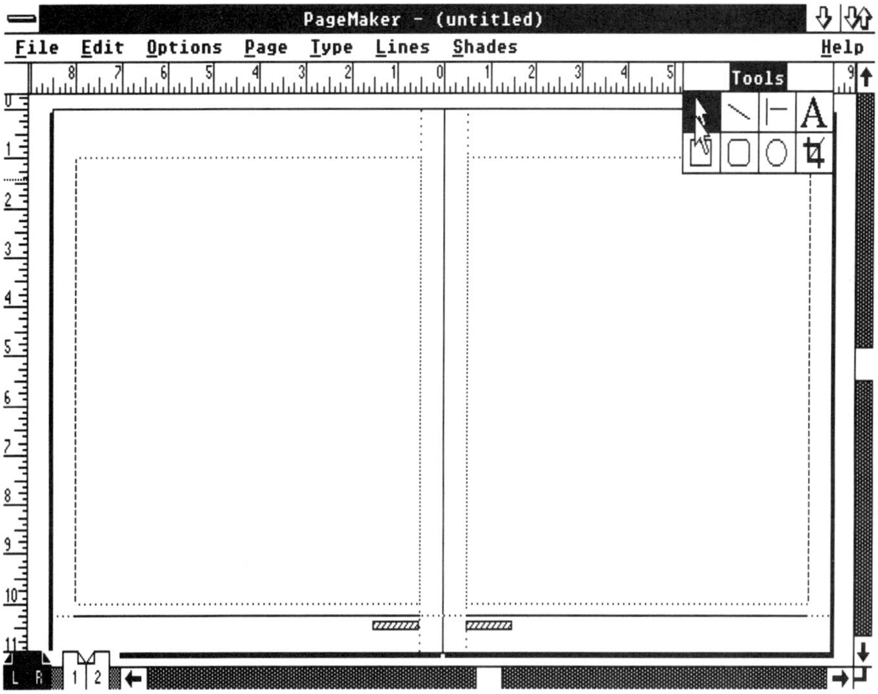

Figure 6.07: *The left and right master pages as they now appear.*

Adding a flag to page one

Now that we have our master page elements in place, we will want to add a flag to the top of page one. The flag, sometimes incorrectly called a masthead, is the title of your newsletter, represented in some eye-catching manner that visually states your purpose. (A masthead, incidentally, is a publication's staff and copyright listing, often inside a box.)

Creating the flag text

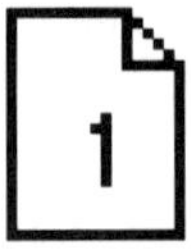

18 Click on the first page icon (labeled "1") to turn to page 1. You could also use the GO TO PAGE... command from the PAGE menu CTRL-G, but it is usually faster to click the page icon.

19 Zoom in to the top area of page one by clicking the secondary mouse button. Select the text tool from the toolbox and position the I-beam cursor in the upper left corner of the page, just inside the top and left margins. Click the mouse button and a flashing vertical cursor will appear against the left margin. This is the **text entry cursor** (also known as the I-beam), indicating that we are ready to enter the text for our flag.

20 Let's say that we decide to call our newsletter "Information!" This is an exciting and utilitarian title with general implications, useful for many different situations. As you type the characters "I-n-f-o-r-m-a-t-i-o-n-!," you will notice that they emerge from the left margin in whatever is the the default type face and type size. In the second sample project, we will see how you can alter the default settings used for type face, type size, and many other PageMaker options.

21 To change the type face and type size of our flag, we must select the text that we wish to alter. PageMaker uses exactly the same principals of selection and modification with which you are probably familiar if you have worked with a Windows word-processor such as Microsoft Write—text must be selected (highlighted) for any of its attributes to be changed. There are several ways to select text in PageMaker:

- Drag the I-beam cursor over the text to be selected.

- Double-click on a word in the text block to select the entire word. Holding the mouse button down after the second click and then dragging selects additional text one word at a time.

- Triple-click on a word to select the entire paragraph.

- After setting the text entry cursor within a text block, choose the SELECT ALL command from the EDIT menu (CTRL-A) to select the entire story, even if it spans many text blocks on many pages.

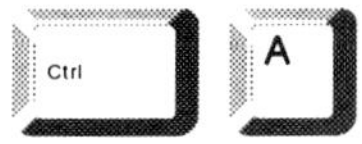

In this particular case we want to select the entire text block, which consists of only the word "Information!," so we can use any of these techniques.

22 Once the text block is selected, choose the TYPE SPECS... command from the TYPE menu, or press CTRL-T. This dialog box contains options for determining the type face, size, and many other formatting options. To select a type face, scroll down the list of fonts on the left side of the dialog box until you see the font you want to use; then click on the font name to highlight it. In this case, select the font name "Helvetica."

23 To select a type size, scroll down the list of point sizes and click on the size you want. If it is not listed, you can type in any custom point size between 4 and 127 points in the "Size" option box. In our case, double-click inside the "Size" option box to select the current value and enter 72, replacing the selected value.

24 Click on the "Bold" option so that a cross (X) appears in its check box, indicating that it's selected. This changes the type style of the current font from plain to bold.

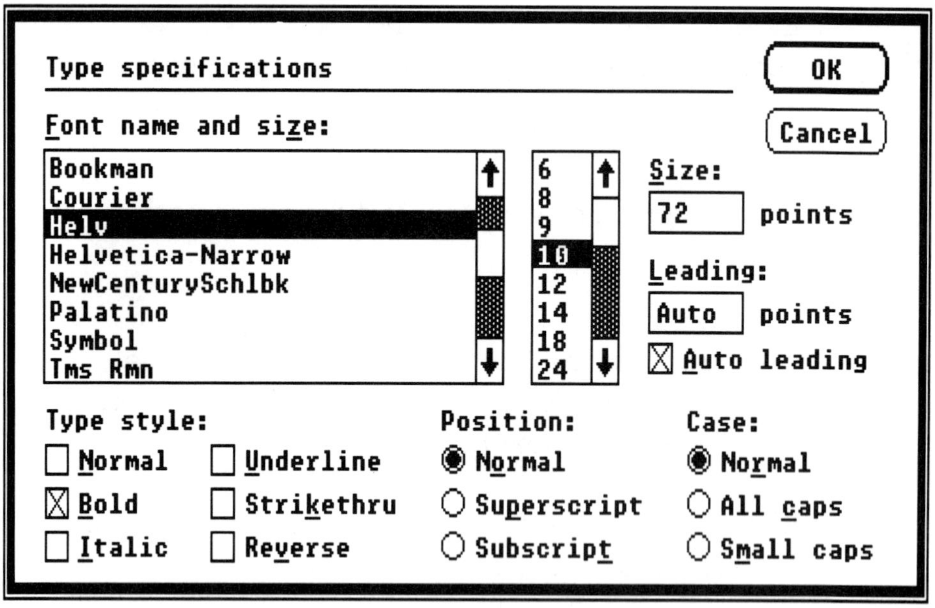

Figure 6.08: *The Type specifications dialog box containing our type face, style, and size specifications.*

25 To apply our font, size, and style specifications to the selected text block, click on the OK button. Notice now that the selected text is much larger than before, due to its larger type size, as well as heavier, due to its bold type style. As a result, it appears very impressive and eye-catching as the flag of our newsletter.

26 Assuming that our text is still selected, center the flag by choosing the ALIGN CENTER command from the TYPE menu (or press CTRL-C).

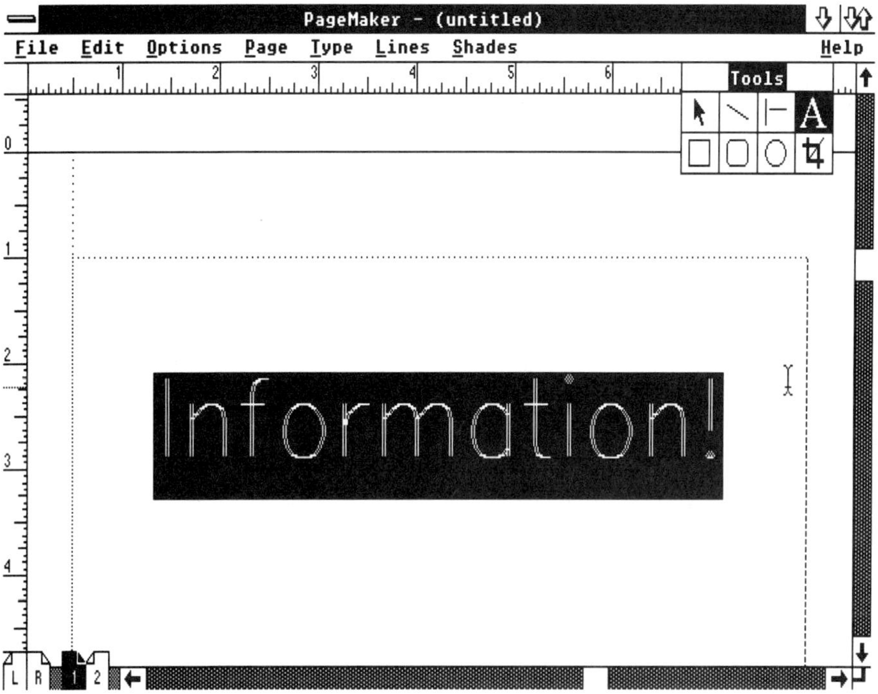

Figure 6.09: *Our 72-point, Helvetica Bold flag as it appears centered on page 1.*

Our flag now appears in the font, type size, type style, and horizontal position that we desire. To adjust the vertical position we must learn a little about PageMaker **text blocks**.

A PageMaker text block is a discrete element that can be selected, moved, sized, and deleted. Text blocks are created automatically when you enter new text after clicking the text tool outside an existing text block, or when text is imported using the PLACE... command from the FILE menu. When selected, text blocks are marked by **handlebars** that appear on the top and bottom of the text block. As we shall see, handlebars can be moved in relation to each other by dragging at the small **tabs** that extend upward or downward from the middle of the handlebar. To see the text block for our flag text, select the arrow tool from the toolbox and click on the word "Information!"

We can now change the position of the text block by dragging it. Press and hold the mouse button down while pointing anywhere in the text block except on its handles or tabs. Since we wish to alter only the vertical positioning of the text block, we may press the SHIFT key to constrain our movement to the vertical axis. Another method of vertically positioning a text block without disturbing the block's horizontal positioning is to drag the tab on the upper handlebar of the text block. By dragging upward on the handlebar and releasing, you cause the text block to rise. Dragging downward on the upper handlebar lowers the text. Note, however, that when you drag the upper handlebar downward, the bottom handlebar will often remain motionless, so that a line or more of text may be hidden. If this happens, drag downward on the lower handlebar, which should show a plus sign in its tab (The later portion of this chapter includes more information on using the tab on the lower handlebar of a text block).

27 Move the flag text vertically, either by dragging the text block while pressing the SHIFT key or by dragging the upper handlebar, until the top of the text block snaps to the top margin.

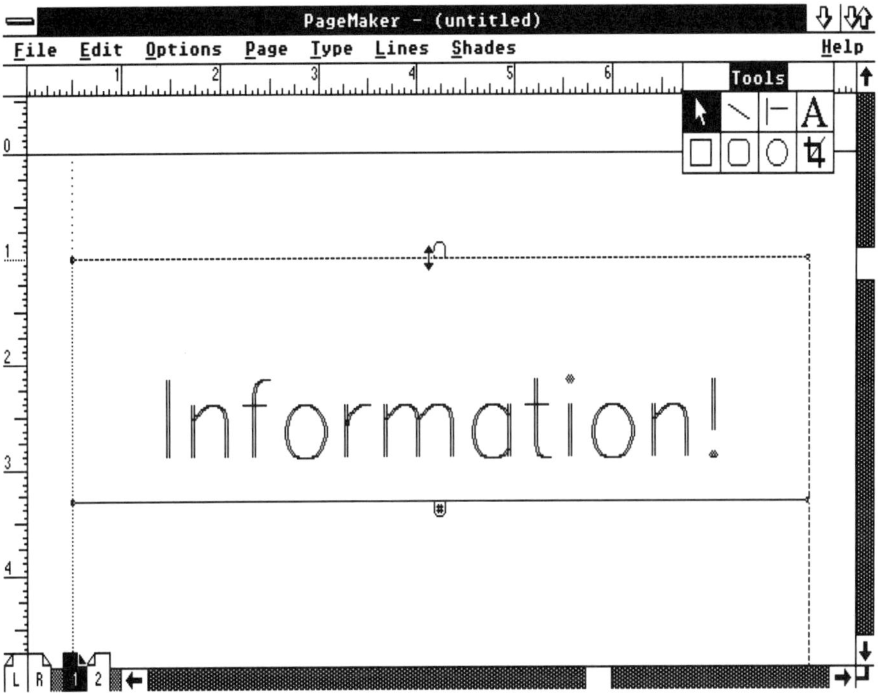

Figure 6.10: *Moving the text block upward by dragging its upper handle until it snaps to the top margin.*

Setting the flag off from the newsletter

If we were to stop now, we would simply have a big word at the top of our page. There is nothing to differentiate our flag from other large blocks of text, such as headlines. Although we won't be creating any 72-point headlines, the sheer immensity of our flag is not necessarily enough to direct a reader concerning the purpose of this text block. A simple graphic can go a long way to visually establishing our flag for what it is. We will be using the simplest of all graphics, a straight line, to set our flag apart from the rest of our newsletter.

28 We will now add an 8-point rule under our "Information!" text. First, with the arrow tool, drag a guide down from the horizontal ruler to a point about one-quarter inch below the flag text. Then select the perpendicular-line tool from the toolbox and position the cursor at the intersection of the left vertical ruler guide (from the right master page) and the horizontal guide. Draw a line to the right margin so that it stretches across the page. If your view size does not display the entire width of the page, PageMaker will automatically scroll your display.

29 With the line selected, choose the 8 PT command from the LINES menu.

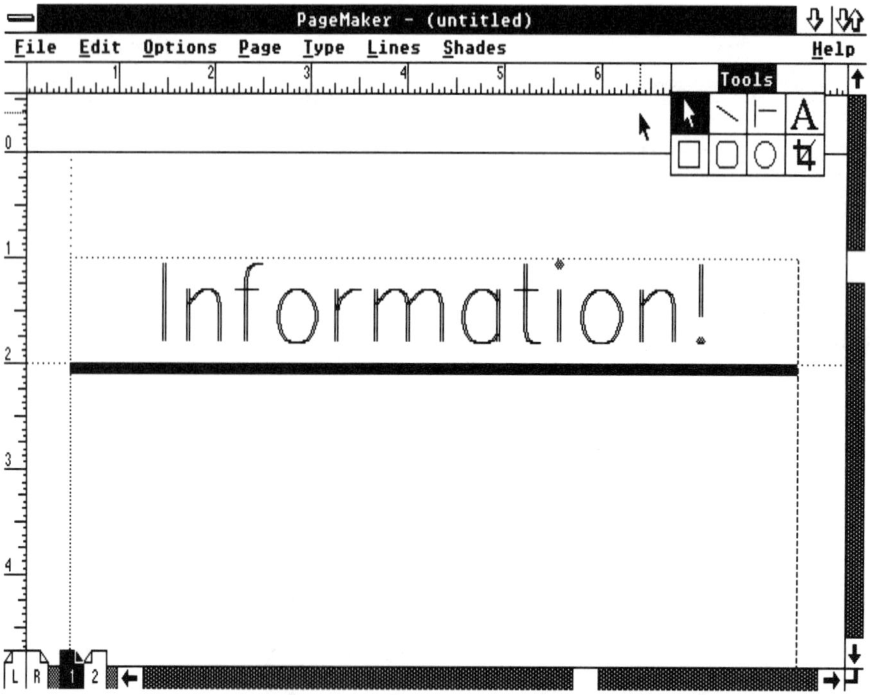

Figure 6.11: *The completed flag with text and an 8-point line.*

Column Guides

Now that we have completed our flag, we are ready to add the first article to our newsletter. The format that we are going to use calls for our lead article to be set in two columns directly below the flag. It is usually advisable to define columns prior to pouring any text, so that is what we will do.

30 Choose the Column guides... command from the Options menu. This command allows us to define up to 20 columns per page as well as specify the amount of space between columns. Choosing this command brings up the Column guides dialog box. This dialog box defines the number and placement of equally-spaced column guides for the current page or pages. Setting the column guides while working on the master pages affects the guides on all corresponding publication pages. In our case, we want to enter 2 for the "Number of columns" option and define the "Space between columns" as 0.5 (assuming we are still in inches). Click the OK button to instruct PageMaker to close the dialog box and add the specified column guides to the page.

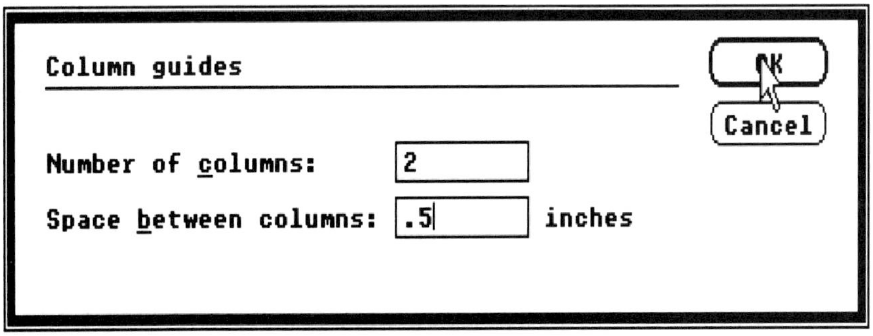

Figure 6.12: *The Column guides dialog box containing the number of guides and gutter specifications.*

In order to define the two columns, PageMaker has added three column guides to our page. One is on top of the left margin guide, one is on top of the right margin guide and one is in the middle of the page with a one-half-inch gutter between its two sides, according to our specifications in the COLUMN GUIDES dialog box. The amount of room between the left and center column guides and the center and right column guides is equal. PageMaker simply subtracts the combined gutters from the total width of a page, and divides that amount by the number of columns. The result is the width of each column. (In later chapters, we will see how you can move column guides to create individually wider or narrower columns.)

Placing Text

As we have discussed in earlier chapters, the majority of text that will be used in PageMaker is prepared in a word-processor and then imported into PageMaker. For the lead article in our newsletter, we will use the LOREM.TXT text file in the TEMPLATE directory on the TEMPLATES disk supplied with PageMaker. This is a dummy text file you can use to fill a layout with text to see how the page will look. The text itself consists of meaningless imitation Latin words.

Importing an article from a word-processor

31 After you choose the PLACE... command from the FILE menu (CTRL-D), the PLACE FILE dialog box will appear. It is here that you select the text file that will be imported for our lead article and specify several things about the way in which it the text is used.

Insert your backup copy of the TEMPLATES disk into drive A, click on the [A] at the end of the list of files, and click the OK button. You will see a list of the files on drive A. If you have a 1.2-Mbyte floppy disk, double-click on the TEMPLATE directory to see its contents, and click on the LOREM.TXT file. Use the scrolling file list in this dialog box to locate files on disks and in directories (remember that you can use any text document that you have available for this exercise, provided it is at least one page long). You may want to examine and perhaps change some of the "Place" and "Options" options.

There are three "Place" radio buttons. The first option, "As new item," is selected by default and is suitable for our purpose. (The remaining two options are useful when replacing existing text.)

There are also three "Options" check boxes. The "Retain format" option is selected by default, instructing PageMaker to use the text and paragraph formatting that the incoming document contains. Deselecting this command would cause the placed document to be stripped of its character formatting (such as fonts, type sizes, and type styles) and paragraph formatting (margins, indents, and tabs). The "Convert quotes" option alerts PageMaker to substitute an opening or closing quote (" or ") in place of a leading or trailing standard quote ("). If this option is deselected, the quotation marks remain unchanged. The "Read tags" option is used when style sheet tags have been entered into a word-processed document. We will discuss style sheets and tags in more detail in later chapters.

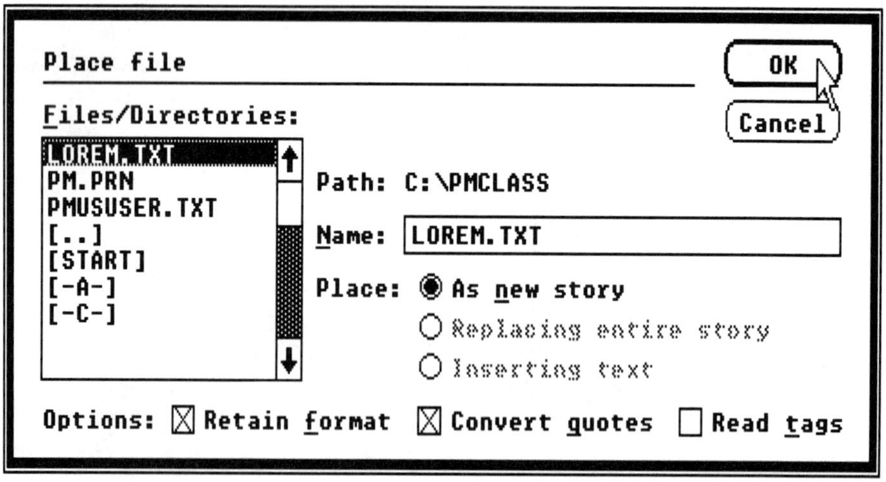

Figure 6.13: *The Place file dialog box showing various options.*

32 With the file you wish to import selected, click the OK button. The dialog box will close and your cursor will change to the manual text flow icon. This indicates that PageMaker is ready for you to pour the selected article. (If you get an error message reading "The placed document may not exactly match the original"—error number 5312—click the OK button and proceed. You may ignore the message, since we will be changing many of the text attributes anyway).

Manually pouring a story

33 In order to make sure our article will be properly aligned on the page, we drag down another ruler guide. Interestingly enough, this is possible, even though our cursor is ready to pour text. Simply drag down from the horizontal ruler to a location about two inches below our flag. Be careful, however—if you position the guide incorrectly, you won't be able to reposition it until you can access the arrow tool cursor.

34 Position the manual text flow cursor at the intersection of the new ruler guide and the leftmost column guide; then click your mouse button. The text from your document will flow into the column, stopping when it reaches the bottom margin. (Now, if you like, you can reposition your ruler guide.) Assuming that your entire document does not fit into a single column, there is now a plus sign (+) in the tab of the lower handlebar of the new text block, indicating that more text remains to be placed.

35 Click on the plus sign (+) and the manual text flow cursor will reappear. Position your cursor in the right-hand column, vertically aligned with the beginning of the text in the left column, and click the mouse button to begin the text flow in this column. If enough text remains in the document, the text will flow down to the bottom margin.

36 Make sure that the tops of both columns are even with each other by selecting each text block and then dragging each upper handlebar flush with the most recently created horizontal ruler guide. If necessary, line up the bottoms of both columns as well by dragging at the lower handlebars.

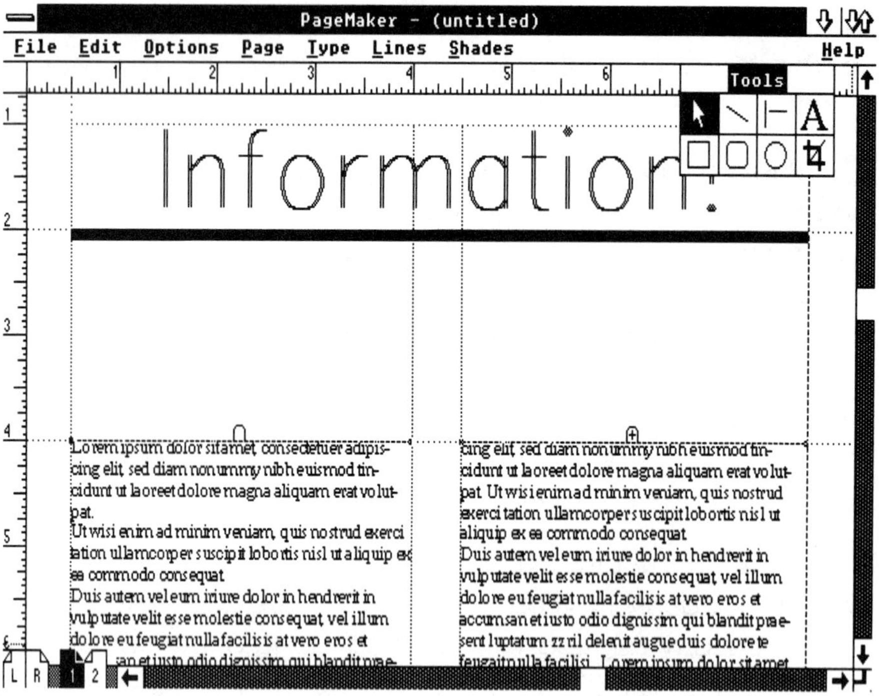

Figure 6.14: *The result of pouring an article into two columns with a one-half-inch gutter.*

Formatting text

Now that we have our first story in position, we can change the character and paragraph attributes of the text to fit both our design scheme and our personal preference. We will change the font for the entire article, set the type size, leading, and the first-line indent, and create a headline as a separate text block.

Changing type specifications

37 Click anywhere inside the first or second column of our text and press CTRL-A or choose the SELECT ALL command from the EDIT menu. This ensures that the changes we make to the text affect the entire article, even those portions we may not have poured yet. Then press CTRL-T to access the TYPE SPECIFICATIONS dialog box. Select "Helvetica" from the font list and 10-point from the size list.

38 Our next step is to change the leading of our article. Like type face, type size, and type style, leading can be changed in the TYPE SPECIFICATIONS dialog box. Double-click in the "Leading" option box or press the TAB key until the current leading value is selected, and type "12.5." This gives us 10/12.5 type, or 10-point type size on 12.5-point leading, an extremely legible combination for most type faces. Click the OK button to apply our new type specs.

Changing paragraph specifications

39 To increase the legibility of our text, we will add some space between each paragraph as well as first-line indents. With your entire story still selected, choose the PARAGRAPH... command from the TYPE menu, or press CTRL-M. This brings up the PARAGRAPH SPECIFICATIONS dialog box, which controls a number of attributes that are applied to whole paragraphs. We will discuss each of the options offered by this dialog very briefly.

The "Hyphenation" options control the way PageMaker hyphenates text. When selected, the "Auto" option instructs PageMaker to automatically hyphenate words in the selected text. If deselected, PageMaker inserts no hyphens. The

"Prompted" option will prompt you to hyphenate words in a selected block of text, and allow you to add these words to the PMUSUSER.TXT dictionary file.

Using the "Pair kerning" options, you tell PageMaker if you want certain letter pairs to be kerned more tightly based on information provided by the selected font. The point size option box allows you to enter a type size. Selected text larger than this type size will be kerned, smaller type will not be kerned. We will discuss both the "Hyphenation" and "Pair kerning" options in more detail Chapter 8, *Editing Text*.

The "Alignment" options allow you to select from four alignments. Text may be flush left, centered, flush right, or fully justified. These options are identical to the options available at the bottom of the TYPE menu.

The "Indents" options allow you to add specified amounts of horizontal space to selected paragraphs. The horizontal space indicated by the "Left" value is added between the left column guide and the selected text; the space indicated by the "Right" value is added between the right column guide and the selected text. The "First" option adds space between the left column guide and the first line of text in the paragraph. We will be using the "First" option to add a first-line indent to our text.

The "Spacing" options allow you to add vertical space between selected paragraphs and their neighbors. The "Before" option inserts space between the first line of a selected paragraph and the preceding paragraph; the "After" option inserts space between the last line of a selected paragraph and the following paragraph.

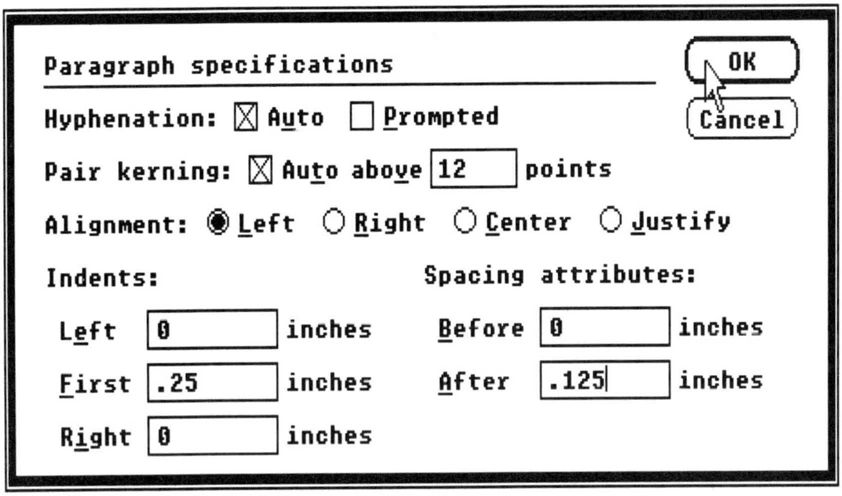

Figure 6.15: *The Paragraph specifications dialog as it should appear before clicking the OK button.*

40 Of the "Indents" options, change the "First" value to 0.25, or one-quarter inch. Also change the "After" value in the "Spacing" column to 0.125, or one-eighth inch. Then click the OK button to apply these changes to the selected text. You can now see how our indents call attention to the beginning of each paragraph. (Incidentally, if your paragraphs already contain introductory tabs or multiple spaces, both of which are common typewriting devices for indicating the beginning of paragraphs, they should be deleted. First-line indents serve the same purpose, and are much easier to implement and manipulate. The space after each paragraph helps to set each paragraph apart slightly. The result is two very readable columns of text.

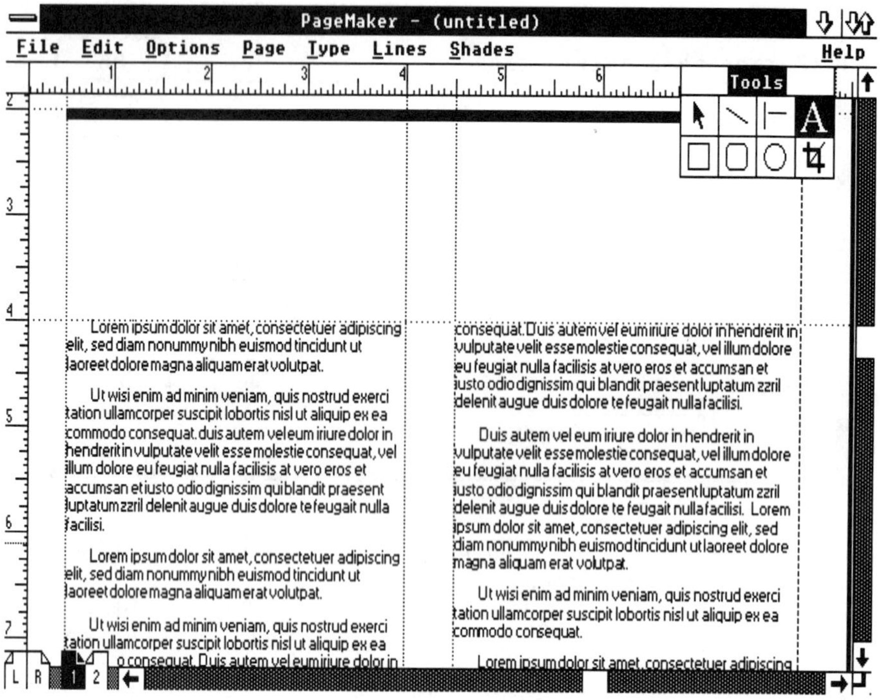

Figure 6.16: *Our two columns of text, fully formatted.*

Creating a stickup initial

We will now create a "stickup initial," a design device for introducing your article to a reader. The first letter of our article will be set in a larger type size, "sticking up" into the white space above the first line of text. Because of the unique way that PageMaker measures leading, stickup initials can be created without adversely affecting surrounding text.

41 Select the first letter in the first paragraph of your article. Press CTRL-T to access the TYPE SPECIFICATIONS dialog box, and type "36" in the "Size" option to increase the size of the letter. Then select the font "Times" from the list of fonts, and click the OK button. Our stickup initial is complete, but notice how it sticks way up above our horizontal ruler guide—so much so, in fact, that you can't even see the top of the character. PageMaker has a problem displaying type that exceeds the boundaries of a text block.

42 If your initial is still selected, press the LEFT CURSOR ARROW key to move your text entry cursor back to the very beginning of the text. If not, click with the text tool just to the left of the initial. Then press the RETURN key. This inserts a carriage return before the first paragraph, lowering your text enough to allow for the extreme height of the stickup initial.

43 You probably still cannot see the top of your initial. If you could, you would notice that it looks awkward when it is indented like the other paragraphs. We will remedy both of these problems in one step. With your text entry cursor still in front of the first character, press CTRL-M to access the PARAGRAPH SPECIFICATIONS dialog box. Change the "First" value under the "Indents" column to 0 and click OK. Now the first-line indent has been removed from the stickup-initial paragraph. In addition, PageMaker has fully refreshed the screen to display the stickup initial in its entirety.

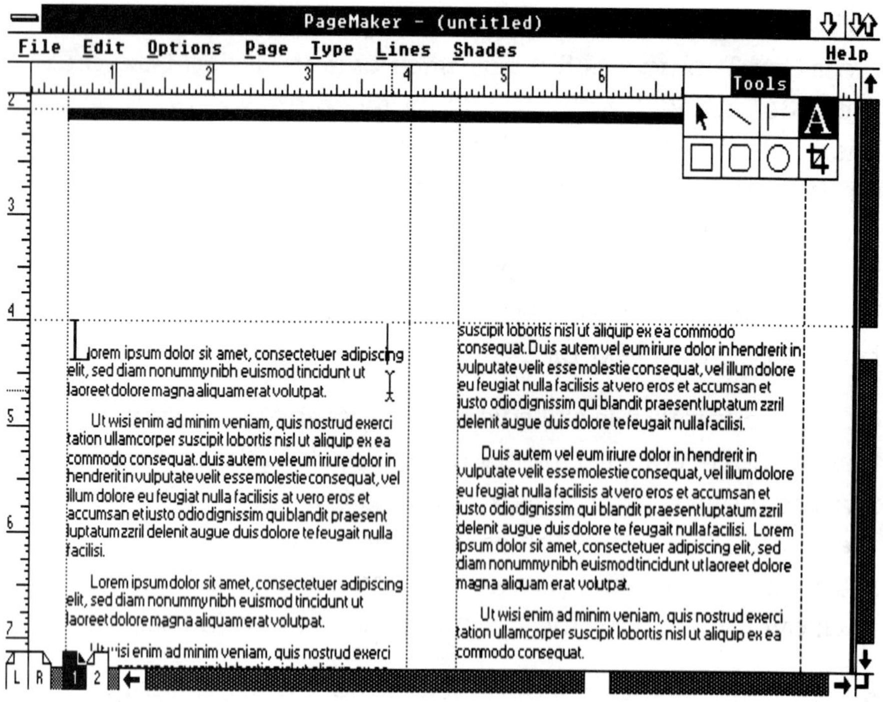

Figure 6.17: *The 36-point stickup initial as it appears when completed.*

Adding a headline

The only element that this article still lacks is a headline. A headline is needed to introduce the article and summarize its purpose. We'll add this headline similarly to how we created the flag—by typing it directly into PageMaker. Generally, headlines are as wide as the text they introduce. If an article is poured into a single column, the headline should be one column wide. If the article is poured into two columns, like ours, then the headline should stretch across both columns, and so on. Therefore, we need to create a headline that extends the entire width of the image area, from left margin to right margin.

The problem here is that we have set up two columns. If we were to click with the text tool in one of these columns, our headline text block would only be one column wide. There are three ways to rectify this situation:

- Choose the COLUMN GUIDES... command from the OPTIONS menu, and change the "Number of columns " option to 1. This would return your page to a one-column format without changing the size of the existing text blocks, and allow you to create a headline the width of the page.
- Override the column guides by drawing the width of your column with the text tool. This is the quickest and easiest method, and we will demonstrate it in a moment.
- Click in one of the two columns and type in your headline text. When you are finished, you can stretch the width of this existing text block to whatever width you choose. (This method is demonstrated in the second sample project in Chapter 11.)

44 We will be using the second method of overriding the column guides by dragging with the text tool. When you drag with the arrow tool on an empty portion of your page, you create a marquee, which is useful for selecting multiple elements. By dragging with the text tool, you also create a marquee of sorts. The dotted rectangle drawn with the text tool, however, determines the width and height of your column of text. Within the two-inch-high area between the flag and the columns of type, click on the left column and, without releasing the mouse button, drag the entire width of the page, to the right edge of the right column. Figure 6.18 demonstrates how your drag should appear.

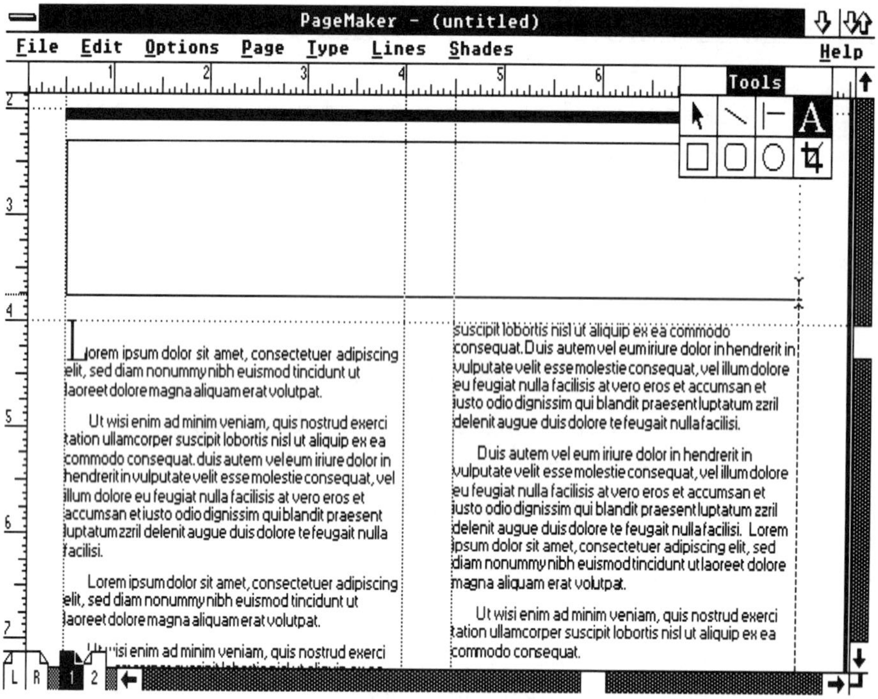

Figure 6.18: *Drag the entire width of the image area with the text tool to define the width of the text block.*

45 Once you have defined the width of your text block, you may type in your headline. We recommend, "Rise In Mortgage Rates Blamed For Drop In Housing Starts." This headline may not match the contents of your story, but as we mentioned earlier, the contents of your story are unimportant to this project.

46 Press CTRL-A to select all text in the headline. Change the typeface to Helvetica and the type size to 36-point using the same methods described throughout this chapter. Also, make sure the leading is "Auto." You can set automatic leading by clicking in the "Auto leading" check box in the TYPE SPECIFICATIONS dialog box or by typing "auto" into the "Leading" option box. Center the headline by pressing CTRL-C or choosing the ALIGN CENTER command from the TYPE menu.

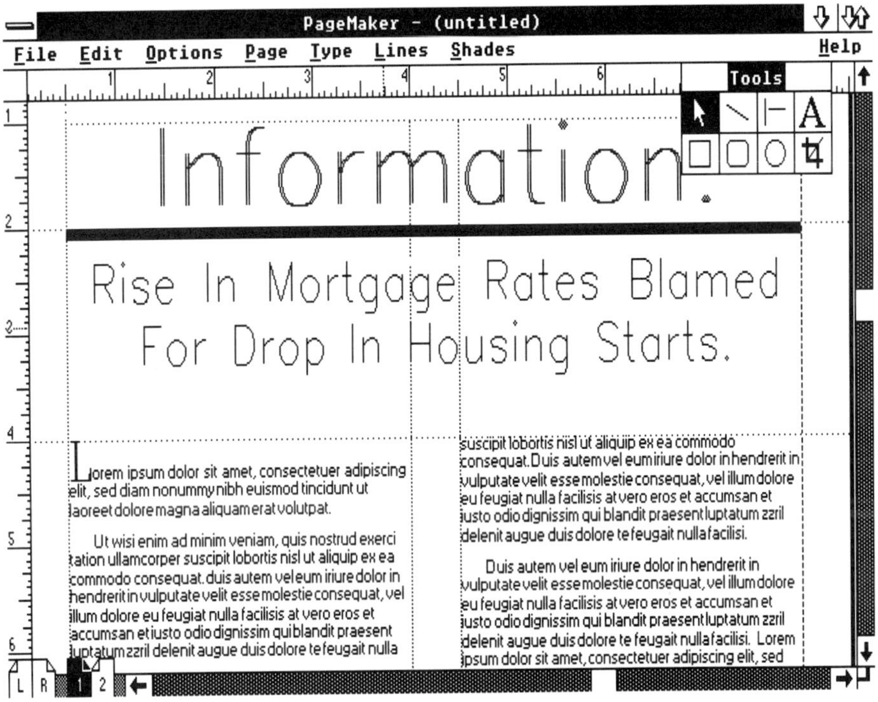

Figure 6.19: *The fully formatted headline for our two-column article.*

47 Vertically position the headline text block evenly between the flag and the two-column article by SHIFT-dragging with the arrow tool.

This ends our discussion of page 1. We have successfully created a flag to announce our newsletter, a lead story to inform our readers, and a headline to introduce the lead story. On page 2, we will pour two more stories and give each article a headline. We will also draw a box around one of our stories for visual emphasis.

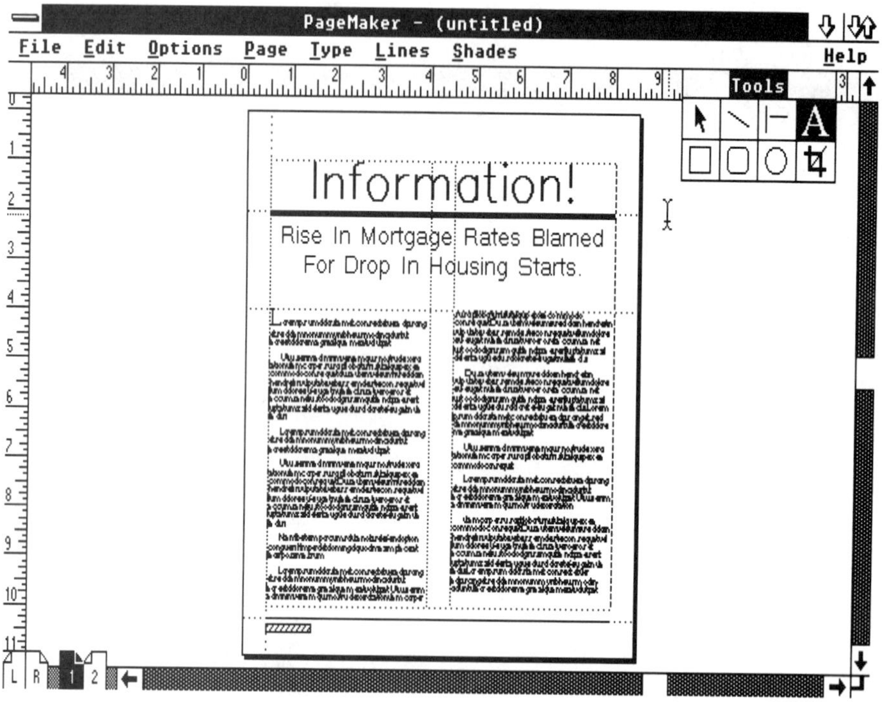

Figure 6.20: *The first page of our newsletter is complete, including flag, headline and two-column story.*

Creating the second article

We are now ready to create our second page of this two-page newsletter. We will be placing two more stories, both created using a word-processor. Again, you may use the LOREM.TXT text file or any text files that you have saved to disk, regardless of their content. For the first article, choose a file that is at least two pages long. The second article should be slightly shorter.

Placing and formatting a three column story

48 Click on the page 2 icon (labeled "2") to turn to the second page.

49 When your screen displays page 2, you will notice that it matches the left master page. The rule is at the bottom, the company logo rectangle is in the bottom right corner, and there is only one column defined. On this page, we will be changing our format slightly to accommodate three columns of text. Therefore, we choose the COLUMN GUIDES... command from the OPTIONS menu. After the COLUMN GUIDES dialog box appears, replace the "Number of columns" value with a 3 and the "Space between columns" value with 0.5, or one-half inch. Then click OK. Four column guides appear on our page, defining three equal columns.

50 Drag a horizontal ruler guide down to a point two inches below the top margin. Assuming that you have not moved the zero point of your rulers, this point will correspond to the 3-inch tick mark on your vertical ruler. The area above this guide designates the area where we will create the first headline. Drag another horizontal ruler guide down to a point corresponding to the 6-inch mark on the vertical ruler. Both guides will help you to position the first article on this page.

51 Now that we have defined the boundaries for our article, we are ready to pour. Choose the PLACE... command from the FILE menu. Then double-click on an appropriate text file from the PLACE FILE dialog box.

52 Position your manual text flow cursor up against the top ruler guide inside the first column and click. After PageMaker has poured the first column of your article, click on the tab of the lower handlebar of the text block. (If your lower handlebar tab does not contain a plus sign, your story is not long enough and you will need to find another.)

53 Next, click with the manual text flow cursor at the intersection of the top ruler guide and the second column. The text will again flow to the bottom margin. For our purpose, however, we only want this column of text to extend down to the lower horizontal ruler guide. This means that you must lift the lower handlebar of the second text block up to the lower ruler guide and click on the plus sign. (Again, if the tab below the handlebar does not contain a plus sign, or the second column fails to extend to the lower ruler guide, you will need to find a longer text file.)

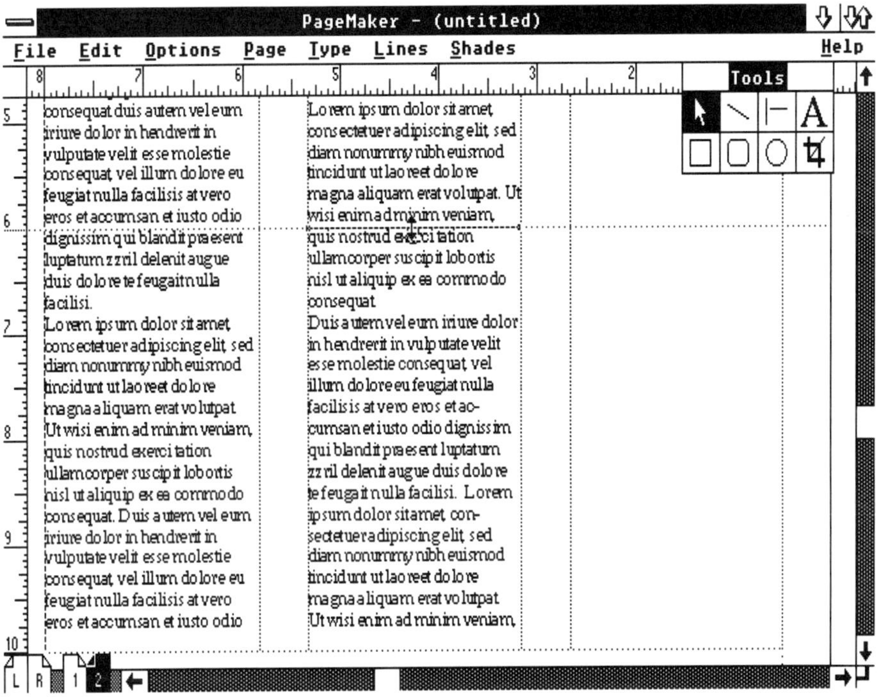

Figure 6.21: *Shortening the second column by lifting up on the lower handlebar of the text block.*

54 Finally, position your manual text flow cursor flush with the top ruler guide and click inside the third column. Like the second column, this column should only extend to the lower ruler guide. If your third column ends with a plus sign, indicating that there is more text to pour, ignore it. For this project, the end of the story may remain unpoured.

55 Now it is time to format the text. Select the text tool, click inside any one of the columns of text, and press CTRL-A to select all the text. Then change the type specifications to 10/12.5 Helvetica using the TYPE SPECIFICATIONS dialog box as described earlier in this chapter. Also, add a first-line indent of 0.25 inch and an "After" spacing of 0.125 inch to your paragraph formatting. If your text is not ragged right, choose the Align left command from the Type menu.

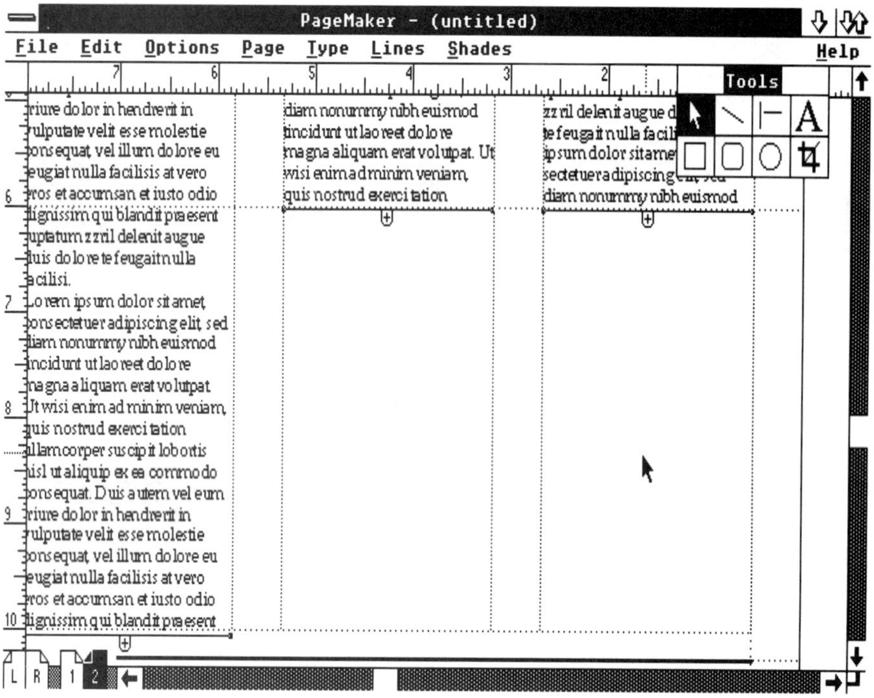

Figure 6.22: *Each of the three columns selected to show how each ends in reference to the bottom margin and lower ruler guide.*

This article is now poured into three columns and fully formatted. Notice that the format exactly matches the article on page 1. It is generally a good idea to keep your body text consistent throughout a newsletter or other document. This gives your pages a homogeneous design structure, which helps your readers by reducing potential confusion. The best type, after all, is type that goes unnoticed.

Creating a headline with subhead

Our next step is to add a headline for this story, as well as a subhead. As we mentioned earlier, a headline serves as an introduction to an article. A subhead further elucidates the story, often related very closely to the headline both visually and conceptually. A headline might ask a question that is answered in the subhead. The headline might make a statement to which the subhead poses a logical question that is answered in the text. In our case, we will create a direct, two-word headline designed simply to attract the reader. Our subhead will summarize the article and state its purpose.

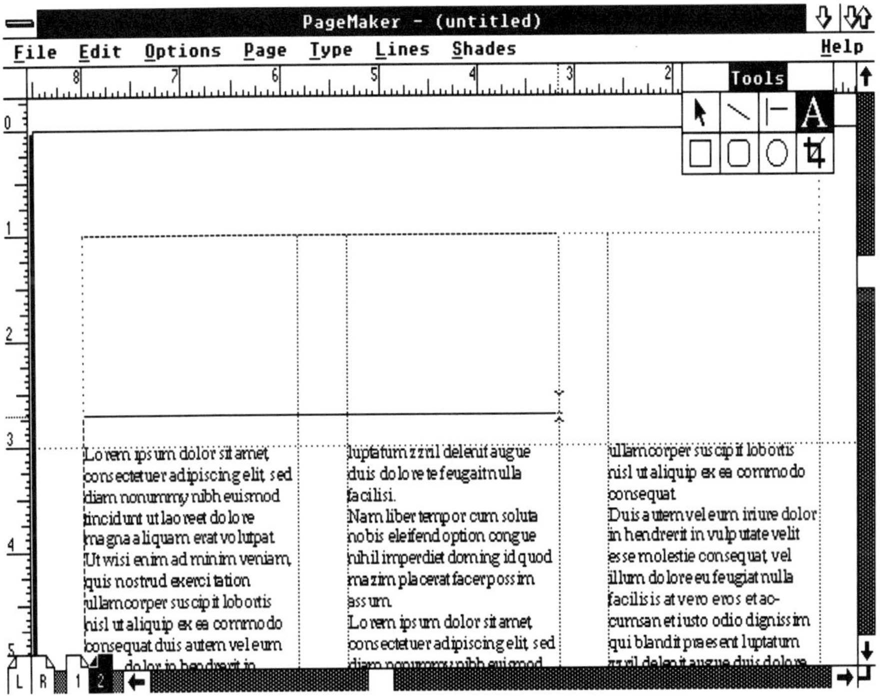

Figure 6.23: *Dragging with the text tool to create a two-column headline.*

56 First we will create a two-column headline. If you haven't already done so, we suggest that you magnify your screen display to "Actual" view size and position your display so you can see the top of the page. Select the text tool and position your cursor at the intersection of the top and left margins. Drag from this point to the right edge of the second column, as shown in Figure 6.23.

57 Type in the words "Good Times." Then select both words and format the entire text block to 48-point Helvetica Bold. Move the headline up until it is flush with the top margin.

58 To visually link our two-column headline with our three-column text, we will add a three-column subhead. Again, use the text tool to drag from an empty point between the headline and text on the left margin all the way across the page to the edge of the right column. (Be careful not to click inside an existing text block if you are trying to create a new text block.) Then type the subhead, "Company's domestic revenues rise for last three quarters despite recent textile market fluctuations." Select the whole text block and format the subhead to 24-point Helvetica. To further differentiate the subhead from the headline, select the "Italic" option box in the TYPE SPECIFICATIONS dialog box, giving the subhead a visually interesting slant. Vertically position this text block between the headline and the article.

Figure 6.24: *The completed headline and subhead shown with three-column article.*

Creating a side bar

The last article that we will place into this newsletter will obviously have to fit in the empty area occupying the bottom right third of the page. This area is intentionally much smaller than the area containing the three-column article, since the next story that we pour will visually act as a supporting story, or side bar, to the feature story. A side bar includes additional information along the same lines as the feature story—information that is interesting, although not necessarily as important as that in the feature story.

To differentiate it from the feature story, a side bar is often surrounded by a box. To further highlight the article, its box might have a drop shadow. A drop shadow is a black or gray box, largely hidden in back of the first box, that gives your page a sense of dimension, as if the box surrounding the article is sitting above the page and casting a shadow onto the page.

Drawing a box with drop shadow

59 We will begin to create our side bar by establishing a border and a drop shadow. But first, we must set another ruler guide to help us position our article and the graphic elements that surround it. Drag a horizontal ruler guide down to three-quarters inch below the lower horizontal ruler guide. This should be at the 6¾-inch tick mark on the vertical ruler, if you have not moved the zero point of the ruler.

60 Before we create our box, we must create our drop shadow. Select the rectangle tool and drag from the intersection of our new horizontal ruler guide and the left edge of the second column to the bottom right margin corner, as shown in the Figure 6.25. While the shape is still selected, choose the 40% screen from the SHADES menu and the NONE command from the LINES menu. The result is a rectangular, medium-gray-value screen with no outline.

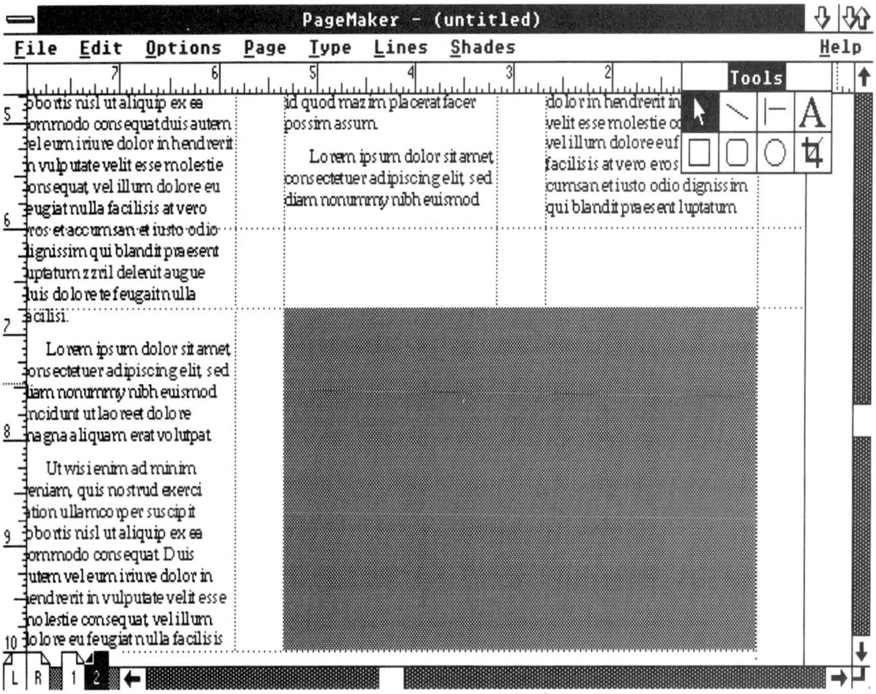

Figure 6.25: *This gray rectangle with no outline will act as the drop shadow to our side bar box.*

61 The next step is to create the box in front of the shadow. The box should be the same vertical and horizontal dimensions as the shadow to ensure a consistent and realistic relationship between them. The shadow is, after all, being cast by the box. Therefore, we will create the box as a copy of our existing shadow. Assuming the gray rectangle is still selected, choose the COPY command from the EDIT menu, or press CTRL-INSERT. Then immediately bring a copy of the shadow from the Windows Clipboard to your page by choosing the PASTE command from the EDIT menu, or pressing SHIFT-INSERT. The pasted rectangle will appear in the center of your screen display and is automatically selected.

62 Drag the selected rectangle to within one-eighth inch above and to the left of the bottom right margin corner. In this way, it is just slightly offset from the original rectangle behind it. While the forward shape remains selected, choose the PAPER command from the SHADES menu and the 1 PT command from the LINES menu. The box is now completed, appearing to be in front of the drop shadow. We are now ready to place the text into the box.

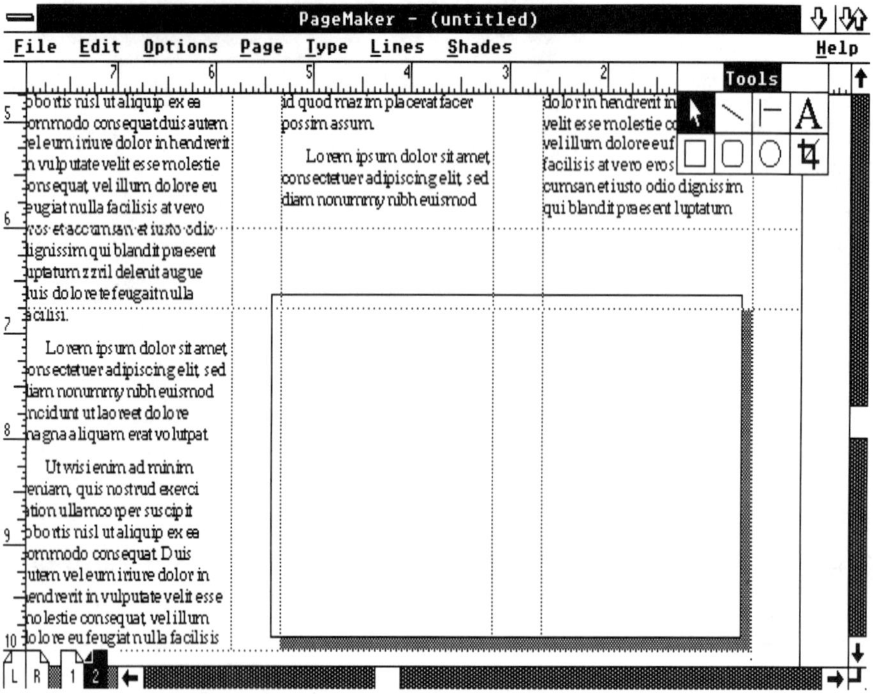

Figure 6.26: *The completed box with offset drop shadow.*

Pouring and formatting the side bar text

63 Before we place our text, we need another ruler guide. Drag a vertical guide to a point one-quarter inch to the left of the right margin. This will define the right side of our text.

64 Choose the PLACE... command, or press CTRL-D, select the LOREM.TXT file (or any one-page story) to be imported, and click OK. When your manual text flow cursor appears, do *not* click. This time, we will draw the column width of our text with the text tool, just as we have done when creating headlines and subheads. Drag with the manual text flow cursor from the intersection of the left edge of the second column and the lowest horizontal ruler guide (just inside the box) to our new vertical ruler guide, as shown Figure 6.27.

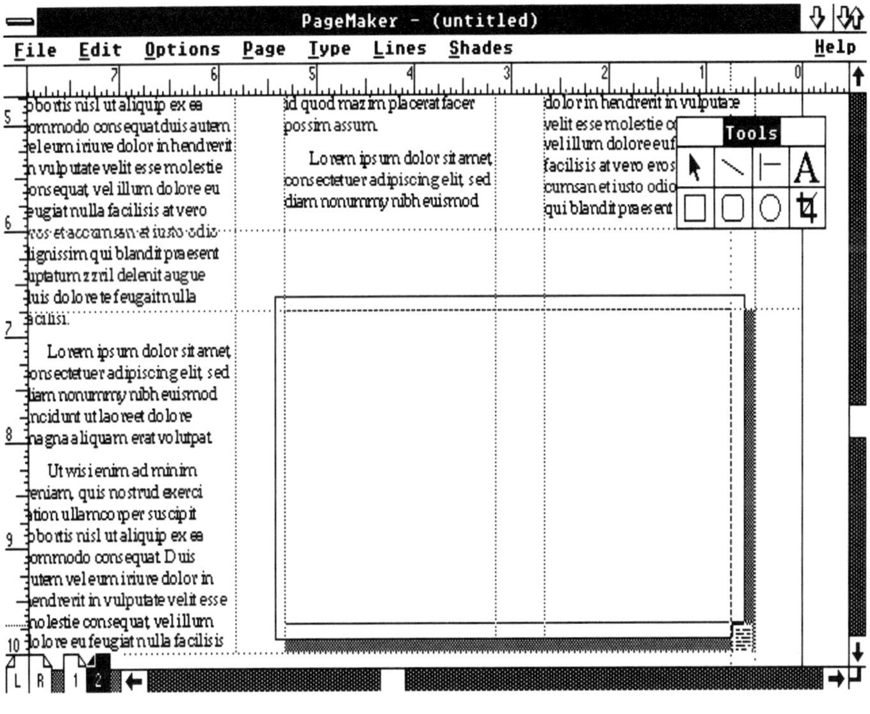

Figure 6.27: *Dragging with the manual text flow cursor to define the column width of the side bar text.*

65 After PageMaker pours your text, select all the text with the text tool and change the type specifications, or specs, to 12-point Helvetica with "Auto" leading. Also make sure the text is flush left and give each paragraph one-quarter-inch first-line indent, as described earlier in this chapter. Incidentally, we have made this text slightly larger than other text in this newsletter to further highlight the side bar. Because it is a small article with large text, it seems friendly, and your reader is more likely to read it. If it is well written, a side bar can interest readers in the main article as well.

66 Click on the text with the arrow tool and, if necessary, move the lower handlebar of the text block until it is within one-eighth inch of the bottom edge of the box. The upper handlebar may need to be adjusted as well so that it touches the horizontal ruler guide.

Creating the side bar headline

67 Now that the text is finished, it is time to create the headline for this side bar. The headline will be in the area between the feature article text and the side bar box. Select the text tool and drag in this empty area from the left edge of the second column to the vertical ruler guide on the far right of the page, defining the headline column width. Then type, "Stocks also looking bullish," and change the specs to 24-point Helvetica Italic (known as Helvetica Oblique). If necessary, adjust the position of the headline vertically to match the position shown in Figure 6.27.

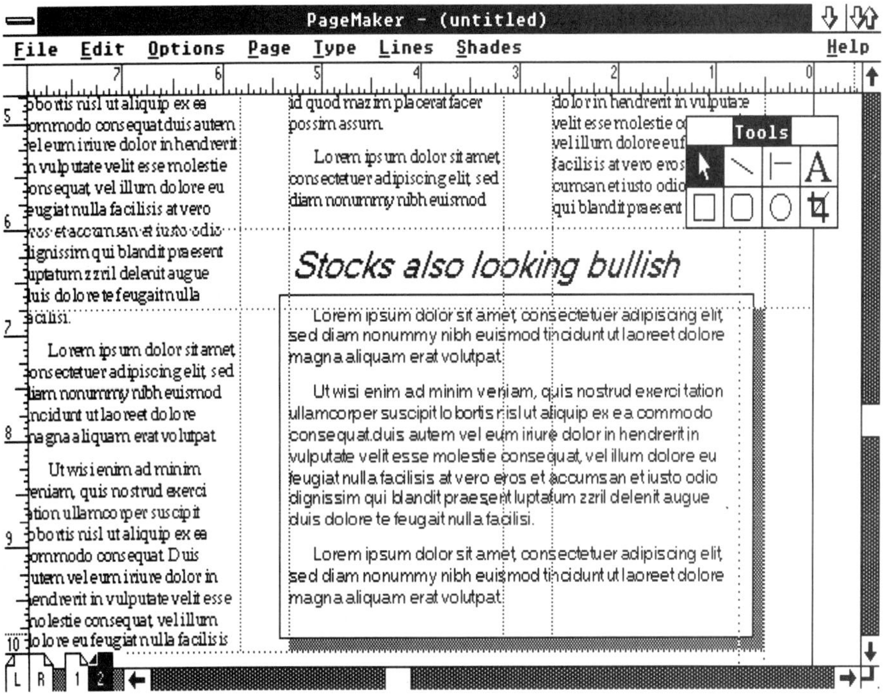

Figure 6.28: *The headline accurately positioned above the side bar drop shadow box.*

Our newsletter is now complete. If you wish, reduce your display to "Fit-in-window" view size. It should closely match the page shown in Figure 6.29.

All that is left to do is save our newsletter to disk for future reference and print the file to an output device.

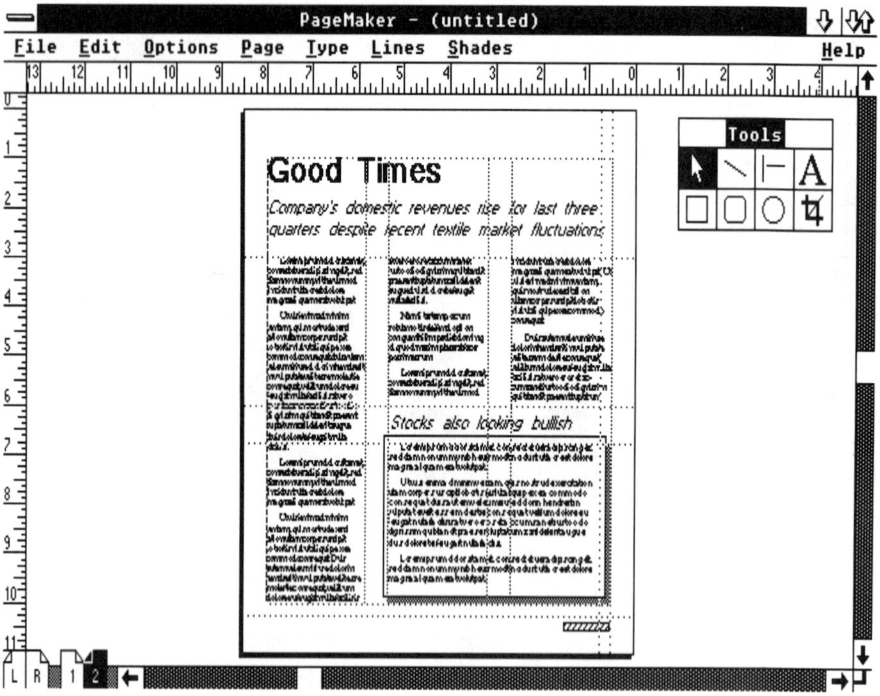

Figure 6.29: *Page 2 displayed at the "Fit-in-window" view size.*

Saving the newsletter to disk

You always want to store files that you create to disk. Generally, you want to save a file frequently while you are creating it. We have postponed our discussion of the SAVE command to this point so that the focus of the sample project is the newsletter creation process itself. We recommend that when you create files of your own, however, that you execute the SAVE command frequently. This way, you won't lose very much information if your computer crashes.

When you save a file to disk, all of the work that you have done, which has been stored in memory up to this point, is transcribed to disk. The file that you save can be transferred to other floppy or hard disks, and will remain available if you want to use it again. You never know when you may want to use this file again, especially in the case of a periodical publication like a newsletter. Once you have established a certain visual style, you will want to build on it again and again. For example, in future versions of our newsletter, we could open this same file to spare ourselves the time and effort of recreating our master page items and the flag text. Considering that the creation of these items alone consumed the first third of this chapter, there is much to be gained by saving this file.

68 Choose the Save command from the File menu, or press Ctrl-S. Since we have never saved this file before, the Save publication as dialog box will appear. Use the "Directories" list to tell PageMaker where to save the file. Double-click on the letters in brackets at the end of the list to change drives, and double-click on the [..] option to move to the parent directory. You must also enter a name for your file in the option box to the right of the "Directories" list. The "Path" option shows the currently chosen destination. We have chosen the name "SAMPLNWS," but you can enter any name that you like, up to eight letters long.

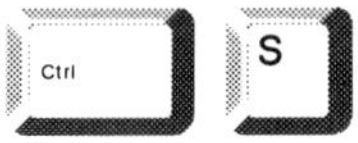

Determining a filename and location is a very important process. First-time users often make the mistake of giving their early files very general or obscure names and saving them to arbitrary disks. In the short run, this can be fine. You may not have many files, only two or three disks worth, and you can easily find them and tell them apart. But you would be surprised how little time it takes to amass a very large number of files. If you use PageMaker often, you can easily create enough files to fill many disks every month, making random file storage an organizational nightmare. Here are a few tips when saving your files:

- Save similar files to the same disk or directory. In other words, save newsletters to one disk or set of disks, flyers to another, business letters to another, and so on.

- When naming a file, remember that MS-DOS only allows eight characters in a filename, not including the suffix, which in PageMaker is always ".PM3." Be as specific as possible so that after several months or even a few years you will be able to identify it. Because eight-character file names tend to be necessarily cryptic, it is particularly important that you keep files organized in different directories or on different floppy disks.

- How will you be able to differentiate this version of your document from previous or future versions? You don't need to date your file, since the MS-DOS already provides this information, but adding a version or issue number to the end of a filename can help.

After determining a file destination and entering a filename, click the OK button. Your file is now saved so you can reuse it in the future.

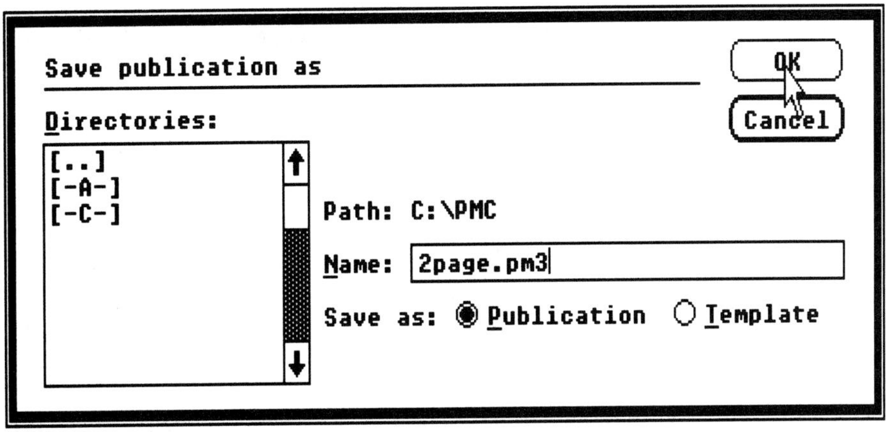

Figure 6.30: *The Save publication as dialog box, used to name our file and determine the drive and directory where it will be saved.*

Printing a two-page document

The last step in producing a document in PageMaker is to print it. PageMaker files can be printed to any PostScript-language-based laser printer, such as the Apple LaserWriter; to a typesetter with a PostScript-language interpreter such as the Linotronic series; or to a standard PC-compatible dot-matrix printer such as an Epson. If you are on a tight budget, we recommend that you print proofs of your documents to a dot-matrix printer to make sure that your page layouts are both attractive and effective. If you have a compatible laser printer, you may print final outputs of your documents at a resolution of 300, or even 600 dots-per-inch (DPI), suitable for photocopying and distribution to a professional readership. If you do not own or do not have access to a laser printer, you can usually find a service bureau that can provide outputs from your disk. You might also consider typesetting your files, another service provided by many service bureaus. This makes it possible to print your files on output devices with resolutions of 1270 DPI or 2540 DPI. Files may be submitted either on disk or via modem for this purpose.

If you are printing a file yourself, whether it is a final or proof version, you may make use of PageMaker's built-in printing options. The printing process can be very complicated, so we will only discuss those options that are relevant to printing our newsletter. (Incidentally, these options are all you will need to know to print most files.)

69 Make sure your printer is turned on. If you have more than one printer available, select the appropriate printer using the PRINTER SETUP...command on the FILE menu.

70 Choose the PRINT... command from the FILE menu or press CTRL-P. This brings up the PRINT dialog box, shown in Figure 6.31. At the "Copies" option, enter the number of copies you want to print. Usually, this number will be 1. If you want to print large quantities of copies, it is more financially efficient to print a single original and have photocopies or offset prints made from these. The "Page range" option controls which pages in your file will print. Select the "All" radio button to print the entire file, or enter the page range in the "From" and "to" option boxes. For example, if you wanted to print only page 1, select the "From" radio button and enter 1 for both the "From" and "to" values.

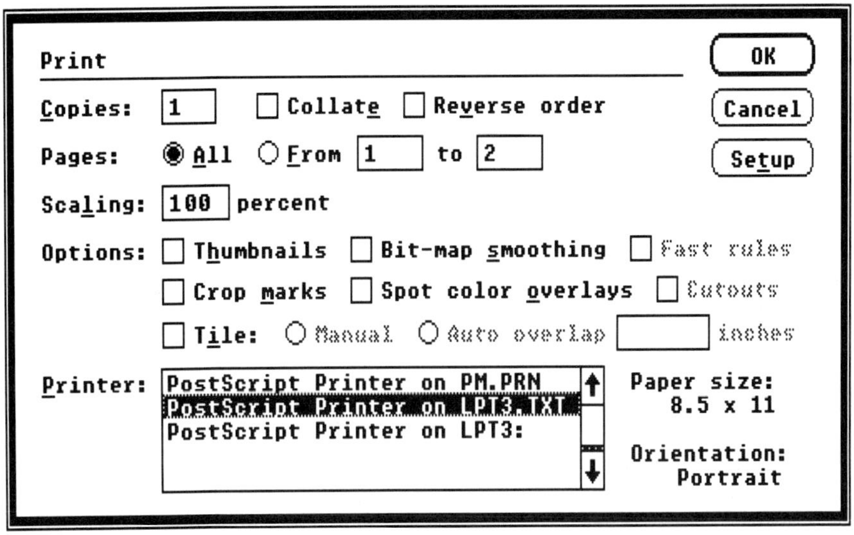

Figure 6.31: *The Print dialog box, containing our printing specifications.*

71 PageMaker highlights the type of printer that you have chosen and the output port in the "Printer" option at the bottom of the dialog box. Click on the desired printer name to change printers. If you have more than one printer of the same type, for instance, you have a laser printer and a typesetter, click on the Setup button to choose the specific brand of printer.

72 Clicking the Setup button takes you to either the PostScript Printer or HP/PCL LaserJet dialog we saw in Figures 6.02 and 6.03, respectively. Scroll down the "Printer" list until you find your brand and model and click on its name, and select the other options in this box, which vary depending on the printer type. When you are satisfied with the settings, click the OK button to return to the Print dialog box.

73 After all your specifications are complete, click on the OK button to instruct PageMaker to print your file. The PRINT dialog will disappear and the PRINT STATUS dialog box and CANCEL button will be displayed. The PRINT STATUS dialog lists various situations regarding your current print job, including PostScript-language and out-of-paper errors. The CANCEL button allows you to cancel the print job if you discover a problem.

After your pages print, examine them and make sure they meet with your expectations. If you see any problems, make the necessary changes to your file. You may even want to make changes to your newsletter that are not outlined in this chapter. Try experimenting with the fonts and other type specifications. Try jazzing up the flag. The newsletter we have created is not designed to be used "as is" for your personal newsletter needs. But it may act as a foundation upon which you can build a more complex, more personalized newsletter. Or, you may wish to develop a newsletter in a completely different style.

In either case, by successfully completing this project you have demonstrated an understanding of the most basic and essential commands and options offered by PageMaker.

CHAPTER 7

Creating and Adding Text

In this chapter we examine:

- *Preparing word-processed documents*
- *Adding text to publications*
- *Working with text blocks*

The most basic element of any document is text. The text that makes up a PageMaker publication can be created outside of PageMaker in a word-processor or text-editor, or inside of PageMaker using the text tool. Once in the publication, text can be edited extensively and repositioned endlessly. In this chapter, we look at ways of adding text to a publication. In Chapter 8, *Editing Text,* we examine the ways that text can be edited and manipulated within a publication. Finally, Chapter 9, *Using Style Sheets,* focuses on the use of style sheets, an advanced PageMaker feature designed to simplify text editing, publication design, and production.

Word-processing vs. the text tool

Since PageMaker can accept text created in a word-processor, and create text with its own text tool, it is often difficult to decide which method is most suitable for a particular document. In general, word-processors are preferred, because they offer comprehensive text-editing features and are designed to perform editing quickly. PageMaker's ability to create and edit text is provided merely as a convenience, supporting PageMaker's page-layout capabilities. The text tool should be used only to create short blocks of text and to edit existing text.

There are three specific factors that you should consider when deciding how to best create text:

- **Length**. Any text more than one page long should definitely be created in a word-processor. If you require text of this length, you will almost certainly benefit from the additional editing features provided by a word-processor. In most cases, text of less than half a page long can be input directly into PageMaker.

- **Importance of the document**. The more important your text, the more we recommend that you create it in a word-processor. This is true for two reasons; First, the additional editing features of the word-processor, such as spell checking, will probably help you do a better and faster job of editing the text than you could in PageMaker. Secondly, in PageMaker you may be less likely to notice weak writing when it is obscured by an attractive layout.

- **Required editing**. When you are sure that a document will require substantial revisions before it is at a final-draft stage, continue editing in a word-processor. Again, the editing features of a word-processor are superior to those available in PageMaker and should be used whenever possible. Also, the more heavily you edit text in PageMaker, the greater the risk of **corrupting** either the text of that story or of the entire publication.

It is often tempting to place documents into PageMaker as soon as the first text drafts are completed. Laying out the pages of a publication provides a sense of progress and accomplishment and usually makes the project seem closer to completion. We do, however, recommend restraint. While there is no denying the satisfaction of seeing your publication take shape, in the long run it may take longer to complete the publication, and you may forfeit quality because text editing will be slower and perhaps less accurate when done in PageMaker.

TIP 3

Another reason publications are often created prematurely is that their length can be estimated only by positioning text documents and graphics in PageMaker. In this case, approximate the length of your publication in PageMaker, and then return to your word-processor to complete the editing process. Later, either recreate the publication from scratch or replace the first-draft stories in the existing publication with the final word-processing documents. (For more information, see the section *Using the Place... command to replace or insert text*, later in this chapter).

Introducing Text Blocks

In PageMaker, text exists only within a **text block**. The text block is an object that can be sized, positioned, or deleted, and is filled with text. A text block is created whenever new text is added to a publication, whether imported from a word-processor, pasted from the Clipboard, or added with the text tool.

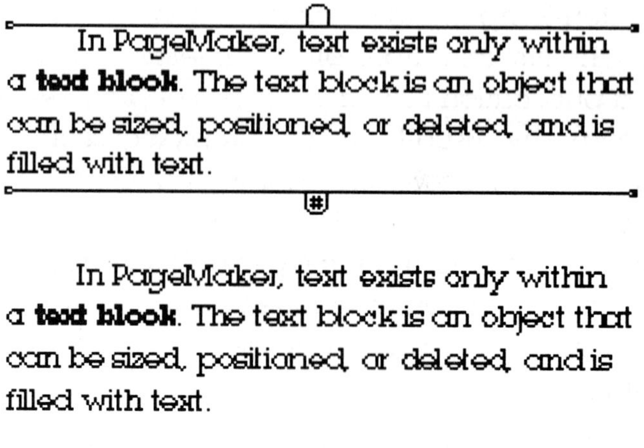

Figure 7.01: *A selected and unselected text block.*

Sizing text blocks

When a text block is selected (clicked on with the arrow tool), **handlebars** appear at the top and bottom of the block, marking the block's beginning, end, and width.

The size of a text block depends upon how it is created:

- A new text block created between two column guides will be as wide as the column (see Figure 7.02). It will begin where the insertion point was set, or where the text flow icon was positioned when the mouse was clicked. It will end when no more text remains, or when it encounters either the bottom margin or certain graphic objects.

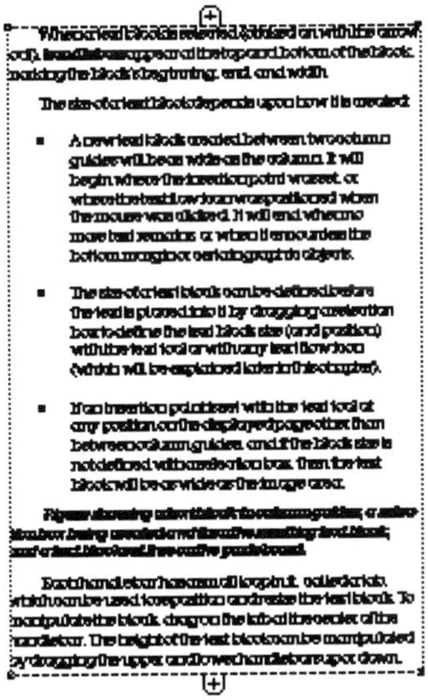

Figure 7.02: *Text placed or created between column guides takes the width and length of the column.*

- The size of a text block can be defined before the text is placed into it by dragging a box with the text tool (or with any text flow icon) defining the text block size and position. This method is known as **drag-placing**.

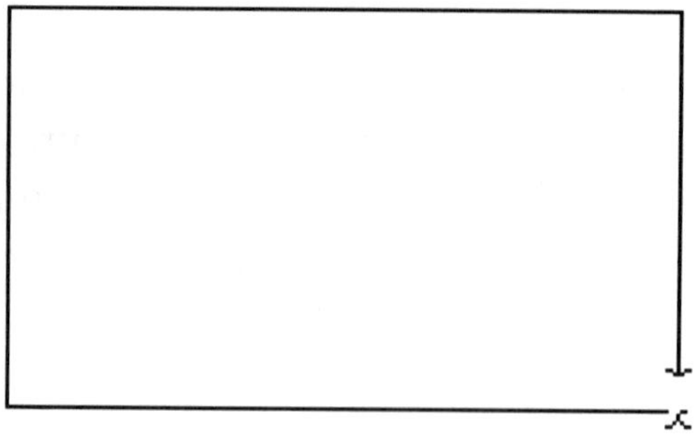

Figure 7.03: *A text block's size can be specified by drag-placing with the text tool or any of the text placement icons.*

- If an insertion point is set with the text tool at any position on the displayed page other than between column guides, and if the block size is not defined with a selection box, the text block will be nearly as wide as the image area.

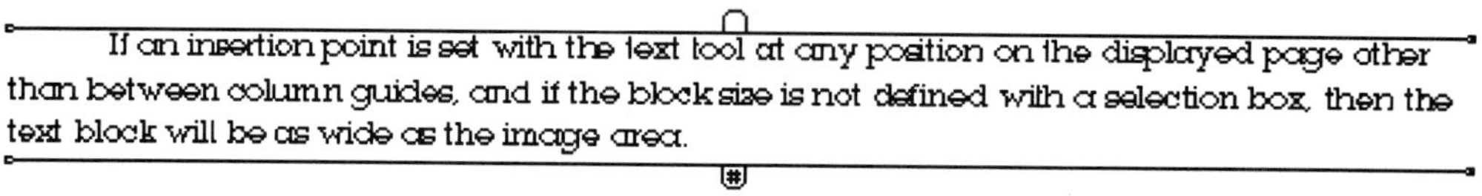

Figure 7.04: *A text block that is not restrained by column guides or drag placing can be nearly as wide as the page itself.*

Each handlebar that appears above or below a text block has a small loop in it, called a **tab**. Using the arrow tool, you can drag these tabs up or down, manipulating the size and position of the text block.

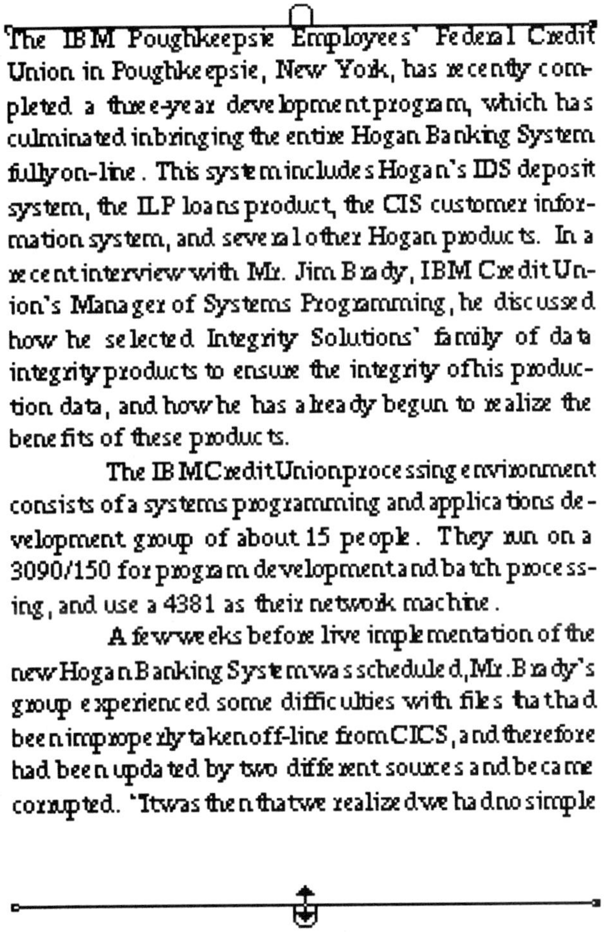

The IBM Poughkeepsie Employees' Federal Credit Union in Poughkeepsie, New York, has recently completed a three-year development program, which has culminated in bringing the entire Hogan Banking System fully on-line. This system includes Hogan's IDS deposit system, the ILP loans product, the CIS customer information system, and several other Hogan products. In a recent interview with Mr. Jim Brady, IBM Credit Union's Manager of Systems Programming, he discussed how he selected Integrity Solutions' family of data integrity products to ensure the integrity of his production data, and how he has already begun to realize the benefits of these products.

The IBM Credit Union processing environment consists of a systems programming and applications development group of about 15 people. They run on a 3090/150 for program development and batch processing, and use a 4381 as their network machine.

A few weeks before live implementation of the new Hogan Banking System was scheduled, Mr. Brady's group experienced some difficulties with files that had been improperly taken off-line from CICS, and therefore had been updated by two different sources and became corrupted. "It was then that we realized we had no simple

Figure 7.05: *Dragging the tabs that appear in the upper and lower handlebars of a selected text block changes the size and position of the text block.*

7

Creating and Adding Text

- **Dragging the top handle upward or downward** will change the vertical position of the first line in the text block. As a result, all text in the story will be moved upward or downward through all the text blocks in the story.

- **Dragging the lower handle upward** will shorten the text block, hiding all text below the lower handle of the block. If this is not the last text block in the story, the hidden text will appear at the top of the next text block, and all text will flow appropriately.

- **Dragging the lower handle downwards** will lengthen the text block, displaying additional text in the text block when the mouse button is released. If this is not the last text block in the story, the new text is flowed back from the top of the next text block, and all text in the story will reflow appropriately. If no more text remains in the document (the # sign is visible in the lower handlebar) dragging the handlebar downward will have no effect—when you release the mouse button, the handle will return to its previous position at the end of text.

The tabs in the handlebars will often display symbols that inform you of the relationship between text blocks. The end of a story is designated by a pound (or number) symbol (#) in the tab of the bottom handlebar. A plus sign (+) in the bottom handle indicates that all of the text cannot fit within the text block at its current size, and the remaining text is hidden until you designate where it should be placed. A plus sign (+) in the top handlebar tab indicates that this text block is continuation of a story from another text block.

The ends of each handlebar have small solid rectangles, called **handles**, which are used to resize the text block. When one of these rectangles is dragged, a box representing the new text block size will be displayed (see Figure 7.06). When the mouse button is released, the text inside the block will reflow to fill the new text block size. This is exactly the same process used to resize any graphic object.

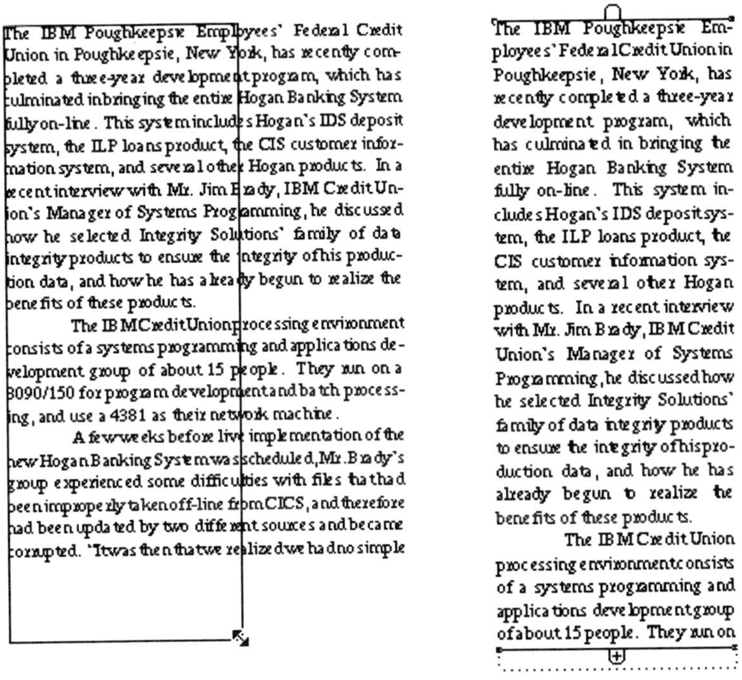

Figure 7.06: *Dragging the handle on the end of a text block handlebar resizes the text block.*

Moving text blocks

To reposition a text block, select the arrow tool from the toolbox, point the arrow cursor inside the text block, and press and hold the mouse button. Now drag the text block to its new position. If you hold down the mouse button for a second or two before you begin to drag, you will be able to see your text as you reposition it. If you begin dragging immediately after clicking the mouse button, you will only see a box marking the outline of your text block. The display will scroll if you drag to the edge of the display. Release the mouse button when the text is in position. You can adjust the text block position again by repeating this process. Holding down the SHIFT key during a move will constrain your movement to either the vertical or horizontal axis, as described in Chapter 5.

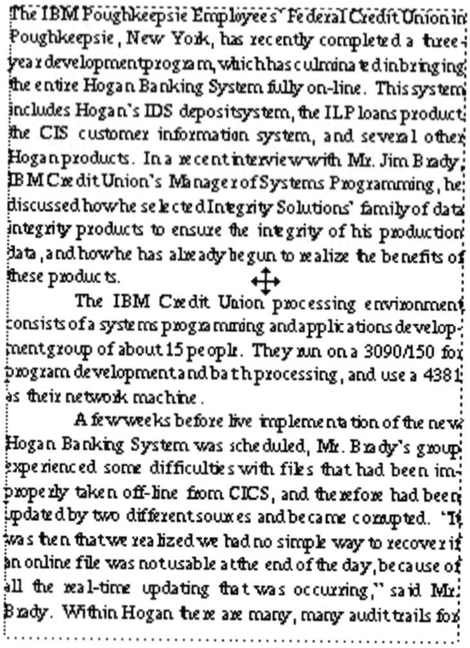

The IBM Poughkeepsie Employees' Federal Credit Union in Poughkeepsie, New York, has recently completed a three-year development program, which has culminated in bringing the entire Hogan Banking System fully on-line. This system includes Hogan's IDS deposit system, the ILP loans product, the CIS customer information system, and several other Hogan products. In a recent interview with Mr. Jim Brady, IBM Credit Union's Manager of Systems Programming, he discussed how he selected Integrity Solutions' family of data integrity products to ensure the integrity of his production data, and how he has already begun to realize the benefits of these products.

The IBM Credit Union processing environment consists of a systems programming and applications development group of about 15 people. They run on a 3090/150 for program development and bath processing, and use a 4381 as their network machine.

A few weeks before live implementation of the new Hogan Banking System was scheduled, Mr. Brady's group experienced some difficulties with files that had been improperly taken off-line from CICS, and therefore had been updated by two different sources and became corrupted. "It was then that we realized we had no simple way to recover if an online file was not usable at the end of the day, because of all the real-time updating that was occurring," said Mr. Brady. Within Hogan there are many, many audit trails for

Figure 7.07: *Dragging a text block to a new position.*

Threaded text blocks

In many publications, text that is imported from a word-processor or created in PageMaker will not fit into just one text block. A single text document, or *story*, as it is called in PageMaker, that fills more than one text block, is said to be **threaded** through multiple text blocks, as seen in Figure 7.08. We will see how threaded text blocks are created in the next section of this chapter.

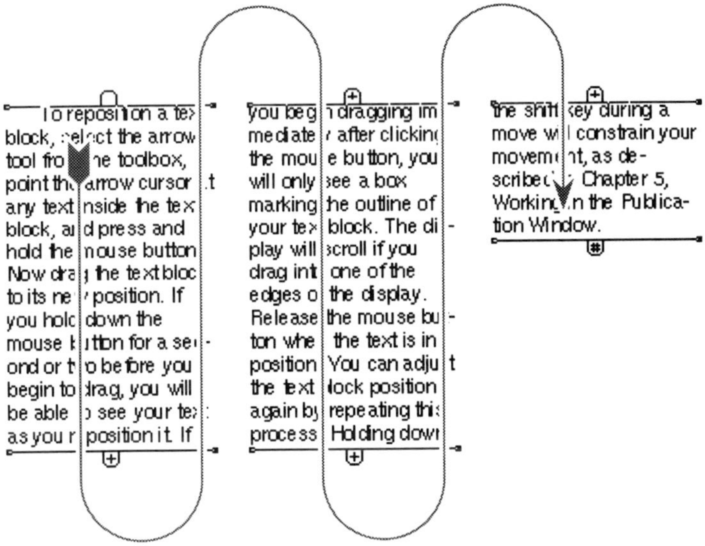

Figure 7.08: *A story threaded through several text blocks.*

Once the threaded text blocks are created, the text in the story flows through the blocks, from the bottom of one column to the top of the next column, and from the bottom of one page to the top of the following page. You can change the length of each block; however, changing one block will affect the content of all other text blocks in a story.

Here are some examples of how a change can affect multiple text blocks:

- **If the bottom of one text block is moved up two lines**, those two lines appear at the top of the next block, and every block in the thread will gain two lines at the top and lose two lines at the bottom. If the last text block cannot hold all lines of text that flow into it, the plus sign (+) will appear in the lower handlebar tab when that block is selected. You may either lengthen the block to accommodate the remaining text or pour the remaining text into a new text block.
- **If the bottom is moved down two lines**, two lines are pulled from the top of the following text block, which gains two lines from the text block following it, and so on. Any text block that loses all its text to the preceding text block is automatically deleted.
- **If text is cut out of the middle of a text block**, the text in all the text blocks following the cut will move up to fill the void. Any text block that loses all its text to the preceding text block is automatically deleted.
- **If text is inserted in the middle of a text block**, the text in all the text blocks following the addition will move down to create space for the new text. If the last text block cannot fit all lines that flow into it, the plus sign (+) will appear in the lower handlebar tab when that block is selected. You may either lengthen the block to accommodate the remaining text or pour the remaining text into a new text block.

- **If one text block in a threaded story is deleted,** the text in that block will either be deleted from the story, or transferred to the the previous block, depending on how you delete the block. This will be explained in detail later in this chapter.

Placing imported text

Now that we understand the basic idea of the PageMaker text block, we are ready to import some word-processed documents into a publication. The process of placing imported text into a publication consists of several steps:

- Preparing the word-processed document.
- Deciding whether to replace existing text and preparing to replace it.
- Executing the PLACE... command and selecting the file.
- Flowing the text into the publication.

Preparing word-processed documents

When instructed to import text from a word-processed file into a publication, PageMaker reads the file from disk and brings a copy of it into the publication. As this copy is being made, the text passes through an **import filter**, which converts the formatting from the word-processed file into formats used by PageMaker. PageMaker 3.01 has built-in import filters for MICROSOFT WORD versions 3.0, and 4.0, MICROSOFT WORKS, WORDPERFECT version 4.2 (not 5.0 as of this writing), WORDSTAR (PC version 3.3), XYWRITE III, WINDOWS WRITE, MULTIMATE, and all DCA-format files, including those created by SAMNA WORD and IBM DISPLAYWRITE 3. PageMaker comes with several import filters for less popular software that can be installed when you install PageMaker or added later on.

Of course, you can also import any ASCII or text-only files as well. Optional import filters may be provided when you purchase other word-processors, and these can be added to your PageMaker application using the FILTER INSTALLER application included with PageMaker 3.0.

PageMaker will not recognize or be able to use word-processed files for which an import filter does not exist. If you have a file from a word-processor that is not supported by PageMaker, try to convert the file into the format of a word-processor PageMaker does support, or save the file as a text-only file (ASCII).

There are several common methods of converting file formats:

- Many word-processors include conversion utilities that can change files from one format to another.
- Many word-processors to allow you to save files in formats other than the wordprocessor's normal format. For example, WORDPERFECT 5.0 users can save their files in version 4.2 or text-only format, which can be imported into PageMaker. The DCA file format is also a common file format option.

- Utility applications such as WORD FOR WORD convert files between many file formats.

- Documents can be sent out to professional conversion services, although this does add both time and expense to the process.

- To convert files created on the Macintosh, conversion software such as APPLE FILE EXCHANGE by Apple Computer, or MACLINK by Dataviz are available.

Import filters may not be able to convert every formatting attribute correctly from the word-processed file. In the following list we describe how PageMaker's built-in import filters handle the most common text-formatting attributes and offer a few suggestions about the use of each in the documents you will be importing into PageMaker.

- **Carriage returns**. Each carriage-return character in a word-processed document will be converted successfully by PageMaker, which assumes that each indicates the end of a paragraph. Therefore, try not to use carriage returns to force line breaks within a paragraph. It is unlikely that the width of your text will be the same in PageMaker as it was in your word-processor, so the carriage returns may not fall at line endings after they are imported. Also, rather than using multiple carriage returns to add space between lines, use paragraph formatting techniques to add space within the paragraph.

- **Tabs**. Tab characters and their positions plus the tab leaders will be used in PageMaker. However, PageMaker may not recognize special tabs such as center and decimal tabs. Check the chart in your *PageMaker Reference Manual* to find what formatting features can be imported from your wordprocessor. Changes in text width will often mean that tab positions need to be adjusted once text is placed in PageMaker. As a rule, use only one tab and correctly position the tab location, as shown in Figure 7.09, rather than a series of tabs on the same line.

- **Spaces**. Spaces will transfer, of course, but be sure not to use spaces to align objects in your word-processor. PageMaker's proportional spacing method will undoubtedly move these elements out of alignment. Tabs are the recommended method of positioning text.

- **Left and Right indents**. Indents will transfer, but they will be transferred as specifications for the distance that PageMaker indents the text from the edges of the text block rather than from the page margins.

- **First-line indents**. First-line indents will transfer, determining the position of the first line of text in a paragraph relative to the left edge of the paragraph. The value can be positive or negative. PageMaker ignores first-line indents that are wider than the PageMaker column.

- **Nested indents**. Paragraphs that are indented using the "Nested indent" option will transfer from some word processors, such as MICROSOFT WORD. Files from some word-processors, such as WORD PERFECT 4.2 and WORDSTAR, must be specially prepared, and indents from MULTIMATE or LOTUS MANUSCRIPT will not transfer at all. See the conversion chart in the *PageMaker Reference Manual* for more information.

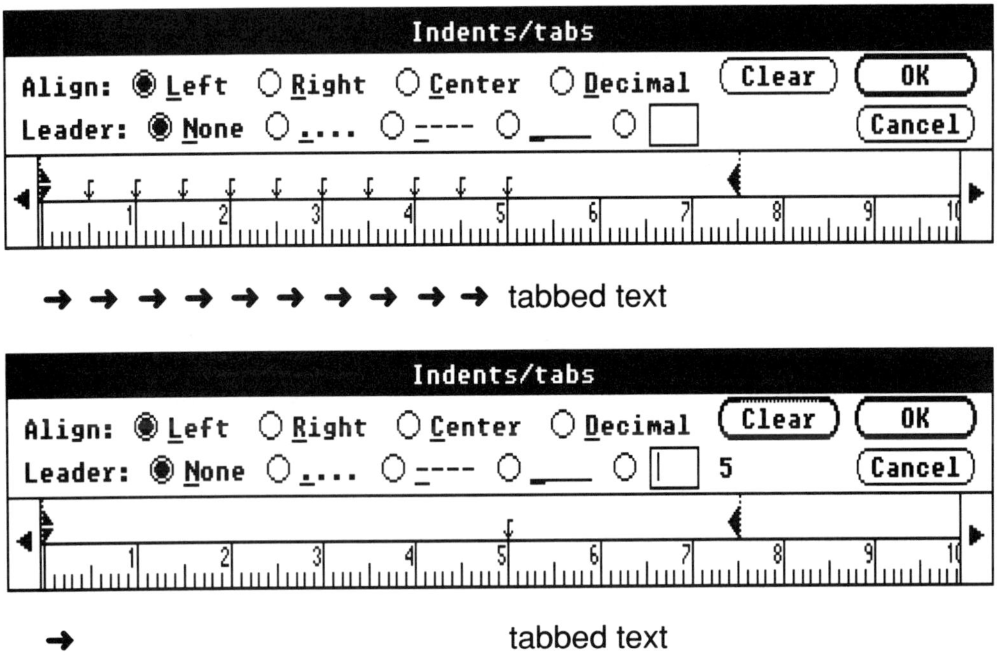

Figure 7.09: *In the top example, multiple tabs are inserted in order to force the text to the correct tab stop. In the lower example, the extra tab stops have been deleted so that only one tab character is necessary.*

- **Margins**. The top, bottom, right, and left margins defined in your word-processor will not transfer into PageMaker. (Neither will most other page setup specifications.) As text is placed into PageMaker, it assumes the margins of the text block into which it is placed.

- **Line spacing, Paragraph spacing**. Line spacing (leading) will transfer from most word-processors, and paragraph spacing (space before and after paragraphs) will transfer into PageMaker successfully, except for WORD PERFECT 4.2 files.

- **Paragraph alignment.** PageMaker will recognize and use left, right, centered, and justified paragraph alignment from all applications except WORDSTAR 3.3.

- **Type faces**. PageMaker will import type face information from most word-processors that support different typefaces, such as MICROSOFT WORD, MULTIMATE, and WINDOWS WRITE.

- **Type sizes**. Text files from MICROSOFT WORD, MULTIMATE, and WINDOWS WRITE will retain the same point size when they are transferred into PageMaker, except for any type set in a fractional point size, in which case its size is rounded up to the next whole number. Files from WORDPERFECT 4.2 and WORDSTAR 3.3 will not retain their type size specifications.

- **Type style (Bold, Italic, Underline, Strikethru).** All text will retain the same type style specified in the word-processor when it is transferred into PageMaker, with the following exceptions: All word underlines will be changed to single-stroke underlines, and superscripts and subscripts will be changed to 7/12 the normal type size and will be positioned a distance above or below the baseline equal to 1/3 the current point size.

- **Special characters**. Most special characters, including MICROSOFT WORD's hidden text, formulas, and line numbers, will not transfer with the text document into PageMaker.

- **Headers/Footers, Page numbers**. PageMaker will completely ignore all information contained in the headers or footers of the word-processed document.

- **Footnotes**. In most cases, footnotes are not included in placed documents, although in some cases they might be placed at the end of the word-processed document as it appears in PageMaker.

- **Columns**, **Page breaks.** PageMaker completely recomposes all text, ignoring column settings and all page breaks.

Placing a new story

Once your word-processed documents have been prepared and you have created your PageMaker publication, you are ready to begin importing word-processed documents. Choose the PLACE... command from the FILE menu (CTRL-D) to bring up the PLACE FILE dialog box (shown in Figure 7.11). In this dialog you may select a file to import and then specify several options for its placement in your publication.

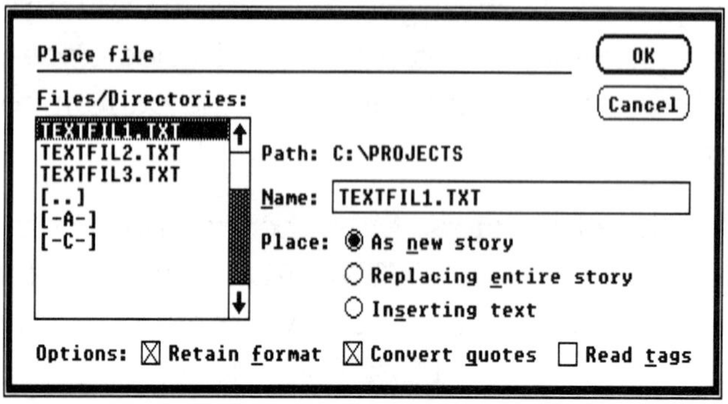

Figure 7.11: *The Place file dialog box.*

The scrolling file listing on the left side of the dialog box displays the names of all text or graphic files that PageMaker can use from the current drive and sub-directory, as well as all other sub-directories and drives available. Remember that this list does not include every file in the directory, only those that PageMaker can import. The drive and directory whose contents are currently being displayed appears next to the "Path." option.

As we've mentioned earlier, there are several methods of moving between directories and drives:

- Double-click on any drive letter (enclosed in brackets [A]) to change to that drive.
- Double-click on a sub-directory name (enclosed in brackets [*sub-directory*]) to view files in that sub-directory.
- Double-click on the [...] line to move up the folder hierarchy (out of the current sub-directory and into the parent directory).

Once you've located the file you wish to place, select its filename from the scrolling list. When an eligible filename is selected, PageMaker determines whether a text or graphic file has been selected, and the first "Place" option appears as either "As new graphic" or "As new story."

When a text document is selected in the scrolling file listing, three text placement options along the bottom of the PLACE DOCUMENT dialog box will become selectable:

- **The "Retain format" option**. This option is selected by default whenever the selected file is from a word-processor for which an import filter is available. As long as this option remains selected, PageMaker will convert and utilize the paragraph and character formatting of the word-processed text. If the selected file is an unformatted text file, this option will not affect it. If this option is deselected, even for a file that can be handled by an import filter, most character and paragraph formatting is removed from the text as it is placed in PageMaker.

Figure 7.12: *The "Options" options become available when a text document is selected for placement in the Place document dialog box.*

- **The "Convert quotes" option**. This option causes PageMaker to scan the file being imported and attempt to intelligently change straight double quotation marks (") into typesetting (opening and closing) quotation marks (“ and ”).

- **The "Read tags" option**. This option causes PageMaker to look for *tags*, the names of PageMaker style sheets which are contained between the characters < and > in the word-processed file. PageMaker reads these tags and applies the style formats to the text following each tag. Style sheets and tags are more completely discussed in Chapter 9, *Using Style Sheets*. If this option is not selected, PageMaker treats tags as normal text, printing the tags character for character: <*tag name*>.

After you have selected a file and set all the available options, click the OK button or double-click on the file name. PageMaker will then read the file from disk and prepare to position the text into your publication.

Flowing text

When PageMaker is finished reading the word-processed file, the cursor will become one of two *text flow icons*: the manual text flow icon or the autoflow icon. It will become the autoflow text icon if the AUTOFLOW command is selected (marked with a check mark in the OPTIONS menu), or a manual text flow icon if not. We can use either one of these add text to our PageMaker publication.

Figure 7.13: *The manual, semi-automatic, and automatic text flow icons.*

Text from an imported document may be placed (added) anywhere on any publication page, on the master pages, or on the pasteboard. In most cases, the text will belong on pages of the publication. Text is usually placed on the pasteboard only if it is a small amount of text and you are unsure of its content or size. Placing it on the pasteboard allows you to read the text and then decide where it should be positioned.

If necessary, use the page icons, the keyboard equivalents (ALT-TAB and ALT-SHIFT-TAB) or the GO TO PAGE... command to turn to the appropriate page, or reposition the screen display using the scroll bars, grabber hand, or view-size commands. Any of these may be accessed without affecting the text flow icon.

If you decide that you do not wish to place the imported text at this time, click on the arrow tool in the toolbox and the text flow icon will disappear. Later, when you are ready to place the file, you will have to begin again by choosing the PLACE... command from the FILE menu. This same technique can be applied anytime that a text flow icon appears—clicking on the arrow tool will always discard it.

The process of actually placing text into a publication involves flowing the text into a text block or between column guides. Text flow can be controlled manually (using the manual text flow icon), automatically (using the autoflow text flow icon), or semi-automatically (using the semi-automatic text flow icon):

- **Manual text flow**. When flowing text manually, you decide where to begin each block of text. At the end of the text block, if more text remains to be placed, you must manually *reload* the text icon to continue the text flow process. You will have to turn the page when necessary and use the INSERT PAGES... command to add pages if more pages are required.

  Manual text flow is the default setting when the AUTOFLOW command from the OPTIONS menu is *not* selected. If AUTOFLOW is selected (indicated by a check mark before the command on the menu bar), manual text flow can be accessed temporarily by pressing the CTRL key.

- **Fully automatic**. When using automatic text flow, you only have to begin the text flow once, and the flow will continue, column by column, page after page, until the entire document is placed. Pages will be turned automatically, and if required, new pages are added automatically (until the document reaches its 128-page limit). It is possible to stop automatic text flow at any time by clicking the mouse button. When the AUTOFLOW command is selected, fully automatic text flow is the default setting. When AUTOFLOW is *not* selected, fully automatic text flow can be accessed temporarily by pressing the CTRL key.

- **Semi-automatic**. Semi-automatic text flow is identical to manual text flow except that the text icon is automatically reloaded when the end of a text block is reached. This loaded text icon must then be positioned manually at the location where the next text block is to begin. Semi-automatic text flow is initiated by pressing the SHIFT key, regardless of whether or not the AUTOFLOW command is selected.

Manually placing imported text

When the manual text flow icon appears, PageMaker is ready to begin flowing text into a new text block. You can initiate text flow by positioning the icon between any column guides at the vertical location where you would like the text block to begin and clicking the mouse button, or by drag-placing to create a marquee that will define the text block, and then releasing the mouse button.

Either of these methods will create a new text block, which will be filled with the first portion of the text from the file being imported. Text will flow down the new text block until either all the text has been placed, the bottom margin of the column or the bottom of the pasteboard is reached, or the text is interrupted by a graphic that has been formatted to stop text.

When the text flow stops, the text block is selected (as indicated by the presence of handlebars at the top and bottom of the text block), and the lower handlebar tab indicates whether any text did not fit in the text block: the plus sign (+) indicates that more text remains and the pound symbol (#) indicates that all the text has been placed. The arrow tool is automatically selected, allowing you to easily reposition the text block, resize the text block, or reload the text flow icon to continue flowing the text.

If more text remains to be placed, point the arrow tool at the plus sign (+) and click the mouse button. This reloads the text icon so that it is ready to place the additional text. The remaining text may be flowed into existing columns, placed into a new text block that is created manually, or placed onto the pasteboard. You can either turn the page or insert new pages into your publication without disturbing the loaded text icon. Position the text icon where you want the top of the next text block to begin, and click the mouse button to flow the remaining text into the new text block. Repeat this process until all the text in the document has been placed, indicated by the pound symbol (#) in the lower handlebar tab of the final text block.

Remember that manual text flow is the default setting unless the AUTOFLOW command is selected (marked with a check mark) in the the OPTIONS menu. If the AUTOFLOW command is selected, and the automatic text flow icon appears, you can still change the flow to manual mode temporarily by holding down the CTRL key.

Figure 7.14: *Using manual text flow, the text flow icon must be manually reloaded after each text block flows.*

Using the Autoflow command

In longer documents, the process of positioning the text cursor icon, initiating the text flow, reloading the flow icon, and repositioning the text cursor icon (including turning or creating pages) may become slow, boring, and repetitive. In these cases you will want to use the AUTOFLOW command to automate the process of flowing text documents. Autoflowing text works much like manual text flowing except that PageMaker automatically reloads the text icon cursor and initiates the flow in the next available column (moving left to right). PageMaker will turn pages as necessary, and will even insert new pages until all the text in the file is placed or the 128-page limit of the publication is reached.

Automatic text flow is initiated with the automatic text flow icon, which appears when the AUTOFLOW command is chosen from the OPTIONS menu. Choosing the AUTOFLOW command toggles a check mark (✓) on and off in front of the command. When the check mark appears before this command, the loaded text cursor will by default become the automatic text flow icon, and text flow will be automatic. You can choose the AUTOFLOW command at any time—before choosing the PLACE... command or even after the manual text flow icon has appeared. The automatic text flow icon also appears when the CTRL key is pressed down while the manual text flow icon is displayed.

Once the autoflow text icon is displayed, position it at the top of the column where the text document is to begin, and click the mouse button. Text will flow through each subsequent column in the publication, turning and adding pages as necessary, until all text in the placed document has been positioned. You may interrupt automatic text flow at any time by clicking the mouse button. To restart automatic text flow, click the plus sign (+) to reload the text flow icon, position the autoflow icon at the top of the next column, and click the mouse button to restart automatic text flow.

The drag-place method of defining a new text block (described in detail later in this chapter), can also be used while the autoflow text icon is displayed. Position the autoflow icon at the point you want the upper left corner of the new text block to begin, press and hold the mouse button, and drag the lower-right to create a box as large as your desired text block. Release the mouse button and text will flow into the box you have defined. Drag-placing with the autoflow icon will create one text block only—you will have to reload the autoflow icon if all of the available text does not fit into this new text block.

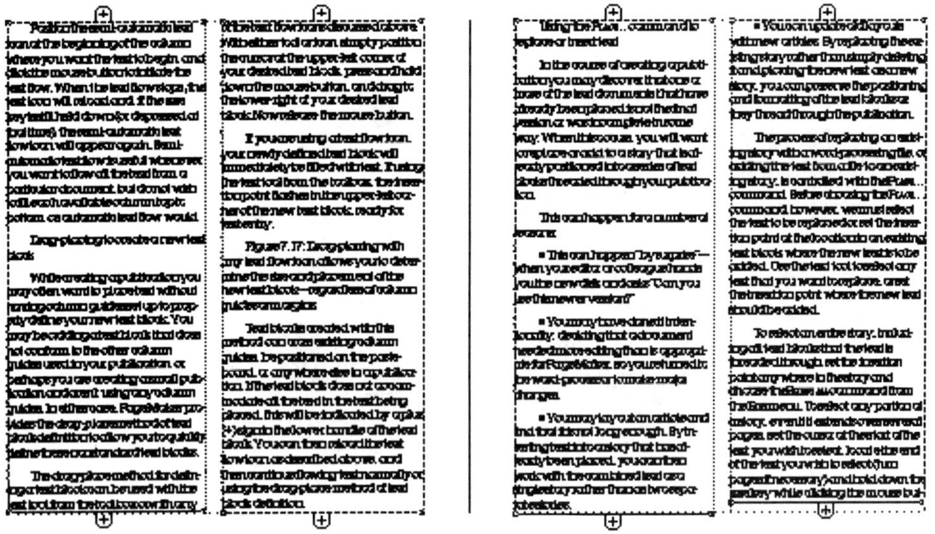

Figure 7.15: *Using automatic text flow, text automatically continues to flow from column to column, page to page.*

Semi-automatic text flow

A third method of text flow is semi-automatic, in which each column of text flow must be initiated individually, but the text icon is reloaded automatically if additional text remains when the text block is full. Semi-automatic text flow is initiated with the semi-automatic text flow icon, which is displayed by pressing the SHIFT key and holding down the mouse button when *either* the manual or automatic text icon is displayed.

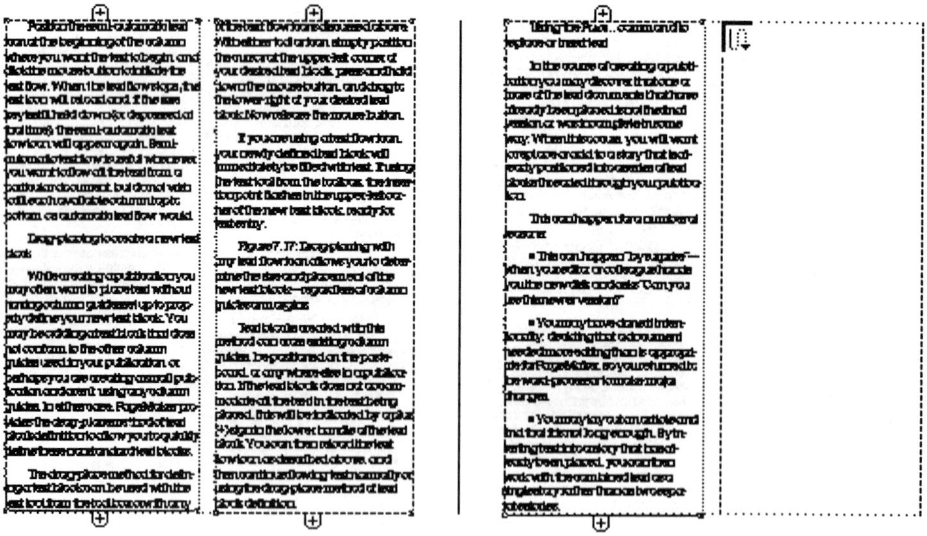

Figure 7.16: *Using semi-automatic text flow, you decide where each text block begins, but you do not have to reload the text flow icon after each new text block is created.*

To begin semi-automatic text flow, position the semi-automatic text icon at the beginning of the column where you want the text to begin, and click the mouse button to initiate the text flow. When the text flow stops, the text icon will reload and, if the SHIFT key is still held down (or depressed at that time), the semi-automatic text flow icon will appear again. If the SHIFT key is no longer being held down, then either the manual text flow icon or the automatic text flow icon will appear, depending on the current setting of the AUTOFLOW command in the OPTIONS menu.

Semi-automatic text flow is useful whenever you want to flow all the text from a particular document, but do not wish to fill each available column top to bottom, as automatic text flow would.

Drag-placing to create a new text block

While creating a publication you may often want to place text without having column guides set up to properly define your new text block. You may be adding a text block that does not conform to the other column guides used in your publication, or perhaps you are creating a small publication and aren't using any column guides. In either case, PageMaker provides the *drag-place* method of text block definition to allow you to quickly define these nonstandard text blocks.

The drag-place method for defining a text block can be used with the text tool from the toolbox or with any of the text flow icons discussed above. With either tool or icon, simply position the cursor at the upper left corner of your desired text block, press and hold down the mouse button, and drag to the lower right corner of your desired text block. Now release the mouse button.

If you are using a text flow icon, your newly defined text block will immediately be filled with text. If using the text tool from the toolbox, the insertion point flashes in the upper left corner of the new text block, ready for text entry.

Text blocks created with this method can cross existing column guides, be positioned on the pasteboard, or anywhere else in a publication. If the text block does not accommodate all the text being placed, this will be indicated by a plus sign (+) in the tab of the lower handlebar of the text block. You can then reload the text flow icon as described above, and continue flowing text normally or by using the drag-place method of text block definition.

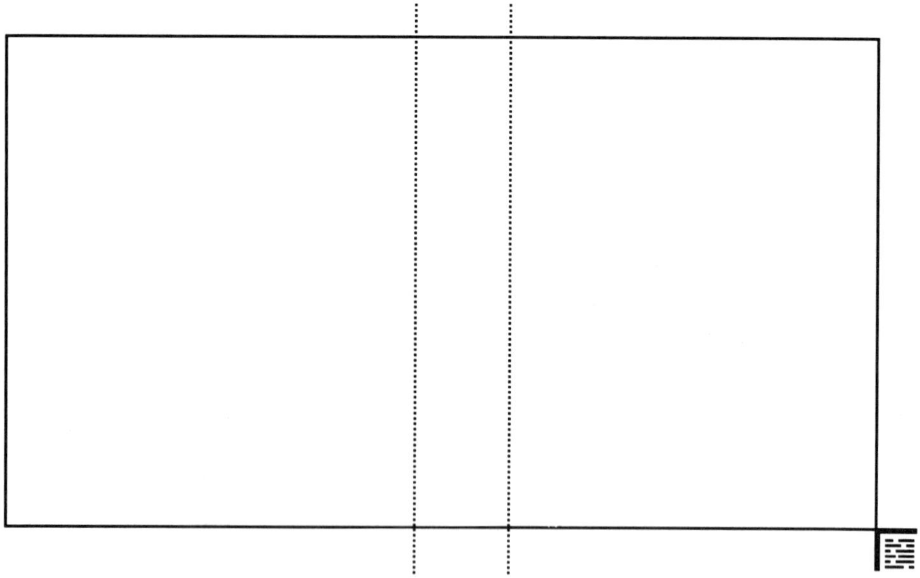

Figure 7.17: *Drag-placing with any text flow icon allows you to determine the size and placement of the new text block—regardless of column guides or margins.*

Using the Place... command to replace or insert text

In the course of creating a publication you may discover that one or more of the text documents that have already been placed is not the final version or was incomplete in some way. When this occurs, you will want to replace a story that is already positioned in your publication, or add additional text to an existing story.

This can happen for a number of reasons:

- This can happen "by surprise"—when your editor or colleague hands you the new disk and asks, "Can you use this newer version?".
- You may have done it intentionally, deciding that a document needed more editing than was appropriate for PageMaker, so you returned to the word-processor to make major changes.
- You may lay out an article and find that it is not long enough. By inserting text into a story that has already been placed, you can then work with the combined text as a single story rather than as two separate stories.
- You can update old layouts with new articles. By replacing the existing story rather than simply deleting it and placing the new text as a new story, you can preserve the position and size of the text blocks as they thread through the publication.

The process of replacing an existing story with a word-processing file or adding the text from a file to an existing story is controlled with the PLACE... command. Before choosing the PLACE... command, however, we must select the text to be replaced or set the insertion point at the location in an existing text block where the new text is to be added. Use the text tool to select any text that you want to replace, or set the insertion point where the new text should be added.

To select an entire story, including all text blocks that the text is threaded through, set the insertion point anywhere in the story and choose the SELECT ALL command from the EDIT menu (CTRL-A). To select any portion of a story, even it it extends over several pages, set the cursor at the start of the text you wish to select, locate the end of the text you wish to select (turn pages if necessary), hold down the SHIFT key, and click the mouse button. All text between the original insertion point and the SHIFT-click will be selected.

After deciding where your text is to go, and selecting any text to be replaced or setting the insertion point, choose the PLACE... command from the FILE menu (CTRL-D), and the PLACE FILE dialog box will appear (as shown in Figure 7.11). The scrolling file list on the left side of the dialog box displays the names of all text or graphic files that PageMaker can use from the current drive and sub-directory, as well as all other sub-directories and drives available. Remember that this list does not include every file in the directory, only those that PageMaker can import. The name of the drive and directory whose contents are currently being displayed appears after the "Path" option. For more information about moving between directories and drives, see the *Placing a new story* section, earlier in this chapter.

Once you've located the file you wish to place, select its filename from the scrolling list. When an eligible filename is selected, PageMaker determines whether a text or graphic file has been selected, and the first "Place" option appears as either "As new graphic" or "As new story." If the selected file is a text file, and the text insertion point was placed inside an existing text block in the publication, the last two "Place" options will become selectable in one of two possible configurations.

If any text is selected, the second option will read "Replacing entire story" and the third will read "Replacing selected text." If you want to replace the entire story with the imported text document, select the "Replacing entire story" option. To replace only the currently selected text, leaving all text before and after the selection intact, select the "Replacing selected text" option.

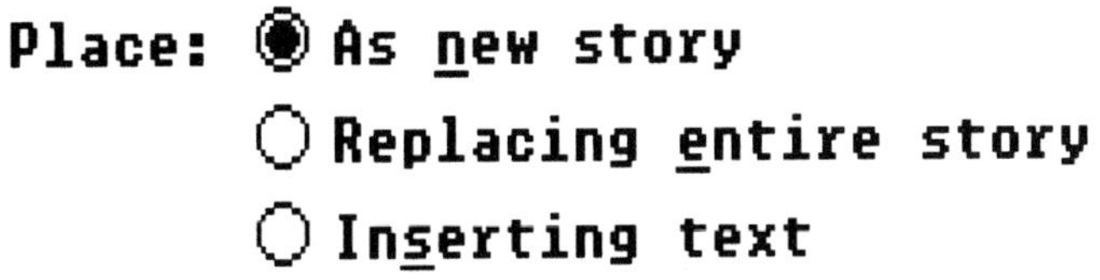

Figure 7.18: *The "Place" option from the Place document dialog box.*

If no text is selected, but the insertion point has been set inside a text block, the second option will read "Replacing entire story" and the third option will read "Inserting text." Again, selecting the "Replacing entire story" option will remove the entire story in which the cursor is set, replacing it with the newly imported document. Selecting the "Inserting text" option will add the text from the selected file to the existing story beginning at the current insertion point. Text below the insertion point will be forced through any threaded text blocks and, if the combined story is longer than the text blocks already created (indicated by a plus sign in the tab of the lower handlebar of the last text block), you will have to create a new text block in order to flow the remaining text.

In addition to the "Place" options, the "Options" options along the bottom of the PLACE dialog box will become available as soon as a text document is selected in the scrolling file listing. The operation of these options was discussed earlier in this chapter in the section *Placing a new story*.

When the correct file is selected and all the options are correctly set, click the OK button or double-click on the filename. The new text file will now replace the existing text, or add to it, as you have specified. Replacement text uses the exact same text blocks as the replaced text. If the new or added text makes the story longer than the existing text blocks can contain, you will have to create additional text blocks to hold the end of the story.

Pasting text from the Windows Clipboard

Another way of adding text to a publication, or of creating a new text block is to paste it from the Windows Clipboard. As you probably know, virtually any text or graphic element in any Windows application can be transferred to the Clipboard using the CUT and COPY commands on the EDIT menu.

Text (or graphics) on the Clipboard may have been cut or copied from one of several places:

- **Elsewhere within the current publication**, or even within the current text block.
- **Another PageMaker publication** that was closed before the current publication was opened.
- **A document in another Windows application**, perhaps one whose files cannot otherwise be transferred into PageMaker. The contents of the Clipboard are kept, even when one Windows application is closed and another Windows application, such as PageMaker, is opened.

- **A desk accessory**, such as the NotePad, which is a very simple text editor. NotePad, and many other similar desk accessories, allow you to access files stored on disk without opening the application that created those files. Once these files are opened, their contents can be transferred to the Clipboard. If the text was cut or copied from any source other than PageMaker, it will probably appear in the default type specifications currently set in the publication.

There are two ways to create a new text block for the pasted text. The first involves simply choosing the PASTE command from the EDIT menu (SHIFT-INSERT). A new text block will appear in the center of the publication window, containing all the text from the Clipboard, selected and ready for repositioning. The cursor will automatically become the arrow tool. If the text was cut or copied as a text block (with the arrow tool) from within PageMaker, the new text block will retain its original size. If text was selected with the text tool and then cut or copied, or if the text came from any source other than PageMaker, the size of the new text block will be determined by PageMaker according to its usual procedure (as described at the beginning of this chapter). In either case, the text block can be moved and resized as explained below.

The second way of creating a new text block for pasted text allows you to specify the size and location of the text block before it is created. This technique uses the drag-place method for text block creation, which we described earlier for placing a new story. To create a text block by this method, select the text tool from the toolbox, position the text tool where you want the upper left corner of the text block to be, press and hold the mouse button and drag to the lower right, creating a box that defines the width and height of the new text block. Release the mouse button and the insertion point will flash at the upper left position of original placement. No text block or box will be visible. Choose the PASTE command from the EDIT menu (SHIFT-INSERT), and the text will flow into the new text block. If the entire selection of pasted text will not fit within the text block, a plus sign will appear in the handlebar tab of the at the bottom of the now-selected text block. The remaining text can be flowed by reloading the text block and placing the additional text, as described earlier. If there is not enough text to fill the entire length of the text block, the block will be shorter than the selection box that has been created.

The drag-place method will not work if the Clipboard contains more than one text block or both text and graphics.

To add text to an existing story via the Clipboard, simply set the insertion point at the position where you want the new text inserted, and choose the PASTE command from the EDIT menu (SHIFT-INSERT). The text will be added, just as if it had been entered at that spot from the keyboard (all subsequent text in the story will flow downward through the text blocks).

Creating text with the text tool

As we've seen, PageMaker makes it very easy to import text files created in compatible word-processors. In many cases, however, we may want to create a publication with a very small amount of text, which would not require the editing features of a word-processor. Or, while working in a publication we may find that we need to create such a small amount of additional text that it is not worth quitting the application to create the text in a word-processor and then import it into our PageMaker document. For these cases, PageMaker allows us to create text directly in our publication using the text tool.

The text tool can be used to:

- add text between column guides or on the pasteboard, automatically creating a new text block.
- add text to an existing text block.
- create a new text block, then add text to it.

To add text between existing column guides, select the text tool from the toolbox, position the I-beam cursor between any two column guides, and click the mouse button. The insertion point will blink on the left edge of the column. You may now enter text from the keyboard. Text will automatically **wrap** at the right margin of the column, or carriage returns can be inserted manually. As much text can be entered as will fit between the original insertion point and the bottom of the current page. This text will automatically wrap around any graphic that has a **graphic boundary**.

If the text tool is selected and the I-beam cursor is positioned at any location that is *not* between two column guides, you may still enter as much text as you wish, but the new text block will be nearly as wide as the current page. Text may be entered into this text block until the bottom of the pasteboard is encountered. This text will also automatically wrap around any graphic that has a graphic boundary.

As we've seen, when placing text from a word-processor or pasting text from the Clipboard, we can define the size of a text block using the drag-place method. This also works with the text tool. To define the size of a text block before entering the text from the keyboard, position the I-beam cursor anywhere in the publication window, except over an existing text block, press and hold the mouse button, and drag to create a box of the size that you wish the new text block to be. When you release the mouse button, the insertion point will flash in the upper left corner of the new text block. Begin entering your text before clicking the mouse button again. This new text will be in a text block of the size defined by your drag with the I-beam.

Text created with the text tool can also be threaded through multiple text blocks. After creating a new text block, the pound sign (#) will display in the bottom handlebar tab. To thread the text, move the bottom handle up a few lines and release the mouse button. The plus sign (+) will now appear in the tab in the lower handlebar. Select the arrow tool from the toolbox and click the plus sign (+) to reload the text flow icon. You may now flow this text into another column, as described earlier in this chapter.

To add text to an existing text block, select the text tool from the toolbox, position the I-beam cursor, and click the mouse to set the flashing insertion point. You may now enter text at this position. As you add new text, all following text flows downwards through the text blocks. If the last text in the last text block no longer fits in that text block, the plus sign (+) will appear in the tab in the lower handlebar of the last text block, and you will have to reload the text flow icon and manually place the remaining text, or pull down on the tab to extend the text block.

How text wraps around graphics during text flow

Many times in the course of adding text to your publication, you will encounter graphic objects that have already been positioned on the pages of your publication. When flowing text, creating new text blocks, or moving existing text blocks, the placement of text may be interrupted by a graphic that has been assigned a **graphic boundary** via the TEXT WRAP dialog box (accessed from the TEXT WRAP... command in the OPTIONS menu).

Graphic boundaries and the TEXT WRAP command are discussed more completely in Chapter 10, *Using Graphics.* In this section, however, we will briefly introduce the effects graphic boundaries have on existing text blocks and on new text blocks as they are being created.

Graphic boundaries are created for any graphic object by selecting the graphic object, choosing the TEXT WRAP... command from the OPTIONS menu, and choosing the "Rectangular wrap" icon. A graphic boundary is initially a rectangle that is slightly larger than the graphic. The distance between sides of the graphic boundary and the graphic is determined in the "Standoff" option boxes in the TEXT WRAP dialog box. Graphic boundaries can be edited and manipulated to follow any irregular shape, as shown in Figure 7.19

Whenever a graphic boundary is positioned to overlap a text block, text will be positioned automatically so that is does not flow inside the graphic boundary. When a text block is in place before a graphic boundary is assigned to a nearby graphic, the text in the text block immeadiately reacts to the graphic boundary when it is created. When a graphic is in place before text is positioned near it, text flowing near the graphic reacts to it based on the setting of the "Text flow" option in the TEXT WRAP dialog box.

"That particular night", adds Mr. Brody, "we had another problem later on in the night which was application oriented. Had it not been for that failure, the online system would have come up close to on-time in the morning, even though we had to pull together a lot of data from scratch." Concluded Mr. Brody, "It is my feeling that we could probably recover a file no matter how heavily it is updated in approximately an hour, and most of that time would be spent storing the original back-up material to tape."

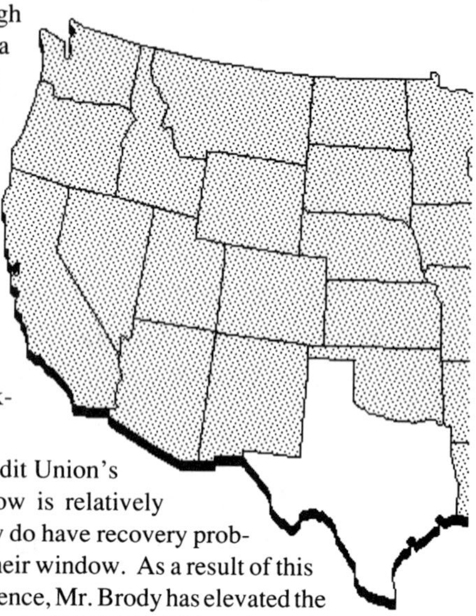

The ATC Credit Union's batch processing window is relatively tight at night, and if they do have recovery problems, it is easy to miss their window. As a result of this positive recovery experience, Mr. Brody has elevated the priority of implementing the DRS/BATCH product. In addition, he has more thoroughly evaluated the powerful functions of DRS/BATCH through a series of on-screen briefing programs designed in excite interest in the product throughout the corporate

Figure 7.19: *A custom graphic boundary causes text to wrap exactly as you specify.*

The three "Text flow" options are:

- **None**. When this option is selected, graphics will not impede the flow of text. Text will flow directly over the graphic.

- **Column break**. This option causes flowing text to jump over any graphics encountered, even if the text could wrap around the graphic boundary.
- **Wrap around**. This option causes flowing text to wrap around the graphic boundary. Text will wrap around this boundary whether it has been customized or conforms to the original values in the "Standoff" option in the TEXT WRAP dialog box.

Either of the "Text Wrap" options or the "Text Flow" options may be set or reset at any time by selecting the graphic and choosing the TEXT WRAP... command from the OPTIONS menu. Again, all aspects of the TEXT WRAP... command are discussed more completely in Chapter 10, *Using Graphics,*

Editing Text in PageMaker

In this chapter we examine:

- *Formatting characters*
- *Formatting paragraphs including indents and tabs*
- *Using hyphenation and word and letter spacing*

After adding text to a publication, you will often need to edit text (change the characters and words used, and their positions) and format that text (alter the way the text looks). Although most text editing and formatting might have been done in a word-processor before the text was placed into PageMaker, as our publication takes shape we will very often continue to alter the text. Sometimes this will be necessary because of space constraints or other limitations posed by our layout, and sometimes we will continue to edit our text because we just want to "try it a different way."

A very wide range of text editing and formatting control is provided by PageMaker. We can add, delete or move text, and we have control over character attributes such as type face, type size, and leading: paragraph attributes, such as margins, paragraph spacing, and tabs: and document attributes, such as hyphenation and character spacing.

Setting the insertion point and selecting text

Before learning to perform any text editing or formatting, we must learn two basic operations: moving our cursor within text blocks, and selecting text. As we shall see in the following sections, positioning our cursor is the first step in selecting, adding, deleting, formatting, or moving text.

Moving inside a text block

In Chapter 7, *Creating and Adding Text*, we learned that text in PageMaker exists within text blocks. The determination of which text block we are working in is made by selecting the text tool and clicking inside an existing text block. There is no other way to move from one text block to another.

Once we are inside a specific text block, however, there are several ways to move the **insertion point** (flashing vertical cursor):

- **With the mouse.** This allows us to reposition the text tool anywhere in the text block (or in any text block), and then click the mouse button to set the insertion point anywhere we desire.

- **With the arrow keys on the keyboard**. The right or left arrow key move the insertion point one character forward or backward, while the up or down arrow keys move the insertion point one line up or down. Pressing the CTRL key and the right or left arrow key moves the insertion point one word forward or backward, while the CTRL key and the up or down key moves the insertion point one paragraph up or down.

- **With the number pad keys**. The HOME and END keys move the cursor to the beginning and to the end of the line, respectively. Press CTRL-HOME to move to the beginning of a sentence, and CTRL-END to move to the end of a sentence. The PAGE UP and PAGE DOWN keys moves the cursor up or down one screen at a time, and pressing CTRL-PAGE UP or CTRL-PAGE DOWN moves the cursor to the beginning or end of a story.

Selecting text

Text is selected in PageMaker in order to apply some command or action to that text. Selected text is displayed on-screen in reverse video or in color, as shown in Figure 8.01. There are several ways to select text in PageMaker:

- **With the mouse**. Drag over the characters that you want to select, character by character. Dragging upward or downward will select additional lines of text, and dragging across columns of a threaded story will select portions of each threaded block. Double-clicking the mouse on a word selects that word and the space following it; triple-clicking inside a paragraph will select the entire paragraph. Holding down the mouse button after the second or third click and dragging will select additional words or paragraphs.

This utility allows you to look at every field (data item) in a time or A/R record. This includes fields which are hidden within the record and which are accessible only through this utility. Data items within these records can be viewed or changed, or the entire record can be deleted. We suggest that you use this utility to view records, or possibly delete them, but do not change items within these records except as a last resort.

Figure 8.01: *Selected text is displayed as white on black.*

- **With the mouse and the keyboard**. Set the insertion point at the beginning of the text you want to select, move the mouse cursor to the end of the text you want to select, press the SHIFT key and click the mouse button. All text between the original insertion point and the SHIFT-click will be selected.

- **With the SELECT ALL command**. Set the insertion point anywhere in the text block and choose the SELECT ALL command from the EDIT menu (CTRL-A) to select all the text in the story, including all text threaded through text blocks on all pages.

- **With the keyboard**. Use keyboard equivalents to select text. Holding down the SHIFT key while pressing the right or left arrow keys selects one character at a time; holding down the SHIFT key and pressing the up or down key selects one line at a time. Holding down the CTRL and SHIFT keys and pressing the right or left arrow key selects one word at a time. Holding down the CTRL and SHIFT keys and pressing the up or down arrows select one paragraph at a time. You can also used the SHIFT key to select text in conjunction with the HOME, END, PAGE UP, and PAGE DOWN keys.

Text editing basics

Editing text in PageMaker is very much like editing text in a standard word-processor—you can add text anywhere in the existing text, delete any of the existing text, or move sections of text from one place to another.

Before beginning to edit text in PageMaker, remember that PageMaker is not intended to be used as a word-processor. If your document needs extensive editing, return to your word-processing software to perform the text editing. If changes have already been made to the text as it appears in PageMaker, you can export the text back into word-processing format, as described later in this chapter. In either case, you will be able to use PageMaker's ability to replace existing text, as described in the Chapter 7, to bring your text back into PageMaker after editing is complete.

PageMaker's text editing abilities are ideally suited to both relatively minor text editing and to the creation of smaller text blocks, such as those used in headlines, captions, and flyers. By recognizing and respecting the limits of PageMaker's text editing abilities, you save yourself time and improve the overall quality of all your publications.

Adding text in a text block

To add text in an existing text block, position the insertion point at the position where you want the text to begin (using the methods discussed above), and enter the new text from the keyboard. If you are inserting text in a text block that is not threaded to other text blocks, all text following the newly inserted text will move down in the text block, and some text might become hidden below the lower handlebar of the text block. If this occurs, you may drag downward on the tab in the lower handlebar to expose the hidden text, or click the plus sign (+) in the lower handlebar tab and then flow the additional text into another text block.

If you are inserting text into a text block that is threaded to other text blocks, the lines below your insertion will move downward and all lines in the thread will flow accordingly. If the last text block in the thread cannot contain the extra text, you must either extend that text block or click the plus sign (+) in the tab in the lower handlebar and flow the remaining text into another new text block.

Moving text from one place to another

Text can be moved from one place to another by selecting the text to be moved using one of the selection techniques discussed above, and then using some combination of the CUT, COPY and PASTE commands.

Choosing the CUT command (SHIFT-DELETE) from the EDIT Menu will delete the selected text from its current location and transfer it to the Windows Clipboard. Choosing the COPY command (CTRL-INSERT) from the EDIT menu will leave a copy of the text at its current location but also add a copy to the Clipboard. Once a copy of the text to be moved is on the Clipboard, position the insertion point at the location where you want the text to be moved to, and choose the PASTE command (SHIFT-INSERT) from the EDIT menu. This transfers a copy of the Clipboard's contents to the insertion point.

Text from the Clipboard may be pasted into an existing text block, or into a newly created text block. When pasting text into an existing text block, if any text is selected when the PASTE command is chosen, the selected text will be deleted replaced with the pasted text.

Deleting text

To delete any text from your publication, select the text to be deleted (using one of the selection techniques described above) and choose the CUT command from the EDIT menu (SHIFT-DELETE) or press the DELETE key. If you use the CUT command, the deleted text is placed on the Clipboard, making it easy to retrieve the deleted text (until something else is cut or copied). Deletions made using the DELETE key are not transferred to the Clipboard, leaving the contents of the Clipboard unaffected. Text deleted in this manner, however, can only be retrieved by choosing the UNDO command immeadiately after making the deletion. Either method of deletion can be undone using the UNDO command from the EDIT menu immediately after it is executed.

You can also delete text by selecting it and replacing it with text from the keyboard (typing over it) or Clipboard (pasting over it).

Text formatting basics

PageMaker supports character-level formatting (type face, type size, leading, and other attributes that are set on a character-by-character basis), paragraph-level formatting (alignment, margins, and other attributes set on a paragraph-by-paragraph basis), and document-level formatting (in the case of PageMaker, "story level" formatting, which includes attributes such as hyphenation and spacing that can be set only for an entire story).

- **Character** (font, type size, leading):*Each character must be selected to be changed.*
- **Paragraph** (alignment, indents, tabs): *Any part of paragraph must be selected to be changed.*
- **Story** (spacing, hyphenation): *Any part of story must be selected to be changed.*

Figure 8.02: *The levels of text formatting, example attributes, and how they must be selected in order to be reformatted.*

In order to change character formatting, specific text characters must be selected before the options are reset. In order to change any paragraph-level formatting attributes, the insertion point must be set in any paragraph to be modified, or at least one character of the paragraph must be selected. To change story-level attributes, some text in the story must be selected, or the insertion point must be set somewhere in the story.

If no text is selected when any character specifications are changed, and the insertion point has been set in a text block, the new settings will apply to new text entered at the insertion point (as long as the insertion point is not reset). If the insertion point has not been set, or if the text tool is not selected, any changes to character, paragraph, and story specifications become the default settings for any new text blocks later created with the text tool. In this case, existing text blocks are not affected.

Formatting text characters

Each character in your publication, regardless of whether it was created in PageMaker or imported from a word-processor, can be set in a variety of fonts, type sizes, and other text characteristics. The commands used to set the type specifications are found in the TYPE menu. The TYPE menu provides several commands to quickly change type styles and paragraph alignment, as well as the TYPE SPECS... command, which brings up the TYPE SPECIFICATIONS dialog box containing the complete set of character formatting options.

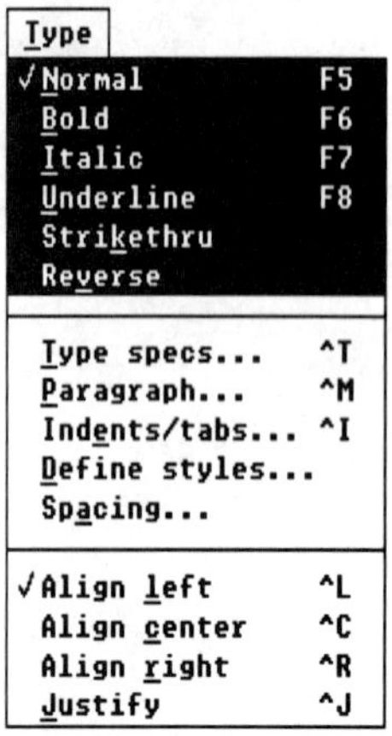

The "quick" type styles

The first six commands in the TYPE menu are used to quickly access the most common type styles used in publications: NORMAL (F5), BOLD (F6), ITALIC (F7), UNDERLINE (F8), STRIKETHRU, and REVERSE. These type styles can also be selected in the TYPE SPECS... command, described below.

To use any of these commands, first select the text to which you wish to apply the type style, and then simply choose the appropriate style command or keyboard equivalent. Any styles that are applied to the currently selected text are indicated with a check mark (✓). If none of these styles apply to the selected text, or if the currently selected text is not all set with the same type style, none of the commands will display the check mark (✓). To cancel a type style that has been applied to the selected text, select the appropriate type style command, and the style will be removed and the check mark will disappear from before the command.

The Type specs... command

Choosing the TYPE SPECS... command in the TYPE menu (CTRL–T) brings up the TYPE SPECIFICATIONS dialog box, as shown in Figure 8.03, which contains options offering full control over the attributes of the currently selected text.

The "Font" option displays a scrolling list of all type faces currently available. If the selected text is set in one of these type faces, its name is highlighted. If the currently selected text is not set in one of these type faces, or if all of the currently selected text is not set in the same font, no type face is highlighted. Clicking on any font name applies that font to all of the currently selected text. If you load a publication that contains fonts no longer installed on your computer, the font name will appear, dimmed, on the font list. You cannot select a dimmed font.

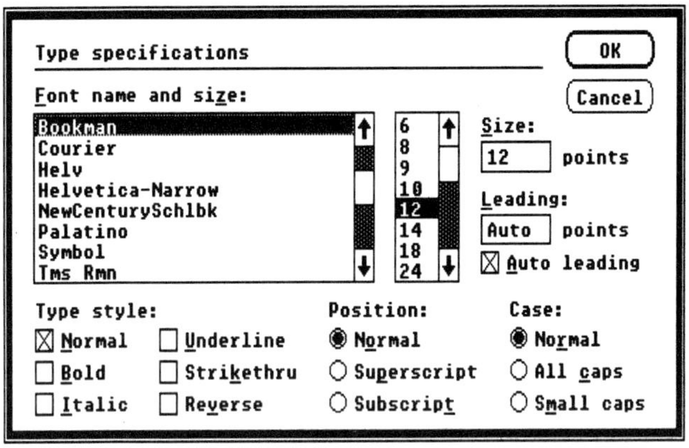

Figure 8.03: *The Type specifications dialog box.*

Font names in the scrolling list are listed alphabetically, with the listing centered on the currently selected typeface. For example, if the current font is "Aachen," most of the listing will be below; if the current font is "Zapf Dingbats," most of the listing will be above. Scrolling up or down the list will allow you to see all available fonts.

The "Size" option controls the type size, in points, of the currently selected text. The "Size" option lists available type sizes, and the option box lists the size of the currently selected text. The type size of the currently selected text is displayed in the option box unless the selected text is not in the same type size. If you are using a PostScript printer, you can enter any value between 4 and 127 in single-point increments in the option box. Non-PostScript users must use only the font sizes provided in the scrolling list, because most non-PostScript printers cannot scale fonts and must use only specific font sizes that are loaded or available for downloading.

The "Leading" option includes only an option box. This option box displays the leading as set for the currently selected text, unless the selected text includes more than one leading option. Any value between 4 and 127 in .5-point increments may be entered in this option box, or the word "Auto," which stands for *automatic leading*. "Auto" is, by default, 120% of the current type size (10-point type would use 12-point leading, 14-point type would use 17-point leading). Using the "Auto leading" option in the SPACING dialog box, you can control the percentage used to calculate "Auto" leading, setting it to any value between 100% and 200%.

Leading controls the amount of vertical space between lines of text. Leading was originally named after the lead shafts that were placed between lines of type on old typesetting and printing machines. PageMaker can apply leading in two ways. "Proportional" leading applies two-thirds of the space above the baseline and one-third of the space below the baseline, while "Top of caps" leading is measured from the top of a capital letter to the top of a capital letter in the line below. You can select which of these leading measurement methods PageMaker will use in the SPACING dialog box, using the "Leading method" option.

Leading control allows you to significantly affect the amount of space taken up by your text, and the "look and feel" of the text. Type set with loose leading is often easier to read than type set with a tight leading, but of course requires more space. You should always feel free to experiment with leading—it is one of the easiest and most significant ways to change any publication. If you are uncertain as to what leading to use, the "Auto" leading option is usually appropriate.

Any time that one line of text contains characters with two or more different leading specifications, the largest leading setting will prevail. When making a large initial capital letter, for example, you might have a 24-point character on the same line as 12-point characters. If both the 24-point character and the 12-point character use "Auto" leading, then the entire line will be set at 29-point leading (the "Auto" leading for the 24-point character), and the leading will be larger than required for the body text. This can be corrected by changing the leading for the 24-point character to 14-point or smaller, so that the "Auto" leading of the 12-point character will be the larger leading and therefore will prevail.

The "Case" option provides three alternatives for the case of the selected text: "Normal," which sets the text in upper and lower case; "All Caps," which sets the text in all capital letters, regardless of how it was input originally, and "Small Caps," which sets all characters entered as capital letters as full size capital letters and all characters entered as lowercase letters in capital letters that are only 70% as tall as full size capital letters.

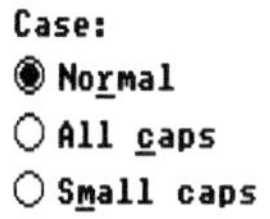

The "Position" option also offers three alternatives: "Normal" positions characters with their **baselines** on the same baseline as all other characters on the line. "Superscript" positions the characters' baselines slightly above the baseline, and "Subscript" positions the characters' baselines slightly below the baseline. Often, in addition to superscripting or subscripting characters, you will want to make them a few point sizes larger or smaller for additional emphasis.

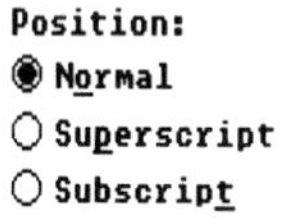

The "Type style" option consists of six options, each of which has a check box in front of it. Any of these options may be selected by clicking the check box or clicking on the

style name. Most of these type styles have keyboard equivalents, as listed in at the end of Chapter 3, *Terms, Tools, and Menus*. Selecting the "Normal" option deselects all other options. Selecting any of the options other than the "Normal" option deselects the "Normal" option.

The "Type style" option, generally speaking, alters the current type face mathematically to produce the requested style effect. If you select a style for which there is a corresponding stylized screen and printer font (such as selecting the bold type style for the type face Helvetica instead of selecting the type face Helvetica Bold), the true stylized type face is not used—the mathematically created type style is used instead. This is important because these mathematically achieved effects are not as accurate as the specifically designed stylized type faces. They do, however, offer some effects not otherwise available (such as underline and strikethru). In general, try to use the stylized fonts themselves (Helvetica Bold) rather than using the plain screen font (Helvetica) and applying the type style (Bold).

After setting the options in the TYPE SPECIFICATIONS dialog, click the OK button to apply the changes that you have made, or click the CANCEL button to negate them and return to the previous settings.

Formatting Paragraphs

PageMaker's paragraph-level formatting includes margins, tabs, space before and after paragraphs, and alignment. Some of these attributes are controlled in the PARAGRAPH SPECIFICATIONS dialog box, others in the INDENTS/TABS dialog box.

Controlling paragraph indents

Every paragraph has left, right, and first-line indents. These settings force the offset of the text in the paragraph from the text block margins. Paragraph indents can be set using options in the PARAGRAPH SPECIFICATIONS dialog (accessed by choosing the PARAGRAPH... command from the TYPE menu, or pressing CTRL-M), or using the ruler and options in the INDENTS/TABS dialog (accessed by choosing the INDENTS/TABS... command from the TYPE menu, or pressing CTRL-I). Either of these methods applies only to the paragraphs within the current selection.

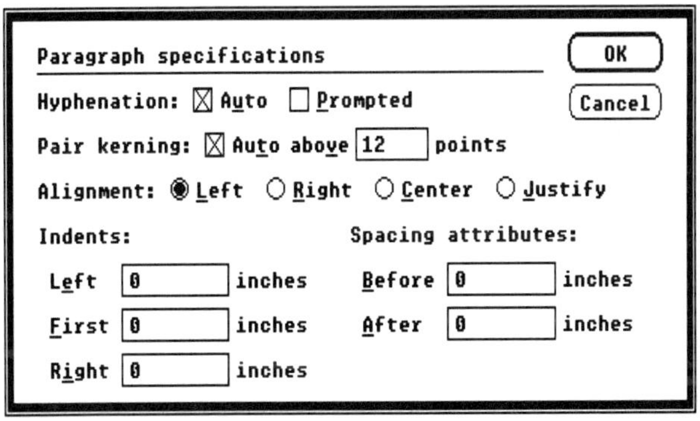

Figure 8.04: *The Paragraph specifications dialog box.*

The PARAGRAPH SPECIFICATIONS dialog includes three options governing the indents for any particular paragraph:

- The "Left" indent option specifies the position of the left edge of each line in the paragraph relative to the left edge of the text block. The first line of the text block is also positioned according to the "First" indent option as described below.

- The "Right" indent option specifies the position of the right edge of every line in the paragraph relative to the right edge of the text block.
- The "First" indent option specifies the position of the left edge of the first line of type in a text block relative to the left edge of the other lines in the paragraph (as specified by the "Left" indent option).

  To create a paragraph where the first line has a more pronounced indent than the other lines of the paragraph (an effect which is traditionally accomplished by placing a tab character before the first line of a paragraph), enter the indent distance in the "First" indent option box. To create a paragraph where the first line begins to the left of all other lines in the paragraph (as in the previous paragraph), the "First" indent value should be given a negative value relative to the left margin. Note that the "First" line indent can only be as negative as the "Left" indent is positive, or the specification would call for the first line to begin outside the text block.

The ruler inside the INDENTS/TABS dialog box (see Figure 8.06) provides a more direct method of altering the indents for selected paragraphs. This ruler always uses the current unit of measure and is magnified to the current view size (the larger the view size the less measure the ruler can display). Although only a portion of the ruler is displayed within the dialog box, it can be scrolled by clicking on the arrows at either end of the ruler. The INDENTS/TABS dialog box can be repositioned on the screen by dragging on its title bar. This allows you to position the ruler so that its zero point is aligned with the left edge of the current text bock. Regardless of the actual on-screen position of the ruler, its zero point represents the left edge of the current text block.

This utility allows you to look at every field (data item) in a time or A/R record. This includes fields which are hidden within the record and which are accessible only through this utility. Data items within these records can be viewed or changed, or the entire record can be deleted. We suggest that you use this utility to view records, or possibly delete them, but do not change items within these records except as a last resort.

- This utility allows you to look at every field (data item) in a time or A/R record.
- This includes fields which are hidden within the record and which are accessible only through this utility.
- Data items within these records can be viewed or changed, or the entire record can be deleted. We suggest that you use this utility to

Figure 8.05: *The paragraph on the left has a positive first-line indent; the paragraphs on the right have negative first-line indents.*

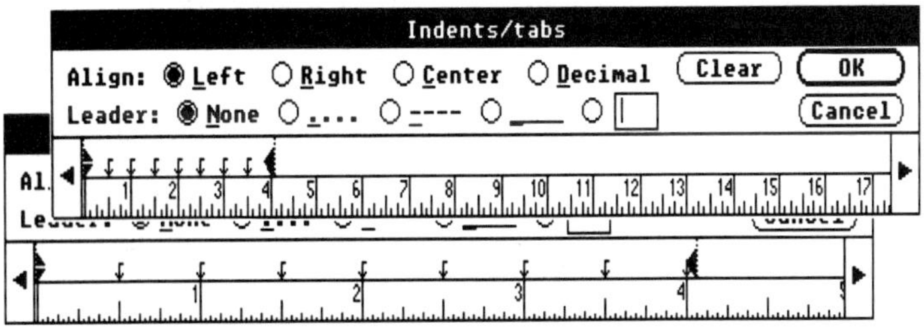

Figure 8.06: *The Indents/Tabs dialog as it appears at two different view sizes. The first-line indent arrow is above and to the right of the left indent arrow .*

Three triangles appear inside the ruler representing the "Left" indent, "Right" indent, and "First" indent. The position of these markers, and therefore the settings of these indent options, can be adjusted by dragging them within the ruler. As an indent is dragged, its location is displayed in the current unit of measure below the Clear button. When the Indents/Tabs... command is chosen, the indents of the currently selected paragraphs are displayed above the ruler in the Indents/Tabs dialog box. If all the selected paragraphs do not have the same indent settings, the indents of the first selected paragraph are displayed. After adjusting the indent markers as required, click the OK button to apply the changes made to the indents, or click the Cancel button to return to the publication window without changing the indent settings.

Working with tabs

The Indents/Tabs dialog box is also used to manipulate the tab settings for any paragraph or group of paragraphs. Like margins settings, tab settings are applied to any paragraph that is fully or partially selected when the Indents/tabs... command is chosen from the Type menu.

The Indents/Tabs dialog displays the current tab settings for the selected paragraph(s) when it is opened. Tabs appear in the space just above the ruler tick marks. If the selected paragraphs do not all have the same indent and tab settings the space above the ruler bar is dimmed, indicating that all currently selected paragraphs are not identical and that the positions of the indent and tab markers in the ruler do not correspond to all the selected text. You can still manipulate tab settings if this occurs, and any changes made will apply to all selected paragraphs.

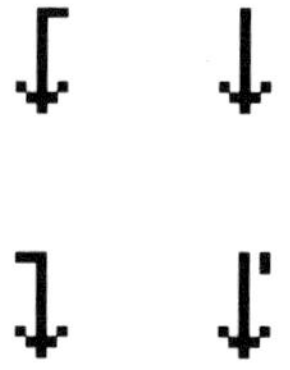

PageMaker supports four types of tabs; "Left," "Right," "Center," and "Decimal." Each of these tabs has a unique icon, which is displayed in the ruler when the tab is set. Any PageMaker tab can have a *tab leader*, which fills the space between the position where the tab key is pressed and the tabbed text is positioned. PageMaker supports a dotted leader, a dashed line leader, an underline leader, and a custom leader, that allows you to enter any character, or characters, to be used as the tab leader. Leaders serve as a visual reference between items on a line, making it easier for the eye to follow the line to the tabbed item. Tabs must be created with leader characters—you cannot assign a leader to an existing tab.

Tab leader none

Tab leader .... dot leader

Tab leader-------------------------------- dash leader

Tab leader ______________________ underline leader

Tab leader zzzzzzzzzzzzzzzzzzzzzz character leader

Figure 8.07: *Tab leaders begin where the tab key is pressed and end where the tab stop is positioned.*

By default, each PageMaker paragraph has a left tab stop, with no leader, positioned at each ½-inch increment in the paragraph.

You may reset these tab stops, add new stops, delete specific stops, or manipulate existing stops.

- **To remove all the existing tabs** and reset the paragraph indents, click the CLEAR button.
- **To add a new tab**, click the radio button next to the icon representing the kind of tab that you want to create, click the radio button next to the icon representing the kind of tab leader you want to use (enter the "Custom" leader in the

option box, if appropriate), and then click the mouse button in the ruler to create the new tab. You cannot create a new tab on top of an existing indent marker. Instead, you must create the tab elsewhere and then drag it into position over the indent marker.

- **To check the position and leader of an existing tab**, click on the tab icon in the ruler. The position of the tab will be displayed under the CLEAR button. The radio buttons will become selected, indicating the kind of tab and tab leader that has been selected.

- **To reset an existing tab**, select the tab icon and drag it horizontally in the ruler. As you move the tab icon, its current position will be displayed below the CLEAR button. Release the tab when you are satisfied with the new location. Positioning tabs is made easier by repositioning the ruler so that the zero point corresponds to the left margin of the current text block. This is done by either dragging the title bar of the INDENTS/TABS dialog box or using the scrolling arrow on each end of the ruler.

- **To delete a tab**, drag the tab icon down below the ruler and release the mouse button. The tab icon will fall into oblivion. To remove all the tab stops for the current paragraph, click the CLEAR button and all tabs will be removed.

Paragraph alignment (justification)

Any paragraph in PageMaker can be aligned to the left, to the right, centered, or fully justified. Paragraph alignment is adjusted relative to the width of the paragraph's text block. Paragraph alignment can be adjusted for any paragraph that is fully or partially selected.

There are three ways to change the alignment for a paragraph:

- Use the "Alignment" option in the PARAGRAPH SPECIFICATIONS dialog box, which is accessed by choosing the PARAGRAPH... command (CTRL-M) in the TYPE menu.
- Use one of the "quick" alignment commands in the TYPE menu: ALIGN LEFT, ALIGN CENTER, ALIGN RIGHT, and JUSTIFY.
- Use keyboard equivalents for each of the alignment options: CTRL-L for "Left," CTRL-R for "Right," CTRL-C for "Center," and CTRL-J for "Justified."

Hyphenating text

The professionalism and quality of any publication is substantially affected by the quality of its hyphenation. Many documents produced with early desktop publishing suffered with terrible "rivers" of white space caused by the then-prevalent lack of sophisticated hyphenation capabilities. PageMaker 3.0 provides very powerful hyphenation capabilities that can be easily used to produce professional-looking publications.

In general you will want to hyphenate most body text used in your PageMaker publications. In most cases, headlines, subheads, captions and other short text passages should not be hyphenated.

There are three levels of hyphenation available in PageMaker:

- **Automatic hyphenation** uses the 110,000-word Houghton Mifflin Company hyphenation dictionary to hyphenate your entire publication.
- **Prompted hyphenation** is applied on a paragraph-by-paragraph basis as you require it. Each word eligible for hyphenation is displayed along with suggested hyphenation points, which can be accepted or augmented with an additional hyphenation point.
- **Manual hyphenation** involves the insertion of *discretionary hyphens* into the text. These are inserted manually, wherever you see fit.

Automatic hyphenation

Automatic hyphenation is turned on or off by selecting the "Automatic" option in the Paragraph specifications dialog box. This is accessed by choosing the Paragraph... command (ctrl-M) in the Type menu while the insertion point is anywhere inside one of the text blocks of the story. This option is selected by default, and you will want to leave it on in most circumstances. Automatic hyphenation is applied to an entire story—it cannot be used for a single paragraph within a story. Either every text block in a story is hyphenated, or none is hyphenated.

Automatic hyphenation will hyphenate text as it is placed into your publication, entered with the text entry tool, or any time the size of a text block is modified. If you simply set the insertion point inside the text block, choose the "Auto Hyphenation" option, and click the OK button in the PARAGRAPH SPECIFICATIONS dialog box, the story will not be hyphenated until it is resized.

To delete any hyphens that PageMaker has automatically added to your document, position the cursor to the right of the inserted hyphen and press CTRL-DELETE.

Prompted hyphenation

When automatic hyphenation is not being used, or when you wish to add additional hyphens to a paragraph that has already been automatically hyphenated, the "Prompted Hyphenation" option in the PARAGRAPH SPECIFICATIONS dialog box can be selected. To use this option, select the text to be hyphenated, and then select the "Prompted Hyphenation" option in the PARAGRAPH SPECIFICATIONS dialog box. Prompted hyphenation applies only to the currently selected text. After selecting the "Prompted" option, click the OK button to begin the prompted hyphenation process.

If any words in the selected text are eligible for additional hyphenation, the dialog box shown in Figure 8.07 will then appear. This dialog displays the word to be hyphenated along with several words that appear before and after it in the the text. Any hyphens previously added by automatic hyphenation, manual hyphenation, or earlier prompted hyphenation will be displayed in the selected word. To add new hyphens, simply click between the appropriate characters and a hyphen will appear. You may add as many hyphens as you wish. Click the NEXT button to repeat the process until all words eligible for hyphenation have been viewed. Double-clicking between two characters adds the hyphen and goes on to the next word. You may also click the STOP button at any time to end the prompted hyphenating session.

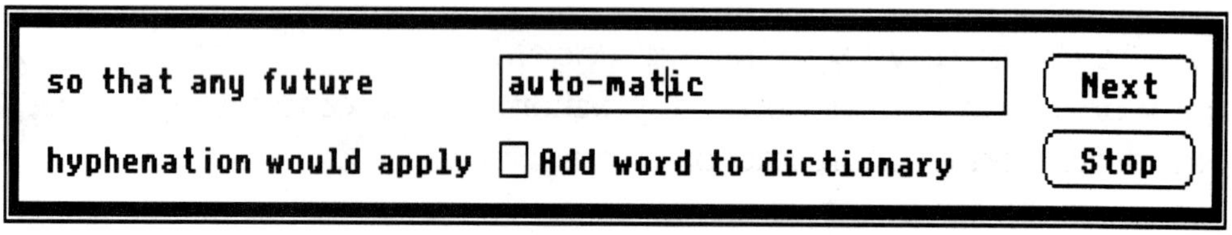

Figure 8.08: The Prompted hyphenation dialog box.

If you wish to add any newly hyphenated word to your personal hyphenation dictionary, so that any future automatic hyphenation would apply the hyphens that you have defined, click the "add word to dictionary" option below the newly hyphenated word. Added words are placed in the PMUSUSER.TXT file on your hard disk. This file will be automatically used in all future hyphenating as long as it is available on your hard disk.

To delete any hyphens that have been added via prompted hyphenation, position the cursor to the right of the inserted hyphen and press the DELETE key.

Manual hyphenation

While PageMaker's automatic and prompted hyphenation provide efficient methods of hyphenating long text passages, quite frequently you will want to manually hyphenate your text to quickly correct obvious hyphenation problems. The best way to do this involves the use of PageMaker's **discretionary hyphens**. Discretionary hyphens are placed between characters by setting the insertion point with the text tool and pressing CTRL-- (hyphen key). A discretionary hyphen will appear only if the word can be successfully hyphenated at the point at which the hyphen is inserted; if the word cannot be hyphenated at that point, the discretionary hyphen remains hidden until the text is changed so that it can be used.

To delete a visible discretionary hyphen, position the insertion point to the right of the hyphen and press CTRL-DELETE. To delete a discretionary hyphen that is not visible, position the insertion point between the two characters where the discretionary hyphen is located and press the BACKSPACE key. No character will be deleted but the invisible hyphen will be removed.

You may also insert normal hyphens into your text by simply pressing the hyphen key. These are called **hard hyphens**. The use of hard hyphens is not advised because if the width of your paragraph changes, or if the text is edited, the hyphen may no longer appear at the end of a line but will still appear in the text. Hard hyphens should be used only when you want the hyphen to appear regardless of its position.

Hyphenating justified vs. unjustified text

In addition to the hyphenation method being used, hyphenation also depends on the current alignment setting of the paragraphs being hyphenated, the settings of the "Word space" and "Letter space" options in the SPACING dialog box, and the setting of the "Hyphenation zone" option in the Spacing dialog box.

When hyphenating unjustified text, the setting of the "Hyphenation zone" option in the Spacing dialog box determines whether or not PageMaker attempts to hyphenate words for a particular line, and if so, where the hyphen is placed. If a word ends within the defined hyphenation zone, PageMaker does not try to hyphenate the next word—it is moved to the next line. If the last complete word in a line ends before the hyphenation zone, PageMaker tries to hyphenate the first word on the next line. The larger the "Hyphenation zone," the more ragged the right edge of unjustified text will remain.

It has been my good fortune the past three years
to have been directly involved in the leadership
of AIESEC. As President, I have traveled exten-
sively, meeting many of our individual members
and those who represent their respective choirs
and national organizations. I have participated in
the planning and administration of the Federa-
tion's activities, most specifically the World
Symposium on Development I. And I have sta-
bilized the financial base of AIESEC. This brief
report will highlight the principal areas of my
work during this three-year tenure.

Figure 8.09: *Unjustified text is hyphenated so that a line ends, whether naturally or with a hyphen, within the hyphenation zone whenever possible.*

When hyphenating justified text, the setting of the "Hyphenation zone" option has no effect. Instead, the determination of which word is hyphenated, and where it is hyphenated, is based in part on the "Word space" and "Letter space" options in the Spacing dialog box. These options, which are described fully in the next section of this chapter, determine how much "play" is allowable in the positioning of characters and words and indirectly, how crucial hyphenation becomes. If hyphenation is impossible according to the current settings of these options, PageMaker overrides the "Word space" settings and positions words in order to correctly justify the text.

Character spacing and kerning

To determine the positioning of each character in a text block relative to the character immediately before and after it, PageMaker relies on information that is included with the screen font or font metric file. This information, determined by the font designer, specifies the amount of space that the character occupies (its width) and the amount of space that should be placed before and after the character (its side bearing), as shown in Figure 8.10. In most cases, characters are positioned according to these specifications, and the result is legible, aesthetically pleasing text. In other cases, however, these default characters spacings are not satisfactory, and you might want to manipulate them.

There are three aspects of character spacing that you may manipulate:

- Spacing between specific pairs of characters.
- Spacing between all characters in a group.
- Spacing between words.

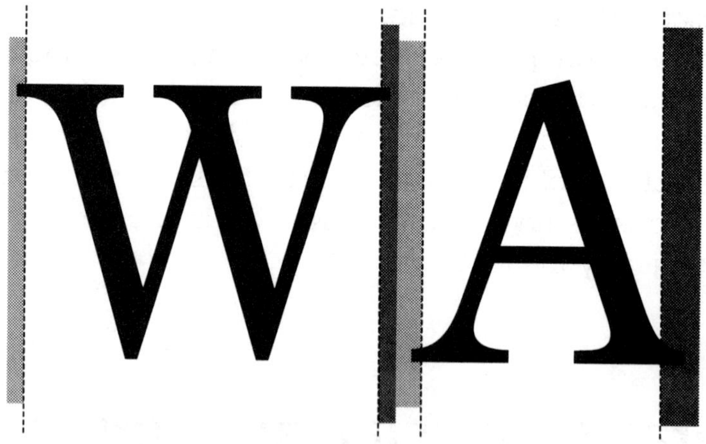

Figure 8.10: *Each character has a width (shown as thin vertical lines) and a left and right side bearing (shown as light and dark gray areas, respectively).*

Pair kerning

In most cases, the space between any two characters is determined by the right bearing of the first character and the left bearing of the second character. However, when font designers specify the width and side bearing of each character in a type face, they also specify certain pairs of letters for which the space between them should be an amount other than the right bearing of the first character and the left bearing of the second character. These letter pairs are called **kerning pairs**. Whenever two characters of a kerning pair appear next to each other, they should be spaced according to the kerning pair information.

PageMaker is capable of using kerning pair information to accurately position characters, but rather than doing so in all cases, it allows you to specify when pair kerning should be performed. Because kerned pairs take longer to display on-screen, you might not always want pair kerning performed. In some cases, you may decide that the improvements in character placement accuracy are not worth the cost in screen refresh rate; therefore you may turn off pair kerning.

Because the benefits of pair kerning are more apparent for larger type sizes, PageMaker allows you to specify a point size above which all kerning pairs will be accurately spaced. Type set in sizes below this threshold does not use the kerning pair information. It is also possible to turn pair kerning off entirely.

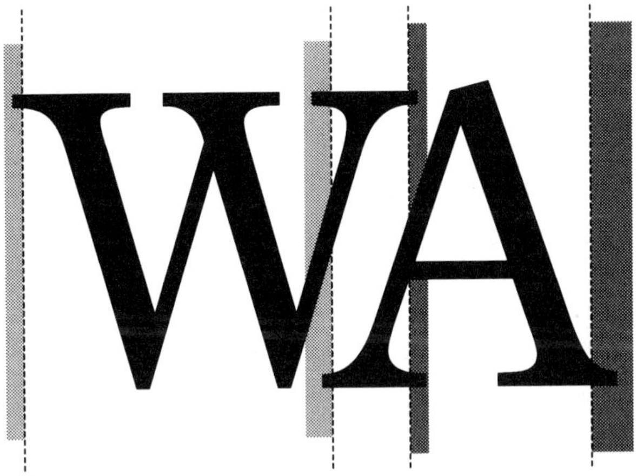

Figure 8.11: *Certain pairs of letters are defined as kerning pairs and have specific spacings when next to each other, regardless of their normal side bearings.*

To adjust the pair kerning used in a document, select the PARAGRAPH... command (CTRL-M) from the TYPE menu. Deselecting the "Pair kerning" option turns off all pair kerning, selecting this option enables pair kerning for type set in sizes larger that that specified in the "above ____ points" option box. By default, PageMaker uses pair kerning on type sizes larger than 12 points. While this is acceptable as a general rule, when creating publications with body copy set in 9-point, 10-point, or 11-point, you might wish to lower the pair kerning threshold.

You can also kern letter pairs manually, adding or removing very small amounts of space between letters. Space can be added or removed between characters in increments of $\frac{1}{48}$ point size. This means that the smallest amount of space you can add or delete between 48-point characters is one point; between 12-point characters, the minimum amount of space that can be added or deleted is $\frac{1}{4}$ point.

To delete space between characters, position the insertion point between the characters and press CTRL-DELETE. To add space between characters, position the insertion point between the characters and press CTRL-SHIFT-DELETE.

In many cases, you will not be able to see a visible difference as you add or delete space because the display is not sufficiently accurate. Whenever possible, zoom in to "200%," or even "400%" view size when kerning characters manually. In any case, the spacing will be adjusted accurately when output on a high-resolution printer.

Space between all characters and words

In addition to manipulating the amount of space placed between a specific pair of characters, you can also control the amount of space between all characters and between all words in a story by using options in the SPACING ATTRIBUTES dialog box. There are two primary reasons for manipulating overall spacing:

- This allows you to give a story a "tighter" or "looser" look or to adjust the amount of space that the story requires. This is primarily controlled with the "Desired" options
- Controlling the amount of spacing indirectly affects the hyphenation. This is primarily controlled with the "Minimum" and "Maximum" options.

The amount of space placed between characters and between words is controlled as a percentage of the amount of space predefined by the font designer.

Theamountof spaceplacedbetweencharacters andbetweenwords iscontrolledasapercentageofthe amountofspace predefinedbythe fontdesigner.

The amount of space placed between characters and between words is controlled as a percentage of the amount of space predefined by the font designer.

Figure 8.12: *Examples of normal letter and word spacing, tight word spacing, and tight letter spacing.*

The amount of space set between characters and between words is specified as a percentage of the default space defined by the font designer. PageMaker allows you to specify the minimum, maximum, and desired percentages for both word and letter spacing. All these options are used when text is being justified, but only the "Desired" options affect unjustified text.

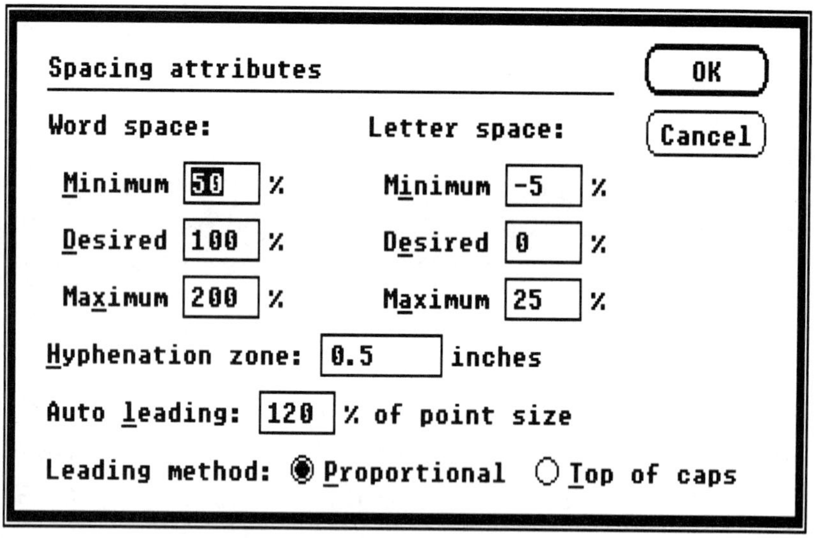

Figure 8.13: *The Spacing attributes dialog box.*

When justifying text, PageMaker attempts to maintain the "Desired" spacing percentage, but will reduce spacing to the amount specified for the "Minimum" option, or expand spacing to the amount specified for the "Maximum" option, if necessary. As discussed in the previous section of this chapter, the current setting of the "Hyphenation" option affects the magnitude of spacing manipulation required to justify text. The more hyphenation that is possible, the closer PageMaker will be able to conform to the "Desired" spacing percentages. If PageMaker is unable to hyphenate text enough to justify any paragraphs while staying within the spacing boundaries defined by the "Word space" and "Letter space" options, it will ignore the "Word space" options and manipulate word space as required in order to justify the text.

For unjustified text, only the "Desired" options are applied. All word and letter spacing will be implemented exactly as the "Desired" option specifies, and hyphenation will depend upon the results of this spacing, the current setting of the "Hyphenation" option, and the current setting of the "Hyphenation zone" option.

Spacing options can be changed whenever some portion of a story is selected. Choose the SPACING... command from the TYPE menu and the SPACING ATTRIBUTES dialog will appear, as shown in Figure 8.13. Enter the values you wish to set for the "Word space" and "Letter space" options. All values are entered in percentages, according to the acceptable ranges listed in Figure 8.14. Click the OK button to apply these settings, or click the CANCEL button to negate them and return to the publication window.

▪ *Minimum Word spacing:*	*0 to 500%*
▪ *Desired Word spacing:*	*≥ min and ≤ max*
▪ *Maximum Word spacing:*	*0 to 500%*
▪ *Minimum Letter spacing:*	*-200% to 0*
▪ *Desired Letter spacing:*	*≥ min and ≤ max*
▪ *Maximum Letter spacing:*	*0 to 200%*

Figure 8.14: *Allowable ranges for spacing options.*

8 Editing Text

Exporting text

After editing text in PageMaker, you will occasionally want to export your text from PageMaker to word-processing (or text-only) format. This allows you to take advantage of the superior text editing features provided by word-processors, or to use the text for some other purpose.

PageMaker allows you to export any amount of selected text, or an entire story, to a disk file in text only, MICROSOFT WORD 3.0, or in the format of any other word-processors for which Import filters (which also contain export filters) have been installed. Files exported to one of the word-processing formats will retain all character and paragraph formatting attributes that were in the PageMaker file. Style sheets used to format text that is exported to MICROSOFT WORD will also be converted and included in the exported file. Style sheet tags can be included in any exported text file regardless of the export format.

To export text, select the text you wish to export. If you wish to export an entire story, it is not necessary to select the entire story, just set the insertion point anywhere in the story. Choose the Export... command from the FILE menu, and the EXPORT TO FILE dialog box will appear, as shown in Figure 8.15. Select the "File format" that you wish to use for your exported file from the scrolling list on the right side of the dialog box. Set the "Export" option to either "Entire story" if you want to export all of the text from the currently selected story, or to "Selected text only" if you want to export only that part of the current story that you selected before choosing the EXPORT... command. If the insertion point was set (with no text selected) when the EXPORT... command was chosen, the "Selected text only" option will be dimmed.

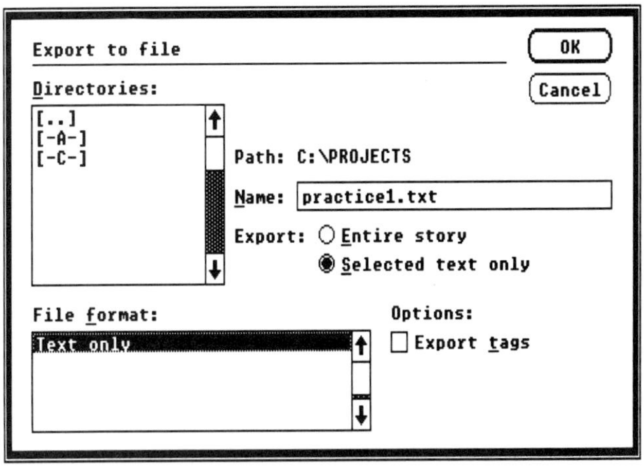

Figure 8.15: *The Export to file dialog box.*

Click the "Export tags" check box if you would like a style sheet tag to be placed before each paragraph in the exported document. Style sheet tags consist of the style sheet name placed between the less than (<) and greater than (>) characters. By exporting style sheet tags, you make it possible to use the "Read tags" option in the PLACE FILE dialog box when importing the document back into PageMaker, thereby retaining all style sheet links. MICROSOFT WORD users do not need to use this option, since style sheets are exported to and imported from MICROSOFT WORD files automatically.

Enter a name for your exported file in the "Name" option box. Remember to specify the destination drive and directory path if you do not want your file saved in the path specified by the "Path" option. Use the drive and directory designators to select a destination for your file, as described earlier. When you are satisfied with all these options, click the OK button to save the exported file. Alternatively, you may click the

CANCEL button to avoid exporting the file and return to the publication window.

After editing your exported file in a word-processor, you can again import it into PageMaker, replacing the existing text with the updated file, or placing it into a new PageMaker publication. Importing text is fully discussed in Chapter 7, *Adding and Creating text in PageMaker*.

Using Style Sheets in PageMaker

In this chapter we examine:

- *What style sheets are and when to use them*
- *The process of creating style sheets*
- *Using and modifying style sheets*

As described in the Chapter 8, PageMaker's text formatting abilities are powerful and comprehensive. For each word or paragraph that is used, we are given control over fonts, styles, alignments, spacing, indents, tabs, colors, and many other attributes. When working in longer publications, or on a series of smaller publications, the process of determining and applying all of these attributes can sometimes become complex and tedious. Fortunately, PageMaker also provides **style sheets** that can help us to quickly and accurately format text.

Style sheets allow us to specify a complex set of attributes with a single click of the mouse button, and then change these attributes globally at any time. A style sheet is composed of a name, which usually describes the kind of paragraph the style sheet defines, and a definition, which identifies the text formatting attributes that the style sheet bestows on any paragraph to which the style sheet is applied. In PageMaker, style sheets may contain attributes from the TYPE SPECIFICATIONS, PARAGRAPH SPECIFICATIONS, INDENTS AND TABS, and COLOR dialog boxes.

As we will see in this chapter, you can use the default style sheets that PageMaker provides, create new style sheets, import style sheets from other PageMaker publications, or import style sheets from word-processed documents as they are placed into PageMaker publications.

The purpose of style sheets

Style sheets are used because they automate the process of text formatting. They allow us to specify the formatting attributes of a paragraph only once, and then use that specification an unlimited number of times. This not only saves time and reduces both effort and complexity, but it also insures consistency. Since style sheets can be imported from word-processing documents, exported to word-processed documents, and shared between PageMaker publications, the benefits of defining and using style sheets can be enormous.

The concept of style sheets is valid because most documents are composed of several kinds of paragraphs, each of which is used repeatedly throughout the publication. This book, for example, is basically made up of five types of paragraph formats:

- **Body Copy**. Set in 11-point Lubalin Graph Book with 15.5 points of leading. Paragraphs are left justified with a 2¼-pica first-line indent.
- **Major Subheads**. Set in 24-point Helvetica Condensed Bold with Auto leading. Paragraphs are left justified with 3 picas of space above each.
- **Minor Subheads**. Set in 18-point Helvetica Condensed Oblique with Auto leading. Paragraphs are left justified with 2 picas of space above each.
- **Cutlines**. These are set in 12-point Helvetica Condensed Light Oblique with Auto leading. Paragraphs are left justified with 4 picas left and right indents and 2½ picas before and after the paragraph.
- **Listings**. These use the same attributes as Body Copy, except they have a 4½-pica left indent, a 2-pica right indent, a 0p6 space before the paragraph, and a 0p9 space after the paragraph.

Without using style sheets, it would be necessary to assign the above attribute sets over and over again during formatting. The process involves several trips to the menu bar and through the dialog boxes each time we need to format any one of these paragraphs. If we later decide to change anything—to make the subheads a little bit larger, for example—we would have to go through our document, page by page, reformatting each subhead paragraph to change the size as desired.

Using style sheets, however, this scenario can be improved dramatically. We need only define the specifications of our five paragraph styles once, as style sheets, and we can then *apply* these styles sheets to our text as needed. Each application of a defined style sheet is quick, simple, and accurate. If we later need to change the attributes of any style of paragraph, such as the subheads mentioned in the previous example, we only have to alter our definition—every paragraph to which that style has been applied will be updated automatically to reflect the new definition.

Using default style sheets

When a new PageMaker publication is created, five style sheets are automatically available (see Figure 9.01). These style sheets are representative of the most commonly used kinds of paragraphs and, although their default specifications will rarely match the exact specifications that you intend to use in your publication, the styles can be easily edited to your specifications. (Editing style sheets is described in detail later in this chapter.)

As they exist when you begin using PageMaker, the default style sheets are useful only when the document that you are formatting is fairly simple (requiring only a few different paragraph types) and you know the specifications for the document in advance. When preparing more complex documents, or when the formatting specifications will not be determined exactly until you begin to format the publication in PageMaker, some of the other methods of defining style sheets are more appropriate.

- *Body text — Times 12/Auto, left aligned, 2-pica first indent, Kern above 12, auto hyphenation*
- *Caption — Times 10/Auto, Italic, left aligned*
- *Headline — Times 30/Auto, Bold, left aligned*
- *Subhead 1 — Times 18/Auto, Bold, left aligned*
- *Subhead 2 — Times 12/Auto, Bold, left aligned*

Figure 9.01: *The original default style sheet specifications.*

It is very important to remember, however, that the default style sheets can modified and reset as application defaults, as described in Chapter 4, *A Brief Tour of PageMaker.* By editing the style sheets when no publication window is open, you can create a set of default style sheets that specifically address *your* document formatting needs. From that time forward, every new publication that you create will have access to the default style sheets that you have defined, providing you with the kind of quick and easy formatting described earlier, and insuring consistency throughout your publications. Of course, you will still need to occasionally edit your customized default style sheets for a specific publication, and even create additional style sheets, but overall a well-thought-out set of default style sheets is an easiest way to save yourself and your colleagues time, and to insure quality and consistency in all your publications.

Creating new style sheets

Whenever it is inappropriate to use an existing style sheet, and required style sheets cannot be obtained from another PageMaker publication or from a word-processing file being imported into PageMaker, a new style sheet must be defined. There are several ways to create new style sheets in PageMaker: new style sheets can be defined from scratch; new style sheets can be defined based on some formatted text that already exists in the publication; and new style sheets can be defined based on another style sheet that already exists.

Defining a style sheet from scratch

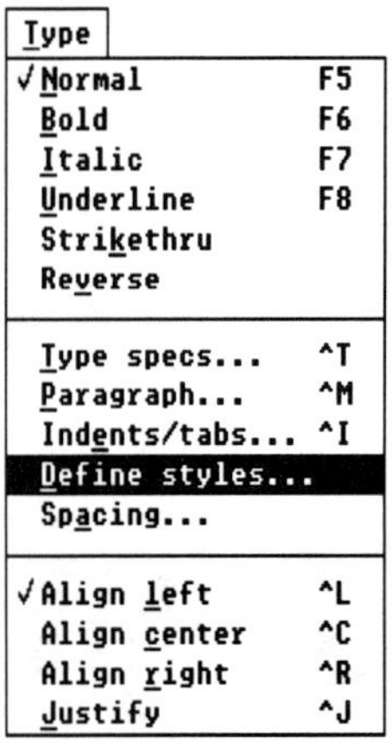

To begin defining a new style sheet, choose the DEFINE STYLES... command from the TYPE menu, and the DEFINE STYLES dialog box will appear as shown in Figure 9.02. If it is not selected already, click on the word *"Selection"* at the top of the scrolling list on the left side of the dialog box, and then click the NEW... button. The EDIT STYLES dialog box will now appear, as shown in Figure 9.03. It is here that we will specify the name and formatting attributes for our new style sheet.

To name the new style sheet, enter any name up to 32 characters long into the "Name" option box (some non-alphabetic characters are not allowed in style names). Try to name your style sheet descriptively, but use as short of a name as possible so that you can see it easily in the Styles palette. The "Based on" option box should remain empty.

We are now ready to define the attributes that our new style sheet will imbue upon any paragraphs to which it is applied. In the lower portion of the EDIT STYLES dialog box is a listing of the current settings of our style sheet's attributes These settings are based on the current default settings from the various options used to define style sheets, or on any text that was selected when we chose the Define Styles... command. Clicking the OK button would assign these attributes to our new style sheet.

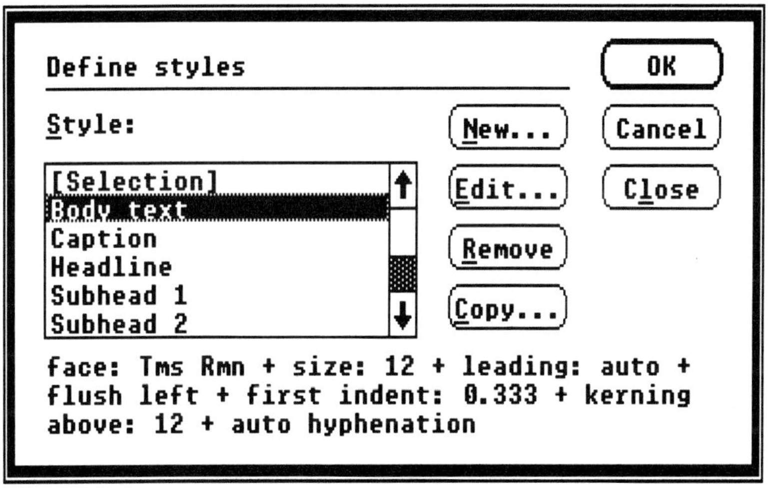

Figure 9.02: *The Define styles dialog box.*

To edit the specifications for this new style sheet we use the Type..., Para..., Tabs..., and Colors... buttons, which access the Type specifications, Paragraph specifications, Indents and tabs, and Color dialog boxes, respectively. Each of these dialog boxes is used exactly as described in Chapter 8, *Editing Text in PageMaker*. As we edit the various options in these dialog boxes, the style sheet specification listing is updated to reflect the current attributes of the style sheet.

When satisfied with the specifications for the new style sheet as listed in the lower portion of the Edit styles dialog box, click the OK button to complete the definition of this new style sheet, or the CANCEL button to abort the creation process. In either case we are returned to the DEFINE STYLE dialog box. The name of our new style sheet now appears in the scrolling style sheet listing. To return to the publication window, click the OK button or click the CANCEL button.

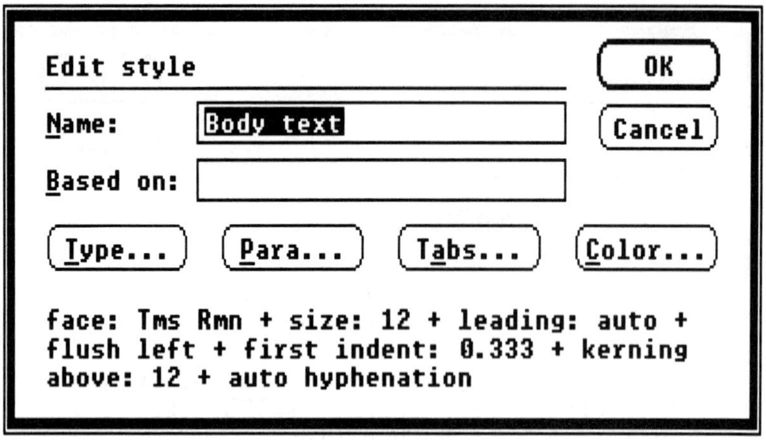

Figure 9.03: *The Edit style dialog box.*

You can also begin the process of defining a new style sheet by holding down the CTRL key and double-clicking on the *No style* line in the Styles palette. (If the Styles palette is not displayed, choose the STYLE PALETTE command from the OPTIONS menu.) This will bring up an empty EDIT STYLE dialog box, where you can name the new style and edit its specifications, as described above. If any text is selected when you CTRL-click on the *No style* line, the new text block will use the specifications of the selected type as its defaults, or the "Based on" option will list the name of the selected text's style sheet, if there is one.

Defining a style sheet based on existing text

The process of defining style sheets from scratch, as described above, requires that you know in advance the specifications that you want to assign to your new style sheets. While this will occur sometimes, many other times you will not know the final specifications for your publication until you create a few pages of it, experimenting with various formatting possibilities until you (and perhaps your colleagues) are satisfied.

In this case, you will want to "capture" the results of your trial-and-error formatting, creating a style sheet for each different kind of paragraph that you have defined. These style sheets can then be used to format the remainder of your publication.

To create a style sheet based on an existing paragraph, select a paragraph that is properly formatted and choose the DEFINE STYLES... command from the OPTIONS menu. The STYLES dialog will appear, and the word *Selection* will be highlighted in the scrolling list (unless the selected paragraph has already been defined as a style sheet). *Selection* refers to the text paragraph that was selected when you chose the DEFINE STYLES... command. The specifications for the selected paragraph are listed in the lower section of the dialog box. These are the specifications that PageMaker assumes you want to use in your new style sheet.

Click the NEW... button, and the EDIT STYLE dialog box will appear. Enter the name you wish to give this new style sheet in the "Name" option box. The "Based on" option box will be blank, unless the paragraph that you selected before choosing the DEFINE STYLES... command had been previously defined using another style sheet.

You may now edit any of the attributes of the style sheet. This is done by clicking on the TYPE..., PARA..., TABS..., and COLORS... buttons, and changing options in the associated dialog boxes. Since the default attributes of this new style sheet came from a paragraph that you formatted, this will probably not be necessary. If however, any attributes of the selected text are not uniform—if there is one italic word within a paragraph of plain text, for example—the word *mixed* will follow the specification of that attribute in the specification listing, as shown in Figure 9.04.

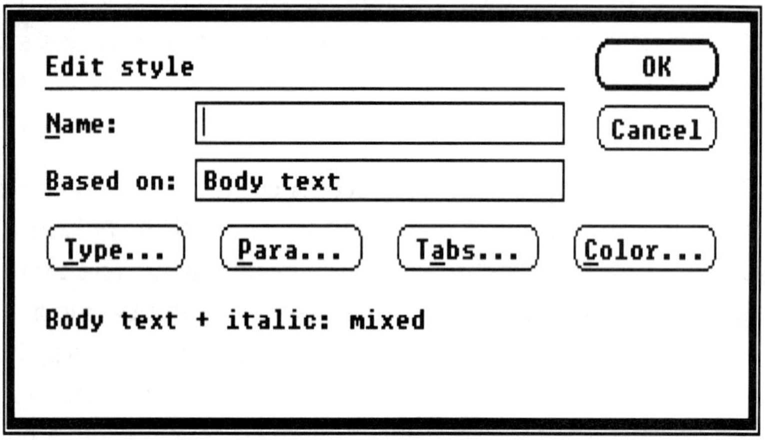

Figure 9.04: *The word "mixed" appears for any attribute that is not uniform in the selected text when a new style sheet is created.*

Any attributes followed by the word "mixed" will have to be reset so that they can be applied uniformly throughout the paragraph. To reset the type style, for example, click the TYPE... button and click either the "Normal" or "Italic" options so that all words will be set in the same type style. The word *mixed* will now disappear from the specifications listing.

When satisfied with the specifications for the new style sheet as listed in the EDIT STYLE dialog box, click the OK button to complete the definition of this new style sheet, or click the CANCEL button to abort the creation process. If any conflicts remain in the specifications, one of the dialog boxes shown in Figure 9.05 will appear when you click the OK button, and you will have to resolve the conflict. If no specification conflicts exist, the DEFINE STYLES dialog will again display, with your new style added to the scrolling list. To return to the publication window, click the OK or CANCEL button.

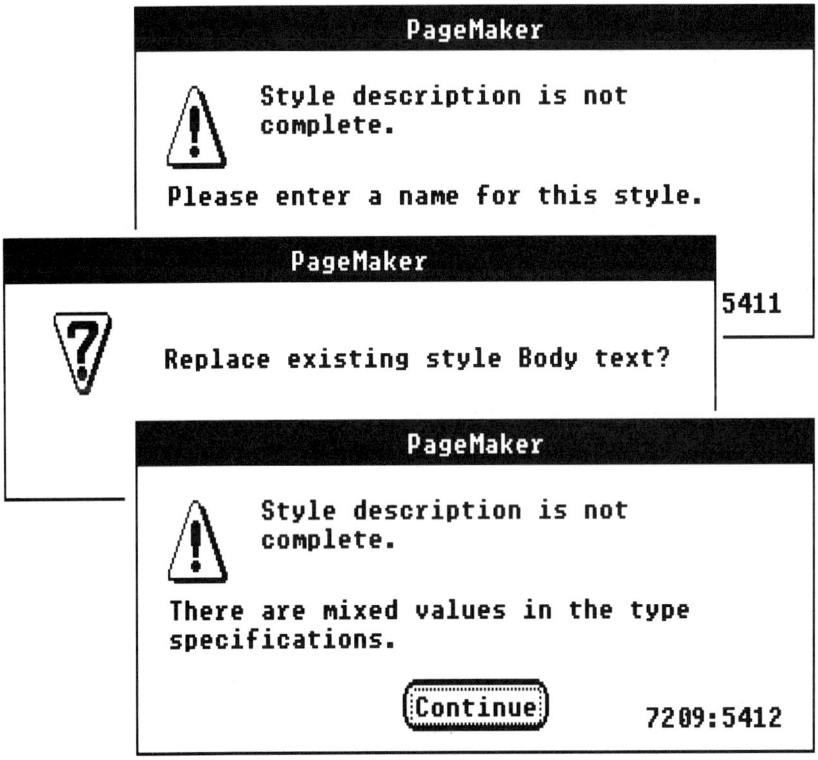

Figure 9.05: *Some of the Alert boxes that appear when a new or edited style sheet contains conflicting specifications.*

You can also define a new style based on existing text by selecting the text and holding down the **CTRL** key while double-clicking on the *No style* line in the Styles palette. (If the Styles palette is not displayed, choose the STYLE PALETTE command from the OPTIONS menu.) This will bring up the EDIT STYLE dialog box, where you can name and edit the attributes of the style, as described above. Click the OK button after defining the new style sheet, or click the CANCEL button to abort the creation, and you will return immediately to the publication window.

Defining a style sheet based on an existing style sheet

Many paragraph styles used in a publication are very similar, but not identical, to other paragraphs used in the publication. For example, the major and minor subheads in this book have the same type face and alignment as the major headlines, but different type sizes and type styles.

In PageMaker you can create style sheets that are "based on" existing style sheets. When one style sheet is based on another, it has exactly the same attributes as the style sheet upon which it is based, except the few attributes that are set differently. This technique reduces the amount of effort required to define the "based-on" style sheet, and creates a dynamic link between the two style sheets—if an attribute is changed in the first style sheet, it is automatically changed in the second style sheet.

For example, suppose we define a style and name it "Headline," giving it the attributes of Times Bold 30/auto, left aligned. We then define another style, which is "Based on" "Headline," and name it "Subhead 1." The only attribute that we change for "Subhead 1" is its type size, which is set as 18. Figure 9.06 displays the EDIT STYLE dialog boxes for these two styles.

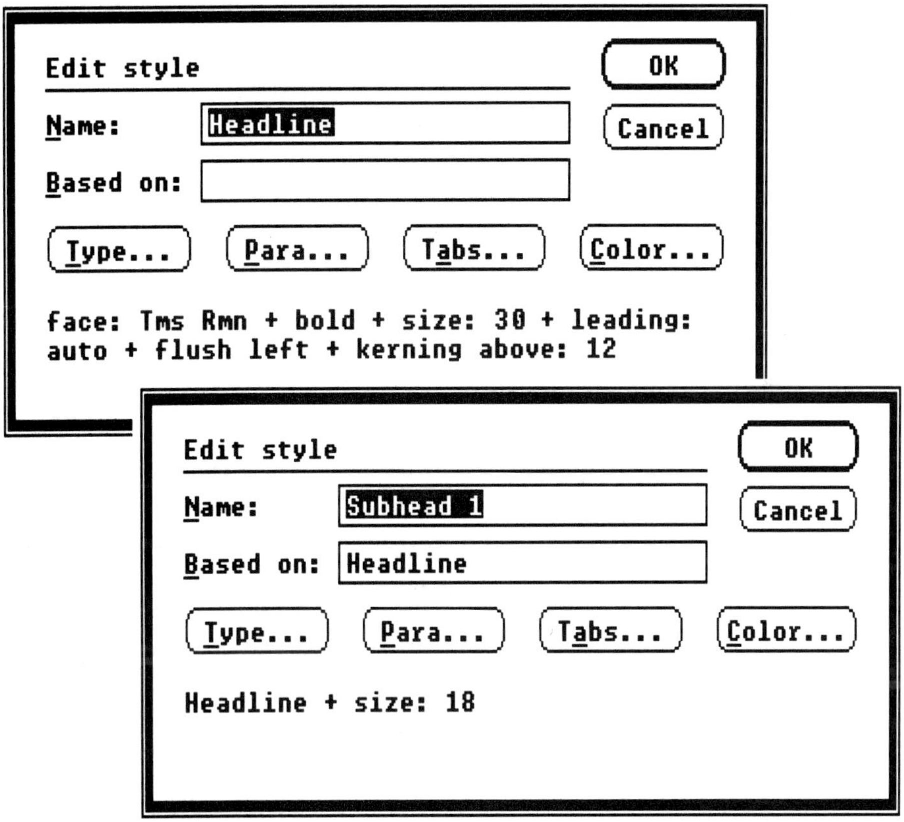

Figure 9.06: *When one style sheet is based on another, the second sheet uses all the attributes of the first.*

Notice that "Subhead 1" does not display a type face, leading, or type style in its attribute listing. Instead, it simply reads "Headline + 18." All paragraphs to which "Subhead 1" is applied will be Times Bold auto leading left aligned, as long as "Headline" is so defined, or until the type face, type style, or leading, are specifically edited in the definition of "Subhead 1" style sheet. If the definition of "Subhead 1" is edited, so that Helvetica is the specified font instead of Times, all paragraphs to which "Subhead 2" has been applied will immediately become Helvetica as well. The link between a style sheet and the sheet on which it is based is dynamic—changes made in the attributes of a style sheet are passed directly to any style sheets based on the changed style sheet.

If we create a third style sheet, called "Subhead 2," and base it on "Subhead 1," a change to an attribute in "Headline" would affect "Headline," "Subhead 1," and "Subhead 2."

To create a new style sheet that is based on an existing style sheet, choose the DEFINE STYLES... command from the TYPE menu. The DEFINE STYLES dialog will appear. Depending on the currently selected text in the publication window, either one of the style sheet names or the word *Selection* will be selected. If the style sheet that you want to base your new style sheet on is not selected, select it from the scrolling list. Next, click the NEW... button and the EDIT STYLE dialog box will appear. The "Name" option box will be empty, but the "Based on" option box will display the name of the style sheet selected when the NEW... button was clicked. Enter a name for your new style sheet in the "Name" option box.

The specification listing for the new style sheet will contain only the name of the "Based on" style. At this point the new style is exactly the same as the style on which it is based. By using the TYPE..., PARA..., TABS..., and COLOR... buttons and their associated dialog boxes, you can specify the attributes of this new style sheet that are different from the "Based on" style sheet. The specifications listing will reflect these changes as they are made.

When satisfied with the specifications for the new style sheet as listed in the EDIT STYLES dialog box, click the OK button to complete the definition of this new style sheet, or the CANCEL button to abort the creation process. The DEFINE STYLES dialog will again display, with the name of your new style sheet added to the scrolling list. To return to the publication window, click the OK button or click the CANCEL button.

You can also create a new style sheet that is based on an existing style sheet by selecting a paragraph that uses the existing style sheet, holding down the CTRL key and double-clicking on the *No style* line in the Styles palette. Or you can select the name of the style in the Styles palette that you want to base the new style on, and then hold down the CTRL key and double-click on the *No style* line. Either of these methods will bring up an empty EDIT STYLE dialog box, with the "Based on" option box already filled in, where you can name the new style and edit its specifications. Click the OK button after defining the new style sheet, or the CANCEL button to abort the creation process, and you will return immediately to the publication window.

TIP

To break the link between a style sheet and the style sheet that it is based on, delete the entry in the "Based on" option box. This removes the name of the based on style from the specification listing, and replaces it with the specifications themselves. This does not change any of the specifications for the style sheet, only the way that they are listed. This does, however, break the link between the style sheets so that if the style sheet on which this style sheet was based is edited, this style sheet will not be affected. You can also change the "Based on" style sheet from one to another by entering the name of any current style sheet in the "Based on" option box.

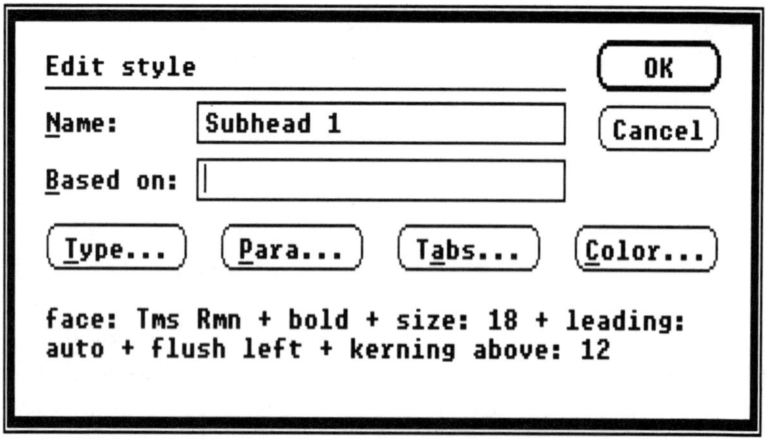

Figure 9.07: *When the name of the "Based on" style is removed, all the attributes of the "Based on" style appear in the new style sheet's specifications in place of the "Based on" style's name.*

Importing style sheets from other PageMaker publications

After defining style sheets using any of the methods described above, it is a good idea to get as much use from those style sheets as possible. In PageMaker, style sheets defined in any publication can be imported for use in any other publication. This allows us to maximize the benefits discussed earlier—consistency between documents and a reduction of the time and trouble required to format documents.

In some ways, the ability to import style sheets from one publication to another appears to make it unnecessary to reset the application default style sheets. You can, however, import style sheets from PageMaker publications, as described in the remainder of this section, so that they become application defaults. This allows you to make any number of commonly used style sheets available to all new publications that you create.

To import style sheets into your publication, choose the Define styles... command from the Type menu to bring up the Define styles dialog box. Click the Copy... button and the Copy styles dialog will appear, as shown in Figure 9.08. Locate the publication containing the style sheets that you wish to import, using the drive, sub-directory, and parent directory markers in the scrolling file listing as discussed earlier. When you have located the publication, select its name in the file listing and click the OK button, or double-click the publication name.

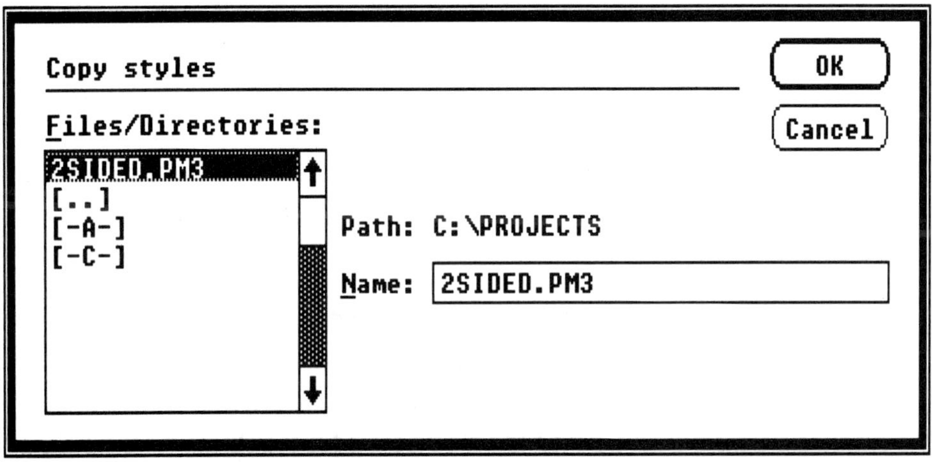

Figure 9.08: *Copy styles dialog box.*

All style sheets from the opened publication will then be added to the list of style sheets in the current publication. If the names of any imported style sheets have already been assigned to styles in the new document, those style sheets will not be added. Existing style sheets always override those being imported. If you know that an existing style sheet name is duplicated in the style sheets being imported, and you want to use the version of the style sheet being imported rather than the one that already exists, either delete the existing style sheet (using the REMOVE... button), or rename the existing style (in the EDIT STYLES dialog box) before importing the new style sheets.

Importing style sheets from word-processors

The concept of style sheets is not unique to PageMaker. Several popular word-processors use style sheets, and although these style sheets are implemented slightly differently than PageMaker's style sheets, they provide basically the same function—by assigning a group of formatting attributes to a named style sheet, those attributes can quickly be applied and edited.

Word-processing style sheets are converted into PageMaker format when the word-processed file is placed into PageMaker. The conversion is done by the same import filter that converts all other document formatting. Currently only MICROSOFT WORD's import filter can convert its style sheets into PageMaker format, although improved import filters for other word-processing software may become available.

```
1=¦•••[•••••1•••••••••2•••••••••3•••••••••4•••••••••5•••••]•••6•••••••••7•••••
  1   NL Paragraph 2                                 BODY COPY
          Bookman (roman a) 10/12. Flush left, Left indent 0.4" (first line
          indent -0.4"), right indent 0.4", space before 1 li, space after 1
          li (keep in one column).
  2   TI Paragraph 3                                 SUBHEAD 2
          Helvetica (modern i) 14/12 Bold. Centered.
  3   SH Paragraph 7                                 SUBHEAD 3
          Helvetica (modern i) 12 Bold Underlined. Flush left.
  4   RH Paragraph 8                                 RUNNING HEAD
          Bookman (roman a) 10/12 Italic. Centered.
  5   LE Paragraph 1                                 LIST 5
          Bookman (roman a) 10/12. Flush left, Left indent 1" (first line
          indent -1"), right indent 0.4", space after 2 li (keep in one
          column). Tabs at: 1" (left flush).
  6   SP Paragraph Standard                          CHAPTER TITLE
          Helvetica (modern i) 18/12. Centered.
  7   H1 Paragraph Heading level 1                   HEAD LEVEL 1
          Helvetica (modern i) 14/12 Bold. Flush left, space after 1 li (keep
          with following paragraph).
                                                                   SAMPLE.STY
COMMAND: Copy Delete Exit Format Help
         Insert Name Print Transfer Undo
Select style or press ESC to use menu
GALLERY          {Paragraph Hea...} ?          CL               Microsoft Word
```

Figure 9.09: *Microsoft word's style sheet gallery.*

When placing word-processed documents that use style sheets (and that are supported by an import filter), the names and definitions of all style sheets defined in the word-processor become PageMaker style sheets and remain tagged to the appropriate paragraphs. Once in PageMaker, these style sheets can be used and edited as if they had been created in PageMaker. If the PageMaker publication already contains a style sheet with the same name as an imported style sheet, the existing PageMaker style dominates—it is not replaced and all paragraphs in the word-processed document that have been formatted with that style sheet name will take the attributes of the PageMaker style sheet.

<Headline>Importing Style Sheets

<Body Copy>Once you have created style sheets for a publication, you can use those style sheets in other publications.

<Analytic Comment>The most common use for imported style sheets will be in sections or chapters of a large publication, but this feature will also be useful in more general cases. For example, by reusing the style sheets from one technical data sheet or brochure, you can ensure consistency in all similar publications.

Figure 9.10: *A text document with style sheet tags before each paragraph.*

When using a word-processor that does not have a style sheet feature or whose style sheets cannot be imported into PageMaker, it is possible to manually **tag** paragraphs so that predefined PageMaker style sheets are applied to the text as it is being placed into PageMaker. This is done by adding the name of the style sheet, between less than (<) and greater than (>) symbols, to the beginning of each group of paragraphs of a particular style. For example, suppose our word-processed document looks the one in Figure 9.10.

This document contains three style sheet tags: "Headline," "Body Copy," and "Analytic Comment." As long as our PageMaker document contains defined style sheets named "Headline," "Body Copy," and "Analytic Comment," our text can be formatted with the style sheet attributes as it is placed into the PageMaker publication.

Importing Style Sheets

Once you have created style sheets for a publication, you can use those style sheets in other publications.

The most common use for imported style sheets will be in sections or chapters of a large publication, but this feature will also be useful in more general cases. For example, by reusing the style sheets from one technical data sheet or brochure, you can ensure consistency in all similar publications.

Figure 9.11: *The text from Figure 9.10 after it is poured.*

To import a tagged word-processed document, use the PLACE... command exactly as described in Chapter 7, *Creating and Adding Text*, but be sure to select the "Read tags" option in the lower right corner of the PLACE DOCUMENT dialog box. This instructs PageMaker to remove all paragraph tags and format the paragraph that contains them according to existing style sheet definitions. After placing the word-processed document shown in Figure 9.10 in this way, the text will be formatted (according to the style sheets) as shown in Figure 9.11.

If the "Read tags" option is not selected, tags are treated like any other text, and the text will appear in PageMaker as shown in Figure 9.12 (exactly as it appeared in the word-processed file).

In actual practice, the "Read tags" option may have limited application, since it is often easier to simply apply style sheets after placing the text than to manually enter the tags into the word-processing document. Of course, users who wish to consistently apply tags in their word-processing documents could automate the process using some type of macro software, such as SMARTKEYS.

<Headline>Importing Style Sheets

<Body Copy>Once you have created style sheets for a publication, you can use those style sheets in other publications.

<Analytic Comment>The most common use for imported style sheets will be in sections or chapters of a large publication, but this feature will also be useful in more general cases. For example, by reusing the style sheets from one technical data sheet or brochure, you can ensure consistency in all similar publications.

Figure 9.12: *Tagged documents imported without using the "Read tags" option are treated as normal text files.*

Both style sheets and tags can be exported back to word-processing format, as described in the section *Exporting style sheets*, later in this chapter.

Applying Style Sheets

After we have created our style sheets, using any of the methods described above, it is very easy to apply these style sheets to any text in our document. Like all other paragraph attributes, style sheets apply to all paragraphs that are partially or fully selected when the style name is selected. Even if the insertion point is simply set in a paragraph, with no text selected, a style sheet can be applied to that paragraph.

Once a paragraph or group of paragraphs has been selected, select the style sheet name from the Styles palette, or choose the DEFINE STYLES... command, select the style sheet name from the scrolling list in the DEFINE STYLES dialog box, and click the OK button. The paragraph will immediately reformat to the specifications of the selected style sheet.

Problems applying style sheets (overrides)

PageMaker style sheets, as we have defined them, operate like other paragraph level formatting—a single paragraph can have only one style sheet applied to it, and a style sheet is by definition applied to an entire paragraph, not just a portion of a paragraph. When creating style sheets based on existing text, we saw that any inconsistencies that exist within a paragraph—one bold word, for example—had to be corrected before the style sheet could be defined.

Similarly, when applying a style sheet to existing paragraphs, problems can occur if the paragraphs to which the style sheet is being applied contains formatting inconsistencies such as one word with a different type style,type face, or leading than the rest of the paragraph.

PageMaker calls these formatting inconsistencies (in the paragraphs that have been formatted using style sheets), *overrides*. All overrides are temporary—they will be removed when the style sheet is reapplied—*except* type style overrides. Type style overrides remain active even when a style sheet is reapplied to a parargraph or when a different style sheet is applied to the paragraph.

For example, suppose we have a line of text that contains one bold word (the rest are plain), one 14-point word (the rest are 12-point), and one word in the Times font (the rest are Helvetica) as shown in Figure 9.13. If we reapply the current style sheet or apply a new style sheet to this sentence, the Times font and the 14-point type size will disappear (conforming instead to the specifications of the applied style sheet), but the bolded word will remain distinguished from the other words. If the style sheet that we apply has "bold" defined as its type style, all the words in our sentence will become bold *except* the previously bolded word (see Figure 9.13), which will become plain: applying style sheets toggles the setting of any override type styles on and off if they are included in the applied style sheet. If the overriding type style is not included in the applied style sheet, the override is unaffected.

This is a ***sample*** paragraph.

This is a *sample* **paragraph.**

Figure 9.13: *All inconsistencies in formatting are overridden by style sheets except type style overrides, which are unchanged or are reversed when a new style sheet is applied.*

To preserve any non-type style overrides—for example our Times font or 14-point type size—hold down the SHIFT key while appying a new style sheet. All overrides will remain intact and all non-overridden text will be formatted according to the style sheet specifications.

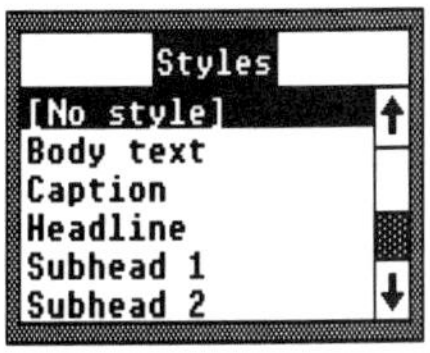

The Styles palette

The Styles palette is a window that lists the names of all currently defined style sheets plus the entry *No style*. The palette can be displayed at any time by selecting the STYLE PALETTE command from the OPTIONS menu. When the Styles palette is displayed, a check mark (✓) appears before the STYLE PALETTE command. Selecting the STYLE PALETTE command when the palette is already being displayed will remove it from the publication window. The Styles palette can be moved, sized, and closed using the window title bar, size box, and close box, respectively.

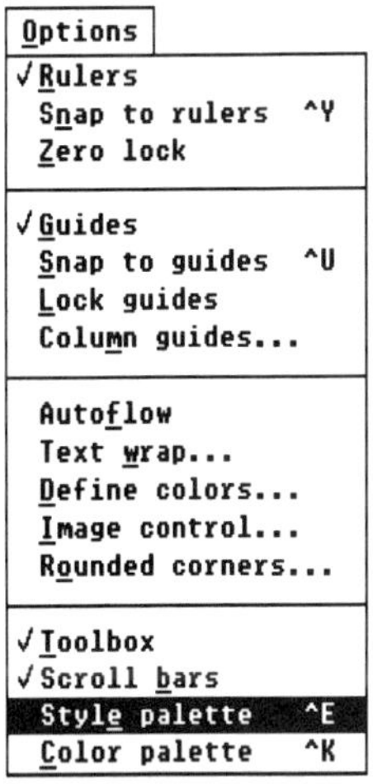

The Styles palette serves many functions:

- **Applying style sheets**. To apply a style sheet to any number of paragraphs, select the paragraphs and then click on the appropriate style sheet name in the Styles palette. The paragraphs will immediately format as specified by the selected style sheet. More information about the application of style sheets is included in the preceding section *Applying style sheets*.

- **Checking style of text**. As soon as any paragraph is selected, or the insertion point is set, the Styles palette highlights the name of the style that has been applied to the selected text. If the selected text contains text of more than one style sheet, no name is highlighted. If the selected text has not been formatted using a style sheet, the *No style* line is highlighted.

  If the selected text contains formatting overrides for any attributes other than type style, a plus (+) sign appears after the style sheet name. Type style overrides cause the plus sign to appear only if overridden text is selected exclusively. If both type style overridden text and non-overridden text is selected, no plus sign will appear.

- **Reformatting edited style sheet text**. To remove non-type style overrides from formatted text, select the text in question (a plus sign will appear after the style sheet name in the Styles palette) and reselect the style sheet name. The plus sign will disappear and the text will return to the pure style sheet specifications. Type style overrides must be removed manually.

- **Disassociating text from a style sheet**. There are times when you want to dissassociate a particular paragraph from the style sheet that has been applied to it. The most common reason for this is that you intend to edit the style sheet specifications, but you want this particular paragraph to retain it current formatting. To remove the style sheet, select the text to be disassociated, and then select the name *No style* from the Styles palette. The formatting of the selected text will not change, but the text is no longer associated with the style sheet—any editing done to the style sheet will not be applied to the disassociated text.

- **A shortcut to editing an existing style sheet**. To edit a style sheet, hold down the CTRL key and then double-click on the name of the style to be edited. The EDIT STYLE dialog box will appear. Editing a style sheet is described fully in the next section of this chapter.

- **A shortcut to creating a new style sheet.** The STYLE palette can be used to create a new style sheet from scratch, based either on formatted text or on an existing style sheet.

  To create a new style sheet, make sure that no text is selected. Hold down the CTRL key and then double-click on the name *No style* in the Styles palette. The EDIT STYLE dialog box will appear. Here you can name the new style sheet and specify its attributes, as described in the next section of this chapter.

  To create a new style sheet based on formatted text, select the text, hold down the CTRL key, and double-click on the name *No style* in the Styles palette. The EDIT STYLE dialog box will appear, listing the attributes of the selected text. You can then name the new style sheet and, if required, edit its attributes.

To create a new style sheet based on an existing style sheet, select any paragraph (or set the insertion point within any paragraph) to which the "based-on" style sheet has been applied. Hold down the CTRL key and then double-click on the name *No style* in the Styles palette. The EDIT STYLE dialog box will appear, listing the name of the selected style sheet both in the "Based on" option box and as the only attribute listing. You can then name the new style sheet and, if required, edit its attributes.

Editing Style Sheets

One of the biggest advantages of using style sheets is that their attributes can be edited at any time. When a style sheet is edited, all of the paragraphs to which that style sheet has been applied—throughout the current publication—are instantly updated.

There are two ways to begin editing a style sheet. The first is to choose the DEFINE STYLES... command from the TYPE menu, select the name of the style to be edited from the scrolling list, and then click the EDIT... button. The second is to hold down the CTRL key while double-clicking on the style sheet name in the Styles palette. Either method will bring up the EDIT STYLE dialog box. Once the EDIT STYLE dialog appears, you can edit any attributes of the selected style sheet. The current specifications of the style sheet are listed in the lower portion of the dialog.

The "Name" option box is used to edit style sheet names. Names can be up to 32 characters long, although some special characters may not be used in style sheet names. You can also edit the "Based on" option. To change the current style sheet so that it is based on an existing style sheet, enter the name of any other existing style sheet in the "Based on" option box. If the current style sheet is based on another style sheet, you can break the link between the style sheets by deleting the entry in the "Based on" option box. This will remove the name of the "Based on" style from the specification listing and replace it with the specifications themselves.

Edit the specifications for the current style sheet using the TYPE..., PARA..., TABS..., and COLOR... buttons and their associated dialog boxes. Click OK to close each dialog box and return to the EDIT STYLE dialog. The specification listing will reflect these changes. When you are satisfied with the name and specification for the style sheet, click the OK button (twice if you began with the DEFINE STYLES... command). The STYLES dialog will again display. If you have edited the style sheet name, the new name appears in the scrolling list. You can perform any other functions available, click the OK button to save all style sheet changes, or click the CANCEL button to negate all style sheet changes. In either case you will return to the publication window. If changes were saved, the publication window and Styles palettes will be updated.

Editing style sheet text

Even after a style sheet has been applied to a paragraph, it is still possible to edit the paragraph or any of its text. This is done using the same text- and paragraph-editing techniques described in Chapter 8, *Editing Text.* For example, you can select a word and make it bold, center the paragraph, add tabs in the INDENTS/TABS dialog, or make any other editing changes. These edits will apply only to the word(s) or paragraph to which they are applied and will not affect any other paragraph using the same style sheet. To edit every paragraph that has been formatted with a particular style sheet, use the style-sheet editing techniques described in the preceding section.

An edited paragraph (or any of its text) is still associated with its style sheet—any changes made to the style sheet attributes will be applied to the paragraph. When an edited paragraph (or any of its text) is selected, a plus sign (+) appears after its style sheet name in the Styles palette.

Once a paragraph has been edited, you can create a new style sheet that reflects the current specifications of the paragraph by selecting the paragraph, and then either CTRL-double-click on the word *No style* in the Styles palette or choose the DEFINE STYLES... command from the TYPE menu and click the NEW... button. Either method will produce the EDIT STYLE dialog, which will display the name of the original style in the "Based-on" option box and complete specifications for the modified paragraph listed below. You can then name the new style sheet and, if required, edit the style sheet specifications.

To return the specifications of an edited paragraph to the original specifications of the style sheet applied to it, select any portion of the paragraph and click on the style sheet name in the Styles palette or select the style sheet name from the STYLES command from the TYPE menu. This will correct any inconsistencies in the paragraph *except* type style changes. Type style changes must be corrected manually.

Exporting style sheets

When exporting text documents using the EXPORT... command from the FILE menu, there are two ways to export style sheet information. If you are exporting to a word-processor that supports style sheets, such as MICROSOFT WORD, style sheet information is automatically included in the exported file as long as you do not check the "Export tags" option in the EXPORT dialog box. You can then edit the text in the your wordprocessor, continuing to take advantage of the style sheet information. This document can then be placed back into the same PageMaker publication that exported it, or it can be placed into a new publication.

Remember that modifications made to the style sheet definitions while in your wordprocessor will be lost when the file is again placed into a PageMaker publication that already has those style sheets defined. This is true because existing style sheets always overide incoming style sheets.

If you are exporting to a word-processor that does not support style sheets, select the "Export tags" option in the EXPORT dialog box and style sheet tags, as described earlier in this chapter, will be appended to the start of each paragraph in the exported file. This tagged file can then be edited in any word-processor, and later replaced into any PageMaker publication which has a defined style sheet corresponding to each tag. This is done using the "Read tags" option in the PLACE DOCUMENT dialog box.

More information about exporting files is included in Chapter 9, *Editing Text in PageMaker.* More information about placing documents into PageMaker is included in Chapter 7, *Creating and Adding Text.*

CHAPTER 10

Using Graphics in PageMaker

10 Using Graphics

In this chapter we examine:

- *Importing graphics from other applications*
- *Creating graphics in PageMaker*
- *Manipulating imported and created graphics*

As with text, graphics can be brought into PageMaker from other applications or created directly with PageMaker's own tools. Graphic applications provide an incredible range of creative capabilities so that you can create virtually any type of image—logos, technical illustrations, and halftone scans are only a few of the possibilities. PageMaker's own graphic capabilities, on the other hand, are limited to the creation of simple line and shape elements; however, the graphic tools can be accessed conveniently during the process of publication design and are adequate for adding basic graphic images to publications.

Importing graphics

The process of importing graphics into PageMaker is similar to the processes we discussed in the previous chapter regarding the importation of text:

- Graphic documents are prepared in their original application.
- Graphics can be placed anywhere in a PageMaker publication.
- The graphic file to be imported is selected with the PLACE... command.
- A graphic placement icon appears after the graphic file is selected. This icon is then positioned, the mouse button is clicked, and the graphic "flows" onto the page. Graphics may be placed on any publication page, master page, or on the pasteboard.
- After being placed, the graphic may be repositioned, sized, or cropped.

An important difference between text files and graphic files that are imported into PageMaker is that graphic files cannot be edited once they are placed in PageMaker as text files can. Graphic files can only be positioned, scaled, and cropped. To change the content of a graphic image, you must return to the original application, modify the graphic, and then re-place it into PageMaker. To facilitate this process, PageMaker's PLACE dialog box provides a "Replace existing graphic" option that allows you to replace an existing graphic with an updated copy while maintain the positioning, scaling and cropping. This feature is described in detail later in this chapter.

Preparing graphics

PageMaker can directly import graphics created in most popular PC graphic applications. PageMaker can also import graphics created on the Macintosh. The determination of whether or not PageMaker can directly import a graphic is made based on the file format used to store the graphic, and the filename extension used in the graphic's name. Graphic images that cannot be imported directly can often be used in PageMaker after they are converted into a format that can be directly imported, or by being transferred via the Windows Clipboard. Both of these alternative methods are described later in this chapter.

The following graphic formats, and associated filename extensions, are supported by PageMaker:

- **Paint-type graphics**. These graphics, also known as bit-mapped graphics, are created by applications such as PC PAINT, PC PAINT-BRUSH, WINDOWS PAINT, and MACPAINT. Paint-type graphics must use the appropriate filename extension, as listed in Figure 10.02. Paint-type graphic applications provide a wide range of graphic capabilities, but the bit-mapped images created in such applications are usually limited in resolution to 72 dots per inch (DPI). When output at the higher resolutions of laser printers and imagesetters, bitmapped graphics usually have a jagged look that is not entirely pleasing. However, a tremendous amount of pre-drawn clip-art is available in this format, giving the non-artist access to a variety of images that can be placed in PageMaker quickly and easily. TIFF Format graphics are a specialized form of paint-type graphics, as explained below.

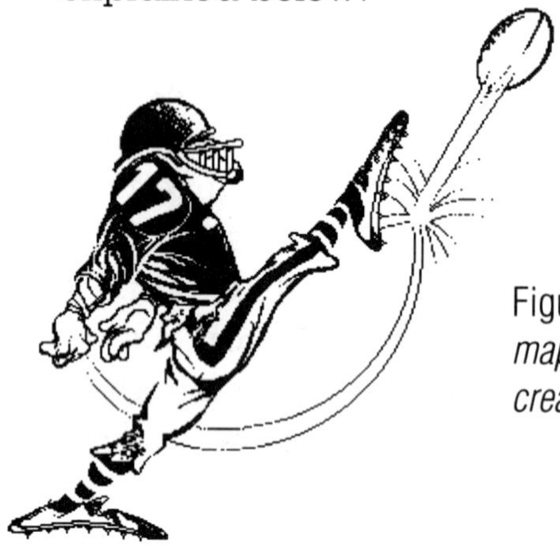

Figure 10.01: *A bit-mapped graphic image created in MacPaint.*

PC Paint, PC Paint Plus	*.PIC*
PC Paintbrush, PC Paintbrush Plus, Publisher's Paintbrush	*.PCX*
Windows Paint	*.MSP*
MacPaint and most other Macintosh paint applications	*.PNT*

Figure 10.02: *Applications that create paint-type files, and the filename extension that each must use.*

- **TIFF format documents**. Most graphic scanning software, and some image editing software, save their files in the **Tagged Image File Format** (TIFF). The TIFF format is a specialized form of the paint-type file format, capable of containing high-resolution images with or without gray scale information. TIFF format documents can be manipulated inside PageMaker using the IMAGE CONTROL... command described later in this chapter. TIFF images must use the filename extension .TIF.

Figure 10.03: *An scanned graphic, saved in TIFF format.*

- **Draw-type graphics**. Draw-type graphics are created by a number of applications, such as AUTOCAD, WINDOWS DRAW, MIRAGE, LOTUS 1-2-3, and SYMPHONY. Many applications that create draw-type graphics can save those graphics in a number of graphic file formats. PageMaker can accept draw-type graphics from any of the file formats listed in Figure 10.05, as long as they use the appropriate file-name extensions.

Graphic applications that create draw-type graphics tend to be best suited to the creation of geometric images consisting primarily of regular lines and shapes, such as technical illustrations, business graphics, and architectural renderings. In general, you should try to create your draw-type graphics without any text, instead adding the text after it is imported into PageMaker. If this is not possible, be sure you have the application that is creating the draw-type graphics configured to use the same printer and fonts that you will be using with PageMaker. Draw-type images will print at the full resolution of most output devices, even when scaled larger or smaller than their original sizes.

Figure 10.04: *A draw-type, or object-oriented, graphic.*

HP-GL format	*.PTL*
CGM format (including Lotus Freelance Plus)	*.CGM*
Videoshow (NAPLPS) format	*.PIC*
Windows GDI Metafiles	*.WMF*
*In*A*Vision and Windows Draw*	*.PIC*
AutoCAD	*.PTL*
Zenographics' Mirage	*.IMA*
Lotus 1-2-3, Symphony	*.PIC*

Figure 10.05: *Applications that create draw-type files, and the filename extensions that each must use.*

10 Using Graphics

- **Encapsulated PostScript (EPS) graphics**. Many high resolution drawing packages, such ADOBE ILLUSTRATOR WINDOWS, LOTUS FREELANCE PLUS, and some graphic scanning applications are capable of creating EPS files. EPS files describe any kind of image using the full power and precision of the PostScript language—they can therefore be used only when you will be printing your files on a PostScript printer. Some EPS files do not contain the information required to display their images on-screen, and will instead display only a box marked with the name of the graphic being represented. These images will, however, print correctly.

Figure 10.06: *An encapsulated PostScript graphic, created on the Macintosh with Aldus FreeHand.*

When using applications that can save files to one of the formats discussed previously, no special preparation of the files is required. PageMaker will recognize and utilize all aspects of the graphics, except color, and the graphics will not be distorted in size or quality as they are imported into PageMaker. Graphic files created in applications that cannot directly save files in a format that PageMaker can import are slightly more difficult to bring into PageMaker. There are two ways of importing these kinds of files into PageMaker:
(1) Convert the file format into one of those listed previously, or (2) transport the graphic into PageMaker using the Windows Clipboard, as described later in this chapter.

To convert the file format of an unusable graphic you must use an application that supports the conversion of your particular file format into one of those accepted by PageMaker. Several popular conversion utilities are available, and a number of graphics applications include some conversion abilities. The most popular application for graphic conversions is THE GRAPHICS LINK from PC-Quick Art Inc. This software can convert graphic files between many popular formats, including .PNT, .TIF, .PCX, .EPS, and others accepted by PageMaker.

The use of Macintosh graphics in PC PageMaker requires simply that the files be transferred to the PC and that they use one of the file formats (and filename extensions) described above. Most Macintosh graphic applications can either save directly into one of these formats or can be converted into an acceptable format using a utility program such as THE GRAPHICS LINK.

Using the Place... command

Once you have created a graphic document and saved it in the proper format, you are ready to import the graphic into PageMaker. Exactly as with text, the process of selecting a file to import is done in the PLACE FILE dialog box, shown in Figure 10.07, which is accessed by choosing the PLACE... command from the FILE menu.

The scrolling file listing on the left side of the dialog box displays the names of all text or graphic files that PageMaker can use from the current drive and directory. Remember that this list does not include every file that is in the drive or directory, only those that can be placed in a PageMaker document. The path whose directory is being displayed is listed after the "Path" option.

As we've mentioned earlier, there are several methods of moving between directories and drives:

- Double-click on any drive letter (enclosed in brackets, [A]) to change to that drive.
- Double-click on a sub-directory name (enclosed in brackets, [*sub-directory*]) to view files in that sub-directory.

- Double-click on the [...] line to move up the folder hierarchy (out of the current sub-directory and into the parent directory).
- Click in the NAME: option box, type the path of the directory you want to see, and click the OK button.

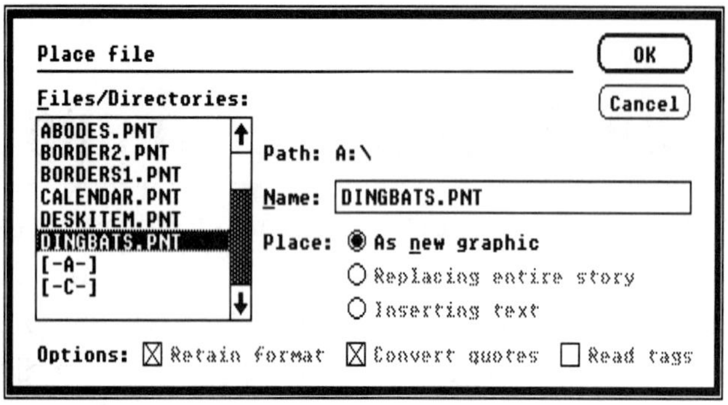

Figure 10.07: *A graphic file selected in the Place file dialog box.*

Once you've located the file you wish to place, select its filename from the scrolling list. When an eligible filename is selected, PageMaker determines whether a text or graphic file has been selected, and the first "Place" option appears as either "As new graphic" or "As new story." If the selected file is a graphic file, and a graphic is currently selected in your publication, the second "Place" option will read "Replace entire graphic." This option positions a placed graphic in the space of an existing graphic (and removes the existing graphic). The effect of this option is discussed fully later in this chapter. None of the text placement options are applicable to graphics and are dimmed whenever a graphic file is selected.

After you have selected a file, click the OK button or double-click the filename. PageMaker will then read the file from disk and prepare to position the graphic into your publication. Graphic files that are less than 64k in size are completely duplicated, and the copy becomes part of the publication. Graphic files of more than 64k (including most TIFF files and some EPS files) are not copied. Instead, a link is created between the PageMaker publication and the original graphic file on your disk. To preserve this link when moving your publication to another disk or directory, you must also move the graphic file, or a copy of the file, as described later in this chapter.

Adding the graphic

When PageMaker is finished reading the graphic file, the cursor will become one of four *graphic placement icons* shown in Figure 10.08.

Figure 10.08: *The paint, draw, EPS, and TIFF graphic placement icons.*

Armed with one of these, we are ready to add the graphic to our publication. The graphic can be placed on any page of the publication, on the master pages, or on the pasteboard. By placing the graphic on the pasteboard, at its original size, rather than directly on a page, you can scale it appropriately before positioning it on the page.

If necessary, turn to the appropriate page using the page icons, the GO TO PAGE... command (CTRL-G), or the keyboard shortcuts (CTRL-TAB or CTRL-SHIFT-TAB) or reposition the screen display using the scroll bars, grabber hand, or view size commands. Any of these may be accessed without affecting the graphic placement icon.

You can now place the graphic using either of two methods:

- Position the graphic placement icon at the position on the page where you want to locate the upper left corner of the graphic, and click the mouse button, as shown in Figure 10.09. The graphic is then placed at its original size, flowing over any text or existing graphic elements, column or ruler guides, or edges of the electronic pages. The graphic is immediately selected, ready to be sized and, if necessary, repositioned.

Figure 10.09: *Position the graphic placement icon where you want the upper left corner of the graphic, and then click the mouse button to place the graphic.*

- Position the graphic placement icon at the position on the page where you want to locate the upper left corner of the graphic. Click and hold the mouse button down while dragging to create a marquee of the final size for the imported graphic. This marquee can be created across column guides, onto the pasteboard, over existing text, or anywhere else. Release the mouse button when the marquee is correctly sized and positioned, and the graphic will flow into this defined area. If necessary, the graphic will be scaled to fit within the space defined by the marquee.

Manipulating graphic objects

Like any other element in PageMaker, a placed graphic can be resized or repositioned. Imported graphics can also be cropped with the cropping tool.

Moving graphic objects

Any placed graphic can be positioned by simply dragging it with the arrow tool: point the arrow tool anywhere on the graphic *except* on the graphic's handles, click and hold the mouse button, and drag the graphic into position. If you begin to drag the graphic as soon as the mouse button is depressed, a box shape will mark the graphic's location while you position it. If you hold down the mouse button for a few seconds before beginning to drag the mouse, the graphic itself (instead of the box) will be displayed as it is positioned.

If you need to position the graphic on an area not currently displayed on-screen, dragging into the edges of the display will cause the display to scroll automatically.

Figure 10.10: *Graphics can be resized by dragging on any of the graphic handles that appear when the graphic is selected.*

Sizing the graphic

To resize a placed graphic, select one of the graphic's handles with the arrow tool, and then drag as required. Every graphic has eight handles, and dragging any one of them will stretch the graphic, distorting it only in the direction of the drag. Be sure that the pointer turns into a double-headed arrow when you select the handle, confirming that you have selected the handle rather than the edge of the graphic. You may have to hold the mouse button down for a few seconds before beginning to drag the mouse to allow the double-headed arrow icon to display.

As you resize any imported graphic, an empty box is displayed representing your resized graphic, while the graphic itself remains visible at its original size. To see the graphic at any new size, hold the mouse still for a few seconds while keeping the mouse button pressed. The graphic will temporarily redraw at its new size—but you can then continue to resize it if you are not yet satisfied with its appearance. When you finally are satisfied, release the mouse button and the graphic will be permanently redrawn. If you want to return the graphic to its original size after resizing it, use the UNDO command from the EDIT menu.

To proportionally resize a graphic, avoiding any distortion to the original image, press the SHIFT key and drag one of the four *corner* handles of the selected graphic. Since the graphic snaps back to its original proportions as soon as the mouse button is clicked, a proportional resizing will eliminate any distortion created by a previous nonproportional resizing. It is impossible to resize a distorted graphic proportionally and maintain the distortion.

Figure 10.11: *Proportionally resizing graphics is accomplished by pressing the shift key while scaling.*

When resizing paint-type or TIFF graphics, hold down the CTRL key while dragging, with or without the SHIFT key (depending on whether or not you want to resize proportionally), and PageMaker will allow you to reduce or enlarge the graphic only to sizes that can be printed at the best possible resolutions on the currently selected output device (as specified in the "Target Printer" option in the PRINTER SETUP dialog box).

PageMaker makes these determinations based on the resolution of the graphic and the resolution of the current output device. For example, since many paint-type graphics are created at a resolution of 72 DPI, and most laser printers print at 300 DPI, these graphics should be printed only at sizes that are 96%, 72%, 48%, or 24% of the original size At these sizes the 72 DPI can be divided evenly into the result of the resolution times the reduction percentage ([300 × 0.96] ÷ 72 = 4). At a percentage at which the DPI could not be divided evenly, the resulting image would not be as smoothly reproduced. You will find that 300-DPI graphics cannot be reduced when you are printing to a 300-DPI printer, but they can be reduced to a number of different sizes when a printer with resolution of 1270 DPI or higher is selected. Especially when working with gray-scale scanners, you might want to reduce the DPI at which you scan to allow yourself more freedom in high-quality reductions and enlargements.

Draw-type graphics and EPS graphics, on the other hand, can be sized to any percentage of the original size and still print with the highest quality possible because their original definitions are mathematically described rather than being based on a particular resolution.

Cropping graphics

Any placed graphic can be cropped using the cropping tool from the toolbox. Cropping removes a portion of the placed graphic, reducing the space occupied by the remaining graphic without resizing the graphic.

To crop a graphic, select the cropping tool from the toolbox and click anywhere on the graphic (if it is not already selected). Position the cropping tool on any handle so that the handle shows through the middle of the cropping tool, and press and hold the mouse button down. The cursor will become a two-headed arrow. You can now drag the handle to trim off the edge of the graphic as desired. You can also de-crop the graphic to reinstate any previously trimmed portions of the graphic: using the cropping tool, drag a handle back over the previously trimmed portions of the image.

Once a graphic has been cropped, you can reposition the graphic within the remaining graphic frame. By repositioning the graphic within its frame you can expose previously trimmed parts of the image and hide previously exposed portions. This is accomplished by positioning the cropping tool *inside* the graphic borders, rather than on any handle or on the graphic frame, and pressing and holding the mouse button down so that the grabber hand appears. While still holding the mouse button down, drag the mouse to reposition the graphic within the frame. This technique is useful for cropping a graphic in order to reduce the amount of space it occupies rather than to eliminate any particular portion of the graphic. Once you have determined the correct size for the graphic frame, you can position the underlying graphic for best display within the available space.

Figure 10.12: *After being cropped, a graphic can be repositioned within its remaining borders.*

Replacing graphics

After you have positioned, sized, and cropped a graphic, you may find it necessary to replace the graphic with a newer version or with an entirely new graphic. Also, you may sometimes use black boxes to hold the place of graphics while laying out your publication, adding the graphics meant to occupy these positions when your design is finalized. In any case, if you want the new graphic to occupy the same space as the one being replaced, select the "Replace existing graphic" option in the PLACE FILE dialog box while placing the graphic.

If the size of the graphic that is being placed is the same as the original size of the existing graphic (before any scaling or cropping), the new graphic will be scaled and cropped to exactly the final size of the graphic being replaced. If the size of the graphic being placed differs from the original size of the existing graphic, the new graphic will be scaled so that the size of one of its edges matches exactly the size of one of the edges of the graphic being replaced.

The graphic boundary of the graphic being replaced is transferred to the new graphic along with any irregular text wrapping and text placement attributes that have been assigned to the boundary. The graphic boundary, which controls the way that text wraps around a graphic, is described completely later in this chapter.

To replace an existing graphic, use the arrow tool to select the graphic anywhere on its boundary. Then choose the PLACE... command from the FILE menu. This will bring up the PLACE FILE dialog box. Select the name of the graphic file to be imported from the scrolling list on the left side of the dialog box. (More information about selecting the filename is included earlier in this chapter.) Select the "Replace existing graphic" option, and click the OK button.

The selected graphic will replace the existing graphic at the size determined according to the rules we have described. The graphic will be selected immediately after being placed. If you are not satisfied with its size, you can resize it or crop it. If the graphic has been sized non-proportionally, hold down the SHIFT key and select one of the corner handles with the arrow tool to snap the graphic to a size that is proportional to its original size.

Creating graphic elements

The PageMaker toolbox contains five tools that can be used to create simple graphic elements directly in your publication:

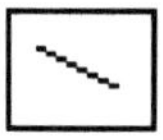

- **The diagonal-line tool** is used to create line segments.

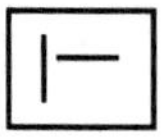

- **The perpendicular-line tool** is used to create line segments at 45° angles.

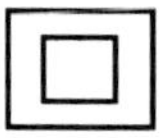

- **The square-corner** (rectangle) **tool** is used to create rectangles and squares.

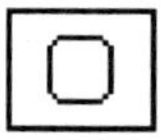

- **The rounded-corner tool** is used to create rectangles and squares.

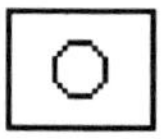

- **The oval tool** is used to create ovals and circles.

The line tools

A straight line is a basic design element that will be required in almost every publication that you will ever create in PageMaker. Two tools can be used to draw straight lines in PageMaker—the diagonal-line tool and the perpendicular-line tool. Using the diagonal-line tool, you can draw a continuous straight line between any two points on any page or on the pasteboard. The direction of the line can be constrained to any 45° angle by holding down the SHIFT key. The effect of constraining the diagonal-line tool is exactly like using the perpendicular-line tool, which draws lines only at 45° angles.

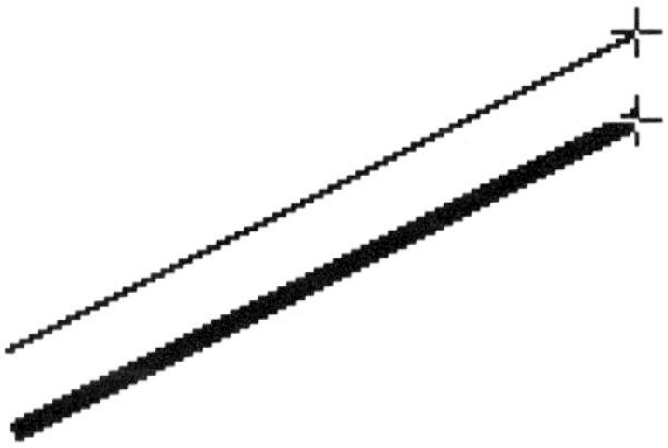

Figure 10.13: *The diagonal-ine tool in action.*

To use either line tool, select it from the toolbox and then position the crossbar cursor at the position where you wish to begin the line. Drag the mouse in the direction of the proposed line until the line is the proper length. If you drag into the edge of the display while drawing a line, the screen will automatically scroll in that direction. Use the ruler tick marks and dotted lines that track the cursor position to check the length of the line. Whenever drawing lines that follow column guides, or start or stop at a column guide, use the SNAP TO GUIDES command to ensure accuracy. In most cases the precision of your drawing will be greater at more enlarged view sizes and is best at "Actual" or "200% size."

When you draw a horizontal or vertical line, the line is created on one side of the crossbar or the other. You can flip the line to the opposite side of the crossbar by moving the crossbar itself to the opposite side.

Figure 10.14: *The perpendicular line tool in action.*

Lines can be drawn only at the current default line width, which is indicated by the check mark (✓) in the LINES menu. You can change the current default line width by selecting a new line width whenever a line or shape is not currently selected. A line width selection made while a line or shape is selected will apply only to the selected element and will not become the new default.

Immediately after it has been drawn, the line is selected, as indicated by the handles that appear at each end of the line. You can manipulate a selected line in several ways:

- **The line weight can be changed** by selecting any of the options from the LINES menu. If a line's weight or style is changed, the line remains centered on its original position.

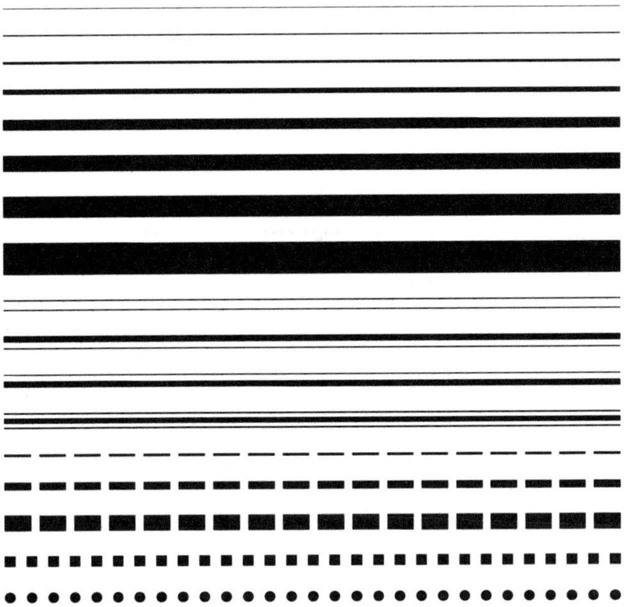

Figure 10.15: *Available line styles in PageMaker.*

- **The lines length can be changed** by dragging one of its handles with the arrow tool. When one of the handles is selected, the cursor will become a two-headed arrow. If the two-headed arrow does not appear, dragging at a handle will move the line rather than change the line length.

Figure 10.16: *Dragging on the handle of a selected line changes its length.*

- **The line can be repositioned** by dragging it with the arrow tool positioned anywhere except on a handle.

Figure 10.17: *Dragging on a line anywhere except at its handles moves the line.*

- **A color can be applied to the line** by selecting a color from the Colors palette.
- **The line can be cut, copied, or deleted** using the CUT (SHIFT-DELETE), COPY (CTRL-INSERT), or CLEAR command (from the EDIT menu) or the DELETE key.

A deselected line can be selected using any of the techniques described in Chapter 4, *A Brief Tour of PageMaker*.

The shape tools

Three tools in the toolbox can be used to create basic shapes in PageMaker. Any shape can be stroked with any of the line weights and styles found in the LINES menu and can also be filled with any of the fill patterns found in the SHADES menu. Shapes are used as basic design elements to create borders around objects, to make drop-out boxes, and to cover up mistakes.

- **The square-corner tool** is used to create a rectangle with square corners. With the SHIFT key pressed, the rectangle is constrained to a square with square corners. The corners of any rectangle or square can be modified by selecting the shape and then choosing the ROUNDED CORNERS... command from the OPTIONS menu, as described later in this chapter. A rectangle can be changed into a square at any time by selecting it, holding down the SHIFT key, and clicking on one of the rectangle's handles.

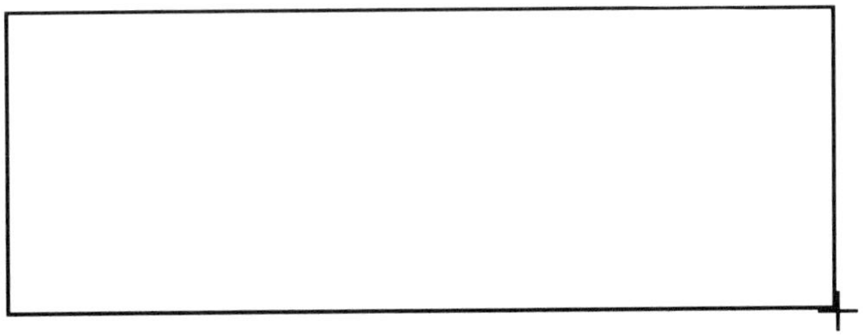

Figure 10.18: *The square-corner tool in action.*

- **The rounded-corner tool** is used to create a rectangle with rounded corners. With the SHIFT key pressed, the rectangle is constrained to a square with rounded corners. The corners of any rectangle or square can be modified by selecting the shape and then choosing the ROUNDED CORNERS... command from the OPTIONS menu, as described later in this chapter. A rectangle can be changed into a square at any time by selecting it, holding down the SHIFT key, and clicking on one of the rectangle's handles.

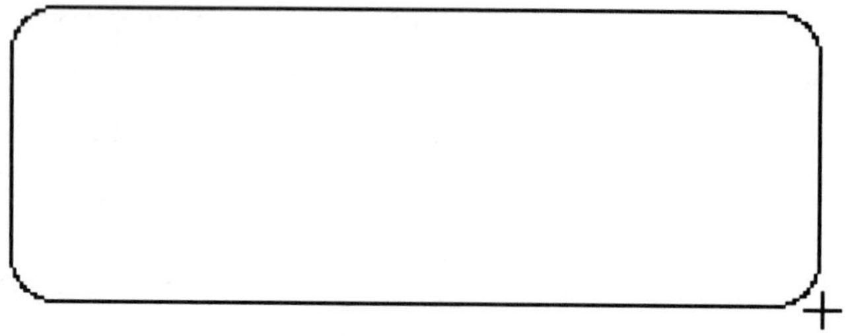

Figure 10.19: *The rounded-corner tool in action.*

- **The circle/oval tool** is used to create ovals and, with the SHIFT key, to create circles. An oval can be changed into a circle at any time by selecting it, holding down the SHIFT key, and clicking on one of the oval's handles.

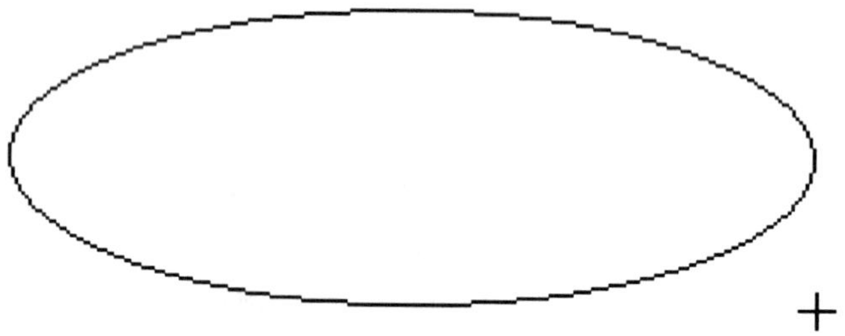

Figure 10.20: *The circle/oval tool in action.*

As any of these shapes is drawn, it is stroked with the current default line as selected in the LINE menu, and filled with the current default FILL pattern as selected in the SHADES menu. Immediately after it has been drawn, the shape is selected, as indicated by the handles that appear on all sides.

You can manipulate a selected shape in several ways:

- **The line weight can be changed** by selecting any of the options from the LINES menu.
- **The size of the shape can be changed** by dragging one of its handles with the arrow tool. When one of the handles is selected, the cursor will become a two-headed arrow. If the two-headed arrow does not appear, dragging at a handle will move the shape rather than change its size.

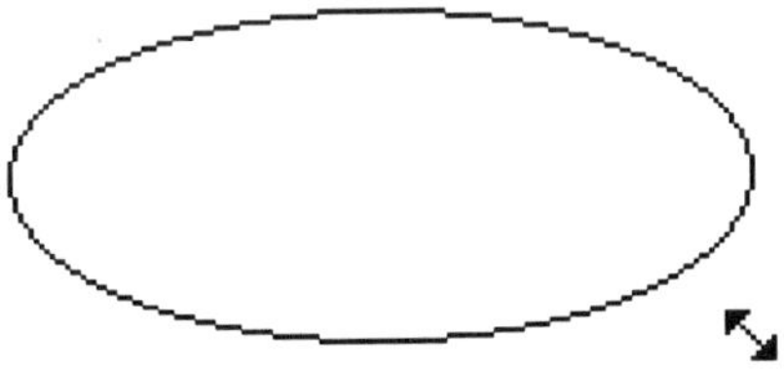

Figure 10.21: *Any shape can be resized by dragging on one of its handles.*

- **The shape can be repositioned** by dragging it with the arrow tool. If "None" is the shape's selected fill pattern (from the SHADES menu), you must drag the shape by the lines that define it, placing the arrow tool anywhere on the line except on a handle. A shape that has any fill pattern other than "None" can be selected and moved by positioning the arrow tool on the lines or anywhere on the fill inside the shape.

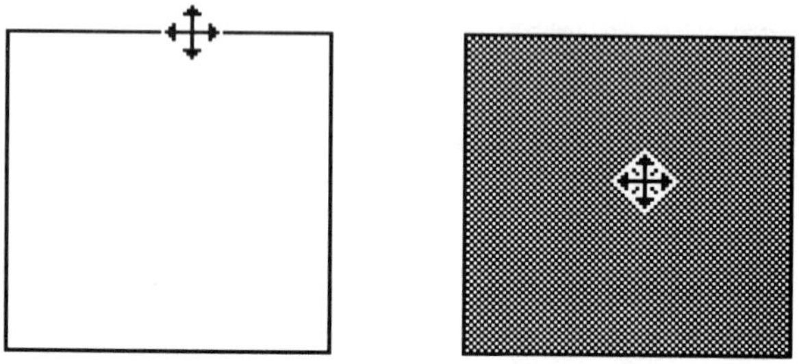

Figure 10.22: *Shapes can be repositioned by dragging anywhere except on their handles. If filled, they can be dragged by their contents as well as their borders.*

- **A color can be applied to the shape** by selecting a color from the Colors palette.
- **The shape can be cut, copied, or deleted** using the CUT, COPY, CLEAR commands (from the EDIT menu) or the DELETE key.

A deselected shape can be selected using any of the techniques described in Chapter 4, *A Brief Tour of PageMaker*.

More about lines and shades

As we have seen, lines and shades are applied to any PageMaker created graphic object by selecting that object and choosing the desired line or shade from the LINES or SHADES menus. The available line weights and line patterns were shown in Figure 10.15; the available shades and fill patterns are shown in Figure 10.23.

The only line widths available in PageMaker are those displayed in the LINES menu: hairline, 0.5 point, 1 point, 2 point, 4 point, 6 point, 8 point, and 12 point. In addition to these solid lines, solid double and triple lines and dashed and dotted line patterns are available. Only one solid line weight or one line pattern may be selected for any line. The "Reverse line" option draws lines in white instead of black, and they will be visible only when drawn on a shaded or solid background. To use any line weight or style not available in PageMaker, create it in another graphic application and then import it as described earlier in this chapter.

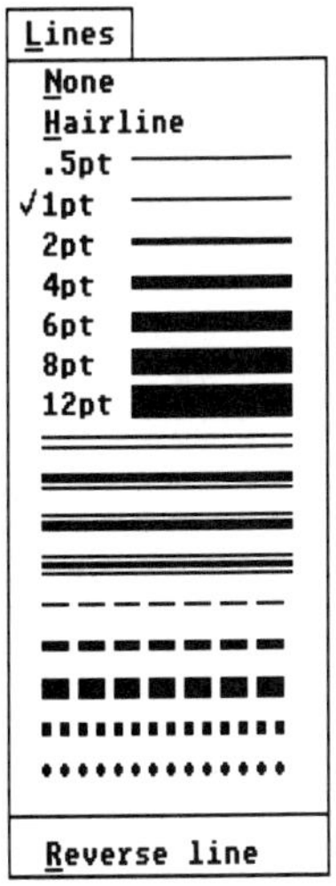

To check the current setting for any line or shape, select the line or shape and check the LINES or SHADES menu; the current line or shade option will display a check mark (✓) in front of it. If more than one object is selected and they do not all have the same line or shade setting, no check mark will display.

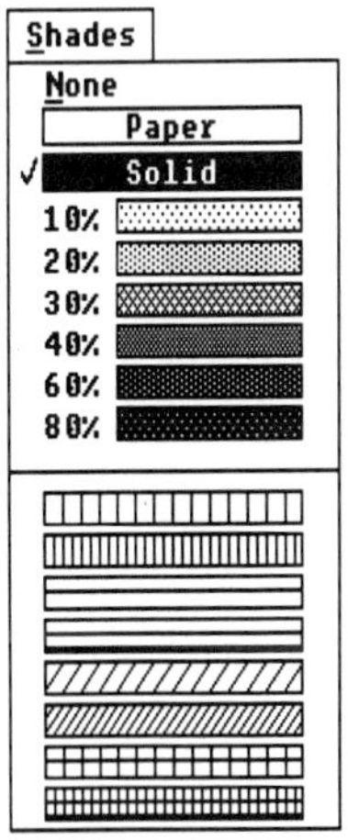

The publication default for the lines and shades can be changed any time that no line or shape is selected. Simply choose the new line or shade option from the appropriate menu. New lines or shapes created therafter using the new default settings.

As soon as a new line or shade is chosen, the display will be updated, approximating the line or shade selected. Very often the display representation for a line or shade will not reflect exactly the specified line or shade. This is true because of the low resolution of most displays. For example, any line weight less than 1 point is displayed on-screen as 1 point. When printed, however, line weights and shades will match their specifications. Of course, the resolution of your final output device will affect the exact thickness of any line or density of any shading, as shown in Figure 10.24.

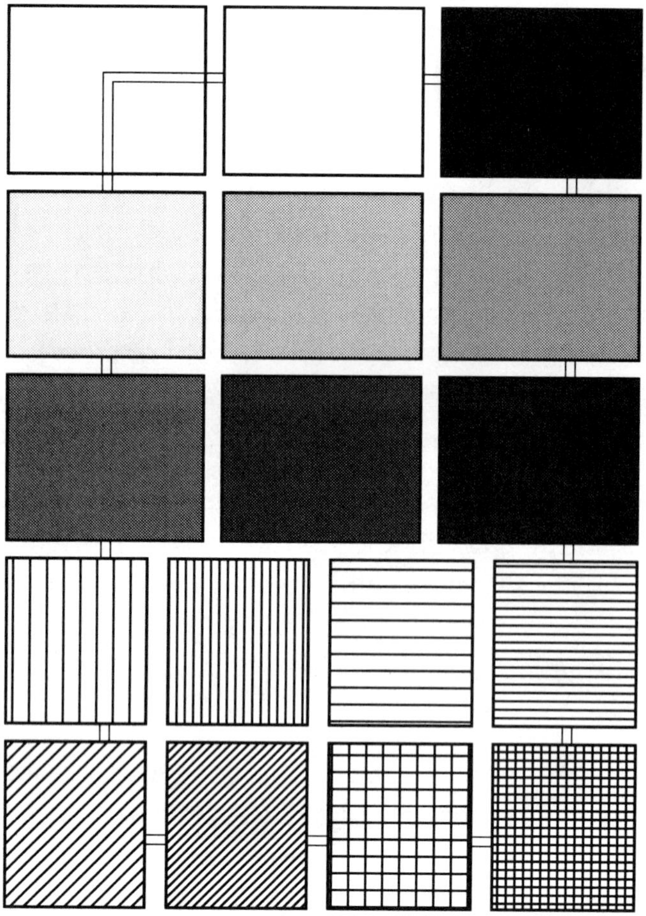

Figure 10.23: *Available shade styles in PageMaker.*

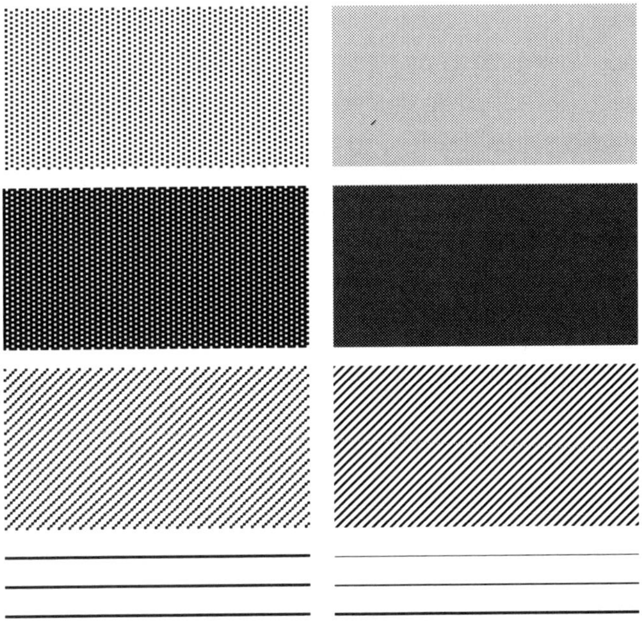

Figure 10.24: *On-screen versions (left) and printed versions (right) of 20%, 60%, and diagonal-line shades style plus hairline, 0.5-point, and 1-point line styles.*

Wrapping text around graphics

When a graphic object overlaps a text block, either partially or entirely, in most cases you will want the text to wrap around the shape of the graphic. You can instruct PageMaker to wrap the text around the graphic automatically, in a rectangular fashion, or you can adjust the text wrap to follow any irregular shape contained in your graphic.

Text wrap can be adjusted for any particular graphic when the graphic is positioned over some existing text or, alternatively the wrapping attributes of a graphic can be predefined so that as text flows into a document it wraps around existing graphics. It is also possible to alter PageMaker's default settings to predefine the wrapping attributes of all new graphics added to a publication.

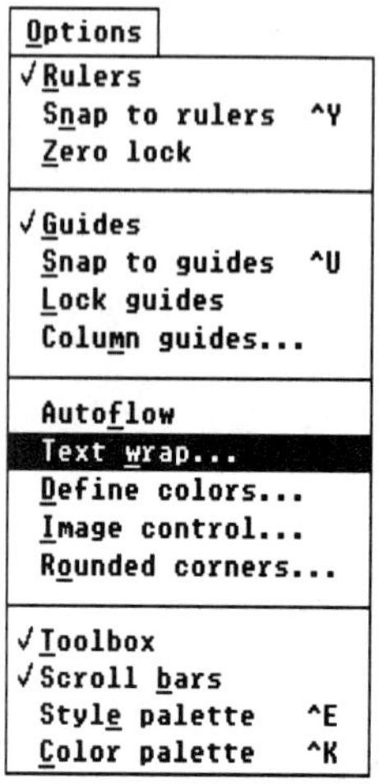

The TEXT WRAP dialog box is brought up using the TEXT WRAP... command in the OPTIONS menu. In this dialog box you can assign two kinds of attributes to any graphic object in PageMaker (whether created in the application or imported from another application):

- How text reacts when it encounters a graphic while being flowed.
- How text from any text block will wrap around a graphic if the text block and the graphic object overlap.

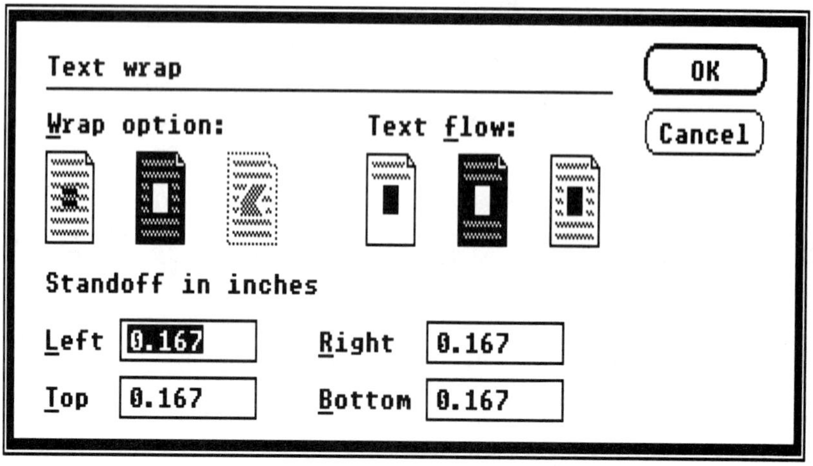

Figure 10.25: *The Text wrap dialog box.*

These attributes can be set after placing both the graphic and text; after placing the graphic, but prior to placing the text; or when no publication is open. In this last case the settings become defaults for all new graphics added to the publication.

Wrapping text automatically

Using the TEXT WRAP dialog box, you can assign any graphic in PageMaker a *graphic boundary*, which defines the minimum space between the graphic and any text. The graphic boundary is represented by a dotted line that appears around the graphic whenever it is selected. Corner points on the graphic boundary have *graphic boundary handles*, which are used to resize and reposition the graphic boundary with respect to the graphic itself. Additional graphic boundary handles can be added so that the graphic boundary can be defined more precisely in order to match the form of an irregularly shaped graphic more closely.

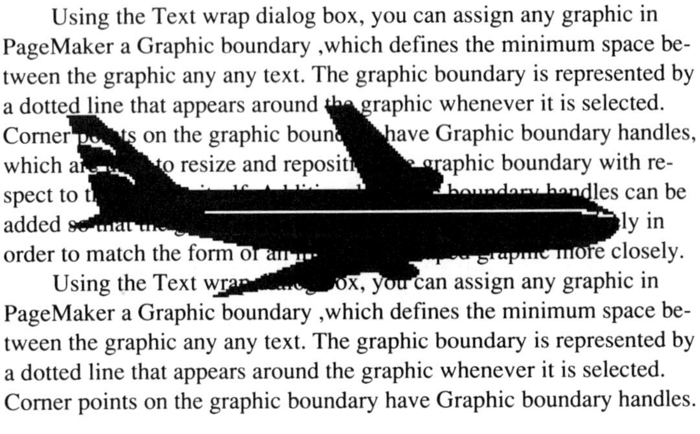

Figure 10.26: *Text with no graphic wrap.*

When a graphic does not have a graphic boundary, text can flow or be positioned directly on top of the graphic.

To create a graphic boundary for a particular graphic, select the graphic and then choose the TEXT WRAP... command from the OPTIONS menu. The TEXT WRAP dialog box contains three options that assign attributes to the graphic boundary. These attributes specify how text will wrap and flow around the the selected graphic.

- **"Wrap option"** One of three "Wrap option" icons are used to specify how text blocks should wrap text that overlaps a graphic element.

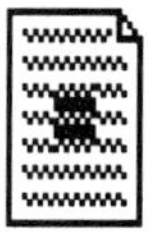

Selecting the "None" icon removes any existing graphic boundary, allowing text to flow directly over the graphic (see Figure 10.26).

The "Regular graphic boundary" icon places a rectangular graphic boundary around the graphic as specified by the "Standoff" option described below. Text will wrap around the graphic according to this rectangular graphic boundary, as shown in Figure 10.27.

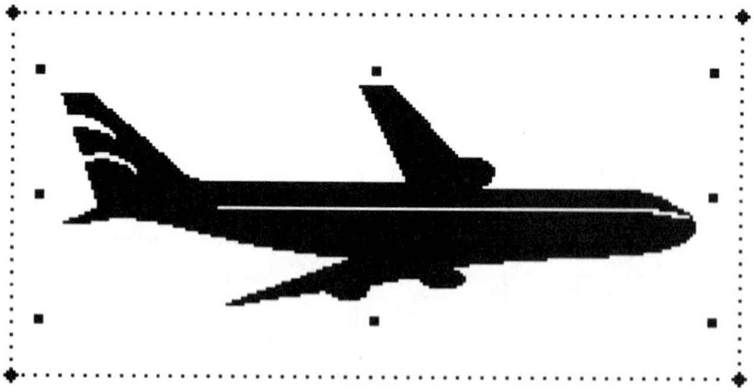

Figure 10.27: *A graphic with a rectangular graphic boundary.*

The third icon is the "Custom graphic boundary," but this icon cannot be selected directly. Instead, it becomes selected automatically when a rectangular graphic boundary is customized, as discussed below. If this icon is selected, selecting the "None" icon or the "Rectangular graphic boundary" icon will remove the custom graphic boundary, replacing it either with no graphic boundary or with a rectangular graphic boundary, respectively.

- **"Text flow"** If either the "Regular graphic boundary" or "Custom graphic boundary" option is set for the "Wrap option," then three "Text flow" options become available for selection. These options determine how text reacts to a graphic that is positioned within the column guides or previously created text block into which the text is being flowed. If the "None" icon is selected for the "Wrap option," then the "Text flow" options cannot be selected, and all three icons will be dimmed.

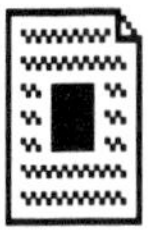

Selecting the "Column break" icon causes text to stop flowing when it reaches the top graphic boundary. If the "automatic flow" option is currently selected, text flow will resume at the top of the next column.

Selecting the "Jump graphic" icon causes the text to stop flowing when it reaches the top of the graphic boundary, and resume flowing under the bottom of the graphic boundary.

The "Wrap around" icon causes the text to continue flowing when it reaches the top graphic boundary, wrapping all sides of the graphic that intrude into the text block, and continuing to flow below the graphic.

- **"Standoff in ______"** The four values entered for this option (in the current default unit of measure) control the distance from the graphic to the top, bottom, left, and right edges of its rectangular graphic boundary. As discussed, the graphic boundary determines the space between the graphic and any text. A different value may be entered for each of the four settings.

  If a graphic boundary is customized, as indicated by the selection of "Custom graphic boundary" icon in the "Wrap option," the values in the "Standoff in" option become irrelevant for that graphic boundary. If a graphic is resized after the graphic boundary and standoff values have been set, the amounts of standoff will remain the same for the scaled graphic as for the graphic at its original size—the values are not reduced proportionally.

When the "Text wrap" options have been set to your satisfaction, click the OK button. The graphic element will now reflect the settings you have specified. If a graphic boundary has been specified, it will be displayed. If text did not previously wrap around this graphic, the text will now wrap around the new graphic boundary according to your specifications. If the text did wrap the graphic previously, the text will rewrap to reflect any changes made in the TEXT WRAP dialog box.

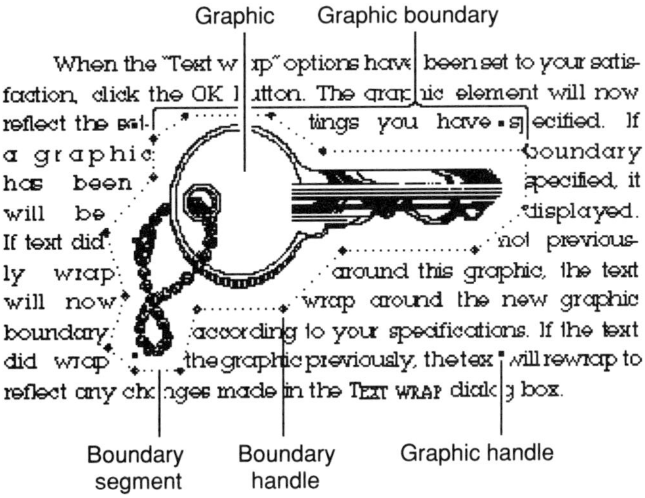

Figure 10.28: *A graphic boundary with handles and segments labeled.*

Customizing a graphic boundary

Once a rectangular graphic boundary has been created for a graphic element (by selecting the "Rectangular graphic boundary" icon in the "Wrap" option of the TEXT WRAP dialog box) or a graphic is created while the "Rectangular graphic boundary" is the default setting, the position and shape of the graphic boundary can be customized to better fit the graphic. A graphic boundary may be customized by manipulating it in any of four ways:

- Drag a boundary segment
- Drag a boundary handle
- Create additional boundary handles by clicking on the graphic boundary. You can then drag the new boundary sections or any of the boundary handles.

- Delete an existing boundary handle by dragging it on top of another existing boundary handle. You can then manipulate the remaining boundary sections or any of the boundary handles.

Holding down the SPACEBAR while adjusting the graphic boundary will inhibit the text from reacting to changes in the graphic boundary until the SPACEBAR is released. This can substantially speed up the process of customizing the boundary of an irregularly shaped object.

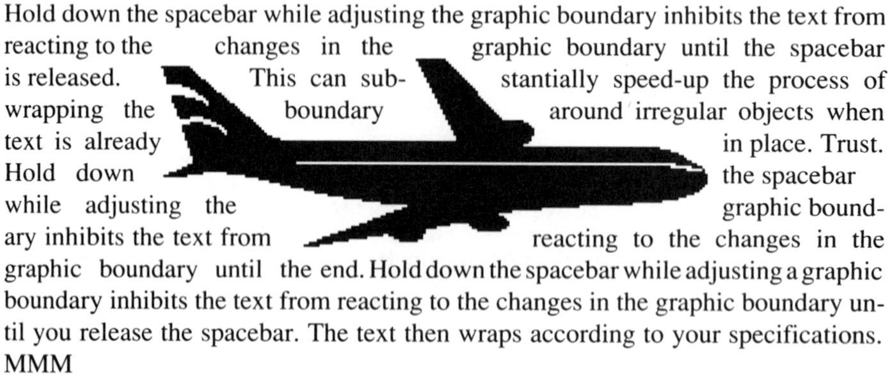

Figure 10.29: *A graphic with a customized graphic boundary.*

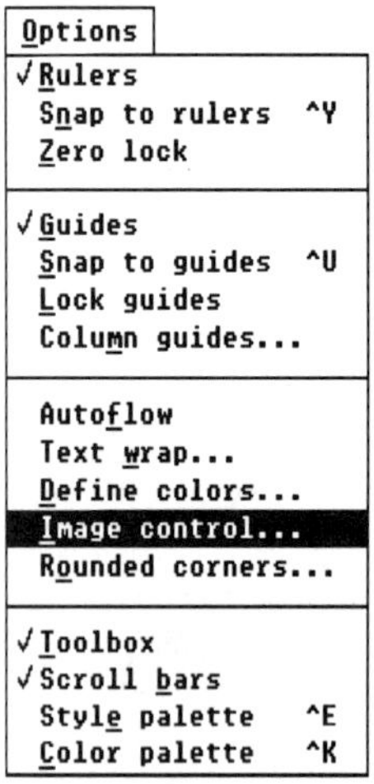

The Image control... command

Although we said earlier that it is impossible to modify graphics imported into PageMaker from other graphic applications, the IMAGE CONTROL command from the OPTIONS menu does make it possible to modify some attributes of paint-type and TIFF format graphics while they are in PageMaker.

Choosing the IMAGE CONTROL command brings up the IMAGE CONTROL dialog box, shown in Figure 10.30.

In the IMAGE CONTROL dialog box, you can:

- Adjust the line-screen and screen angle used to output paint-type or TIFF graphics.
- Adjust the lightness and contrast of these graphics.

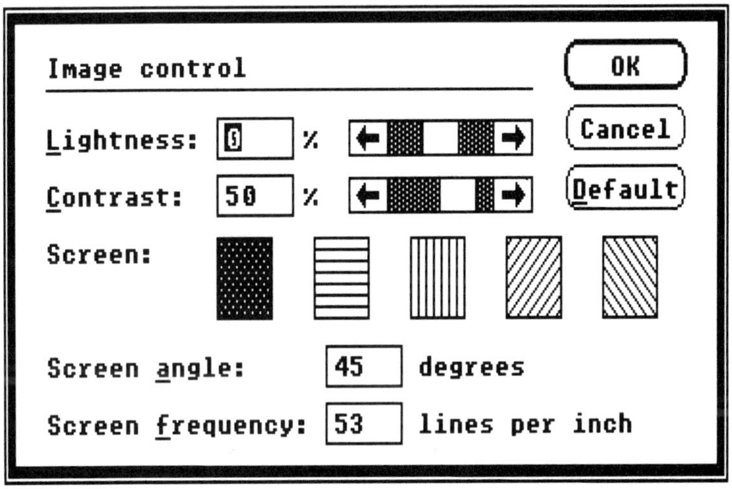

Figure 10.30: *The Image control dialog box as it appears when a paint or TIFF graphic is selected.*

To begin the manipulation, select the graphic that you wish to manipulate and then choose the IMAGE CONTROL... command from the OPTIONS dialog. The IMAGE CONTROL dialog will appear, as shown in Figure 10.30. (If the graphic you select is not a paint-type or TIFF graphic, the IMAGE CONTROL command will be dimmed.)

To understand the control provided by the options in this dialog box, you must understand a little about how printers work. When a document is converted into a print file and sent to a printer, the printing device applies a series of dots to the page in accordance with the instructions given in the print file commands. Since most printers can create only black dots, they utilize a **halftoning** technique to simulate gray areas. In halftones, gray values are simulated by combinations of black and white dots.

To determine which dots should be on and off in order to produce a halftone, printers use the concepts of halftone cells, frequency, angle, and function. Each output device contains some number of **machine pixels**: these are the smallest dots that the printer is capable of producing. Laying a uniform square grid over the printable area divides the machine pixels into **halftone cells**. Each machine pixel belongs to one of the halftone cells and each halftone cell is made up of some number of machine pixels.

The grid that divides the output device has a **frequency**, which is the number of halftone cells per inch into which it divides the imageable area, and an **angle**, which is the number of degrees by which the grid (and thereby each halftone cell) is rotated from being parallel to the bottom of the page. The **function** of a halftone cell is the mathematical expression used to determine in which order the individual pixels that make up the cell will be turned off in order to simulate increasing gray levels.

Each printer has default values for the frequency and angle of its halftone cells, and for the function used to simulate gray values. These defaults are used unless other values are specified in the IMAGE CONTROL dialog box for for the "Screen frequency," and "Screen angle" options.

The first set of options in the IMAGE CONTROL dialog box are the "Lightness," and "Contrast" options. The "Lightness" option allows you to lighten or darken all values in the image at the same time. Pressing on the right lightness arrow darkens all values (except those already at 100%), and pressing on the left lightness arrow lightens all values (except those already at 0%). These changes are reflected in the bar graph as they occur.

The "Contrast" option allows you to adjust the entire range of gray values to compress or expand the range of gray values in the image. Clicking on the right contrast arrow darkens values less than 50% and lightens values greater than 50%. Clicking on the left contrast arrow lightens values less than 50% and darkens values greater than 50%. These changes display in the bar graph as they occur.

The "Screen" option determines whether a line or dot screen pattern is used to create the graphic image. As we mentioned, this is essentially the function used in the halftoning process. When the "dotted" icon is selected, machine pixels in the halftone cell are turned off in an evenly spaced pattern when representing gray values. When one of the "lines" icon is selected, machine pixels are turned off so that the remaining pixels form a linear pattern.

The "Screen angle" option determines the angle of the screen used to create the image when printed. Control over this option is useful when creating special effects in conjunction with the "Screen" option.

The "Screen frequency" option determines the number of lines per inch used to create the image when printed. This controls the frequency of the halftone cells, as discussed earlier. The higher the number used for the "Screen frequency" option, the smoother an image will appear, but the fewer the number of available shades of gray. The lower the number used for the "Screen frequency" option, the coarser an image will appear, but the greater the number of available shades of gray. This is true because the "Screen frequency" and the number of machine pixels that make up a halftone cell are inversely related, and the more machine pixels in each halftone cell, the more shades of gray the halftone cell can represent (but the more room the halftone cell takes up in the imageable area—thereby allowing less halftone cells to fit into the entire imageable area, resulting in coarser images due to dramatic gradiations between halftone cells).

After manipulating any or all of these options, clicking the OK button will redraw the image based on the new settings. Clicking the DEFAULTS button resets all options in the IMAGE CONTROL dialog box to their original settings, while the CANCEL button restores the image to its original values and closes dialog box.

CHAPTER 11

Creating an Intermediate Flyer

In this chapter we examine:

- *Altering PageMaker's default settings*
- *Importing and cropping graphics*
- *Advanced text manipulation techniques*

In this chapter we will use PageMaker to create a two-sided flyer designed for marketing and direct mailing. Our step-by-step creation of this flyer represents the second of three sample projects presented in this book. This chapter focuses on the intermediate level of skill in using the various commands and features of PageMaker, as well as demonstrating how these features can be used to satisfy a wide variety of your publication needs.

Since our flyer is two-sided, we will create it as a two-page document. We will also design the flyer to be folded into thirds so that it can be mailed easily and inexpensively to prospective customers. As an added customer incentive, we will include a clip-out coupon at the bottom of the flyer.

Flyers do not contain superfluous text, so for this project you will need only one fairly short text file such as the LOREM.TXT text file you used in the first sample project. We will also be importing two kinds of graphics: one paint-format graphic (created in MACPAINT) and one EPS illustration (created in ADOBE ILLUSTRATOR). However, your graphics may originate from any graphics application, such as WINDOWS PAINT, AUTOCAD, PUBLISHER'S PAINTBRUSH, or MICROGRAFX DESIGNER. As in our first newsletter project, the contents of your text and graphic files are irrelevant. The focus of this sample project is the construction process, and not the content of the flyer.

Throughout this flyer we will be using the type faces Palatino and Zapf Dingbats. Both type faces can be printed on the Apple LaserWriter Plus and on most other PostScript-language laser printers. If you have a PCL printer, such as a Hewlett-Packard LaserJet, you will need a font cartridge with the Palatino and Zapf Dingbats families, or a downloadable version, such as those made by Bitstream. Use the Windows CONTROL PANEL or the installer included with the screen fonts to load them.

Check your printer manual to learn what type face families it can print. If your printer cannot print Palatino and Zapf Dingbats, substitute Helvetica for all Palatino references. The use of Zapf Dingbat is minimal, and you may simply read the text pertaining to the use of this typeface without actually adding the elements to your flyer.

Creating our publication

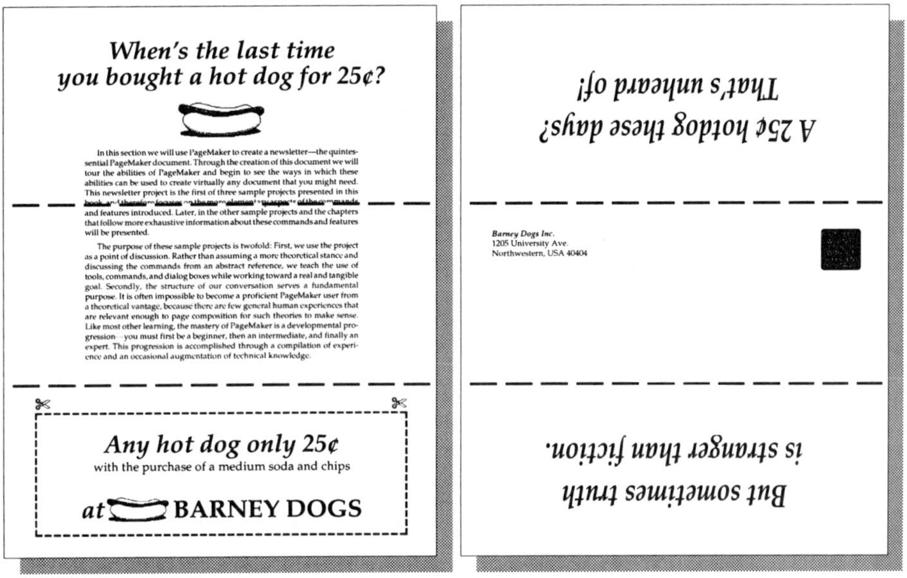

Figure 11.01: *The following pages describe how to create the intermediate, two-sided flyer shown above.*

1 To begin creating our publication, we must first launch the PageMaker application, as described in the first sample project. When PageMaker is loaded, click your mouse button to dispense with the copyright screen.

Changing default settings

Before we create a new file, we will be altering some application default settings in PageMaker. Aldus has set PageMaker defaults to the most commonly used settings for each particular option. By accurately reflecting your needs, customized defaults can save you the time and energy required to change a specific setting over and over again. Here are some examples of the default settings built into PageMaker:

- A new file is created for "Letter"-size paper with "Tall" orientation.
- "Inches" is the default unit of measurement.
- Type specifications are set for 12-point type size, Times type face with Auto leading and flush left alignment.
- Two column guides are set to provide one column per page.
- Line weight is set to 1-point, and shade pattern is set for "None," to provide transparent interiors for graphic objects.

Many of these defaults are useful, but as you continue to work in PageMaker, you will discover more and more defaults that may not be the settings you use most commonly. PageMaker recognizes that an individual's publication needs and page-creation working habits are as unique as the individual, so the application allows you to reset your own defaults. If you create legal-sized pages more often than letter-sized, you may want to change the default setting for the "Page size" option. If you prefer the type face New Baskerville to Times, you may change the "Font" option as well.

There are two ways to change defaults settings. The first method is to choose commands and select options at the PageMaker desktop while no publication is open. This resets the defaults for every new file that you create until you reset the defaults. These are called application defaults. The second method is to choose commands and select options while no element is selected in a specific publication. Resetting defaults in this manner—as publication defaults—redefines settings in the current file only, without affecting future files. By either method, a change in a default setting will affect only a currently active file or a future file. Altering a default setting never has any bearing on an existing file that is not open when the setting is changed.

2 We will alter some defaults at the PageMaker desktop before creating our new file. First, choose the PREFERENCES... command from the EDIT menu to display the PREFERENCES dialog box. This dialog allows you to determine the system of measurement you wish to use in creating a document. The selected "Measurement system" option will affect the appearance of your rulers, as well as the selections offered in many dialog box options.

PageMaker offers five units of measurement:

- **Inches**, the most commonly used system of measurement in America.
- **Inches decimal**, which divides the standard inch into ten equal segments.
- **Millimeter**, a metric unit equal to 1/1000 meter or 1/10 centimeter. The metric system is used commonly throughout Europe.
- **Pica**, a unit of measure that is roughly 1/6-inch. A pica is subdivided into 12 units, called **points**. Picas and points are the traditional unit of measurement for American typesetting and

page composition and are now the preferred system of measurement in desktop publishing applications.

- **Ciceros**, a unit of approximately 4½ millimeters, this is the traditional unit of measurement for European typesetting. Like the pica, a cicero is subdivided into 12 points. (One cicero point is approximately equal to 1.06 pica points.)

You may also select a unit of measure from the "Vertical ruler" column that affects your vertical ruler only. Generally, this option should be set to the same unit of measure selected from the "Measurement system" column.

3 Select the "Picas" option from the "Measurement system" column. The "Vertical ruler" options will then change to those shown in Figure 11.02. The "Picas" option should be selected from this column as well. Then click the OK button.

This change in the default setting for "Measurement system," from inches to picas, has now been saved to the PM.CNF file, which resides in the PageMaker directory. Any new documents created in PageMaker will default to picas instead of inches, as long as "Picas" remains the default setting. Existing documents, however, will retain the same system of measurement that was selected when each document was last saved.

If you wish to alter any other default settings, now is the time to do so. For this project, we will alter type specification defaults, line width and shade settings, and settings in the PAGE SETUP dialog box.

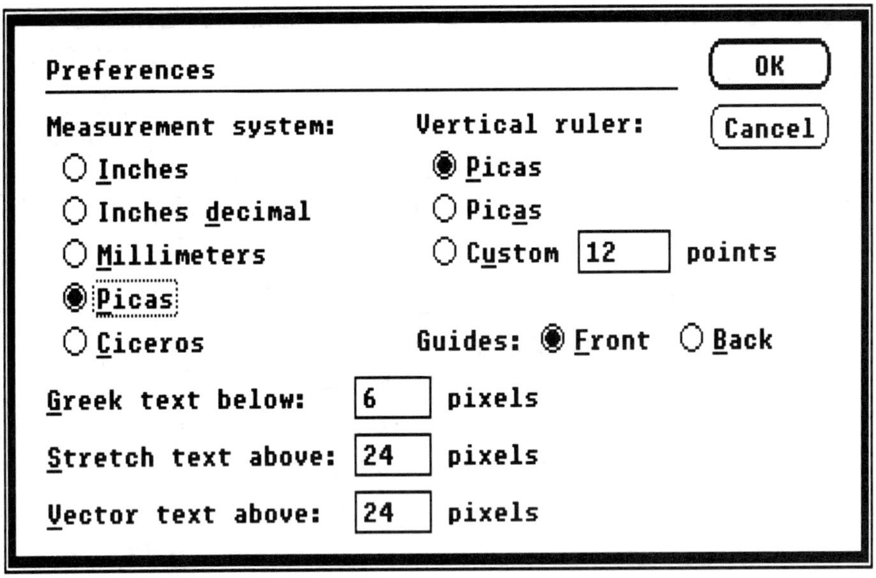

Figure 11.02: *The Preferences dialog box showing our new default settings.*

4 Choose the Type specs... command from the Type menu, or press ctrl-T. This brings up the Type specifications dialog box, where we can change settings for the font, style, size, and leading options. For our project the options in the Type specifications dialog box should be set as follows:

Font: Palatino — **Case**: Normal

Size: 36 — **Position**: Normal

Leading: 37.5 — **Type style**: select "Bold" and "Italic" options

When you have finished entering and selecting the specifications listed above, click on the OK button.

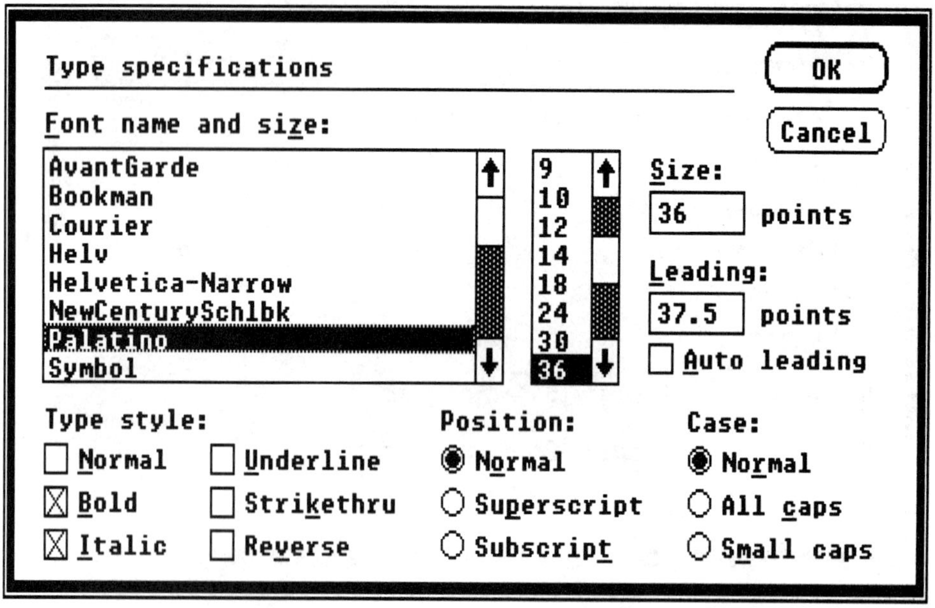

Figure 11.03: *The Type specifications dialog box showing our new default settings.*

5 To set our final default type specification, we will change the alignment of our text from flush left to centered. To do this, choose the "Align center" command from the TYPE menu, or press CTRL-C.

Now that we have altered the default settings for type font, style, size, leading, and alignment, we are ready to move on to other defaults. We will change these settings without accessing dialog boxes, since we can access the settings immediately by simply choosing commands.

6 The coupon at the bottom of our flyer will be surrounded by a fairly heavy dashed line, or coupon border. Click and hold on the LINES menu, and choose the second dashed-line option. Next, choose PAPER on the SHADES menu. Now, any shape that we create in PageMaker will have a coupon border outline and a white interior.

7 Choose the SNAP TO RULERS command from the OPTIONS menu, or press CTRL-Y. This activates PageMaker's snap-to-rulers feature, which constrains the creation and manipulation of elements to a grid determined by your currently selected system of measurement. For example, in our sample project we will be working in picas. Each tick mark on the horizontal and vertical ruler indicates ¼ pica, or 3 points. When SNAP TO RULERS is turned on, you will be able to create or move elements only in increments of 3 points. This 3-point grid will help us to maintain consistency in placement of text and graphics throughout our document.

8 The last group of default settings that we will change will affect the number of master and publication pages, as well as the margins we will use to create our flyer. Flyers generally require only one master page and two publication pages. For our flyer, our margins should be slightly smaller than PageMaker's present settings. To alter these settings, choose the PAGE SETUP... command from the FILE menu. The options in the PAGE SETUP dialog box should be set as follows:

Page size: Letter

Orientation: Tall

Start page #: 1

# of pages: 2

Double-sided: not selected

Facing pages: dimmed

Margin in picas: Left 3, Top 3, Right 3, Bottom 3.

When you have finished entering and selecting the specifications listed above, click the OK button.

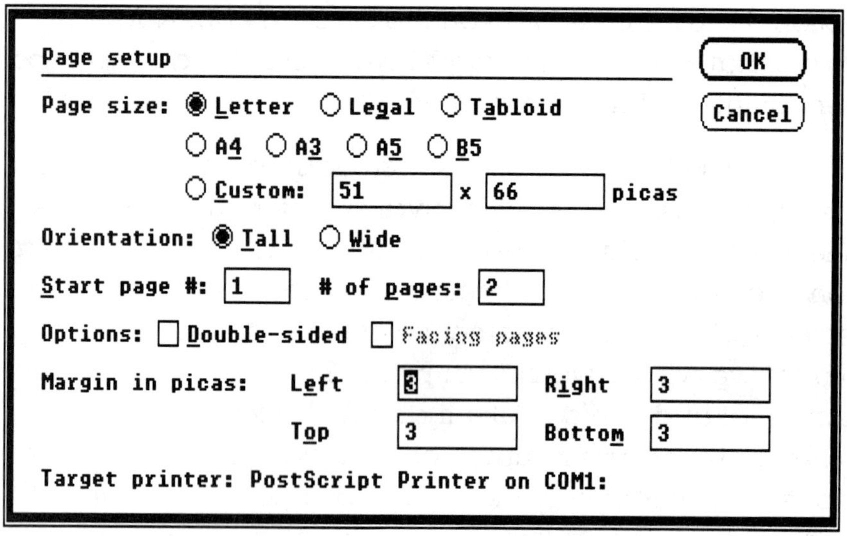

Figure 11.04: *The Page setup dialog box containing our new default settings.*

Creating a new document

We are now finished altering PageMaker's default settings, having changed default settings for commands from every menu except the PAGES menu. Now it is time to see how these altered defaults will affect the creation of a new document.

9 Choose the NEW... command from the FILE menu, or press CTRL-N. Notice that the resulting PAGE SETUP dialog box contains all our new settings. Click OK to confirm these settings and create a new file.

A new publication window now displays, showing the first page of our publication. Vertical and horizontal rulers should also be displayed, both measuring picas. (If there are no rulers, choose the RULERS command from the OPTIONS menu to display them.) Notice that there is now only one master page icon, labeled "R" for "right." Any element or guide that we put on this master page will be displayed on both pages of our flyer.

Preparing the master page

Click on the master page icon in the bottom left corner of your screen display. We will not create any elements on our master page, because no text or graphic items will appear on both sides of our flyer. However, both sides will share to the same basic layout, so we will use the master page to establish a consistent system of ruler guides.

Setting up ruler guides

Creating a two-fold flyer is fairly tricky, because we have to consider how each of three panels (on each side of the paper) will appear when viewed alone as well as when the flyer is fully opened. Therefore, each panel must be marked by fold lines on our electronic pages. We will use horizontal ruler guides to indicate the two fold lines.

We must first determine the size of each panel. This may seem easy. The page is to be folded two times with both folds in the same direction to create three panels; therefore each panel should be one-third page in size. However, our flyer will have the two outer panels folded over on the middle panel, so we must accommodate the thickness of the paper folding over on itself. The bottom panel will be the smallest: it will fold over the middle panel, which should be slightly longer to accommodate the thickness of the paper at the fold and to ensure that the edge of the bottom panel will not touch the second fold line; the third panel must be even larger because it will be folding over the thickness of two layers of paper. For a professional appearance, we will want the edge of the outer panel to be flush with the edge created by the first fold.

To determine the exact size of each panel, we must first establish our overall page size. Our page is 8½ inches wide by 11 inches tall, or 51 picas by 66 picas. We will be folding the flyer lengthwise, so if each panel were exactly one-third page tall, each panel would measure 66 ÷ 3 = 22 picas. The bottom panel is the smallest, so we subtract one pica from it: 22 – 1 = 21 picas. We add this 1 pica to the largest panel—the top one: 22 + 1 = 23 picas.

10 The zero point of our rulers is at the top left corner of the master page. With this in mind, we will drag down two ruler guides from the horizontal ruler at the top of our display to indicate the fold lines in our flyer. Since the top panel is to be 23 picas tall, we drag the first horizontal ruler guide to the 23-pica mark of the vertical ruler (just at the center of the "24"-pica label). The middle panel is to be 22 picas tall, so we drag a second horizontal ruler guide down to the 23 + 22 = 45-pica mark of the vertical ruler (halfway between the "42"- and "48"-pica labels). The bottom panel is to be 21 picas tall, and it is since 66 – 45 = 21 picas. Zoom in to "Actual" size to get a better view of the ruler increments if you are having trouble locating them at the "Fit in Window" size.

From now on, we will refer to these two horizontal ruler guides as the upper and lower *fold lines.*

Now, we need a few more horizontal ruler guidelines to indicate the margins of each panel. Since the flyer as a whole has a 3-pica margin on all sides, each panel should have 3-pica margins as well. You may notice that each panel already has left and right margins of 3 picas. However, the top panel is missing a bottom margin; the bottom panel is missing a top margin; and the middle panel is missing both a top and bottom margin.

11 To establish the bottom margin of the top panel, drag a guide from the horizontal ruler to position 3 picas above the upper fold line, or at the 23 – 3 = 20-pica mark on the vertical ruler. Drag another horizontal ruler guide to mark the top margin of the middle panel. This must be located at the 23 + 3 = 26-pica mark on the vertical ruler. Next, represent the bottom margin of the middle panel by dragging a horizontal ruler guide to 3 picas above the lower fold line, at the 45 – 3 = 42-pica mark on the vertical ruler. And finally, drag a guide to the 45 + 3 = 48-pica mark to mark the top margin of the bottom panel of the flyer.

From now on, we will refer to our four newest horizontal ruler guides as the first, second, third, and fourth *fold margins.*

12 Since we have now created all of the fold lines and fold margins required to help us create our flyer, we are finished working on the master page. Click on the page 1 icon at the bottom of your display to return to publication page 1, which should appear as shown in Figure 11.05.

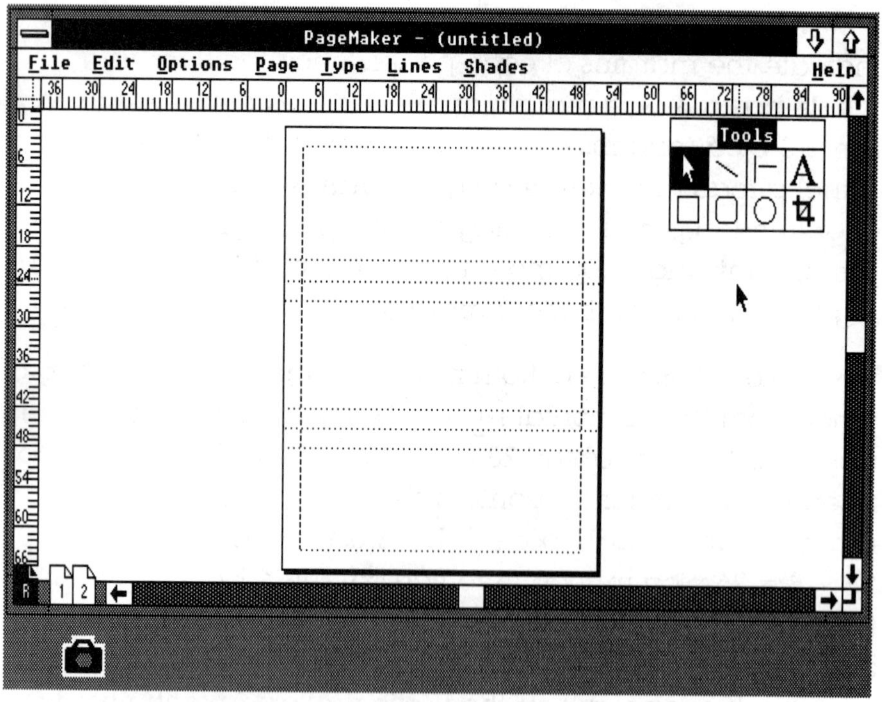

Figure 11.05: *Page 1 of the flyer, containing the fold lines and fold margins that we created as horizontal ruler guides.*

Saving the document to disk

In our first sample project, we waited until we finished our document to save the file in order to isolate our description and execution of the SAVE command. However, you will not normally want to wait until a document is completed to save it to disk. It is a good idea to save a document after each first major step in the creation of your new file. In this case, we may consider our establishment of ruler guides on the master page a major first step, so we are ready to save.

13 Choose the SAVE command from the FILE menu, or press CTRL-S. When the SAVE PUBLICATION AS dialog box appears, enter the name "2side.PM3" or some other appropriate and sufficiently descriptive filename into the option box to the right of the list of filenames in the current directory. Use the drive letters in brackets and the parent directory symbol ([..]) to determine the destination to which your file will be saved, and then click OK. PageMaker will take a few moments to save your file to disk, after which the filename will appear at the top of your screen display in place of the word "Untitled" in the current title bar.

Now that our flyer is saved to disk, we will periodically update the file by choosing the SAVE command, or pressing CTRL-S, after each major step in creating our document. The SAVE command will no longer produce the SAVE PUBLICATION AS dialog box, but will simply overwrite the existing file. If you do wish to produce the SAVE PUBLICATION AS dialog, perhaps to save the file to a different directory or disk, choose the SAVE AS... command from the file menu.

Placing the body copy

Now that we have established our guides and saved the file, we are ready to create the text and graphic elements of our flyer. We will begin by placing the body copy. As we mentioned at the beginning of this project, a flyer does not generally contain a large amount of text, since it is intended to be read quickly. Therefore, you will need to provide a short text file, not more than one page long. For convenience, use the LOREM.TXT text file you used in the first sample project, since the content of this file is irrelevant.

14 Choose the PLACE... command, or press CTRL-D. When the PLACE FILE dialog appears, double-click on an appropriate text filename. When the publication window reappears, click with your manual text flow cursor in the upper left margin corner.

Adjusting column width of existing text

Since we did not set a new application default for the column width, and we did not adjust the column width on our master page, our story pours the entire width determined by the margins we specified in the PAGE SETUP dialog box. However, this does not serve our purpose, since body copy this wide (45 picas) is generally difficult to read. Reducing the width of an existing text block a very simple task. Surrounding your text block (assuming it is selected) are four square **handles**, each located at an end of one of the two handlebars. These handles are useful for adjusting the column width of the text block.

We will also be making use of the small dotted **tracking lines** that appear on the vertical and horizontal rulers, monitoring the location of the cursor. As you move your cursor, you will notice how these tracking lines also move, marking the cursor's distance from the ruler zero point. Tracking lines are very useful in positioning elements.

15 If your text block is not selected, click on it with the arrow tool to display its handlebars and four square handles. Click and hold on the lower left handle, and notice how a rectangle appears surrounding the text, demonstrating its horizontal and vertical dimensions. The tracking line on the horizontal ruler is at the 3-pica mark. Drag the lower left handle until the tracking line aligns with the 9-pica mark, then release. Next drag at the lower right handle of the text block toward the left, following the horizontal ruler tracking line from its initial position at the 48-pica mark until it is at the 42-point marker, as demonstrated in the following figure. Once this move is completed, we will have decreased the column width of our text block by 6 picas (or one inch) on each side. Our new text block width is 33 picas, which is more readable than its previous width.

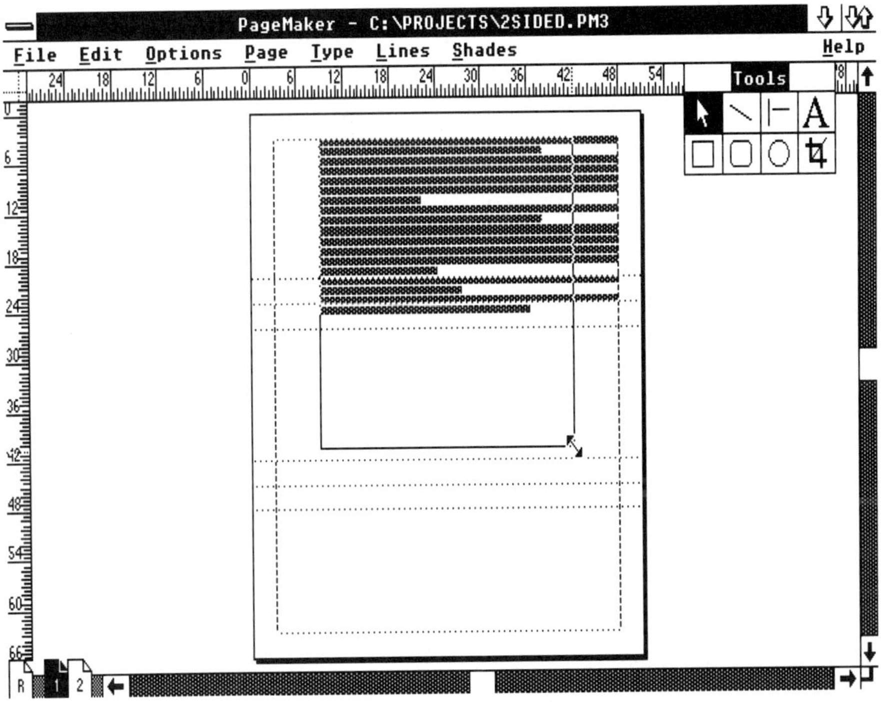

Figure 11.06: *Reducing the column width of an existing text block by dragging at one of its handles.*

Changing type specs

Our next step is to change or adjust the type specifications of our text. Notice that it is in 36/37.5 Palatino bold-italic, which is the setting we specified when we altered the default type specifications. This is because the text was unformatted, and did not have style sheet tags or an accompanying style sheet that PageMaker could use to format the file. (See Chapter 10, *Style Sheets,* for more information about style sheets.) PageMaker has built-in filters for several word-processors, and filters for many more can be installed. These filters enable PageMaker to preserve all or most of the formatting in a text file. However, if a text file, such as the LOREM.TXT file, is unformatted, PageMaker will apply its default type specifications (an exception is a text file with style sheets, as we will demonstrate in the third sample project).

16 Select the text tool, click anywhere inside the text block, and press CTRL-A to select the entire file. Then press CTRL-T to access the TYPE SPECIFICATIONS dialog box. Change the type face, size, and leading to Palatino 12/Auto, using the procedures we used for changing the default settings. Make sure that the "Type style" is set to "Normal" and click OK.

17 This block of text will probably look better if we fully justify it so that the left and right edges of each line of text are flush with the edges of the text block itself. While the type is still selected, choose the JUSTIFY command on the TYPE menu, or press CTRL-J.

18 As usual, the final step in creating our text block is to adjust its position vertically by dragging at its upper and lower handlebars. Select the arrow tool, and drag downward on the tab of the upper handlebar to the 15-pica mark on the vertical ruler (as indicated by the tracking line). Then drag on the lower handlebar to the bottom margin of the middle panel (the horizontal ruler guide 42 picas from the top of the page).

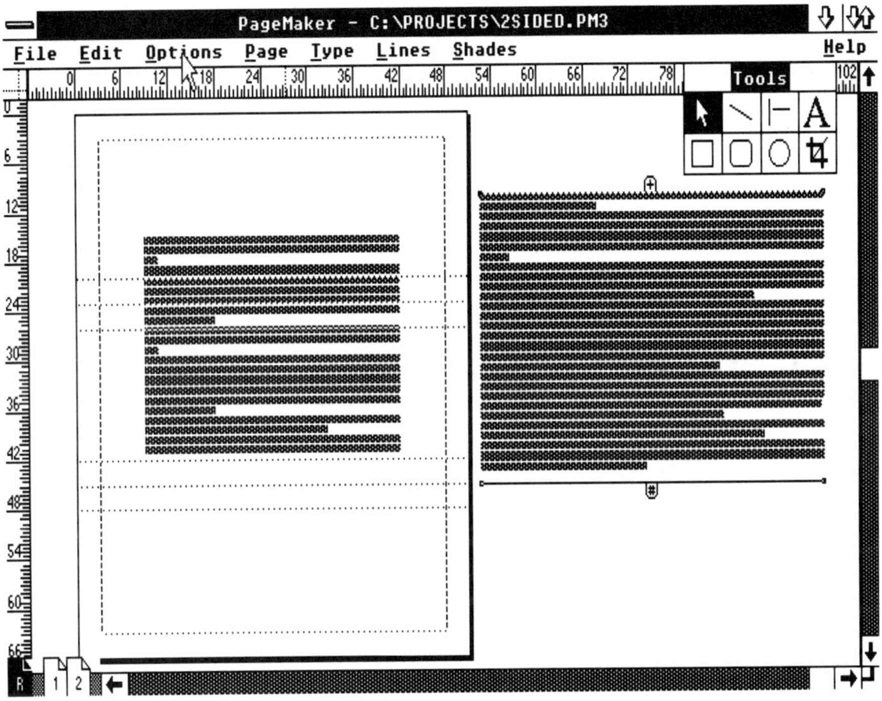

Figure 11.07: *Pouring the excess portion of our story onto the pasteboard.*

19 In the first sample project, we rarely poured an entire text file. If a file contained more text than we wished to display on a page, we simply ignored the remaining text. For this project, however, we will deal with the remainder of our text file by deleting it. With the arrow tool, click on the tag of the lower handlebar. (If your lower tag contains a pound sign (#) instead of a plus sign (+), there is no text remaining in the file, and you may go on to step 20). Your cursor will change to the manual flow cursor. Scroll toward the right, well into your pasteboard, and then click near the top of your display to pour the remaining text. Once the text is poured, press the DELETE key to delete it. Now scroll back to your page (or press CTRL-W) and select our text block. It should now end in a pound sign. If it does not, repeat this step again.

20 Press CTRL-S to update your file on disk.

Adding a headline with default type specs

The area from the top margin to the top of our body copy (15 picas) is allocated for a headline and a simple graphic. We will create the headline first.

21 Select the text tool and click the secondary mouse button at the top of the page to magnify the view size to "Actual" size. Then click with the text tool just below the top margin to establish a text entry cursor, and type "When's the last time ¶ you bought a hot-dog for 25¢?" There are two symbols in this sentence that you may not recognize or know how to access. One is the paragraph sign (¶). The paragraph sign indicates a line return, marking the location at which you should press the RETURN key to set your cursor on the next line before typing the rest of the words. Another symbol is the familiar (but hard to find) cent symbol (¢), which is accessed by pressing the ALT key and typing 0, and then 1-6-2 on the numeric keypad. You may not even recognize that the third symbol is not an ordinary character. It is the apostrophe ('), or closing single quotation mark. You may have instead pressed the

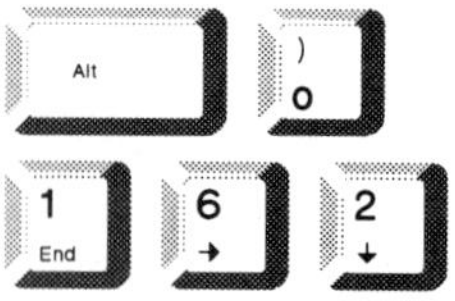

neutral single quotation mark ('). In general, both the neutral single quote (') and the neutral double quote (") should be avoided. In most cases the opening and closing single (‘ and ’) and double (“ and ”) quotes—which are more distinctive and attractive—are the correct symbols. Each quote is accessed by pressing the following key combinations:

- Opening double quote “ CTRL-SHIFT-[
- Closing double quote ” CTRL-SHIFT-]
- Opening single quote ‘ CTRL-[
- Closing single quote (apostrophe) ’ CTRL-]

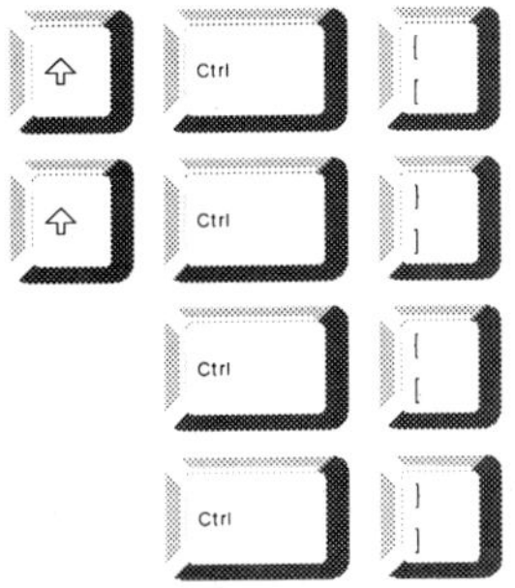

Once you have completed typing in your headline text, notice how it looks. It is centered, 36/37.5 Palatino bold-italic, just as we specified in our default type specs! Because this is exactly what we want, no alterations are necessary. We have saved time and energy by establishing defaults before creating a new file.

22 Select the arrow tool and click on the text block. Then adjust the vertical placement of the headline by dragging its upper handlebar flush with the top margin of the page.

23 Once your headline appears as shown in the Figure 11.08, press CTRL-S to save the file.

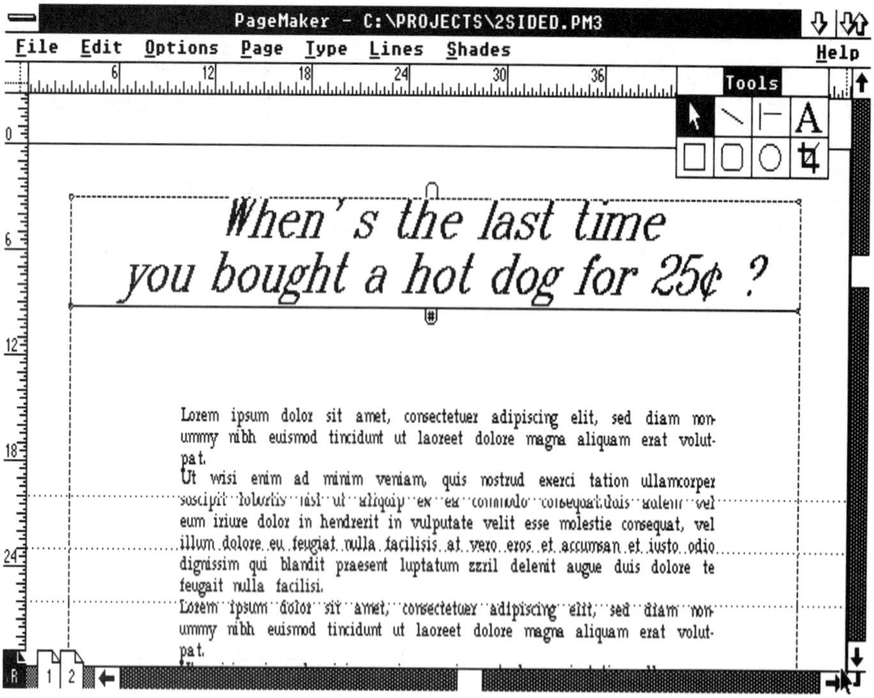

Figure 11.08: *The 36/37.5 Palatino bold-italic flyer headline.*

Adding a simple graphic

Our next steps outline the addition of a simple graphic between the headline text and the body copy on the first page of our flyer. This graphic can originate in any environment. If you own or have access to any electronic clip art, we recommend that you use such a file, since this is what we will be using. Otherwise, use whatever you have.

To use a graphic in PageMaker, or in any other page-composition application, you must first prepare your graphic for importation. This often means that you must save your file in one of the graphic file formats supported by PageMaker—HPGL, PCX, EPS (encapsulated PostScript), or TIFF (tagged image file format). A drawing application generally supports only a single format. Here are a few examples of popular graphics applications, along with the formats supported by each for saving files you intend to import into PageMaker:

▪ MS PAINT	save as .MSP file
▪ PC PAINTBRUSH	save as .PCX file
▪ GRAPHICS GALLERY	save as TIFF (.TIF) file
▪ AUTOCAD	save as .PLT file
▪ ADOBE ILLUSTRATOR	save with IBM PC preview, EPS format
▪ MICROGRAFX IN*A*VISION	save as a .PIC file
▪ MACPAINT	save normally, paint format (.PNT)

Make sure you save your graphic files in one of these formats before trying to import the file into PageMaker, and check your PageMaker manual to determine which file formats are built into PageMaker and which formats require you to install import/export filters.

24 Choose the PLACE... command from the FILE menu, or press CTRL-D. This brings up the same PLACE FILE dialog box that we use to import word-processed files. Select a graphic filename from the file listing. You will notice that as soon as you click on an available graphic filename, some of the "Place" options change. Since we have no graphic currently selected in our PageMaker file, the only option that is not dimmed is the "As new graphic" option. This indicates that our graphic will be placed into our flyer normally, rather than as a replacement for an existing graphic. If we had selected a graphic on our electronic page before choosing the PLACE... command, a second option, "Replacing entire graphic," would also be available. This option would allow us to replace the selected graphic with a placed graphic, including resizing and cropping (both of which we will describe). After selecting a graphic filename to be placed, click OK.

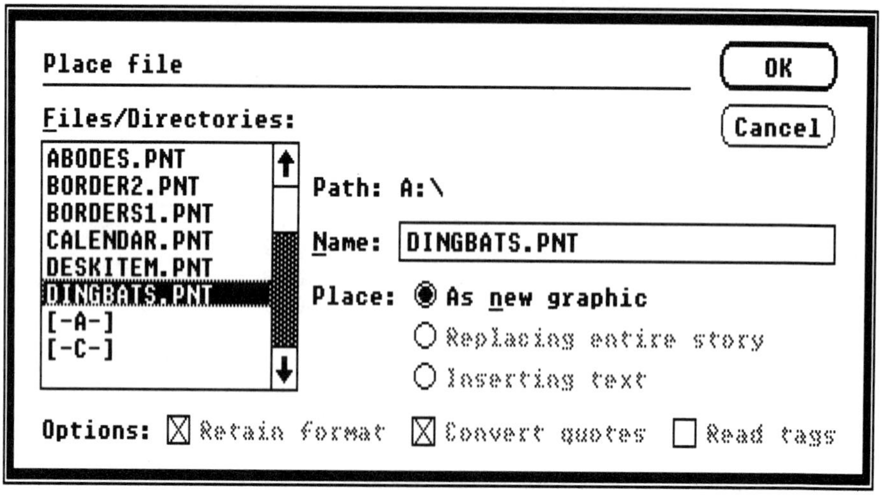

Figure 11.09: *The Place file dialog box demonstrating the options available when importing a graphic.*

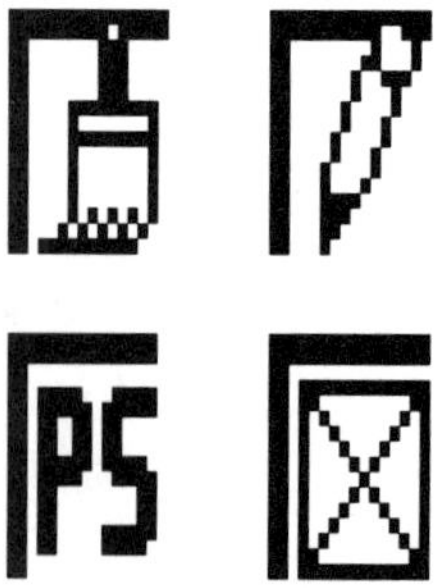

25 Your cursor will change to one of the four graphic importation cursors, depending on the format used to save your graphic—the paint-type icon displays a paintbrush, the object-oriented icon displays a pencil, the EPS-type displays a small "PS," and the TIFF-type displays a small square containing an X. We are importing a paint file, so ours is the paintbrush icon. Whatever your cursor, click in the upper left portion of your window to place your graphic.

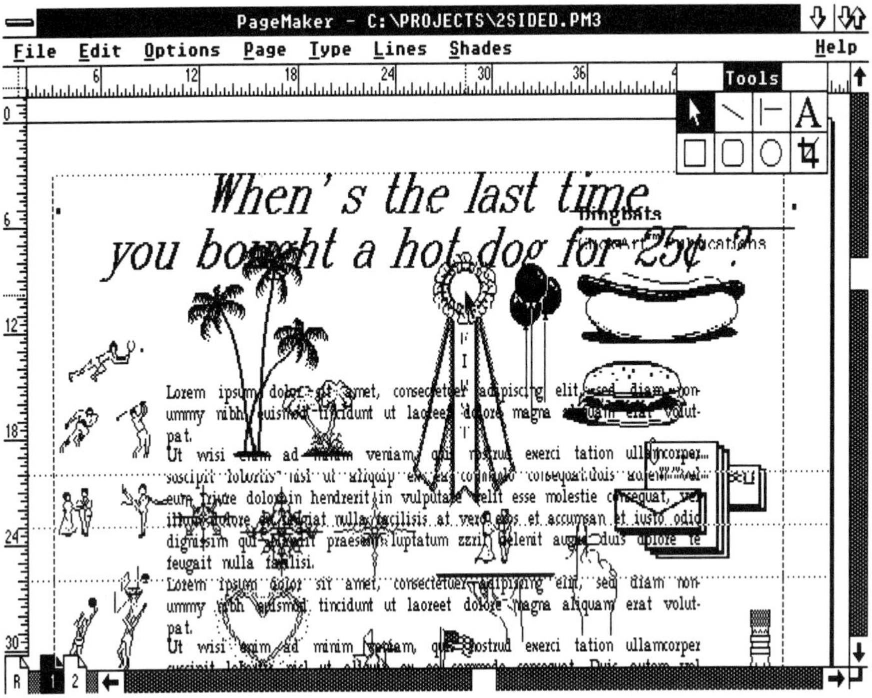

Figure 11.10: *Our selected, imported graphic file displaying handles and extraneous graphic elements.*

Your graphic will now appear on page 1, surrounded by handles to demonstrate that it is selected. Depending on where your file originated, many extraneous graphic elements may be displayed, as shown in Figure 11.10. This is very common when importing clip art files, for example. One page of clip art often contains several drawings, which saves space and decreases the number of files on-disk. Our imported clip art, for example, contains not only a drawing of a hot-dog—the only graphic element we require—but also palm trees, balloons, envelopes, and several other images that are unrelated to our flyer.

PageMaker provides a built-in method by which extraneous images may be removed from a graphic—**cropping**. To crop a graphic is to cut away some portion of the graphic so that it is no longer visible in our document. The cropped portion still exists, and you may access it later if you wish, but it is currently hidden from view.

Your graphic may contain only one image, in which case it will not need to be cropped. If this is the case, read along with the following text and try out the crop tool. Even if you end up destroying the appearance of your graphic, it will help you to learn the lessons contained in this chapter.

26 Select the crop tool (lower right corner of toolbox) and click on your graphic to select it. Eight handles are displayed—one in each corner and one on each side. Click on the bottommost handle and drag upward until the bottom of the graphic is about two picas above the body copy. Then drag downward from the topmost handle until your graphic no longer covers the headline. (Be sure to click on a handle! If you click inside the graphic with the crop tool, you will get a grabber hand icon, as discussed in the next few paragraphs.) Notice that the crop tool cuts off portions of your graphic in horizontal or vertical strips. Therefore, images that jut slightly into each other's perpendicular boundaries cannot be successfully isolated using the crop tool. Such fine-tuning operations must be performed in a graphics application prior to importation.

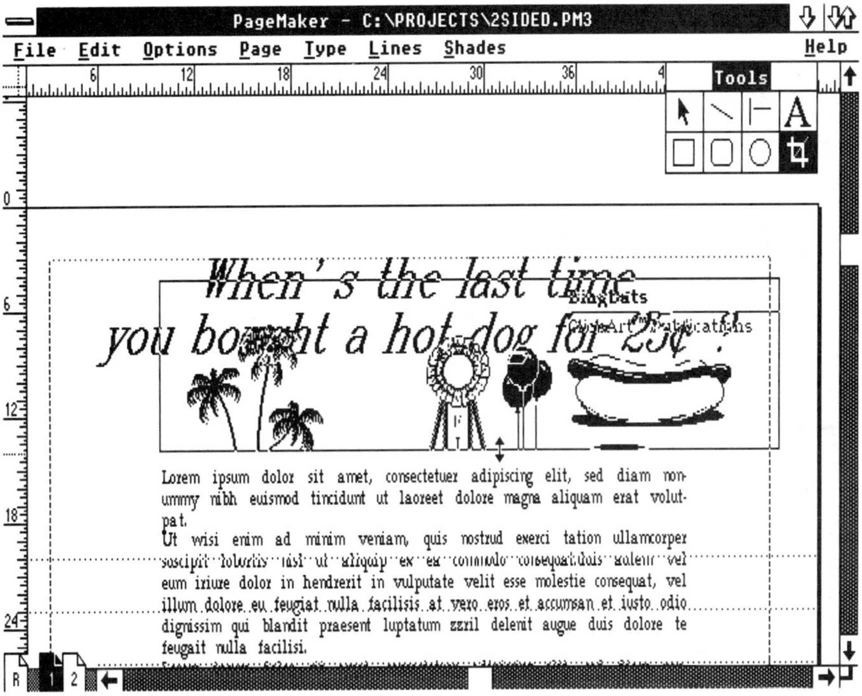

Figure 11.11: *Cropping off the bottom portion of our placed graphic.*

27 After cropping out any extraneous portions of your graphic, select the arrow tool and drag the graphic to center it between the headline and body copy.

28 Once you have established the size of your graphic by cropping and have positioned it correctly, you may find that you have over-cropped or under-cropped, and need to make adjustments. Select the crop tool again and click on the graphic to select it. This time, instead of clicking on a handle, click inside the graphic and hold. Your cursor will change to a grabber hand icon. Now drag with the grabber hand. This moves your graphic within the cropping boundaries. This is especially useful if you have cropped the graphic to an exact size, but aren't quite sure what details of the graphic you would like to see. Dragging with the grabber hand doesn't affect the size of the graphic, as does dragging at the handles; it affects only what portion is visible.

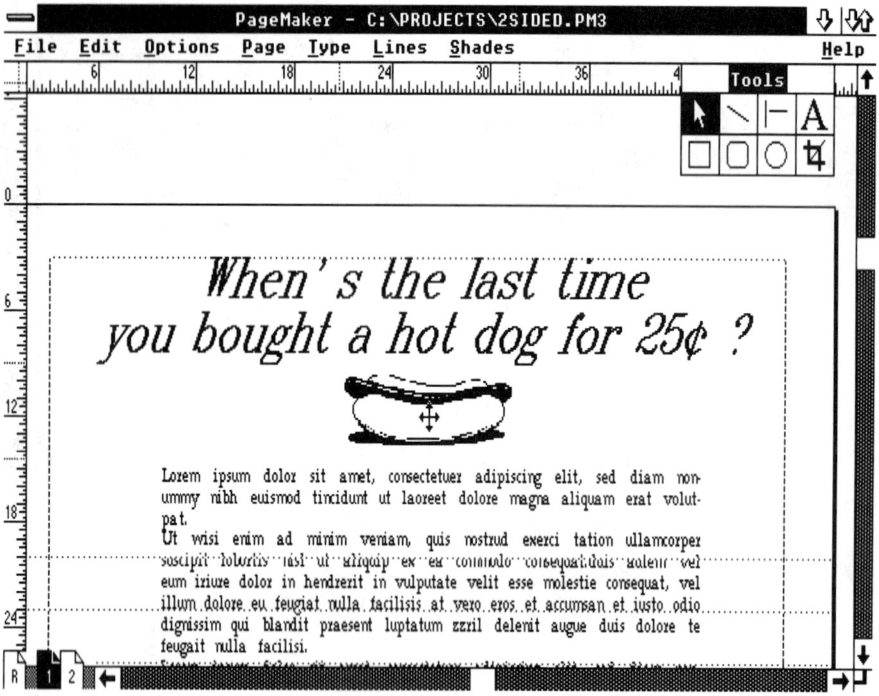

Figure 11.12: *Our hot-dog graphic as it appears after cropping and positioning.*

29 Once you have cropped your graphic until you are satisfied with its appearance, select the arrow tool and click on the graphic to select it. Then press CTRL-INSERT to execute the COPY command. We will be using this copy of our image in a logo at the bottom of the page.

30 Press CTRL-S to update your file on disk.

Creating a clip-out coupon

In the next few steps, we will create a clip-out coupon on the bottom panel of the flyer. Inside this coupon we will type some text using the text tool, and we will add a logo. This logo will also consist of a graphic element, in the form of a reduced version of the image we just copied.

Drawing the coupon border and dragging column guides

31 Scroll down to the bottom panel of page 1. Then select the rectangle tool and drag from the intersection of the top fold margin of the bottom panel and the left margin, to the bottom right margin corner. The resulting box should look like the one shown in the following figure. Notice that the outline of this box is a medium-weight coupon border, the one we selected when setting defaults. The interior is white, also matching our new shade default, PAPER.

Right now, our page has only one column, and both the left and right column guides are flush with the left and right sides of our coupon border. This means that any text that we create inside the coupon will be as wide as the coupon itself, which would make the edges of the text unreadable. Text inside a coupon border must have surrounding margins, just as text on a page must have margins. In order to establish these margins, we will move our column guides.

32 Column guides, like ruler guides, are not permanent. They may be moved by dragging them with the arrow tool. Select the arrow tool and click on the left column guide. You will see a two-headed arrow. Now drag the column guide to the right to the 6-pica mark on the horizontal ruler. If the two-headed arrow doesn't appear, and instead you find yourself dragging the coupon border, check that the "Guides" option is set to "Front" in the Preferences dialog box. Also make sure that the Lock guides command under the Options menu does not have a check in front of it. Next, drag the right column guide to the left to the 45-pica mark on the horizontal ruler.

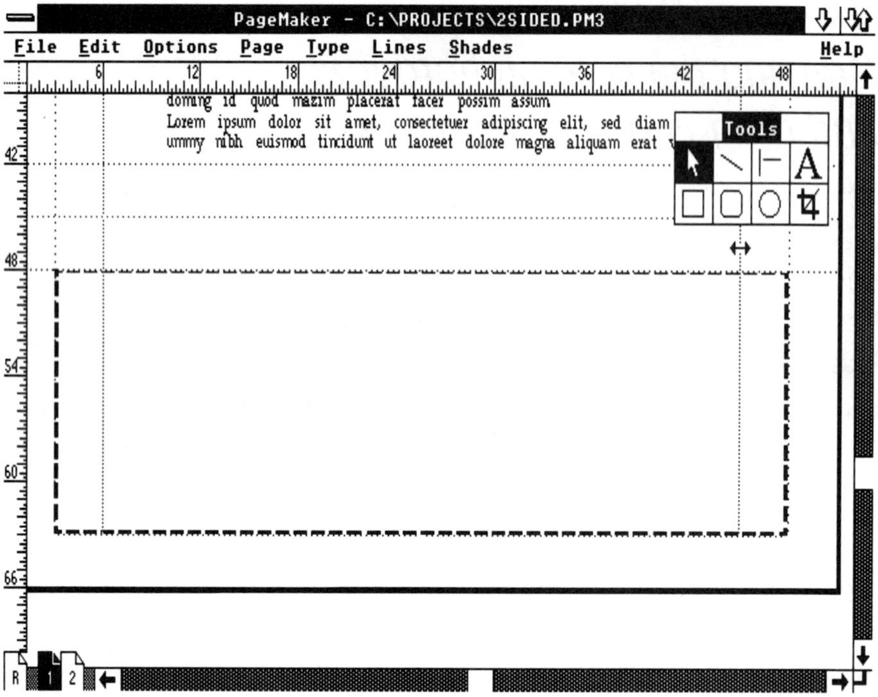

Figure 11.13: *Dragging the right column guide until the tracking line on the horizontal ruler aligns with the 45-pica mark.*

Entering the coupon text

33 Select the text tool and click inside the coupon, anywhere between the column guides. Then type "Any hot dog only 25¢ ¶ with the purchase of a medium soda and chips ¶ at Barney's Dogs." (Remember that the ¶ symbol indicates a line return.)

Our text appears in the default type specs of centered 36/37.5 Palatino bold-italic. This is almost what we want, but some of the text will need to be changed. For example, the second line of text should be smaller to fit it on one line and to downplay its significance.

34 Triple-click on the second line of text with the text tool. This selects the entire paragraph, from line return to line return. Then press CTRL-T to display the TYPE SPECIFICATIONS dialog box. Change the type size to "18 point," change the leading to "Auto," (click in the "Auto" option box), change the type style to "Normal," and click OK.

35 With the second line of text still selected, press CTRL–M to access the PARAGRAPH SPECIFICATIONS dialog box. Press the TAB key until the "After" option is selected and change the value to 3 picas. Then click OK.

36 Now it is time to alter our logo text. Double-click on the word "Barney." Then SHIFT-click on the word "Dogs." This selects both words. Press CTRL-T to access the TYPE SPECIFICATIONS dialog box, and select the "All caps" radio button, one of the "Case" options. Then deselect the "Italic" option and click OK. "Barney Dogs" is now composed entirely of bold, non-italic,uppercase letters.

37 Select the text tool and drag the text block to position it vertically as shown in Figure 11.14. Then press CTRL-S to update your file on disk.

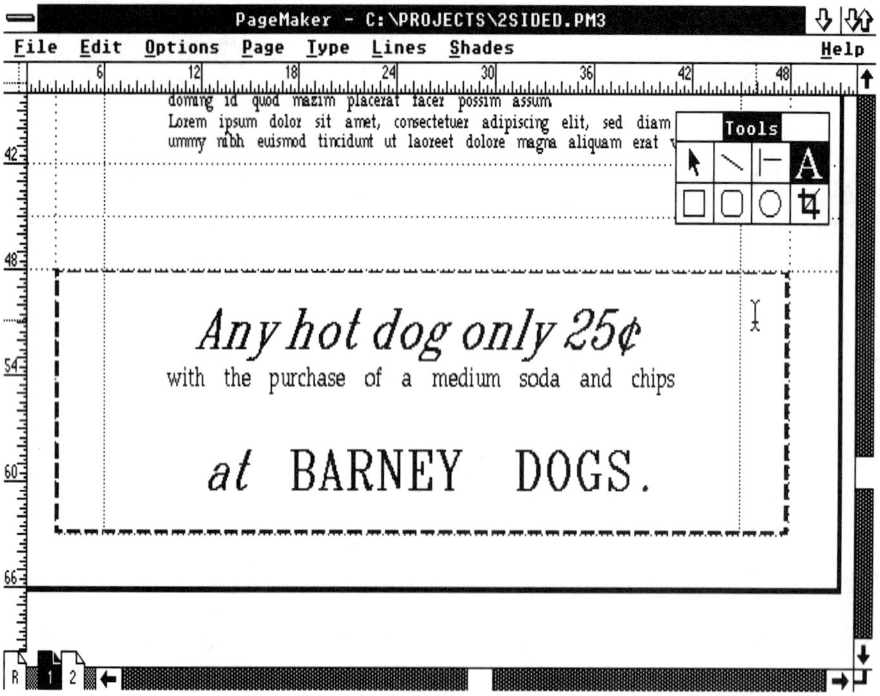

Figure 11.14: *The text for our coupon positioned accurately.*

Enhancing the coupon with graphic elements

Next we will paste our graphic,which we copied to the Clipboard a few moments ago, into the Barney Dog logo. But first, we must make room for it. We want to paste the graphic between the words "at" and "Barney" in the last line of text. We will make room by inserting spaces between these two words. Not ordinary spaces, but **fixed spaces**. When you press the SPACEBAR, you create a *variable* space—a space that may be changed by PageMaker to accommodate the alignment of the text block. This occurs most commonly when you justify text, since PageMaker must stretch or shrink the amount of space between each word in a line of type to fill the column width. Fixed spaces are always the same, regardless of whether the text block is justified, centered, or aligned left or right. These are the three kinds of fixed spaces, followed by the key commands used to access them:

- **Em space**, a space as wide as the point size — SHIFT-CTRL-M

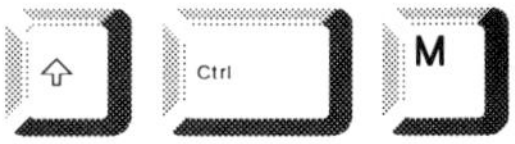

- **En space**, a space half as wide as the point size — SHIFT-CTRL-N

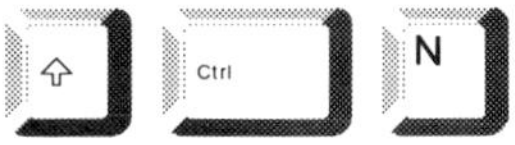

- **Thin space**, one-quarter the width of the point size — SHIFT-CTRL-T

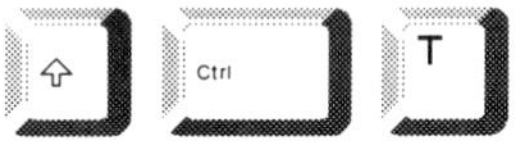

A 12-point em space is 12 points wide, a 12-point en space is six points wide, and a 12-point thin space is three points wide.

38 Click with the text tool between the words "at" and "Barney." Then press SHIFT-CTRL-M twice and SHIFT-CTRL-N once to create two em spaces and one en space. This is the amount of space we want to designate for our logo graphic.

39 Press SHIFT-INSERT to paste a copy of our cropped graphic from the Clipboard. Then drag the graphic with the arrow tool until its lower right corner is just to the left of the B in Barney. Your graphic is no doubt too large to fit in the space we've allotted for it, so you will need to reduce it. Imported graphics are reduced by dragging at their handles with the arrow tool, in the same way you reduce the column width of a block of text. So click and hold on the upper left handle of your graphic. Then drag downward and to the right, pressing the SHIFT key to reduce the graphic proportionally. If you wish to check your progress without ending your drag, stop moving your mouse but don't release your mouse button. PageMaker will refresh your image to display its new size. Once you are satisfied with the size of your graphic in its allotted space, release your mouse button. Because of the way Windows displays screen fonts, you may see large spaces between the words, "Barney" and "dogs." However, the words will be correctly spaced on the printed page. In this sample project it is not important that the graphic be positioned precisely. When you are creating your own publications and you are placing a graphic close to a text block, we recommend you print the page to see the position of type and graphic elements, rather than relying on the display.

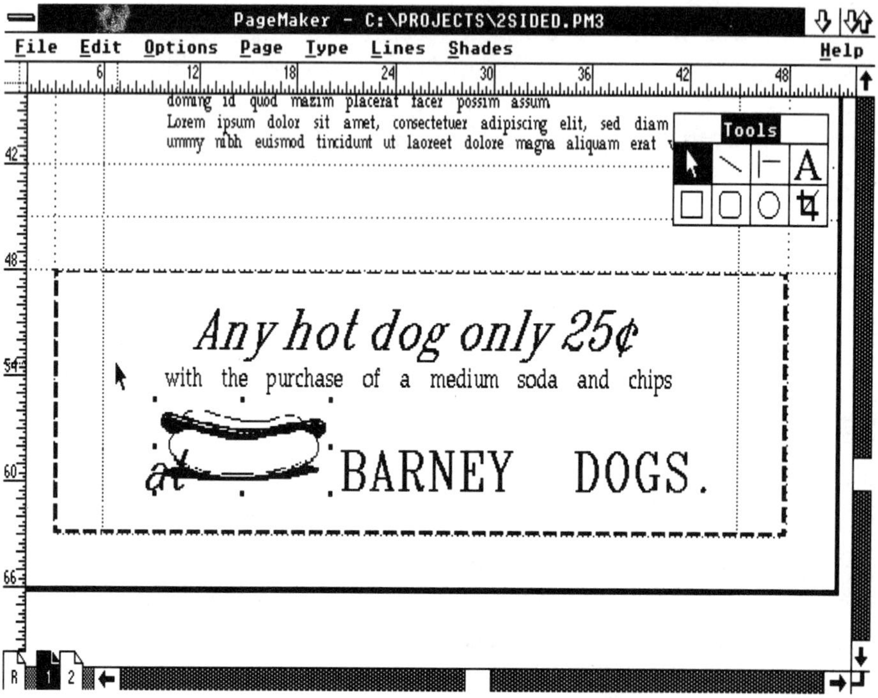

Figure 11.15: *After pasting the graphic, we discover it is too large for its space.*

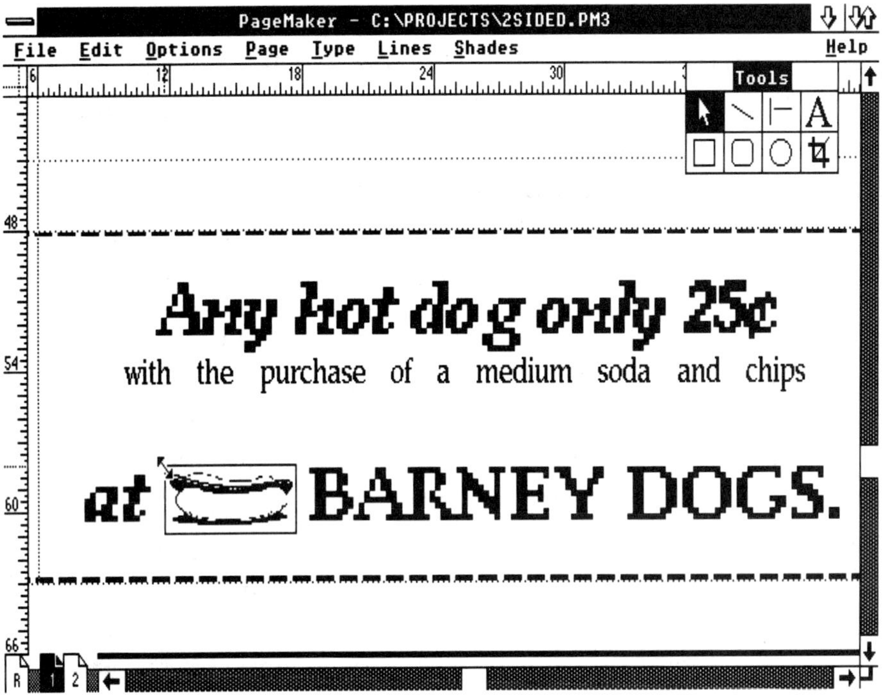

Figure 11.16: *Reducing the graphic proportionally by dragging at one of its handles and pressing the shift key.*

The next two graphic elements we will add are two small pairs of scissors, which will indicate that the coupon is to be clipped from the flyer (and brought into a local Barney Dog franchise for friendly and courteous redemption). These scissors may be accessed as characters of the type face Zapf Dingbats, a standard LaserWriter Plus font that contains various graphic elements and symbols.

40 Select the text tool. Without clicking on-screen, press CTRL-T to access the TYPE SPECIFICATIONS dialog box. Change the type specs to 24/Auto Zapf Dingbats and select the "Normal" type-style option. Then click OK. Since no text is selected, we cannot immediately see the effect of our change. The fact that we did not apply our type modifications to any block of text means that we have altered our default settings for this file. No longer will text default to 36/37.5 Palatino bold-italic, but to 24/Auto Zapf Dingbats. This change does not affect any other files. Existing files will still use the same defaults they used when they were saved, and new files will still default to 36/37.5 Palatino bold-italic, but any text set from now on in this file will have new default type specs.

41 With the text tool, click and drag a little box just above the coupon border from the left margin to the left column guide, a distance of 3 picas. (It does not matter how tall you draw the box.) Then press SHIFT-4. Unless you have the Zapf Dingbats screen font, you will see the dollar ($) character on the screen, rather than the scissors. However, if your printer has the Zapf Dingbats printer font built into it, the scissors will print on the page. We will refer to the "scissors" in the following paragraphs rather than to the dollar sign. Next, press CTRL-L, the keyboard equivalent for flush left text alignment.

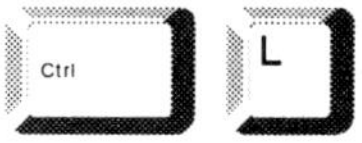

42 Select the text tool and position the text block vertically so that its lower handlebar rides just below the top coupon border. Then press CTRL-INSERT to copy the symbol.

43 Now we want to create a second pair of scissors, horizontally aligned with the first, but positioned on the right side of the page. Press SHIFT-INSERT to paste a copy of the scissors to our page. Next, drag this copy directly over the original scissors. When the dragged copy turns completely white and disappears from view, you have positioned it exactly and may release. This will ensure that the copied scissors are in horizontal alignment with the original scissors. Now press the SHIFT key to constrain movement to the horizontal axis, and drag the text block to the right until it is positioned between the right column guide and right margin, and the handles on its right side snap to the right margin guide.

44 Select the text tool and select the right-hand scissors. Then press CTRL-R, the keyboard equivalent for flush right text alignment.

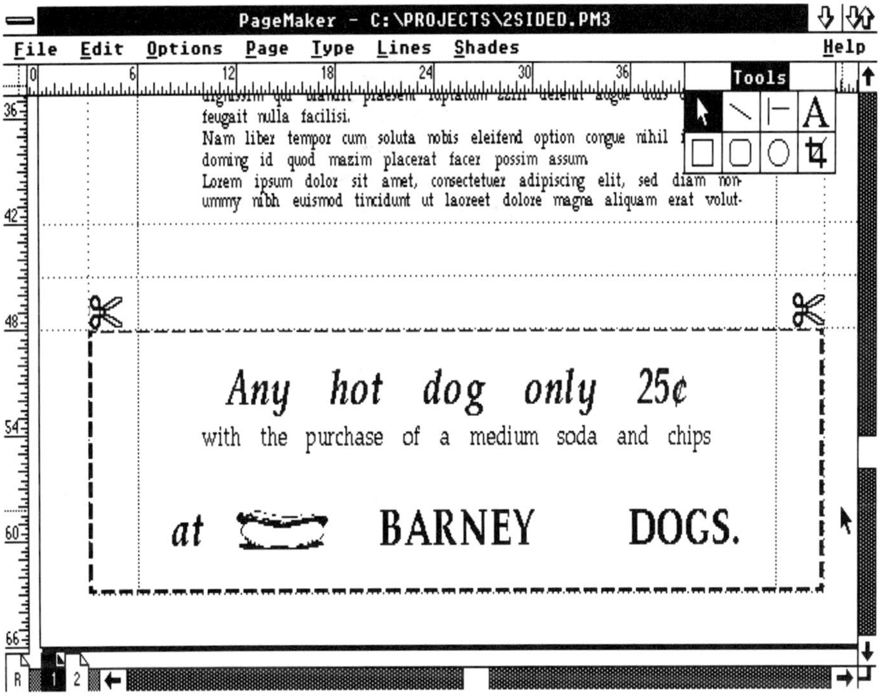

Figure 11.17: *The scissors characters from the Zapf Dingbats type face are positioned to visually indicate the purpose of the coupon border.*

45 Press CTRL-S to update your file on disk. Then press CTRL-W to reduce your view to the "Fit-in-window" size. You have successfully completed the inner side of this two-sided flyer.

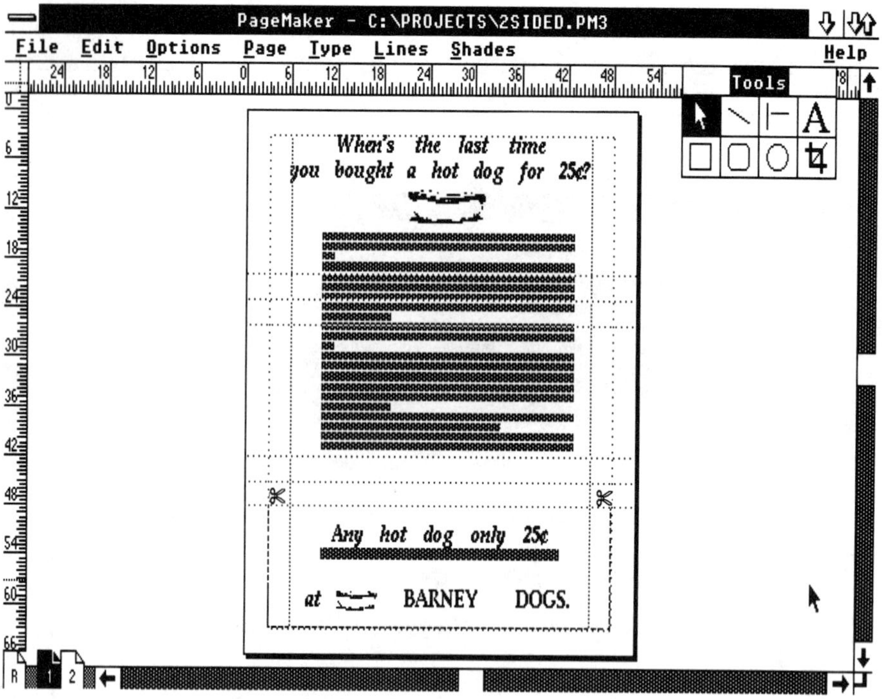

Figure 11.18: *The entire first side of our flyer, viewed at "Fit-in-window" size.*

Building the flyer's outer side

We are now ready to create the second side of our two-sided flyer. The three panels on this side will include a mailer and two blocks of text imported from a graphics program. In building this next page, we will be introducing the concepts of determining the curvature of a rectangle with rounded corners, layering elements in front of and in back of other elements, reversing text, and treating text as a graphic.

46 Click on the page 2 icon at the bottom of your display to go to page 2. Then click the secondary mouse button in the middle of the page to magnify your view to "Actual" size. If necessary, scroll to the right so that the right margin of the page is visible.

Reversing text over a black background

47 Our next step is to create a block of text to exact specifications by paying close attention to the vertical and horizontal ruler while dragging with the text tool. Select the text tool and click and hold down your mouse button at the location where the horizontal ruler tracking line aligns with the 42.5-pica mark and the vertical ruler tracking line meets the 26-pica mark (flush with the top margin of the middle panel). Without releasing the mouse button, drag downward about 5 picas and to the right until the text tool snaps to the right margin. Before typing, change the type specs to 9/9 Helvetica using the TYPE SPECIFICATIONS dialog box as described throughout this chapter. This changes the type specs for this text block only, and does not affect our default settings.

48 Type "Post office will not deliver without sufficient postage." Press CTRL-A to select the entire block of text and press CTRL-T to bring up the TYPE SPECIFICATIONS dialog. Then select the "All caps" option and click OK. The type should already be centered. If any of the words are hyphenated, change the width of the text block so that no words are hyphenated, and it looks like the text block in Figure 11.19.

49 To correctly position the text block vertically, click on it with the arrow tool and SHIFT-drag it downward one-half pica (use the vertical ruler to measure).

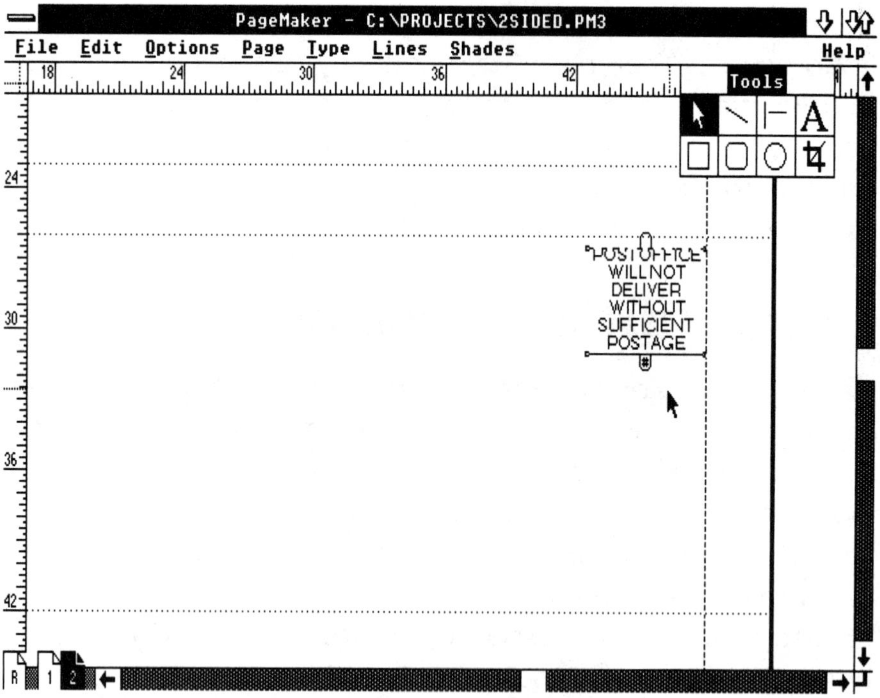

Figure 11.19: *Our new little text block, selected to display column width and vertical positioning.*

50 Select the rounded-corner tool, which is the second tool on the bottom row of your toolbox. We will use this tool to create a small box around our little text block, indicating the dimensions of a typical postage stamp. Position the rounded-corner cursor at the intersection of the top margin of the middle panel and the right margin of the page. Then SHIFT-drag down and to the left five picas to the 43-pica mark on the horizontal ruler and the 31-pica mark on the vertical ruler.

51 Notice that our small square with rounded corners has a fat coupon border and a white interior, as specified by our defaults, covering up our text. We want to change this to a black box, so while the shape is still selected, choose the SOLID command from the SHADES menu and NONE from the LINES menu.

52 Now notice that the rounded corners of our selected shape are too large, so that our square looks almost like a circle. To remedy this, choose the ROUNDED CORNERS... command from the OPTIONS menu, which brings up the ROUNDED CORNERS dialog box. This dialog allows you to select from six corner options, ranging from perpendicular to very rounded. The fourth option is currently selected. Select the second option of the top row, as shown in the next figure, and click OK. Our rounded corners are now much smaller, so that they appear on-screen to be almost perpendicular.

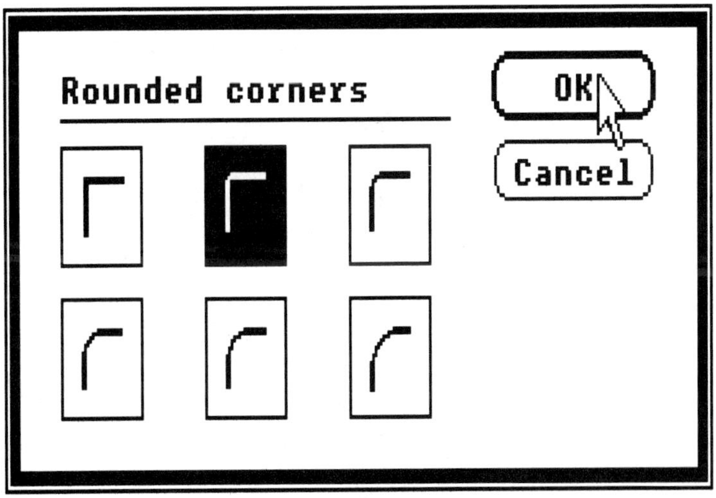

Figure 11.20: *The Rounded corners dialog box with second corner option selected.*

In step 48 we created some text. Unfortunately, we cannot see it because the black square is in front of the text. Like most desktop publishing applications, PageMaker relies on a layering convention whereby any on-screen element is considered to be in front of some elements and in back of others. Thus, when you create a document, you are really creating an electronic collage of lines, shapes, text blocks, and imported graphics. Every time you create a new element, you place it at the front of this electronic collage. New elements are always created in front of their predecessors, so the black square is in front of the text.

You may change the layering relationship between elements using the BRING TO FRONT and SEND TO BACK commands under the EDIT menu. These commands allow you to bring a selected element in front of all other elements on the page or send an element behind all other elements on the page. The next step demonstrates how to use one of these commands.

53 Your black square should still be selected. Choose the SEND TO BACK command from the EDIT menu to send the square to the back of the page, behind the text block.

54 Our text is now in front of the black shape, but it remains invisible because the type is black, the same color as the shape behind it. To be sure that the text block is in front, select the text tool and click in the middle of the black square. A text entry cursor will blink at your exact click point, indicating that there is indeed text there. We will now make this text visible. Begin by pressing CTRL-A to select the entire text block, and choose the "Reverse" option on the TYPE menu. This makes the text white. Click on the arrow tool to deselect the text, and you will see how it is now reversed against a black background. Then press CTRL-S to update your file on disk.

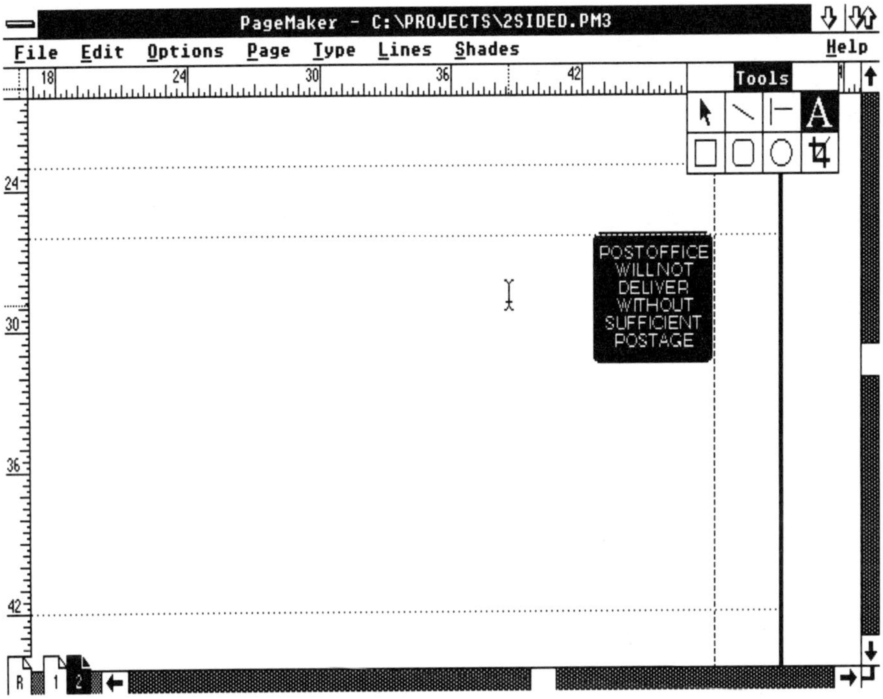

Figure 11.21: *The reversed postage text against a black square background.*

Making plain text

55 No mailer would be complete without a return address. If necessary, scroll to the left until the left margin is clearly visible. Before typing any text, change the default type specs to 12/Auto Palatino bold-italic (use the TYPE SPECIFICATIONS dialog, as we have done before). Select ALIGN LEFT from the TYPE menu, or press CTRL-L, to align our text with the left margin. Now select the text tool and position your cursor at the intersection of the top margin of the middle panel and the left page margin. Click at this point and drag to the right 15 picas (to the 18-pica mark on the horizontal ruler) and downward far enough to accommodate a few lines of text. Now type, "Barney Dogs Inc. ¶ 1205 University Ave. ¶ Northwestern, USA 40404."

56 The name of the restaurant looks nice in Palatino bold-italic type, but it is undistinguishable from the address. So triple-click on the second line of the text block to select the entire first address line. Then SHIFT-click on the third line, selecting it entirely as well. To make this text plain, choose the "Normal" option on the TYPE menu, or better yet, press the F5 function key. The text is now set in Palatino Roman (plain style, without bold and italic), as shown in Figure 11.22. Press CTRL-S to update your file on disk.

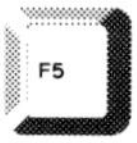

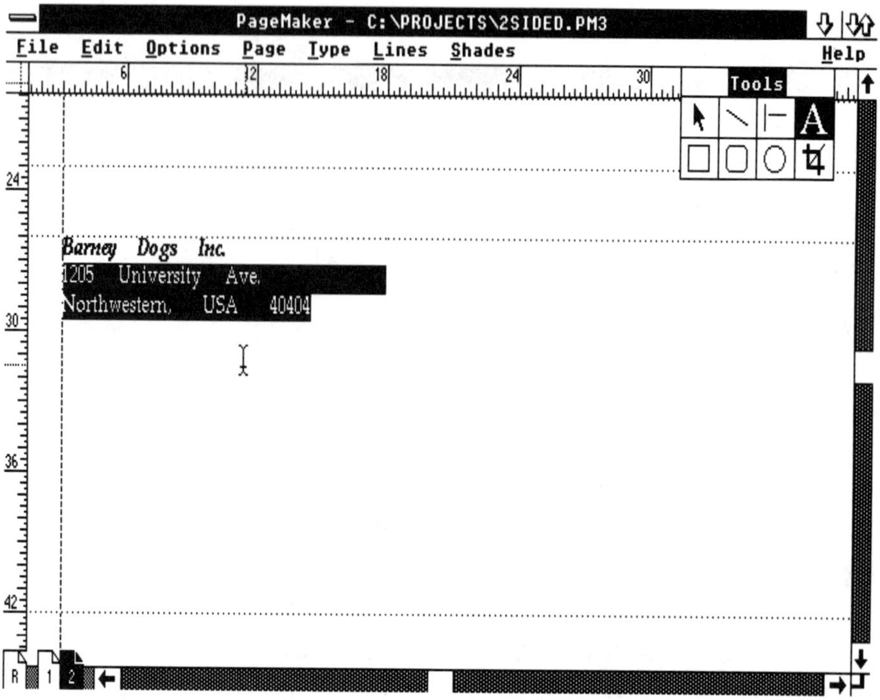

Figure 11.22: *The return address, with selected type in Palatino Roman (plain).*

Importing text as a graphic

The only portions of our flyer that remain incomplete are the top and bottom panels, which present a specific problem. Due to the way in which the folds of our flyer will overlap each other, as demonstrated in the following figure, the text on both the top panel and the bottom panel must be upside down. This ensures that the customer, when unfolding the flyer, can continue to read each newly presented panel without having to turn the flyer upside down at any point. (We recommend that you try folding your flyer after you have printed it to fully understand this concept.)

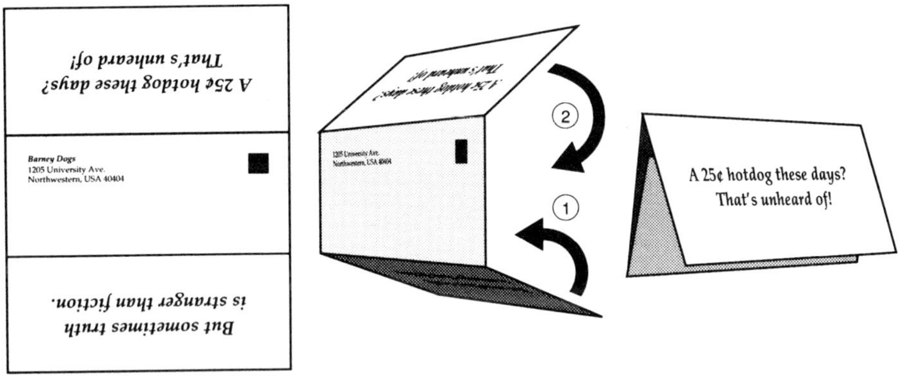

Figure 11.23: *The outer side of the flyer, shown in three phases, demonstrating how it appears flat, in the process of being folded, and fully folded.*

Unfortunately, PageMaker does not allow you to create upside-down text. You may, however, import text from any application that does allow you to create upside-down text. These included the same graphics applications that we mentioned earlier in this chapter (see step 24). You may create upside-down text in WINDOWS PAINT, PC PAINTBRUSH,

ADOBE ILLUSTRATOR, and many other applications. Graphics applications that use Windows have access to the same fonts that PageMaker does, and therefore can print PostScript type faces. Do not use applications that do not support PostScript type faces, since the printed characters will be jagged.

Before we began creating this flyer, we created two files in ADOBE ILLUSTRATOR that contain upside-down text. In one file, we typed the phrase, "A 25¢ hot dog these days? ¶ That's unheard of!" and in the other file we typed, "But sometimes truth ¶ is stranger than fiction." Both text blocks were created in 36-point Palatino bold-italic. We rotated the text block in each file 180° so each was upside down, and saved the files as ".EPS" files.

If you like, you may also create two draw-type text files in this manner, using LOTUS FREELANCE, ADOBE ILLUSTRATOR, or some other graphics application. It is not important that your files exactly match ours. Any PCX or EPS file that contains text will do for our purpose.

57 Scroll to the top panel of your page. Then press CTRL-D to access the PLACE FILE dialog box. Double-click on the graphics file that you want to import into the top panel. (We will be placing the text reading "A 25¢ hot dog these days....")

58 Click with your graphic cursor icon near the upper left margin corner to display the placed graphic. Then drag the text with the arrow tool to center it horizontally and vertically within the panel. Notice that this text has eight square handles like a graphic, rather than text handlebars with tabs (such as text from a word-processor), indicating that PageMaker considers this text to be a graphic.

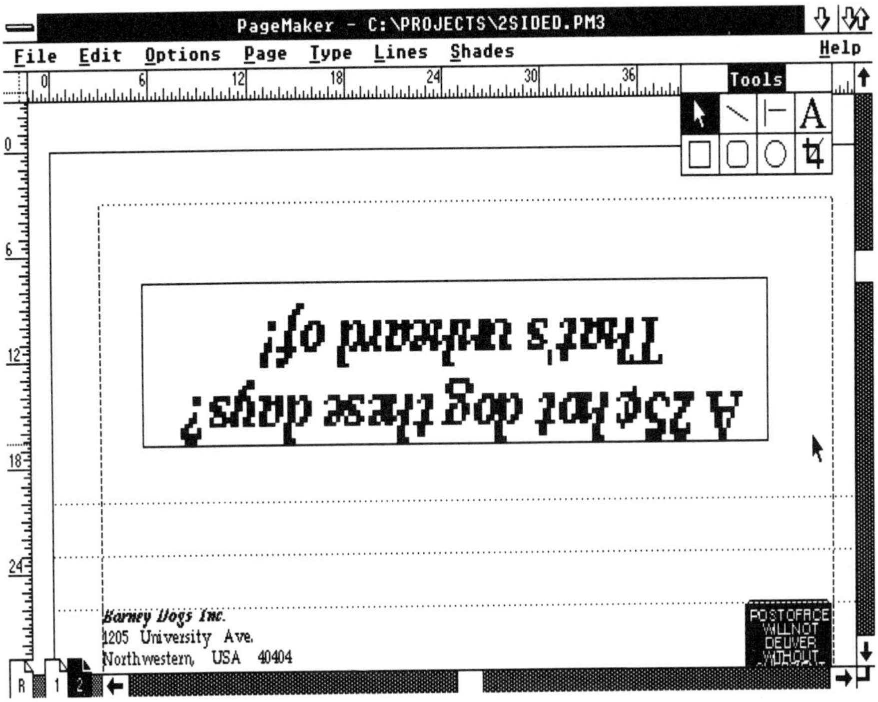

Figure 11.24: *Text imported from a graphics application is surrounded by handles, indicating that PageMaker considers it to be a graphic.*

Text imported as a graphic element (from a graphics program) into PageMaker may be manipulated as follows:

- The text-graphic may *not* be edited in PageMaker.
- The text-graphic may be resized in PageMaker by dragging at one of its handles.

This last point is very important. Normally, PageMaker does not allow you to expand or condense text, that is, stretch or shrink it horizontally while not distorting its vertical size. However, if you import a block of text from a graphics program, you may expand or condense it simply by dragging at its handles.

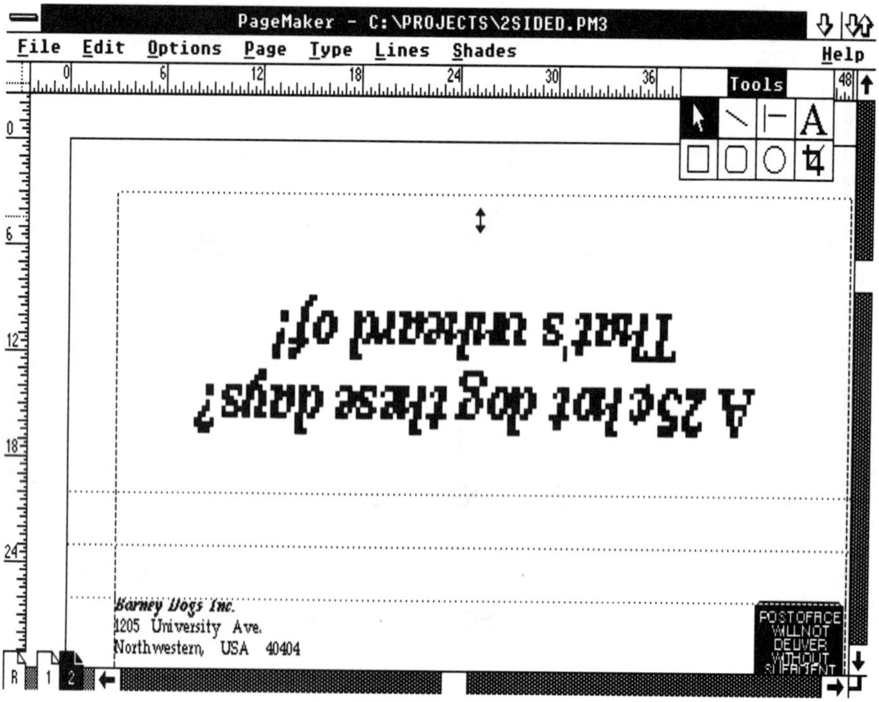

Figure 11.25: *Stretching the text-graphic vertically gives the letters a condensed appearance.*

59 With the arrow tool, drag about two picas upward at the top of the text-graphic. This will give your text a condensed appearance, as shown in Figure 11.25. Our text is still Palatino bold-italic, but its letters are taller and narrower than "normal" Palatino bold-italic. Reposition your text-graphic if necessary. Then press CTRL-S to update your file on disk.

60 Scroll down to the bottom panel and place another block of text created in a graphic application as described earlier. (We import the text reading, "But sometimes truth is stranger than fiction.") Then stretch this text two picas vertically and reposition it to center vertically and horizontally between the panel margins.

61 Press CTRL-W to reduce your page to the "Fit-in-window" view size. Then press CTRL-S to update your file on disk.

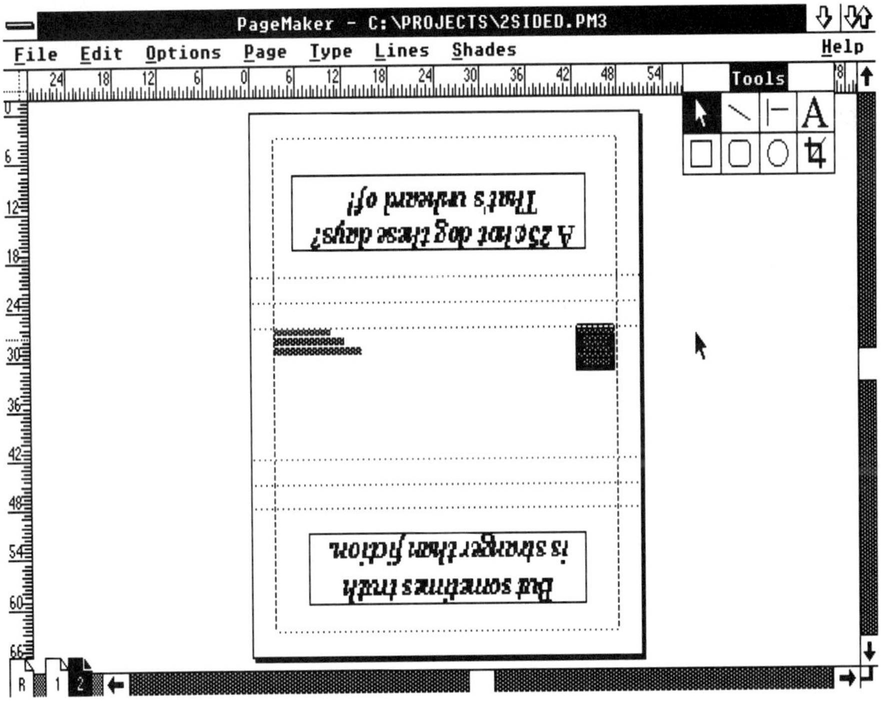

Figure 11.26: *The entire second side of our flyer, viewed at "Fit-in-window" size.*

Printing the two-sided flyer

62 Your flyer is now complete. The only step remaining is to print the finished document. Make sure your printer is on and selected using the PRINTER SETUP... command on the FILE menu. Then press CTRL-P to access the PRINT dialog box. Click on your printer in the list at the bottom of the dialog box, indicate one copy, and print from page 1 to 2 as described at the end of our first sample project (see Chapter 6, *Creating a Simple Newsletter*). When the two pages of your flyer are finished printing, put them back-to-back to simulate the document after it is photocopied or printed commercially. Then try folding it as we demonstrated back in Figure 11.23. This will give you a sense of how a two-fold flyer works.

Examine your pages and make sure they meet your expectations. If you see any problems, make the necessary changes to your file. Successfully completing this chapter demonstrates an understanding of some intermediate functions and operations offered by PageMaker. This will help you to understand future discussions in this book, confirm previous topics, and provide you with a more developed working knowledge of the PageMaker environment.

Using Color in PageMaker

In this chapter we examine:

- *Creating and importing colors*
- *Using colors and the Colors palette*
- *Printing color documents*

Many of the publications that you will create in Page-Maker will be commercially reproduced in color. Traditionally, the process of determining elements to be reproduced in each color occurs *after* the camera-ready publication pages are produced, and your commercial printer creates color separations from the camera-ready pages that you provide. Using PageMaker's color abilities, however, you can specify the color of any element in your publication, and print camera-ready color separations on your laser printer. This allows you to control another step in the document production process, and in some cases can save you time and money.

Colors in PageMaker work very similarly to style sheets as introduced in Chapter 9, *Using Style Sheets*—default colors are provided, you can create new colors, colors can be edited at any time, and colors are applied to objects by simply selecting the object and then selecting the appropriate color name from either a palette or menu command.

Color in publications

There are two methods in which color can be used in commercial printing: spot color and process color. Spot colors are applied to the paper as finished colors—any ink mixtures required are done before the ink is applied to the paper. Documents being printed with spot colors pass through one press roller for each spot color being used. Spot colors are used to highlight specific elements on a page. Although any number of spot colors can be applied to different portions of a single element or page, spot color printing is rarely used when more than two or three colors are needed. Spot-color printing is relatively affordable and can be performed by most commercial printers and quick-print shops.

Process colors, on the other hand, are created by applying varying amounts of each of four colors of ink (cyan, magenta, yellow, and black) to the paper in percentages that mix (or appear to mix) to create the colors required. Documents being printed with process colors pass through one ink roller for each of the four process colors. Process colors are used to reproduce color photographs and other images that require a large number of precise colors, such as in the reproduction of color artwork and photographs. Process color printing is relatively expensive, and only larger commercial printers offer this service.

PageMaker supports the definition and application of spot colors only. You are able to define any needed color using one of three popular color models, or the Apple color wheel, and then apply these colors to any text or graphic element. Once colors have been applied in your publication, you can print composite-color proofs or output your publication as a series of spot-color overlays, ready for reproduction.

Equipment

To use PageMaker's color features, no special equipment of any kind is required—you don't even need a color monitor. If you do use a color monitor, however, PageMaker will accurately display all the colors that you create and assign to the objects in your publication.

Defining colors

There are three ways to obtain colors for use in your PageMaker publications: You can use the default colors available whenever a new publication is created; you can import colors from existing PageMaker publications or templates; or you can define new colors as required.

The default colors

When a new PageMaker publication is created, six colors are automatically available (see Figure 12.01). Three of these default colors are permanent defaults that will be available to all PageMaker publications, and the other three are default colors that you may edit, remove, or replace.

The three permanent default colors are "Black," "Paper," and "Registration." "Black" is initially applied to all text that you create. Black is also used as a replacement color for any objects whose colors are removed at any time. "Paper" is initially set to white, although you can edit it as required. As you know from working with the SHADES menu, "Paper" is used to opaque any underlying elements, and so should usually be set to match the paper on which your document will be printed. "Registration" is not actually a color, but is used like a color to indicate objects that are to be reproduced on every color overlay created. PageMaker's crop marks automatically use this color.

The other three default colors are "Blue," "Green," and "Red." These colors are commonly used, and although they may not be the exact colors that you require, they can be edited easily to your meet your specifications. You can permanently change these three default colors, and add any additional default colors, by editing the colors while no publication is open (see the section, *Defaults and preferences,* in Chapter 4, *A Brief Tour of PageMaker,* for more information.) By editing these defaults, each new PageMaker publication that you create will automatically provide you with the colors you use most often. This will save time and assure consistency among all your publications.

- *Paper—* 0% Cyan, 0% Magenta, 0% Yellow
- *Black—* 100% Cyan, 100% Magenta, 100% Yellow
- *Registration—* 100% Cyan, 100% Magenta, 100% Yellow
- *Blue—* 100% Cyan, 100% Magenta, 0% Yellow
- *Red—* 0% Cyan, 100% Magenta, 100% Yellow
- *Green—* 100% Cyan, 0% Magenta, 100% Yellow

Figure 12.01: *The default colors and their specs.*

Defining new colors

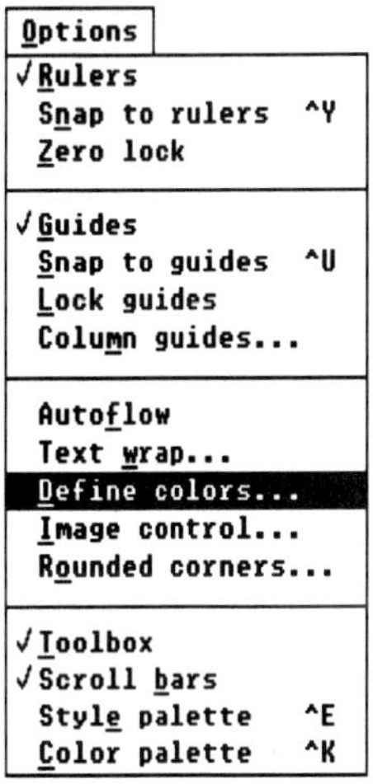

New colors can be defined from scratch in PageMaker, or they can be based on colors that already exist. To begin defining a new color, choose the DEFINE COLORS... command from the OPTIONS menu, and the DEFINE COLORS dialog box will appear, as shown in Figure 12.02. This dialog box contains a scrolling list of all colors that are already available in your publications and a series of buttons that allow you to create additional colors, edit existing colors, remove existing colors, and import colors from other PageMaker publications or templates.

Whenever this dialog box is accessed, the color of the currently selected object is selected, or "Black" is selected if no object is currently selected. To begin defining a new color, click the NEW... button. This will bring up the EDIT COLOR dialog box, as shown in Figure 12.03. New colors always begin with the attributes of the color selected in the scrolling color list when the NEW... button is clicked. This allows you to easily base any new color on an existing color.

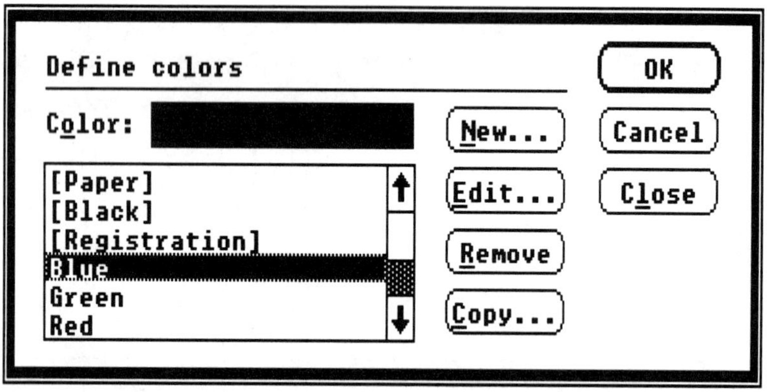

Figure 12.02: *The Define colors dialog box.*

To name the new color, enter any name up to 32 characters long into the "Color" option box. Many special characters cannot be used in color names. Try to name your color descriptively, but use as short a name as possible (so you can see it easily in the Colors palette).

We are now ready to define the attributes of our new color. You can use any one of three available **color models** to define new colors. This variety of color models are provided because each is popular in its own right, and you might recieve the definition for a color that you wish to match in any one of them. These three of the color models are accessed via the "Model" option, which appears just below the "Name" option box. Upon selecting one of these options, the lower portion of the Edit color dialog box will display the options associated with the color model that you select.

The "RGB" color model, shown in Figure 12.03, defines colors based on percentages of "Red," "Green," and "Blue." This is known as additive color definition and is similar to the color model used by most color monitors.

The "HLS" color model, shown in Figure 12.04, defines colors based on percentages of "Lightness," and "Saturation," and degrees (from 0° to 359°) for the "Hue" option.

The "CMYK" color model, also shown in Figure 12.04, defines colors based on percentages of Cyan, Magenta, Yellow, and Black. This is similar to the method of color definition used for four-color printing, and many color definitions are provided in this format.

To manipulate the options in either the "RGB," "HLS," or "CMYK" color model, you can either enter values into the option boxes provided, or use the horizontal scroll bars to adjust the values. On a color monitor, the color will be displayed to the right of the scroll bars as it is defined.

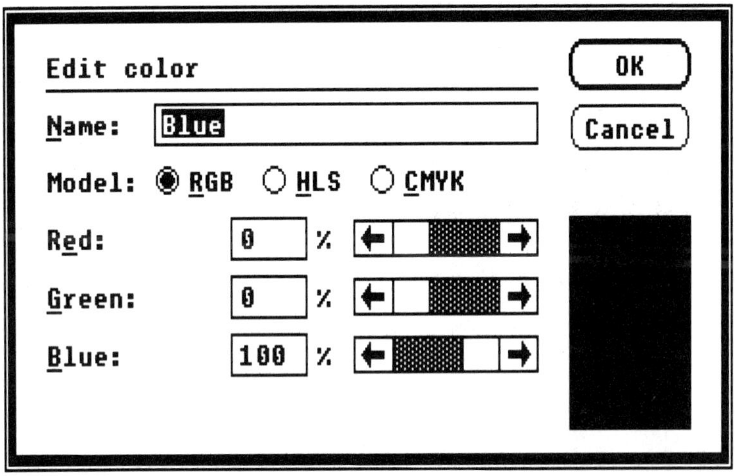

Figure 12.03: *The Edit color dialog box, shown using the RGB color model.*

When satisfied with the specifications for the new color as listed in the EDIT COLOR dialog box, click the OK button to complete the definition of this new color or click the CANCEL button to abort the creation process. In either case we are returned to the DEFINE COLORS dialog box. To return to the publication window, click the OK button or the CANCEL button.

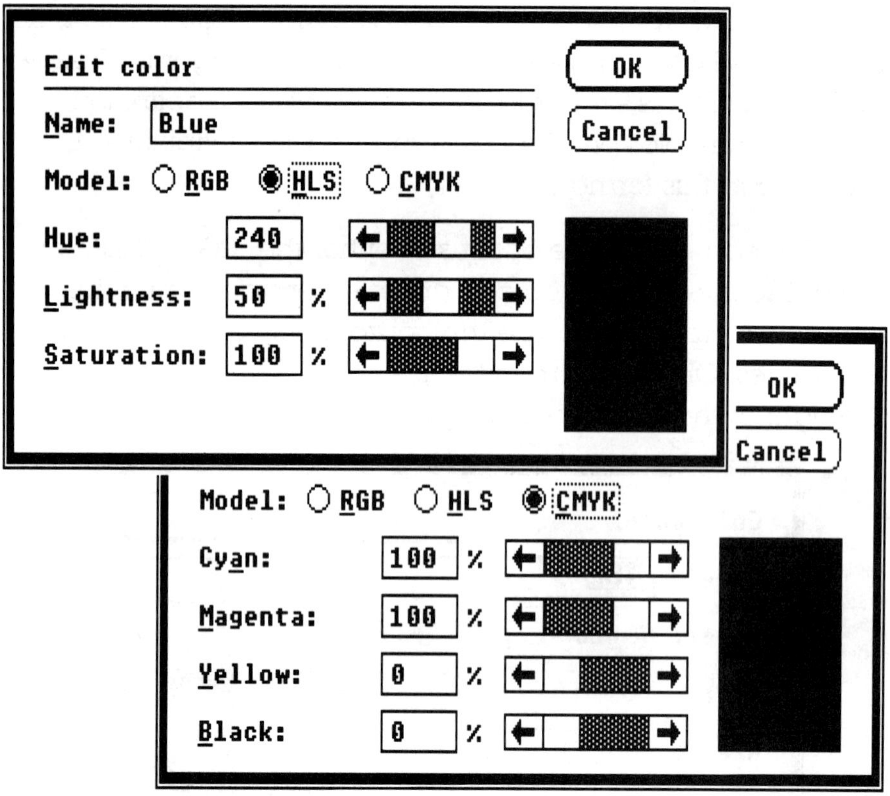

Figure 12.04: *Two other color model definitions of blue.*

Importing colors

After defining colors using any of the methods described above, it is a good idea to get as much use from those colors as possible. In PageMaker, colors defined in any publication can be imported for use in any other publication. This will maximize the benefits of your color-defining efforts and will maintain a consistency among all your publications.

To import colors into a publication, choose the DEFINE COLORS... command from the OPTIONS menu to bring up the DEFINE COLORS dialog box. Click the COPY... button and the COPY COLORS dialog will appear, as shown in Figure 12.05. Locate the publication containing the colors that you wish to import. Select the name of the publication, and click the OK button.

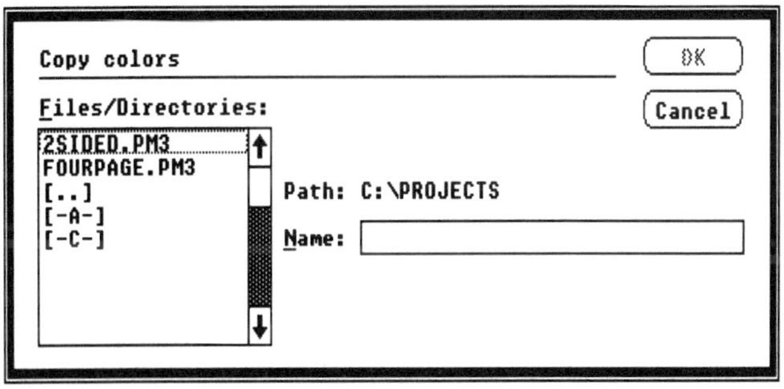

Figure 12.05: *The Copy colors dialog box.*

All colors from the selected publication will then be added to the list of colors in the current publication. If the names of any imported colors have already been assigned to colors in the new document, those colors will not be added. The existing colors override those being imported. If you know that an existing color name is duplicated in the colors being imported, and you want to use the version of the color being imported rather than the one that already exists, either delete the existing color (using the REMOVE... button) or rename the existing color (in the EDIT COLOR dialog box).

Applying colors

After we have created the colors we need for our publication, it is very easy to apply these colors to any text or graphic objects in our publication. Applying a color to any text or graphic overrides any earlier color application. When working on a color monitor, the colors that are applied to text and graphic objects will display on-screen in most cases (see the following section for some exceptions). When printing PageMaker publications to which colors have been applied, you will be able to create color separations by choosing the "Spot color overlays" option in the PRINT dialog box.

To apply colors to a graphic object, select the object (using any one of the selection techniques described in Chapter 5, *Working in the Publication Window*) and then select the name of the color that you want to apply from the Colors palette or the DEFINE COLORS dialog box (which is accessed by choosing the DEFINE COLORS... command in the OPTIONS menu). You may apply a color to any number of selected objects at one time.

To apply colors to any text in your publication, you must select the text to which you want the color applied. Color acts like a character-level formatting attribute—it will be applied only to selected text. Use any of the text selection techniques described in Chapter 8, *Editing Text*, and then select the name of the color that you want to apply from the

Colors palette or the DEFINE COLORS dialog box (which is accessed by choosing the DEFINE COLORS... command in the OPTIONS menu).

Color and imported graphics

Due to the nature and specifications of the many graphic formats that can be imported into PageMaker, not all imported graphics react as you might expect when working with color in PageMaker. EPS graphics from ADOBE ILLUSTRATOR 88 or ALDUS FREEHAND and PICT-format graphics are among the notable exceptions.

Currently, EPS or PICT graphics that include color definitions will display in color on color monitors, but will print as if they are colored "Black" in PageMaker (on the spot-color overlay with the other "Black" text and graphics) unless another color is applied to them. If another PageMaker color is applied to a EPS or PICT graphic, it will not affect the on-screen display, but it will determine the spot-color overlay on which the graphic is printed. If a EPS or PICT graphic does not include color in its definition, it will appear black on-screen regardless of the color applied to it, but it will print on the correct color overlay.

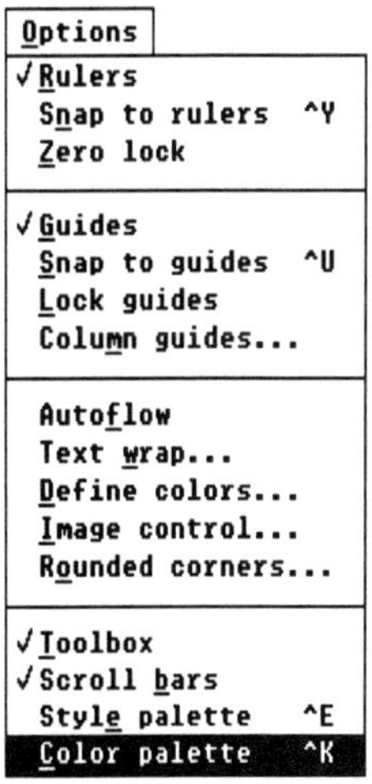

The Colors palette

The Colors palette is a window that lists the names of all currently defined colors. The palette can be displayed at any time by selecting the COLOR PALETTE command (CTRL-K) from the OPTIONS menu. When the Colors

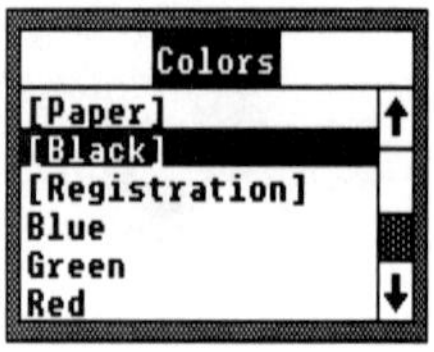

palette is displayed, a check mark (✓) appears before the COLOR PALETTE command. Selecting the COLOR PALETTE command while the palette is already being displayed will remove it from the publication window. The Colors palette can be moved, sized, and closed using the window title bar, size box, and close box, respectively.

The Color palette serves many functions, including:

- **Applying colors**. To apply a color to any number of graphic objects, select the objects and then click on the appropriate color name in the Colors palette. To apply a color to any text in your publication, select the text and then click on the appropriate color name in the Colors palette. More information about the application of colors is included in the preceding section, *Applying colors.*

- **Checking color of text or a graphic object**. As soon as any text or graphic object is selected, the Colors palette highlights the name of the color that has been applied to the text or graphic. Any objects to which no color has been applied will be listed as "Black."

- **A shortcut to editing an existing color**. To edit a color, hold down the CTRL key and then double-click on the name of the color to be edited. The EDIT COLOR dialog box will appear. Editing a color is described fully in the next section of this chapter.

Editing colors

Colors can be edited at any time after they have been created. When a color is edited, all text and graphic objects to which the color has been applied are immediately updated. There are two ways to begin editing an existing color. The first is to choose the Define Colors... command from the Options menu, select the name of the color to be edited from the scrolling list, and then click the Edit... button. The second is to hold down the ctrl key while double-clicking on the color name in the Colors palette. Either method will bring up the Edit Color dialog box.

Once the Edit Color dialog appears, you can edit the attributes of the selected color using either of the three color models available, as described earlier in the section *Defining colors*. You can also edit the name of the color. To save the changes made to the color definition or to the color name, click the OK button (twice if you begin in the Define colors dialog box).

Removing colors

To remove any color that has been defined in your publication (except the colors "Black," "Paper," and "Registration," which cannot be removed), choose the Define Colors... command from the Option menu, select the name of the color to be removed from the scrolling color list, and then click the Remove... button. All text and graphic objects to which the removed color had been applied will now be colored black until you apply another color to them.

Printing color publications

There are two ways to print files that have defined color text and graphic elements. First, you can print a composite copy of your publication, in which all colors for each publication page will be printed on one output page. Composite prints can be used to proof the layout and text of your publication or as final output for a publication that will be color-separated by your commercial printer.

Alternatively, by selecting the "Spot color overlays" option in the PRINT dialog box, you can print color separations of each page in your publication, printing one copy of each page in your publication for each color used on that page. For example, a page that has a red border, black text, and a blue graphic would be printed on three separate pages—one for the red border only, one for the black text only, and one for the blue graphic only. The separations are then provided to your commercial printer, who will use them to prepare printing negatives for each of your specified ink colors.

When using the "Spot color overlays" option, you should also use the "Crop marks" option in the PRINT dialog box. This adds crop marks to your pages, along with the name of each overlay color on each page and additional registration marks that make it easier to align the color overlays during the commercial printing process. An example of a page including all marks output when the both of these options are selected is shown in Chapter 13, *Printing Publications.*

Another option in the PRINT dialog box relating to the output of color documents is the "Cutouts" option. When the "Cutout" option is selected, any portion of any page element that is overlapped by another element will not be printed. If the portion is not cut out on the spot color overlay, ink for the overlapping object will be applied on top of ink for the underlying object in the commercial printing process, thus creating a third color in the area where the inks mix. By cutting out the overlapped portion, the ink for the overlapping area can be applied directly to the paper, and ink color consistency will be better maintained in most circumstances. Be sure to check with the commercial printer who will be reproducing your publication as to their preference regarding the use of this option. See Chapter 13, *Printing Publications,* for a more complete description of all aspects of PageMaker's printing abilities.

CHAPTER 13

Printing Publications

In this chapter we examine:

- *Preparing your system for printing*
- *Printing on PostScript and HP LaserJet printers*
- *Advanced printing techniques*

While creating a publication in PageMaker, you can print one or more publication pages at any time, on almost any printer connected to your computer. In addition to simply printing your publication, PageMaker can also handle a variety of special printing situations—printing oversized pages, creating thumbnails, capturing a print file on disk, and working with downloadable fonts.

PageMaker can print to dot-matrix printers, such as the IBM ProPrinter; to PCL laser printers such as the Hewlett-Packard LaserJet family of laser printers; or to PostScript-equipped printers, such as the Apple LaserWriter II NT or Linotronic 100. The output quality of both text and graphics will vary dramatically between dot-matrix printers and laser printers, so you will usually want to produce camera-ready final prints only on laser printers.

The process of printing PageMaker publications has three parts:

- **Configuring Windows**. Before printing with PageMaker, Windows 2.0 must be properly configured for use with your printer(s) and fonts. This has to be done when you first install Windows and PageMaker, and again when you add any new printers or fonts.

- **Preparing publications for printing**. You must specify the printer that you will be using to print your final document, and your document must then be prepared or adjusted according to the requirements of this printer.

- **Printing publication pages**. To actually print pages from your publication you must specify a number of options in the PRINT dialog box, and then initiate printing.

Configuring Windows

In order to print PageMaker publications, your copy of Microsoft Windows must be configured to include the printer drivers for all printers that you will be using, the communication parameters that will be used by each printer, and all the fonts that you want to use in your publications. You may also, optionally, set a default target printer so that you will not have to reselect a commonly used printer each time you run PageMaker.

Installing and configuring printer drivers

For each type of printer on which you will be printing your PageMaker files you must install a printer driver in Windows. Printer drivers are files used during printing to convert your publication into a format that the printer uses to print publication pages. In addition to copying the printer driver to the Windows directory, the process of installing printer drivers adds information about each installed printer driver to the WIN.INI file, which informs all Windows applications (including PageMaker) of the printer's specifications.

Printer drivers are added to Windows either during its installation or by using the ADD NEW PRINTER... command from the INSTALLATION menu in the Windows Control Panel. Most of the printer drivers that are currently available are included on the DRIVERS floppy disk included with your copy of PageMaker or Windows. If you have a printer for which a driver is not included on this disk, contact Aldus or Microsoft to find out if a printer driver is available.

Once the proper printer drivers are installed, you must specify the port on your computer to which each of your printers is attached, using the Connections... command in the Setup menu of the Windows Control Panel. This is done by simply selecting one of the installed printers from the scrolling list on the left side of the Connections dialog box and clicking on the port to which that printer will be connected in the scrolling list on the right side of the dialog box (see Figure 13.01). Each port can be connected to only one printer, but you can duplicate the installation of any printer type, allowing you to have one printer type connected to more than one port. See the section *Printing to disk* later in this chapter for more information on this feature.

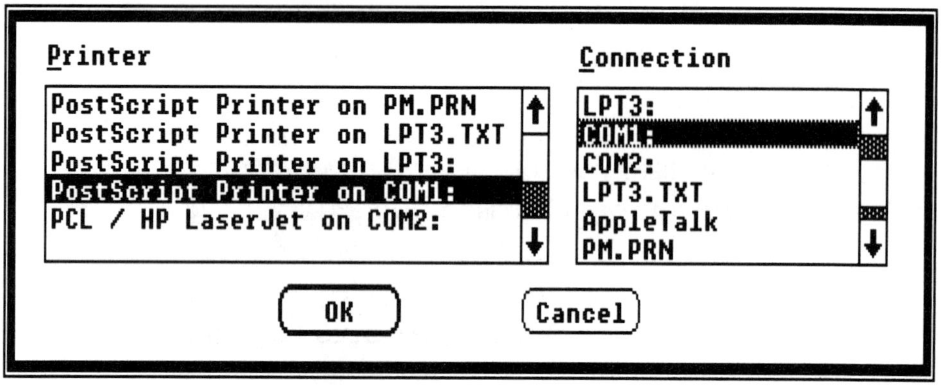

Figure 13.01: *The Connections dialog box.*

It is also important to properly configure your serial (COM) ports using the Communications... command in the Setup menu. The correct specifications for your serial ports depend on your printer and how it has been configured. Check your printer's operation manual or consult your dealer if you are unsure of the correct settings. Serial ports that are configured incorrectly can cause many problems in the printing process and can even make printing impossible.

Setting up PostScript printers

For each PostScript printer installed in Windows, you must specify a number of printer-specific option settings. Information from your configuration is added to the WIN.INI file specifications for your printer and will remain set until you reset the specifications or remove the printer.

There are two ways to access the PostScript printer dialog box (see Figure 13.02), which is used to complete the printer-specific options:

1) Select the Printer... command in the Setup menu of the Windows Control Panel, select the printer to configure, and click the OK button.

2) Choose the Print setup... command from PageMaker's File menu, select the printer to configure from the PostScript printer dialog box, and click the Setup button.

The PostScript Printer dialog box options are:

- **Uncollated copies**. This option allows you specify the number of copies of each page that will be printed on your printer. The "Copies" option in the Print dialog box overrides this option, so in most cases this option is unused.
- **Orientation**. As described for the Page setup dialog box, a page can be "Tall" (taller than wide) or "Wide" (wider than tall). The setting of the "Orientation" option should match the setting of the same option in the Page setup dialog box. PageMaker will not automatically select the same orientation, and most prints made while these settings conflict will not be usable.

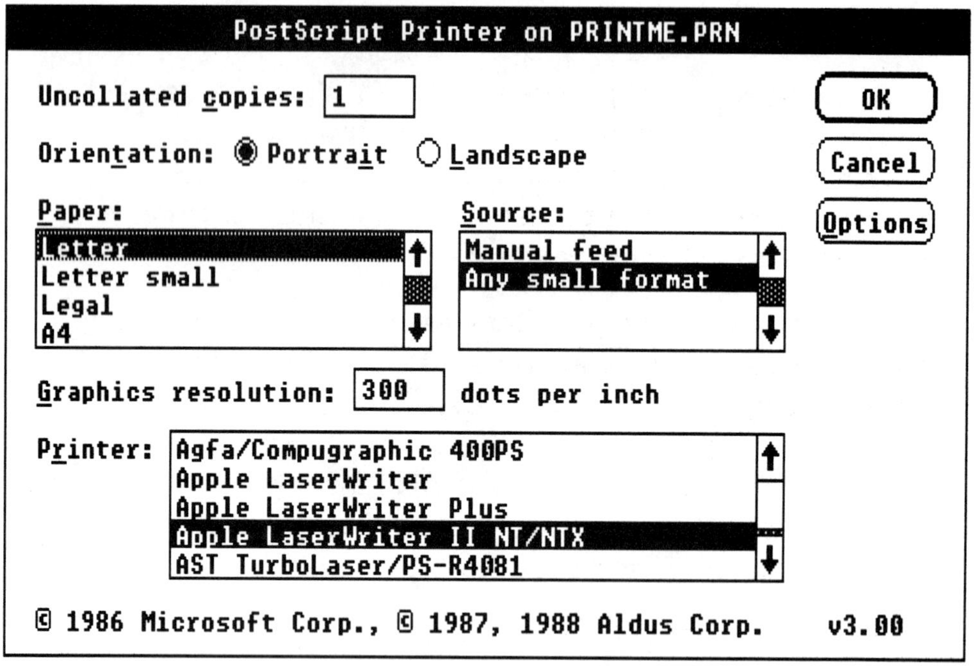

Figure 13.02: *The PostScript printer dialog box.*

- **Paper**. This option lists the paper sizes available for the printer currently specified in the "Printer" option. In most cases, you will want to select a paper size that is the same size as, or larger than, the current setting for the "Page size" option in the PAGE SETUP dialog box. If your "Page size" is larger then your "Paper size," you will have to use either the "Scale" or "Tile" option in the PRINT dialog box to print your publication. When a paper size is selected, the dimensions of the paper are displayed in the "Paper size" option in the PRINT dialog box.

- **Source**. If more than one paper tray option is available for the printer selected in the "Printer" option, you may select the appropriate tray using this option.

- **Graphic resolution**. This option should be set to the resolution of the selected "Printer." The setting of this option primarily affects the quality of paint-type and TIFF graphics. The highest allowable resolution setting is 1270.

- **Printer**. The "Printer" option presents a scrolling list of all printer types included in the Windows PostScript driver. If your PostScript printer is not listed, choose the Apple LaserWriter, since this is the standard PostScript implementation. The setting of the "Printer" option affects the "Paper," "Source," and "Resolution" options, as described earlier.

The OPTIONS button in the upper right corner of the POSTSCRIPT PRINTER dialog box brings up the POSTSCRIPT PRINTER OPTIONS dialog box, shown in Figure 13.03. This dialog box offers additional, more technically specific settings regarding your printer. If an OPTIONS button is not available in your dialog box, you are probably using on older version of the PostScript driver. Copy the file PSCRIPT.DRV from the PageMaker DRIVERS disk into your Windows directory and restart Windows.

The POSTSCRIPT PRINTER OPTIONS are:

- **Job timeout**. This option specifies the amount of time after which PageMaker should cancel a print job, regardless of whether or not the print job is complete. When set to 0, a print job can take as long as necessary to print.

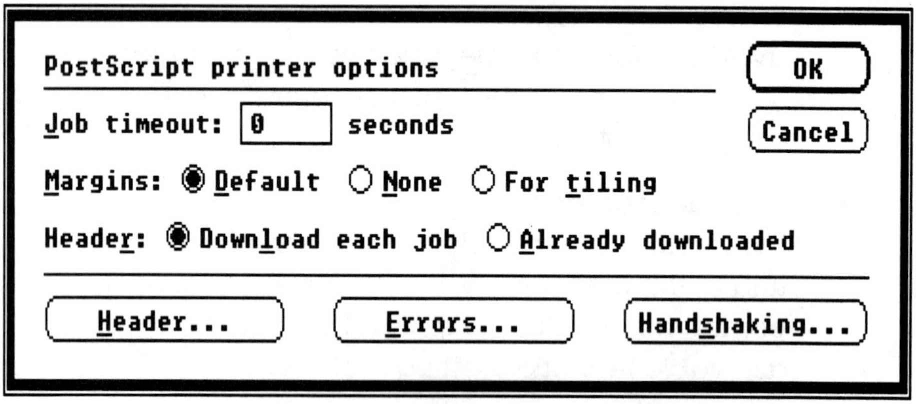

Figure 13.03: *The PostScript printer options dialog box.*

- **Margins**. There are three margins options: "Default," "None," and "Tiling." These options are holdovers from previous versions of the Windows PostScript driver, and really don't do anything.

- **Header**. In order to minimize the size of PostScript files, Windows uses a PostScript dictionary that allows actual PostScript files to be written in a "shorthand" notation. In order for these shorthand PostScript files to be printed, therefore, the dictionary file, which is also known as a header file, must be downloaded into the PostScript printer before the PostScript files are sent for printing.

  This "Header" option allows you to specify whether the PostScript header file needs to be downloaded before each print job or has already been downloaded. When the header file is downloaded before each print job, the process requires time, but the file is automatically flushed from printer memory after the print job, so printer memory is not permanently consumed. This is useful when working with a PostScript printer that has little memory and is being used concurrently with non-Windows applications. The "Already downloaded" option is used when you have "permanently" downloaded the header file, making it unnecessary to download it before each print job. Permanent header downloading is discussed in the next option.

- **Header button**. The Header button is used to either manually download the PostScript header to your PostScript printer or to print the header to a disk file. Clicking the Header button brings up the Header options dialog box (see Figure 13.04), which contains three buttons: Printer, File..., and Cancel.

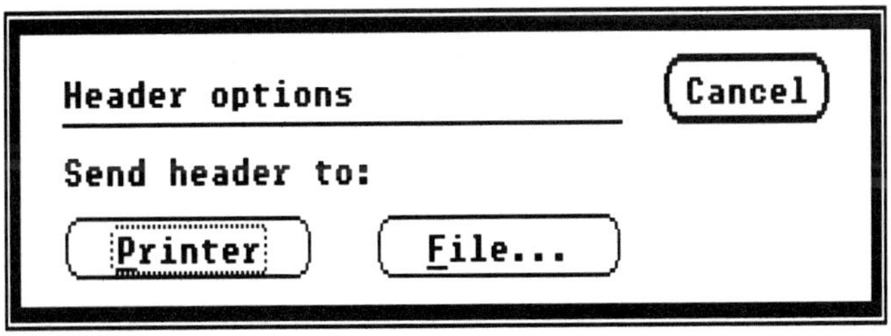

Figure 13.04: *The Header options dialog box.*

Clicking the Printer button brings up the Download header now? dialog box, shown in Figure 13.05, which allows you to download the PostScript header to the selected PostScript printer. This download is "permanent," which means that the header will remain in the printer until it is turned off or rebooted, making it unnecessary to download the header before each print job. This allows you to use the "Already downloaded" option in the POSTSCRIPT PRINTER OPTIONS dialog box, as described earlier.

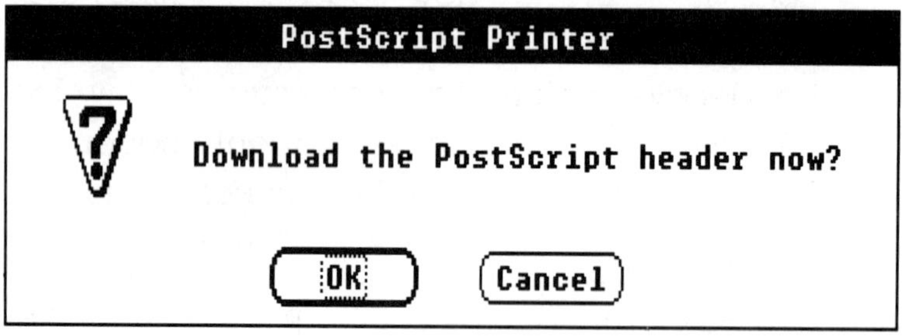

Figure 13.05: *The Download PostScript header now? dialog box*

Clicking the FILE... button allows you to capture the PostScript header on your disk as a file. You can then configure your system so that the header is downloaded permanently when your system is turned on or when PageMaker is run. When the FILE... button is clicked, a dialog box will appear asking you to name the file you are saving. A good name for the header file is PSPREP.TXT. The file should be saved into the same directory as your copy of Windows.

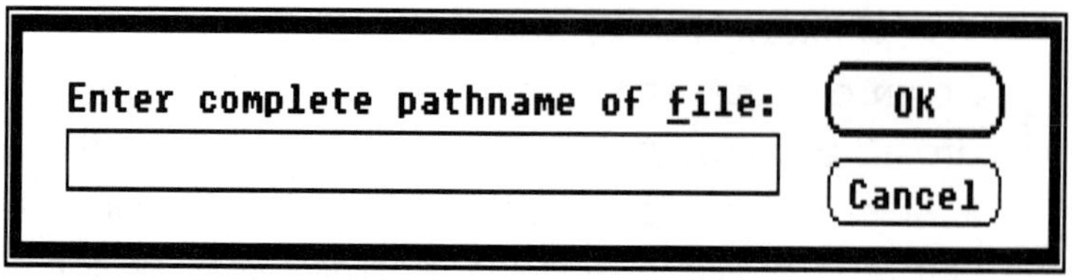

Figure 13.06: *The Enter complete pathname of file dialog box.*

To configure your system so that this header is downloaded automatically when your computer is turned on, add the line COPY C:\BIN\PSPREP.TXT COM1: to your AUTOEXEC.BAT file, where PSPREP.TXT is the filename you saved and COM1: is the port to which your PostScript printer is attached. Alternatively, you can make a separate batch file that downloads this file, download it manually by typing that line at the C: prompt, or add it to a batch file that downloads the header file and then launches PageMaker.

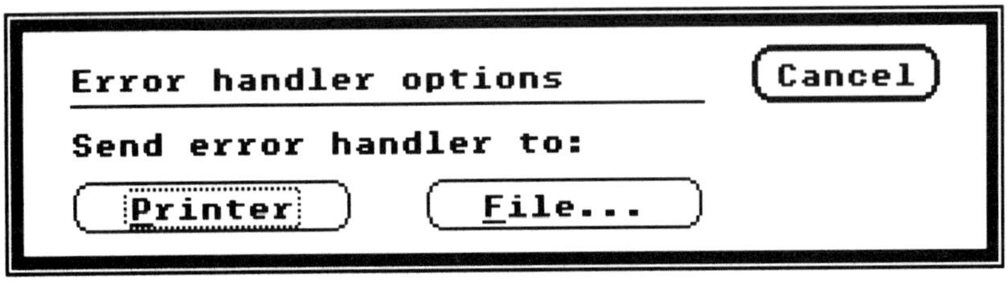

Figure 13.07: *The Errors dialog box.*

- **Errors button**. Normally, when errors occur during PostScript printing, printing is terminated and you receive a generic error message on-screen. By downloading the error handler to your PostScript printer, you instruct the printer to print more specific information about any error that occurs. Like the HEADER dialog box discussed above, the ERRORS dialog box, shown in Figure 13.07, allows you to directly download the error handler to your PostScript printer or to create a disk file containing the error handler. If you create a file containing the error handler, you can download it from the C: prompt or in a batch file (see the discussion in the previous paragraph regarding the PostScript header file.)

- **Handshake button**. Clicking the HANDSHAKE button brings up the HANDSHAKE dialog box, shown in Figure 13.08, which allows you to set the communication between your computer and your PostScript printer to either a hardware or software handshake. With a PostScript printer you usually want to use the hardware handshake, because this allows two-way communication between the PostScript printer and your computer. Note that changes to this option are recorded on an EPROM chip in your PostScript printer, and this chip can be changed only a limited number of times (several hundred) before it wears out. Therefore, do not toggle this option too often.

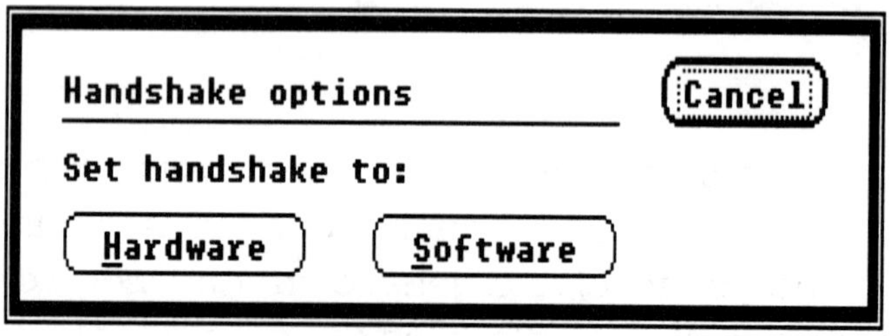

Figure 13.08: *The Handshake dialog box.*

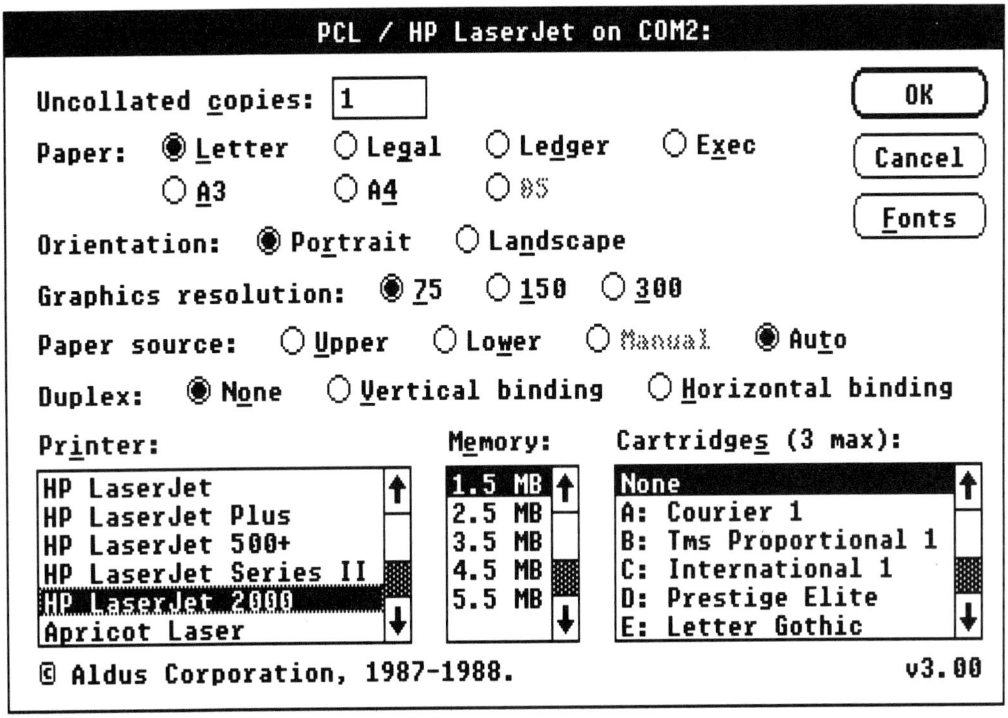

Figure 13.09: *The PCL printer dialog box.*

Configuring PCL printers

For each PCL printer installed into Windows, you must specify a number of printer-specific option settings. Information from your configuration is added to the WIN.INI file specifications for your printer and will remain there until you reset the specifications or remove the printer.

There are two ways to access the PCL PRINTER dialog box (see Figure 13.09) which is used to complete the printer specific options:

1) Select the PRINTER... command in the SETUP menu of the Windows Control Panel, select the printer to configure, and click the OK button.

2) Choose the PRINT SETUP... command from PageMaker's FILE menu, select the printer to configure from the PCL PRINTER dialog box, and click the SETUP button.

The PCL PRINTER dialog box options are:

- **Uncollated copies**. This option allows you specify the number of copies of each page that will be printed on your printer. The "Copies" option in the PRINT dialog box overrides this option, so in most cases this option is unused.

- **Duplex printing**. Check this option if you have a Hewlett-Packard LaserJet 2000 and wish to print on both sides of your paper.

- **Paper**. This option lists the paper sizes available for the printer currently specified in the "Printer" option. In most cases, you will want to select a paper size that is the same size as, or larger than, the current setting for the "Page size" option in the PAGE SETUP dialog box. If your "Page size" is larger then your "Paper size," you will have to use either the "Scale" or "Tile" option to print your publication. When a paper size is selected, the dimensions of the paper are displayed in the "Paper size" option in the PRINT dialog box.

- **Orientation**. As described for the PAGE SETUP dialog box, a page can be "Tall" (taller than wide) or "Wide" (wider than tall). The setting of the "Orientation" option should match the setting of the same option in the PAGE SETUP dialog box. PageMaker will not automatically select the same orientation, and most prints made while these settings conflict will not be usable.

- **Graphic resolution**. This option should be set to the resolution of the selected "Printer." The setting of this option primarily affects the quality of paint-type and TIFF graphics. The highest allowable resolution setting is 1270.
- **Paper source**. If more than one paper tray option is available for the printer selected in the "Printer" option, you may select the appropriate tray using this option.
- **Printer**. The "Printer" option presents a scrolling list of all printer types included in the Windows PCL driver. The setting of the "Printer" option affects the "Paper," "Paper source," "Resolution," "Memory," and "Cartridges" options.
- **Memory**. Select the amount of memory contained in your printer.
- **Cartridges**. This option lists the font cartridges available for the selected printer. Select the font cartridge(s), if any, installed in your printer to add the fonts from that cartridge to the list of available fonts in the TYPE SPECIFICATIONS dialog box. By holding down the SHIFT key you can select more than one cartridge at a time.

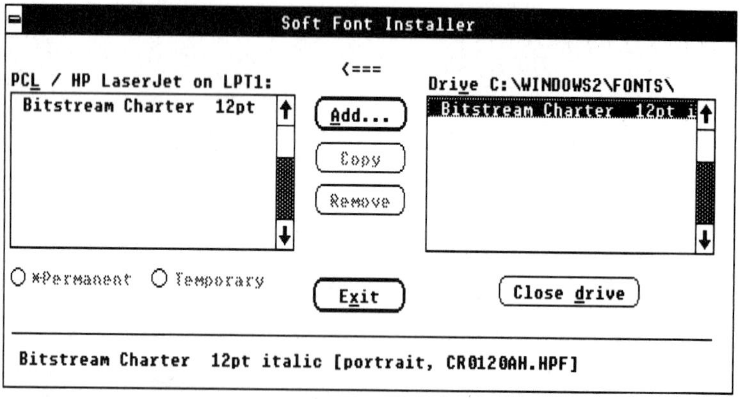

Figure 13.10: *The Soft Font Installer dialog box.*

- **Fonts button**. Clicking the Fonts button brings up the Soft font installer dialog box, shown in Figure 13.10, which is used to install or remove PCL fonts. As described later in this chapter, fonts must be installed in the WIN.INI file for each printer/port combination on which you wish to use them, and printer fonts can be installed so that they are downloaded either manually or automatically. The Soft font installer is an alternative way of accomplishing font installation.

Choosing a default printer

Once your printer drivers are installed and the connections and communication settings complete, you can specify one of your printers to be the default target printer. By doing so, you save yourself the trouble of specifying your target printer in PageMaker whenever you will be using the printer that is specified as the default.

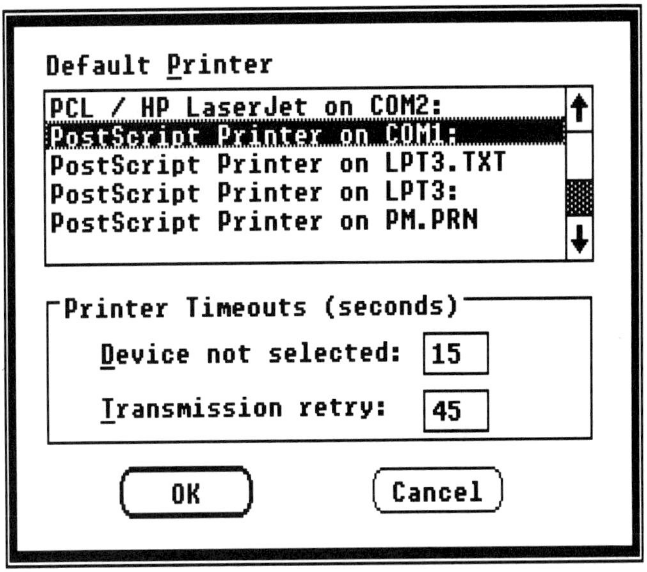

Figure 13.11: *The Default Printer dialog box.*

To set the default target printer, open the Windows Control Panel by selecting the CONTROL PANEL command from the WINDOWS CONTROL menu (any open PageMaker publication must be closed in order to access this command), and then choose the PRINTER... command from the SETUP menu. The dialog box shown in Figure 13.11 will now appear, listing all the printers and their connections as currently configured in your copy of Windows. If you have just added any new printers or adjusted any connections, you might need to reboot Windows in order for this list to be accurate. Click the name of the printer that you wish to set as the default target printer. If desired, you may also change the settings for the "Device not selected" and "Transmission retry" options, although in most cases these options should remain unchanged. Click the OK button to save your new default target printer, or click the CANCEL button to negate any settings or changes. After clicking the OK button, a printer setup dialog box will appear, in which you must specify additional information regarding your particular printer. The printer setup dialog boxes were completely discussed earlier in this chapter.

Adding fonts

Each printer driver installed in Windows includes information regarding the fonts that are built into that particular printer. No special preparation is required to use these built-in fonts after the printer drivers are installed. Additional fonts—either downloadable fonts (often called **soft fonts**) or fonts contained on font cartridges—must be installed separately. Fonts can be installed in Windows either by using the ADD FONTS... command in the SETUP menu in the Windows Control Panel or by using special installation applications provided by the manufacturer of the fonts, such as the SINSTALL program from Adobe or the FONTWARE program from Bitstream.

The font files that you will be installing have three parts: the **printer font metric file** (PFM), the **screen font file**, and the **printer font file**. The printer font metric files (PFMs) provide PageMaker with vital information concerning the character size and spacing of the fonts that you are installing. PFM files are the most important of the font files in terms of using the fonts in PageMaker—it is impossible to use fonts in PageMaker without installing the PFM files. When fonts are installed into Windows, PFM files are copied into the same directory as your Windows application, and one new line for each font is added to each printer/port combination in your WIN.INI file on which the font will be used.

The new line that is added to the WIN.INI file reads:

```
softfont#=path\filename
```

where # represents the sequential font number, and *path/filename* represents the location and filename of the .PFM font file. Also, the line:

```
Softfonts=#
```

must be included before the "Softfonts#=" lines, where # represents the total number of "Softfont#=" lines. It is important to understand that the "SoftFont#=" line must be added to every installed printer on which you intend to use these fonts. Unfortunately, the Windows ADD FONTS... command only adds this line to the default target printer at the time the fonts are installed. To use fonts installed with the ADD FONTS... command with other installed printers, you must manually copy the "SoftFont#=" line to those other printers and manually update the "SoftFont=#" line, or change the default target printer and install the fonts again.

Figure 13.12 shows a portion of a WIN.INI file containing two printer descriptions, one with the Bookman, Zapf Chancery, and Zapf Dignbat fonts installed, the other with just Zapf Chancery and Zapf Dingbat fonts installed. Fonts added with the Adobe SINSTALL program are automatically added to every PostScript printer in the WIN.INI file. Bitstream's FONTWARE, however, requires that you reinstall or manual copy of the font information for each separate printer in your WIN.INI file.

```
[PostScript,PRINTME.PRN]
device=Apple LaserWriter Plus
resolution=300
orientation=0
papersource=1
paper0=Letter
paper1=Legal
paper2=Letter
softfonts=6
softfont1=C:\WINDOWS2\BKDI____.PFM
softfont2=C:\WINDOWS2\BKD_____.PFM
softfont3=C:\WINDOWS2\BKLI____.PFM
softfont4=C:\WINDOWS2\BKL_____.PFM
softfont5=C:\WINDOWS2\ZCMI____.PFM
softfont6=C:\WINDOWS2\ZD______.PFM

[PostScript,COM1]
device=Apple LaserWriter Plus
resolution=300
orientation=0
papersource=1
paper0=Letter
paper1=Letter
paper2=Letter
softfonts=2
softfont1=C:\WINDOWS2\ZCMI____.PFM
softfont2=C:\WINDOWS2\ZD______.PFM
```

Figure 13.12: *A section of a WIN.INI file containing two different printer descriptions, each with different soft fonts installed.*

Once the PFM files are installed in your Windows directory and your WIN.INI file has been updated appropriately, the names of the new fonts will appear in the TYPE SPECIFICATIONS dialog box whenever you use one of the printers for which the fonts have been installed. Optionally, you may install the **screen font files** for some or all of your new fonts so that PageMaker will display them instead of its default screen fonts. To add screen fonts, you must copy them to your Windows directory and add their names to the [Fonts] section of the WIN.INI file as shown in Figure 13.13. PageMaker will automatically use all installed screen fonts for all ports for which their associated PFM files are installed.

```
[fonts]
Bookman-DemiItalic=BKDI____
Bookman-Demi=BKD______
Bookman-LightItalic=BKLI____
Bookman-Light=BKL______
ZapfChancery-MediumItalic=ZCMI____
ZapfDingbats=ZD______
```

Figure 13.13: *A section of a WIN.INI file containing screen font information for the Bookman, Zapf Chancery, and Zaft Dingbat fonts.*

It is not necessary to use and install screen fonts for any of your soft fonts. PageMaker will display one of its default fonts on-screen if no screen fonts are available for any of the fonts that you have installed (relying on the PFM file for character width information). The quality of screen fonts varies dramatically, and in some cases you will actually get better display quality without them. The use of screen fonts also slows down screen display, which is another reason why they are not recommended in all cases.

To control the use of screen fonts at larger font sizes, the PREFERENCES dialog box contains two special options: "Stretch text above," and "Vector text above." The "Stretch text above" option specifies the point size above which available screen fonts are doubled or tripled to create the font size specified. For example, if you set the "Stretch text above" option to 24 pixels (the default setting) any requests for font sizes larger than 24 pixels would be resolved by using the screen font information from a smaller point size. A request to display a 36-point character at "Actual size" would use the 12-point screen

13 Printing Publications

font, tripled. Stretching text allows you to install fewer large point-size screen fonts, saving disk space. The "Stretch text above" option applies only to point sizes below the current setting of the "Vector text above" option.

The "Vector text above" option specifies the size at which PageMaker abandons its efforts to use available screen fonts and instead draws vector fonts. Using vector fonts for larger point sizes increases display speed and also reduces the need to install large point-size screen fonts.

Printer font files contain the actual information used by the printer to create each character of a font. Printer fonts are not used until a document is actually printed. During printing, printer fonts can be made "available" to the printer in one of four ways:

- **As a built-in font**. Printer fonts can be built-in ROM chips in the printer or installed in cartridges inserted into the printer. Most PostScript printers, including Apple's LaserWriter II NT and NTX, have built-in printer fonts for complete families of Times, Helvetica, Courier, Symbol, Avant Garde, Bookman, Palatino, New Century Schoolbook, Zapf Chancery, Zapf Dingbats, and Helvetica Narrow (or in some cases, Helvetica Condensed). Many PCL printers support the use of font cartridges. Built-in fonts are accessed extremely quickly.
- **Installed on a printer's hard disk**. A PostScript printer that has a hard disk—such as the Linotronic Imagesetters or (optionally) the Apple LaserWriter NTX—can hold printer fonts on its hard disk. Fonts are loaded onto a hard disk us-

ing a downloading utility and remain loaded on the disk until removed with the same utility, even if the printer is turned off. Printer fonts are accessed almost as quickly as built-in or manually downloaded fonts, and much faster than fonts that download automatically.

- **Manually (permanently) downloaded**. Using a downloading utility, you can manually download printer fonts to the RAM in your printer. A downloading utility is included with fonts from Adobe, Bitstream, and Hewlett-Packard. When downloaded manually, fonts remain available in the printer's RAM until the printer is rebooted. Once in RAM, fonts are accessed as quickly as built-in fonts, although the downloading process itself is somewhat time-consuming.
- **Automatically (temporarily) downloaded**. PageMaker can automatically download printer font files directly from the hard disk of the computer to the printer, as the fonts are required to process the page. For fonts to be downloaded automatically, the path and filename of the printer font files associated with each PFM file must be added to the "softfont#=" line, in the WIN.INI file for each printer on which a font is installed (see Figure 13.13).

When fonts are downloaded automatically, they are flushed out of RAM as soon as they have been used and therefore must be redownloaded for each use. This feature, however, allows for an unlimited number of fonts to be used on a single page. Automatic downloading of fonts slows down the printing process considerably, because each font requires from 10 to 40 seconds for downloading.

```
[HPPCL,COM2]
prtresfac=0
prtindex=9
prtcaps=-468
FontSummary=C:\WINDOWS2\FSCOM1.PCL
tray=33
softfonts=2
softfont1=C:\WINDOWS2\FONTS\cq0120ah.pfm,C:\WINDOWS2\FONTS\cq0120ah.hpf
softfont2=C:\WINDOWS2\FONTS\cr0120ah.pfm,C:\WINDOWS2\FONTS\cr0120ah.hpf
```

Figure 13.13: *A section of a WIN.INI file with soft fonts specified for temporary downloading.*

Preparing publications for printing

Throughout the preceding chapters we have discussed the overall process of preparing PageMaker publications. We now take a narrower view of publication preparation, looking at only those aspects of preparation that are specifically related to printing.

Selecting the target printer

The first step in preparing a document to be printed is the selection of the target printer. The **target printer** is the printer for which your publication is being prepared. PageMaker must know the target printer for any publication being prepared so that it can offer the correct fonts (and position them correctly on the page), and scale graphics correctly. By default, each new PageMaker publication assumes that the target printer will be the printer you selected as the default target printer (using the Printer... command in the Setup menu in the Windows Control Panel). Whenever the default target printer will not be used, the correct target printer should be selected as early in the publication creation process as possible.

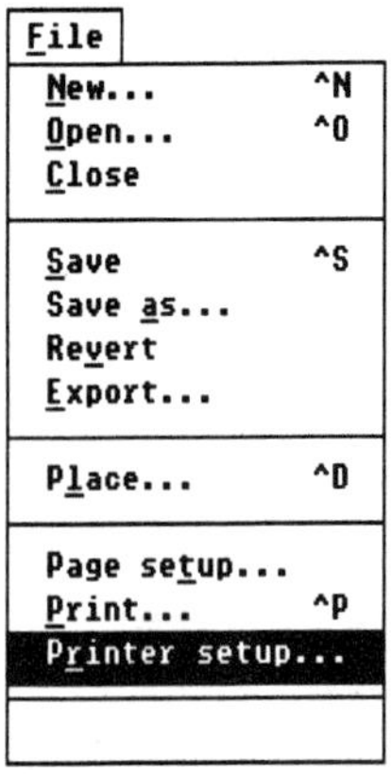

To check the current target printer, or to change the target printer for your publication, choose the Printer setup command from PageMaker's File menu. This will bring up the Printer setup dialog box, shown in Figure 13.14, in which the current target printer is selected. If you would like to change the target printer, select the name of the printer you intend to use for the *final* output of your files.

Your target printer does not have to be the printer on which you intend to print proof copies of your publication—you can print proof copies of your pages on any printer, regardless of the target printer setting. The target printer is the one on which *you will ultimately print your final copy of your publication, and for which you want PageMaker to optimize publication quality*. More information about printing proof copies of publications on printers other than the target printer is provided in discussions of "Printer" option in the Print dialog box later in this chapter.

If the printer/port combination on which you intend to ultimately print your publication is not listed, add additional printer drivers or modify printer connections as discussed earlier in this chapter and in Chapter 2, *Installing PageMaker*.

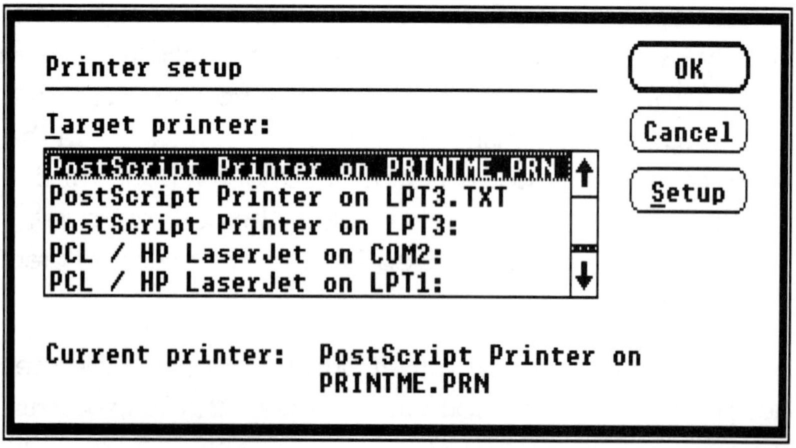

Figure 13.14: *The Printer setup dialog box.*

After selecting the target printer, you may modify that printer's setup (as described earlier in this chapter) by clicking the SETUP button. When you are satisfied with the selected target printer and its setup, click the OK button in the TARGET PRINTER dialog box. If you have changed the target printer, the RECOMPOSE PUBLICATION? dialog box, shown in Figure 13.15, will now appear. Clicking OK in this dialog box allows PageMaker to recalculate all aspects of your page layout based on the new target printer. Clicking the CANCEL button will avoid this recalculation, leaving your publication potentially incompatible with your target printer (in terms of fonts and graphic scaling) but still printable. In most cases, you should allow recomposition whenever you change in the target printer. As we shall see later, PageMaker also asks if you want to recompose your publication when the "Printer" option in the PRINT dialog box is changed, but this recomposition is *not* always recommended.

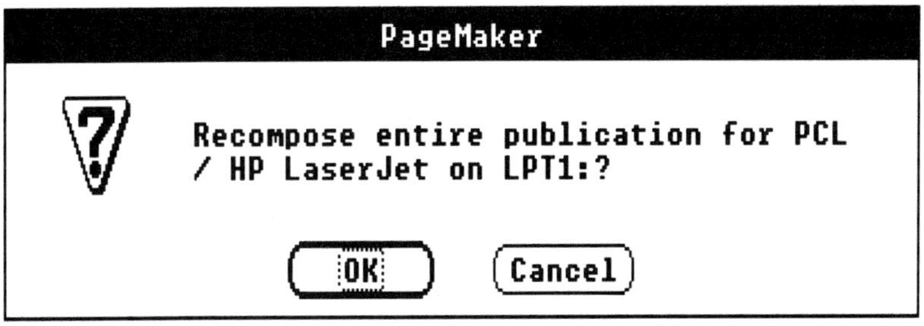

Figure 13.15: *The Recompose Publication? dialog box.*

After recomposing your publication, confirm that all the fonts used in your publication are available in your new target printer, and check the position of all text in the publication. To confirm the presence of any font, select the font name in the TYPE SPECIFICATIONS dialog box: if no font sizes appear in the scrolling list, then the selected font is not installed in the current target printer. You may quit Page-Maker, install the fonts as described earlier, and reopen the publication or change all text in the missing font into a font that is available. Text in many text blocks may wrap differently after a publication has been recomposed for a new printer. Any graphics that have been scaled while holding down the CTRL key should also be resized to match the resolution of the new target printer (if different from the resolution of the former target printer).

Publication preparation

After you have specified the target printer to which your publication will ultimately be printed, you are ready to prepare or adjust your publication. Four aspects of the layout and production of your publication should be considered before you begin the actual printing process. Your choices in these areas will have a direct affect on the quality of your printed publication.

These four pre-printing considerations are:

- **Page size vs. Paper size**. In order to print your publication at full size, the "Page size" you specify in the PAGE SETUP dialog box must be the same size as, or smaller than, the "Paper size" available in your printer and specified in the POSTSCRIPT PRINTER or PCL PRINTER dialog box. If your page size is larger than your paper size, each page of your document will have to be printed using either the "Scaling" or "Tiling" option in the PRINT dialog box.
- **Printable margins**. Most printers cannot print close to the edges of the paper due to an *unprintable margin* area. For laser printers, this area is usually 3/8 inch to 1/2 inch. Check the specifications for your printer before deciding on margins for your document or placing any elements within the margin area. Items positioned in this unprintable margin will not appear on the printed page unless the publication is printed at a reduced size.
- **Scaling graphics**. When scaling imported graphics, PageMaker provides the option of scaling according to the resolution of the output device to which the graphic will be printed, using only reduction or enlargement percentages that will result in the best possible quality. To use this feature, first select the target printer and

then hold down the CTRL key while scaling the imported graphic. The graphic will now resize only to specific percentages that will maintain maximum image quality on your particular printer. This feature is described more completely in Chapter 10, *Using Graphics in PageMaker.*

- **Font selection**. There are two possible problems in font selection: (1) the use of fonts for which PFM files are uninstalled in the target printer (as specified in the PRINTER SETUP dialog box) or the output printer (as specified in the "Printer" option in the PRINT dialog box), and (2) the use of fonts for which printer fonts are not available in the output printer.

  In the first case, the potential for problems is introduced because different printers have different fonts available to them. When changing the target printer or the output printer, you may inadvertently loose access to fonts that were used in our publication. As mentioned earlier, you can check whether or not a font is available for the current printer (the last printer for which the publication was recomposed) by selecting the font name in the TYPE SPECIFICATIONS dialog box. If no font sizes appear in the scrolling list, the selected font is not available for the current printer.

  This commonly occurs when a publication has been prepared for a printer on a .COM or .LPT port and is then output to a printer on a .PRN port. The problem can be avoided, in most cases, by making sure that when you install new fonts they are installed in all printer/port combinations that are installed in your WIN.INI file.

The problem of unavailable printer fonts occurs either when printer fonts are installed improperly (for either automatic or manual downloading) or when PFM files are installed in the WIN.INI file for which printer fonts are unavailable.This may occur intentionally when proofing on a printer other than that which will be used for final output. In this case, the missing fonts will be replaced by either a substitute font or by a bit-mapped version of the missing font.

Printing publication pages

The Print dialog box contains the most basic and frequently used options for the control of the printing process and is used to initiate the actual printing process. The Print dialog box is accessed by choosing the Print... command from the File menu (CTRL P).

The Print dialog box options are:

- **Copies**. Enter the number of copies that you want to print—any number from 1 to 100. In most cases you should only print small quantities of your document directly from PageMaker, since it is usually faster and cheaper to reproduce many copies of the publication by photocopying or offset printing.

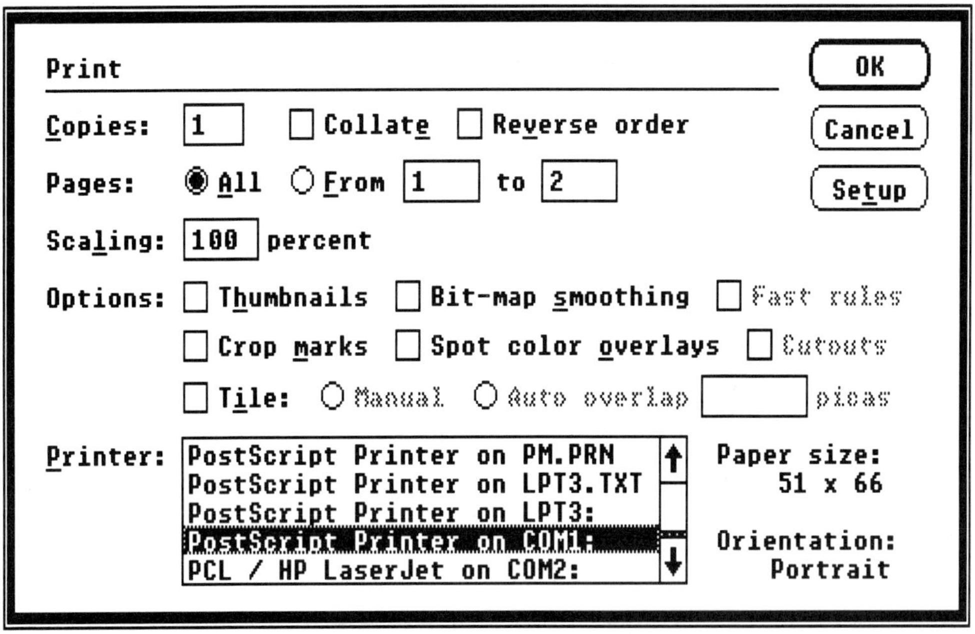

Figure 13.16: *The Print dialog box.*

- **Collate**. When printing more than one copy of a publication, PageMaker normally prints each page as many times as required before going on to the next page. When the "Collate" option is selected, however, one complete copy of the requested range of pages is printed, and then another complete copy, and so on. Although this method eliminates manual collation, it forces the PostScript interpreter inside your printer to recompose each page of the publication every time it is printed, so collated printing is much slower than non-collated printing. This option should be used only when printing a few copies of relatively small documents. In all other cases it will be much faster to print non-collated copies from PageMaker and manually collate the pages.

- **Reverse order**. Depending upon your printer, PageMaker will normally print the range of pages that you specify for output in sequential or reverse sequential order. When the "Reverse order" option is selected, pages are printed in the opposite order than they are normally.

- **Page range**. The "All" option specifies that every page of the publication be printed. The "From" option allows the range of pages to be limited to some subset of the entire publication, as specified in the "From" and "to" option boxes.

  To use the "From" option, enter a value into one or both of the option boxes—the "From" button will then become selected automatically. It is not necessary to enter values in both option boxes; you can specify either a "From" option only or a "to" option only. When the PRINT dialog box is first opened, the "All" option is selected by default. If the "From" option is then selected, it will become the default for the document. Even after quitting and reopening PageMaker, the "From" option remains selected, and the values for the last specified page range are displayed in the option boxes.

- **Scaling**. By default, a publication is printed at its true size (100%). The scaling option can be used to print the publication pages at any reduced size from 25% to 99% or at any enlarged size from 101% to 1000%. When a page is printed at either a reduced size or an enlarged size, the printed page is drawn to the center of the paper. If you are enlarging pages beyond the paper size being used, you will need to use the "Tiling" option, as discussed below, in order to print all portions of your printed pages.

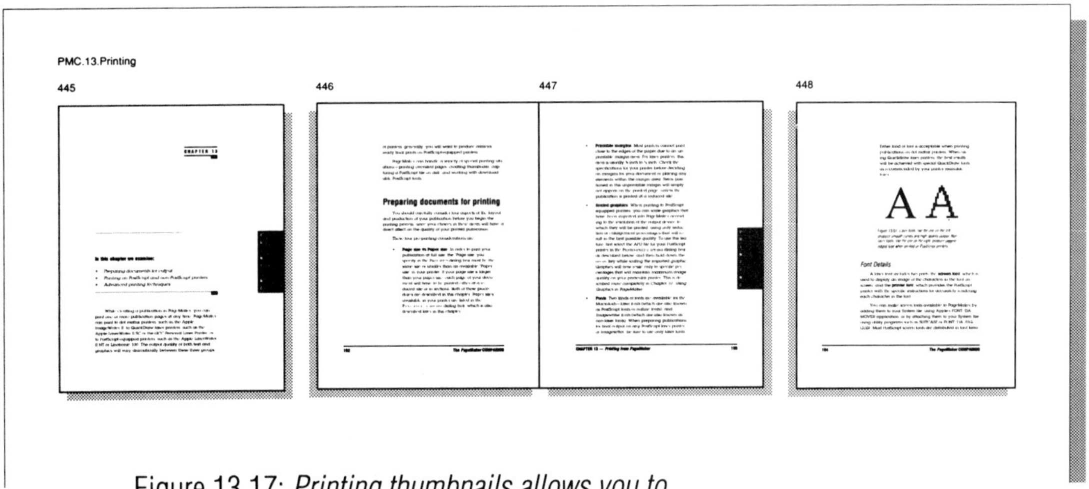

Figure 13.17: *Printing thumbnails allows you to "preview" the general appearance of your publication.*

- **Thumbnails**. Selecting the "Thumbnails" options allows you to print images of several pages of your publication on a single page, at a reduced size. Thumbnails allow you to view several pages simultaneously for design, both individually and in relation to each other. The option box to the right of the "Thumbnails" option specifies how many pages are to be printed on a single sheet of paper—the more thumbnails per page, the smaller the size of each one.

- **Bit-map smoothing.** The "Smooth" option, available only with PostScript printers, instructs PageMaker to try to improve the quality of paint-type graphic images that are included in your file. This is accomplished by using the higher resolution of the PostScript printer to fill in some of the stair-steps along the edges of the bit-mapped graphics. *This option affects* paint-type graphics *only*.

- **Fast rules.** This option, available only when using PCL printers, specifies that mathematical, rather than bit-mapped, descriptions are sent to the printer when boxes are used in a publication. This can slightly increase the speed of printing.

- **Crop marks.** When the "Crop marks" option is selected, small hairline corner marks are printed on the paper. When your publication is printed on paper larger than your page size, crop marks indicate the edges of your page size.

  If the "Spot color overlays" option is used in conjunction with the "Crop marks" option, the name of each color separation is printed on each page, along with additional registration marks that make it easier to align the color separations during the commercial printing process.

CHAPTER 13

PRINTING

In this chapter we examine:

- *Preparing documents for output*
- *Printing on PostScript and non-PostScript printers*
- *Advanced printing techniques*

While creating a publication in PageMaker, you can print one or more publication pages at any time. PageMaker can print to dot-matrix printers, such as the Apple ImageWriter II; to QuickDraw laser printers, such as the Apple LaserWriter II SC or the GCC Personal Laser Printer; or to PostScript-equipped printers, such as the Apple LaserWriter II NT or Linotronic 100. The output quality of both text and graphics will vary dramatically between these three groups

Page 445 - Black overlay

Figure 13.18: *A page output with crop marks and color separation marks.*

- **Spot color overlays.** If you have used color in your publication, as described in Chapter 12, *Using Color in PageMaker,* selecting this option instructs PageMaker to create color separations, printing a separate copy of each publication page for each color used on that page. For example, a page that has a red border, black text, and a blue graphic would be printed on three pages—one for the red border only, one for the black text only, and one for the blue graphic only. You can then provide spot color separations to your commercial printer, who will use them to reproduce your document in the specified ink colors.

When the "Spot color overlays" option is selected, you will usually want to select the "Crop marks" option and the "Cutouts" option, to provide additional support to the color printing process.

- **Cutouts.** This option is only available when the "Spot color overlays" option is selected. When selected, any portion of any object that is overlapped by another object will not be printed—the overlapped portion will be cut out.

  Cutouts are used to avoid the discoloration that would be caused by inks mixing during the color printing process. By cutting out the overlapped portion of all objects, ink from the overlapping object can be applied directly to the paper, and ink color consistency will be better maintained in most circumstances. See Chapter 12, *Using Color in PageMaker*, for a more complete description of all aspects of PageMaker's color features.

- **Tile**. If you specify either a publication page size that is larger than the paper available in your PostScript printer or an enlargement percentage that results in a page size larger than the paper size available, use the "Tile" option to print each publication page in sections (or tiles). The resulting sections are then pieced together so that the entire page can be viewed at once.

Tiling can be controlled manually or automatically. By selecting the "Manual" tiling option, you can print each section of your page individually, manually selecting the exact portion of the page to be printed as a tile. Position the zero point of the ruler to designate the upper left corner of the section to be printed. Then, with the "Tiling" and "Manual" options selected, click the OK button (or press the RETURN or ENTER key) to print the specified section. Adjust the zero point to specify another section of the page to be printed, and repeat the process until all sections of the page have been output. Manual tiling gives you control over how the page is broken into sections so that you can avoid page breaks that would make accurate page reassemply difficult or impossible.

Selecting the "Auto overlap" option instructs PageMaker to automatically create all the tiles required to print each page. PageMaker starts at the upper left corner of each page and continues to print sections of the page until the entire page has been output. Each section overlaps adjacent sections by the amount of space specified in the option box following the "Auto overlap" option. A larger overlap will result in easier reassembly (by avoiding awkward breaks), but will require more sections per page.

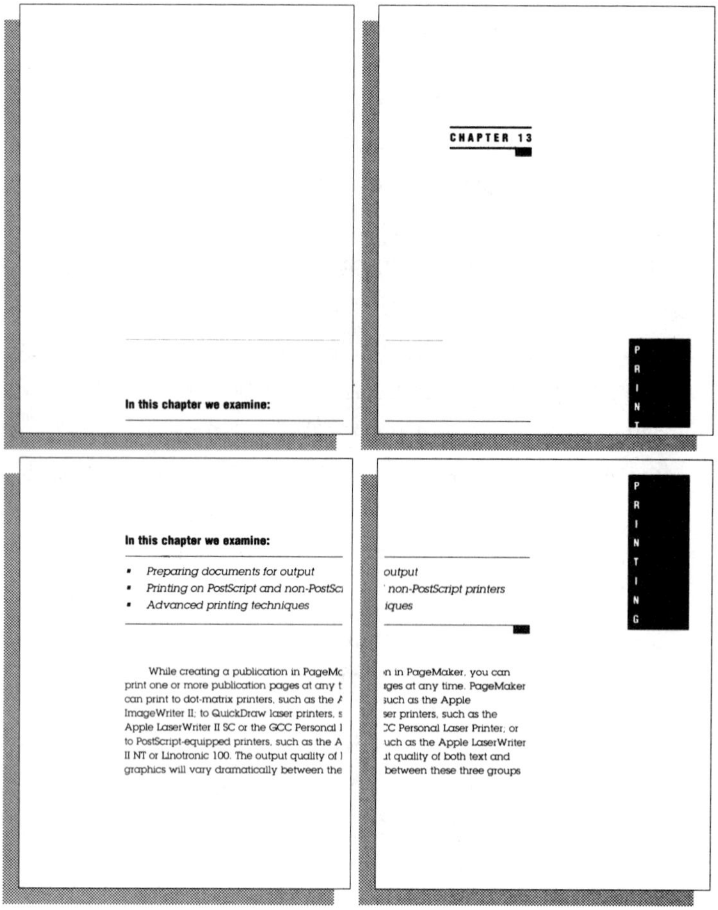

Figure 13.19: *Use the tiling option to print pages that are larger than the available paper size as a series of page sections.*

- **Printer**. This option lists the available printers on which you may output your publication. To select the printer to which your file will be sent, click on the printer name. In most cases, you will choose the printer/port combination that matches the selection you have made for the document's target printer.

You may, however, print to a printer other than the current target printer. For example, suppose that you are preparing a document to be printed on a PostScript imagesetter at a service bureau. Since your document will ultimately be printed to a PostScript printer on the .PRN port (which will create a disk file that you can transfer to the service bureau), the PostScript printer on PRN should be your target printer. To print proofs, however, you will want to use your printer, and so you will choose your printer type in the "Printer" option in the PRINT dialog box.

The same would be true if you were going to print your final publication on a laser printer, but had only a dot-matrix printer available for proofing: you would choose the laser printer as your target printer and specify the dot-matrix for the "Print" option when printing proofs to the dot-matrix printer. Be aware that whenever the printer on which a publication is printed does not match the publication's target printer (or the last printer for which the publication has been recomposed), there is a good chance that the printed output will contain some font substitutions which reduce the accuracy of the publication's representation. The section *Printing files to disk*, later in this chapter, includes an additional discussion on this important topic.

After all the options in the PRINT dialog box have been set, you can proceed in one of two ways:

- **Click the OK button**. This initiates the actual printing process. More information about this process is provided in next section, *Messages during printing*.

- **Click the CANCEL button**. This cancels all entries and returns you to the publication window.

Messages during printing

When the OK button is clicked in the PRINT dialog box the PRINT STATUS dialog will appear, as shown in Figure 13.20, displaying a stream of messages related to the progress of the printing. This dialog box includes a CANCEL button which allows you to cancel printing at any time. As printing begins the lights on your printer will flash. Consult your printer's user manual for specific details concerning the information indicated by the pattern of flashing lights on your printer. For example, on the Apple LaserWriter, a double flash means that data is being received by the printer, and a single flash means that the printer is processing data.

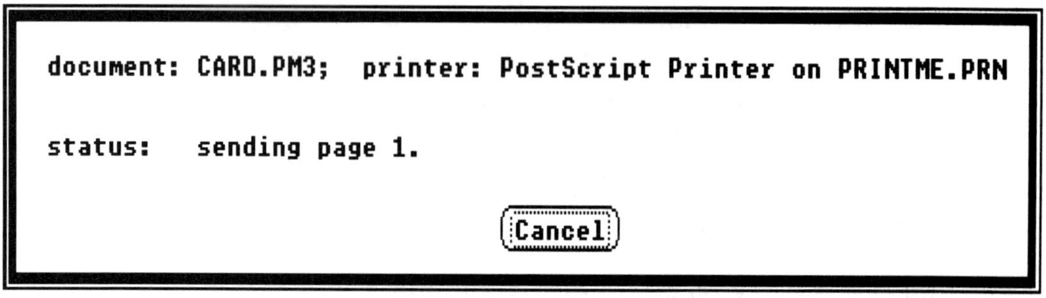

Figure 13.20: *The Print status dialog box.*

Specialized printing techniques

Although each of the commands, dialog boxes, and options relating to the printing of PageMaker publications has been discussed in the earlier sections of this chapter, several common printing situations require additional explanation. This section discusses printing files to disk, printing oversized pages, printing documents that contain color, using downloadable fonts, and using print spoolers.

Printing to disk

Two methods are available for printing a publication on a printer that is not connected to your computer:

1) Save the publication as a normal PageMaker file, transport the file to the computer that is attached to the printer on which you intend to print your publication, open the file in PageMaker, and print the file.

2) Print your publication to disk, transport the file to the computer that is attached to the printer on which you intend to print your publication, and download the print file to the printer.

In the first method, the destination computer must have PageMaker installed on it, and the print file is created on the destination computer (during the printing process), while in the second method the destination computer does not require PageMaker, and the print file is created on the same computer that created the publication. Creating the print file on the computer on which the publication was created ensures that all the fonts used in the publication are available and eliminates the possiblity of introducing unintended changes in the publication. We give up, however, the ability to make any changes to the publication once it reaches the destination computer (because it is no longer a PageMaker file).

When you print your publication to a printer connected to your computer, the printer driver converts the information from the PageMaker file into a format that is understandable to your printer, and sends that information through the selected printer port, directly to the printer. Printing to disk simply routes the same conversion information to a disk file instead of sending it directly to an attached printer. This "printer-ready" information can later be sent to any printer capable of interpreting it.

The procedure for printing a file to disk is as follows:

- Add the line *filename*.PRN= to the [ports] section of your WIN.INI file, as described in Chapter 2, *Installing PageMaker*. The *filename* can be any legitimate DOS filename and will be used as the filename for all files printed to disk. Commonly used filenames include OUTPUT.PRN, PRINTME.PRN, PM.PRN, and PS.PRN.

- Add a new printer of the type that you want to print to disk to your WIN.INI file using the ADD NEW PRINTER... command from the INSTALLATION menu in the Windows Control Panel. Use the CONNECTIONS... command from the SETUP menu to connect this new printer to the .PRN port, and then click the SETUP button to specify the attributes of the printer on which the print files will ultimately be printed. (Use of the CONNECTIONS...

command and SETUP button were discussed earlier in this chapter.) Alternatively, you can just change the connection of one of your existing printers so that it is connected to the .PRN port when you want to print to disk.

- Add all fonts that you will be using in publications that will be printed to disk to the new printer on .PRN. Font installation was also discussed earlier in this chapter.
- Select the *filename*.PRN printer in the "Printer" option in the PRINT dialog box, and click the OK button to print the file to disk. The resulting file will be named *filename*.PRN, and will reside in the same directory as your copy of Windows.

If you do not select the printer on .PRN as your target printer when first composing the publication, it is important to be sure that the printer you do select has all the same fonts as the .PRN printer, and vice versa. In general, you should select the .PRN printer as your target printer, since the printer specified in the "Printer" option in the PRINT dialog box does not have to match the target printer.

You can print proofs of your publication on any printer that is attached to your computer, regardless of the current target printer, although the fonts on the printer used for proofing may not match those in the target printer. To do this, select the printer to which you want to print proofs in the "Printer" option of the PRINT dialog box, click the CANCEL button in the RECOMPOSE FOR NEW PRINTER? dialog box that appears, and then click the OK button in the PRINT dialog box to print your publication. As long as you do not recompose your publication it remains prepared for the target printer, regardless of the type of printer used to print proof copies.

Printing oversized pages

If the "Page size" selected in the PAGE SETUP dialog box is larger than the printable area of the largest "Paper" size available, as indicated in the POSTSCRIPT PRINTER dialog box, you must print each page of your publication either at a reduced size or in sections.

To determine the largest possible reduction at which your page can be printed on the available paper size, divide the horizontal printable area by the horizontal page size (such as $8/8.5 = 0.941$) and the vertical printable area by the vertical page size (such as $10.5/11.5 = 0.913$). The smaller result corresponds to the largest possible percentage of the original size—in this case, 91.3%. Use the "Scale" option in the PRINT dialog box to print your publication at this, or at a smaller, reduction percentage.

The process of printing sections of pages is known as *tiling*. Using the "Auto" tiling option in the PRINT dialog box, you specify the amount by which tiles should overlap in the "Overlap" option box, and PageMaker then calculates the number of sections, or tiles, required and prints all the tiles necessary to output the entirety of each publication page.

Using the "Manual" tiling option in the PRINT dialog box allows you to control how each page is broken into tiles. To use this option, first move the zero point on-screen so that it represents the upper left corner of the section to be printed. Then select the "Manual" tiling option in the PRINT dialog box, and click the OK button. Only the section specified by the zero point will be printed for each page in the specified page range. You then can relocate the zero point to determine a new section, and print again.

Printing colors

If you have used any colors in your publication, two alternatives are available for printing. First, you can print a composite copy of your publication, in which all colors for each publication page will be printed on one output page. Composite prints can be used to proof the layout and text of your publication or as final output for a publication that will be color separated by your commercial printer.

Alternatively, by selecting the "Spot color overlays" option in the PRINT dialog box, you can print color separations of each page in your publication, printing one copy of each page in your publication for each color used on that page. For example, a page that has a red border, black text, and a blue graphic would be printed on three separate pages— one for the red border only, one for the black text only, and one for the blue graphic only. The separations are then provided to your commercial printer, who will use them to prepare printing negatives for each specified ink colors.

When the "Crop marks" option is selected, small hairline corner marks are printed on the paper with your page. When printed on paper that is larger than your page size, crop marks indicate the edges of your page size. These are commonly used when printing to an imagesetter, which prints on large rolls of paper rather than on sheets. If the "Spot color overlays" option is used in conjunction with the "Crop marks" option, the name of each color separation is printed on each page, along with additional registration marks that make it easier to align the color separations during the commercial printing process.

The the "Cutouts" option inhibits the printing of any portions of any page element that are overlapped by another element. If the portion is not cut out on the spot color separation, ink for the overlapping object will be applied on top of ink for the underlying object in the commercial printing process, thus creating a third color in the area where the inks mix. By cutting out the portion, the ink for the overlapping area can be applied directly to the paper, and ink color consistency will be better maintained in most circumstances. Be sure to check with the commercial printer who will be reproducing your publication as to their preference regarding the use of this option. See Chapter 12, *Using Color in PageMaker,* for a complete description of PageMaker's color features.

Using downloadable fonts

If you have used fonts in your publication that are not resident in your printer, either on chips, in cartridges, or on the printer's hard disk, you must make sure that those fonts either are downloaded manually to the printer's RAM or hard disk or are available for automatic downloading during printing.

If your printer has a hard disk, or if font cartridges are available, printer fonts should be kept on the disk as long as there is space for them. Depending on the size of your hard disk or on the number of font cartridge slots available, the disk should hold between 30 and 300 fonts. Fonts can be accessed very conveniently from either the hard disk or cartridge and perform much faster than fonts downloaded automatically during printing.

Fonts that will be used repeatedly should be downloaded manually (also known as permanently) into RAM if they are not already downloaded onto the printer's hard disk. While the process of downloading fonts manually is time-consuming, any time spent will be offset by increased printing speed if the downloaded fonts are used more than half a dozen times. Available printer RAM, however, is a major constraint in deciding how many fonts can be downloaded manually .

In general, printers that have only a few hundred kilobytes of available RAM, such as the Apple LaserWriter Plus, can hold only two or three manually downloaded fonts. Printers having 2 megabytes of RAM, like the Apple LaserWriter II NT, can hold four to six fonts, and printers having 3 megabytes of RAM can hold as many as a dozen fonts. When a printer is holding its maximum number of downloaded fonts, it cannot accept any more fonts, whether downloaded manually *or* automatically. Therefore, before downloading a font, consider not only how many times it will be used, but also how many other downloadable fonts will be used in the same period of time.

Suppose, for example that you intend to print a number of documents that contain different downloadable fonts within a few hours. You will actually save time by allowing the required fonts to download automatically rather than downloading the fonts manually and restarting the printer every time you print a different document. Of course, if you have enough memory in your printer, you may be able to download all the required fonts.

When deciding on your strategy regarding printer fonts, do not forget the requirements of the other users of your laser printer. In a networked situation, fonts should not be downloaded manually unless your printer has adequate memory; a reasonable amount of working memory should be kept available for other users to print documents with automatically downloaded fonts.

If you do not have enough memory to manually download all the fonts that you expect to used repeatedly, or even all the fonts used in a particular document, a good strategy is to download the one or two fonts that you will be using most often. For example, in this book the body copy font, Lubablin Book, would be the most important to download, followed by the subhead font, Helvetica Condensed. The more often a font is used, the more time you will save by manually downloading it into the printer's RAM memory.

Fonts should be allowed to automatically download (also known as temporary download) whenever it is impossible or impractical to download them manually to hard disk or to RAM or to use them from cartridges. In order for fonts to automatically download, the WIN.INI file must be updated to include information specifying the location of the printer fonts, as described earlier in this chapter.

Print spoolers and background printing

Print spoolers, or printer servers, are hardware or software devices that intercept files destined for a printer, and then control the interaction between the file and the printer. The benefit of using a spooler or server is that it can accept the print file from PageMaker much faster than the printer can, freeing the PageMaker application, and thereby freeing you to return to work while the spooler handles the slow process of feeding the data to the printer and waiting for it to print. Some spoolers also perform special functions, such as allowing network administrators to prioritize printing requests, or routing your print job to the first available printer.

One disadvantage of working with print spoolers is that any error messages returned by the printer during actual printing are usually lost, since they are intercepted by the print spooler and are seldom forwarded back to you. In general, whenever you have problems printing your PageMaker files, the first step in correcting the problem should be to either turn off the spooler, or route your printing around the spooler in order to determine if the spooler itself is contributing to the printing problem.

Since PageMaker runs under Windows, the Windows Spooler is most commonly used with PageMaker. In fact, the Windows Spooler is turned on by default during the installation of Windows, and you must turn it off manually if you want to defeat its use. The Windows Spooler is turned off by changing the Spooler=yes line in the WIN.INI file to read Spooler=no, and then restarting Windows.

Using the Windows spooler will return your PageMaker application to you faster than if it were not used. However, PageMaker and Windows are themselves very demanding upon most computing environments (except perhaps an 80386 computer with several megabytes of RAM); therefore, the spooler does not significantly reduce printing times in most cases. It is useful to use the spooler when you wish to print several publications and then leave computer to finish the printing, or spool publications and use the spooler's "Pause" option to delay printing until a later time.

CHAPTER 14

Creating an Advanced Catalog

In this chapter we examine:

- *Autoflowing text and using style sheets*
- *Wrapping text around graphic elements*
- *Applying image control to paint and TIFF graphics*

In this chapter we will use PageMaker to create a four-page catalog including a graphic, a photograph, a price listing, and two spaces for advertisements. Our step-by-step creation of this catalog is the last of three sample projects presented in this book. This chapter focuses on the most advanced commands and operations offered by PageMaker and, as always, demonstrates how these features can be used to satisfy a wide variety of your publication needs.

Because one of the features that we discuss in this chapter is automatic text flow, you will need a sizable word-processing document, between four and five pages in length. You can use the LOREM.TXT text file on the TEMPLATES disk, which is approximately two and a half pages long, but you may need to place the file twice in order to complete the sample project. We will also be importing two kinds of graphic images: one created and saved in the paint format, such as a piece of clip-art, and a photographic TIFF image sampled using a gray-scale scanner. If you are among the majority of persons who do not own a gray-scale scanning device, you will still be able to follow along with our text. The same scan that we use is provided on the GETTING STARTED disk included with your PageMaker application. The file is appropriately named PHOTO.TIFF.

As in our earlier newsletter and flyer projects, the contents of your text and graphic files are irrelevant. It is the construction process, rather than the finished catalog, that is important to successfully completing and understanding this sample project.

Throughout this sample catalog we will be using the typeface Bookman. This is a standard typeface that can be output from the Apple LaserWriter Plus and most other PostScript-language laser printers. You do not need the Bookman screen font family, since Windows will substitute its generic screen fonts, and as long as the Bookman printer font is loaded in your printer, the Bookman family will print correctly. However, the actual Bookman screen font will give you a more accurate screen representation of the shape and spacing of the characters, and we recommend you obtain the screen font and install it into Windows if at all possible. If you absolutely cannot obtain Bookman, substitute Helvetica for all Bookman references included in this chapter.

Creating our publication

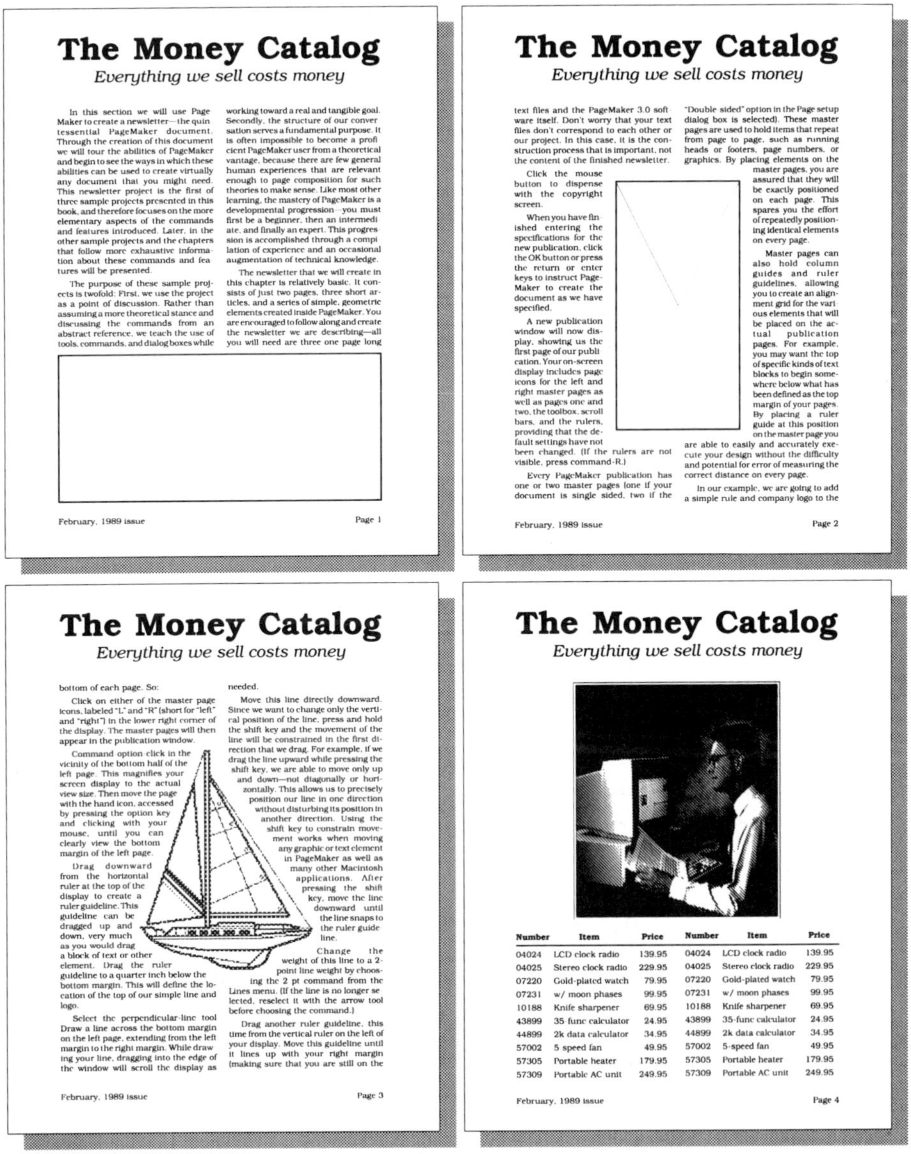

The Money Catalog

Everything we sell costs money

In this section we will use PageMaker to create a newsletter—the quintessential PageMaker document. Through the creation of this document we will tour the abilities of PageMaker and begin to see the ways in which these abilities can be used to create virtually any document that you might need. This newsletter project is the first of three sample projects presented in this book, and therefore focuses on the more elementary aspects of the commands and features introduced. Later, in the other sample projects and the chapters that follow more exhaustive information about these commands and features will be presented.

The purpose of these sample projects is twofold: First, we use the project as a point of discussion. Rather than assuming a more theoretical stance and discussing the commands from an abstract reference, we teach the use of tools, commands, and dialog boxes while working toward a real and tangible goal. Secondly, the structure of our conversation serves a fundamental purpose. It is often impossible to become a proficient PageMaker user from a theoretical vantage, because there are few general human experiences that are relevant enough to page composition for such theories to make sense. Like most other learning, the mastery of PageMaker is a developmental progression—you must first be a beginner, then an intermediate, and finally an expert. This progression is accomplished through a compilation of experience and an occasional augmentation of technical knowledge.

The newsletter that we will create in this chapter is relatively basic. It consists of just two pages, three short articles, and a series of simple, geometric elements created inside PageMaker. You are encouraged to follow along and create the newsletter we are describing—all you will need are three one page long

February, 1989 issue Page 1

The Money Catalog

Everything we sell costs money

text files and the PageMaker 3.0 software itself. Don't worry that your text files don't correspond to each other or our project. In this case, it is the construction process that is important, not the content of the finished newsletter.

Click the mouse button to dispense with the copyright screen.

When you have finished entering the specifications for the new publication, click the OK button or press the return or enter keys to instruct PageMaker to create the document as we have specified.

A new publication window will now display, showing us the first page of our publication. Your on-screen display includes page icons for the left and right master pages as well as pages one and two, the toolbox, scroll bars, and the rulers, providing that the default settings have not been changed. (If the rulers are not visible, press command-R.)

Every PageMaker publication has one or two master pages (one if your document is single sided, two if the "Double sided" option in the Page setup dialog box is selected). These master pages are used to hold items that repeat from page to page, such as running heads or footers, page numbers, or graphics. By placing elements on the master pages, you are assured that they will be exactly positioned on each page. This spares you the effort of repeatedly positioning identical elements on every page.

Master pages can also hold column guides and ruler guidelines, allowing you to create an alignment grid for the various elements that will be placed on the actual publication pages. For example, you may want the top of specific kinds of text blocks to begin somewhere below what has been defined as the top margin of your pages. By placing a ruler guide at this position on the master page you are able to easily and accurately execute your design without the difficulty and potential for error of measuring the correct distance on every page.

In our example, we are going to add a simple rule and company logo to the

February, 1989 issue Page 2

The Money Catalog

Everything we sell costs money

bottom of each page. So:

Click on either of the master page icons, labeled "L" and "R" (short for "left" and "right") in the lower right corner of the display. The master pages will then appear in the publication window.

Command option click in the vicinity of the bottom half of the left page. This magnifies your screen display to the actual view size. Then move the page with the hand icon, accessed by pressing the option key and clicking with your mouse, until you can clearly view the bottom margin of the left page.

Drag downward from the horizontal ruler at the top of the display to create a ruler guideline. This guideline can be dragged up and down, very much as you would drag a block of text or other element. Drag the ruler guideline to a quarter inch below the bottom margin. This will define the location of the top of our simple line and logo.

Select the perpendicular-line tool Draw a line across the bottom margin on the left page, extending from the left margin to the right margin. While drawing your line, dragging into the edge of the window will scroll the display as needed.

Move this line directly downward. Since we want to change only the vertical position of the line, press and hold the shift key and the movement of the line will be constrained in the first direction that we drag. For example, if we drag the line upward while pressing the shift key, we are able to move only up and down—not diagonally or horizontally. This allows us to precisely position our line in one direction without disturbing its position in another direction. Using the shift key to constrain movement works when moving any graphic or text element in PageMaker as well as many other Macintosh applications. After pressing the shift key, move the line downward until the line snaps to the ruler guideline.

Change the weight of this line to a 2-point line weight by choosing the 2 pt command from the Lines menu. (If the line is no longer selected, reselect it with the arrow tool before choosing the command.)

Drag another ruler guideline, this time from the vertical ruler on the left of your display. Move this guideline until it lines up with your right margin (making sure that you are still on the

February, 1989 issue Page 3

The Money Catalog

Everything we sell costs money

Number	Item	Price	Number	Item	Price
04024	LCD clock radio	139.95	04024	LCD clock radio	139.95
04025	Stereo clock radio	229.95	04025	Stereo clock radio	229.95
07220	Gold-plated watch	79.95	07220	Gold-plated watch	79.95
07231	w/ moon phases	99.95	07231	w/ moon phases	99.95
10188	Knife sharpener	69.95	10188	Knife sharpener	69.95
43899	35-func calculator	24.95	43899	35-func calculator	24.95
44899	2k data calculator	34.95	44899	2k data calculator	34.95
57002	5 speed fan	49.95	57002	5-speed fan	49.95
57305	Portable heater	179.95	57305	Portable heater	179.95
57309	Portable AC unit	249.95	57309	Portable AC unit	249.95

February, 1989 issue Page 4

Figure 14.01: *The following pages describe how to create the advanced-level, four-page catalog shown above.*

1 To begin creating our publication, we must first launch the PageMaker application, as described in the first sample project, Chapter 6, *Creating a Simple Newsletter*. Once the launch is completed, click your mouse button to dispense with the copyright screen.

Changing default settings

Before we create a new file, we will be altering a few application default settings in PageMaker, just as we did in the second sample project. The defaults that we will change include the system of measurement, the line weight and shade value, the column guides, and a variety of commands under the OPTIONS menu.

2 Choose the PREFERENCES... command from the EDIT menu to display the PREFERENCES dialog box. Select "Inches decimal" from the "Measurement system" options and click OK. Unlike inches shown on a standard ruler, decimal inches are divided into tenths and twentieths. This means that we might ask you to position your cursor even with the 7.8-inch mark on the horizontal ruler and the 4.15-inch mark on the vertical ruler. All measurements will be given as decimals rather than as fractions.

3 Now choose the COLUMN GUIDES... command from the OPTIONS menu to bring up the COLUMN GUIDES dialog box. Enter 2 for the "Number of columns" option. Then press the TAB key, enter 0.25 to replace the "Space between columns" value, and click OK.

4 Choose the 2 PT weight from the LINES menu and the NONE command from the SHADES menu.

5 Throughout this book, we have described a number of commands available under the OPTIONS menu that are used to toggle various on and off PageMaker attributes. Click and hold on the OPTIONS menu and notice which commands are preceded by check marks. The following list contains the name of the commands that we will use, and the effects of turning on each:

- **Rulers**, displays horizontal and vertical rulers.
- **Snap to rulers**, creates an invisible grid corresponding to each ruler tick mark.
- **Guides**, displays margins and column guides, and allows you to create ruler guides.
- **Snap to guides**, cursor snaps to margins, column guides, and ruler guides.
- **Autoflow**, automatically pours a placed text file into specified columns, adding pages to a document if necessary.
- **Toolbox**, displays toolbox.
- **Scroll bars**, displays scroll bars.
- **Style palette**, displays Styles palette beneath toolbox, containing a scrolling list of all available style sheets.

If any of these commands is not checked, you should choose it at this time. When you are finished, your OPTIONS menu should look like that shown in Figure 14.02.

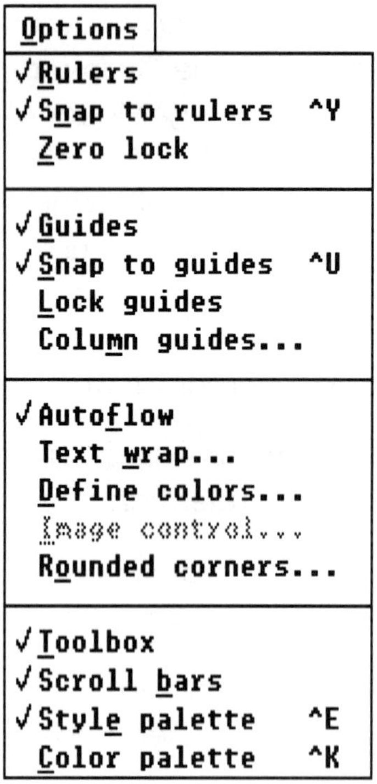

Figure 14.02: *The Options menu displaying the default settings used in this sample project.*

Creating a new document

6 We are now ready to begin creating our catalog. Press CTRL-N to access the PAGE SETUP dialog box. The options in this dialog should be set as follows:

Page size: Letter

Orientation: Tall

Start page #: 1

# of pages: 4

Double-sided: not selected

Facing pages: dimmed

Margin in picas: Left 1, Top 2, Right 1, Bottom 1

When you have finished entering and selecting the specifications listed above, click the OK button, instructing PageMaker to create your new document.

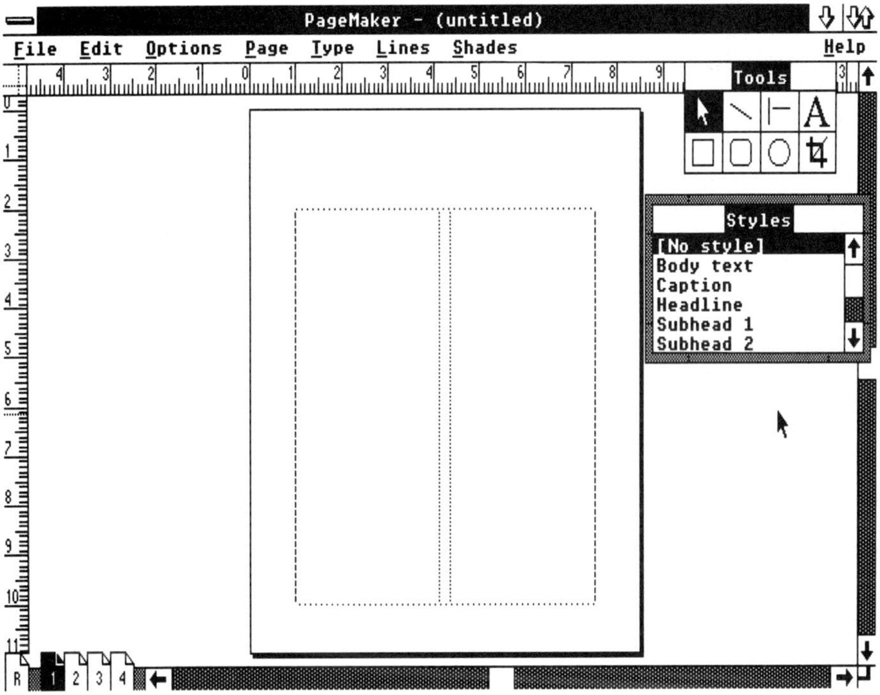

Figure 14.03: *The new document window, displaying default column guides, decimal inch rulers, and the on-screen Styles palette.*

Preparing the master page

As always, our first step is to define and create the master page items. In this case, our master page will be composed of not only a system of ruler guides, but also a catalog flag text block that we will input directly into PageMaker.

The flag, you may remember, is the name of our publication, displayed in an eye-catching manner.

We will also learn how to create a master page folio. A folio contains general information and is positioned at the top or bottom of each page of a document. The text of the folio may include the name of a document or its issue date, along with the current page number.

7 Click on the master page icon, labeled "R" at the bottom of your display. After the master page appears, drag two guides down from the horizontal ruler. One guide should be positioned at the 1.0-inch mark and the other should be positioned at the 1.8-inch mark on the vertical ruler. Next, drag two guides from the vertical ruler, positioning them exactly even with the two outermost column guides (flush with the left and right margins). These guides will provide a grid for text blocks that we will create in the areas above and below our margins.

Creating the flag text

8 Zoom in to the "Actual" size view mode by clicking the secondary mouse button in the center of the two-inch area above the top margin. Then select the text tool. Drag from the intersection of the upper ruler guide and the left margin to the intersection of the lower ruler guide and the right margin. This determines the column width of our flag text.

9 Type "The Money Catalog ¶ Everything we sell costs money." (Remember that the ¶ symbol indicates a line return, accessed by pressing the RETURN key.) This text will display in the current default type and paragraph specifications. If you haven't created anything since our last sample project, this will be 36/37.5 Palatino bold-italic. But it really doesn't matter, since we will be changing the type specs in the next step.

In previous sample projects, we have altered the type specs of one or more selected words either by choosing commands on the TYPE menu or by accessing the TYPE SPECIFICATIONS dialog box. This time, however, we will specify the appearance of our text using **style sheets**. Style sheets are basically PageMaker options that you define. A style sheet contains information controlling an entire paragraph, including its font, type style, size, leading, alignment, indents, tabs, hyphenation, and vertical spacing.

Style sheets in PageMaker are easy to create, edit, and apply. They also provide consistency throughout a document. If you want two paragraphs in a document to be identical in font, style, and so on, you merely choose the same style sheet for each. For example, all of your headlines can be one style, all of your subheads in another, and all of your body text in still another. If you later decide you want to change the type specs of a group of paragraphs, you may edit the style sheet directly. Each paragraph to which that style has been applied will change, even if they are themselves separated by other paragraphs whose specifications you don't want to change. Style sheets save time and help to minimize a user's natural propensity to make mistakes.

10 With the text tool, triple-click on a word at the beginning of our text block to select the entire first line. Then click on the "Headline" option in the Styles palette. Immediately, your first line will change to flush left 30-point Times bold.

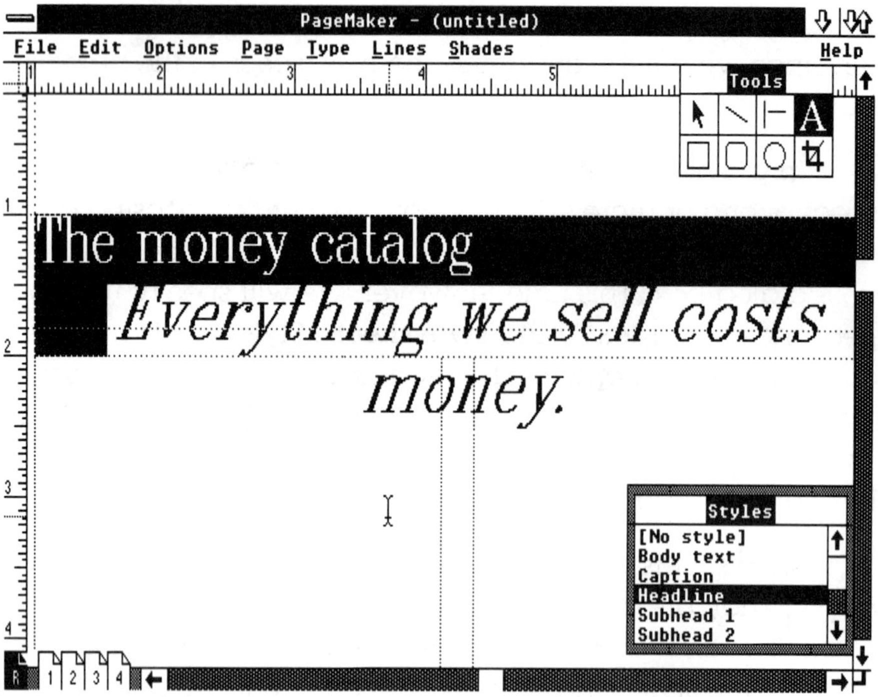

Figure 14.04: *The effect of choosing the "Headline" style sheet for our selected flag text.*

"Headline" is one of PageMaker's default style sheets, available anytime PageMaker is launched. Unfortunately, 30-point Times bold does not really suit our purposes. As we mentioned at the outset of the chapter, the text in our catalog will be set in Bookman. Since Times and Bookman do not generally complement each other, Times would undoubtedly be a poor choice for our flag. We will remedy this by steering the "Headline" style sheet in a more visually harmonious direction.

11 Select the arrow tool to deselect our text. Although this is not an essential step, it will demonstrate that changing a style sheet also changes text tagged to that style, whether or not the text is currently selected.

12 To edit the "Headline" style, choose the Define styles... command from the Type menu. The Define styles dialog box that appears provides full control over the manipulation of style sheets. Here, you may create new styles by clicking the New... button, alter existing styles by clicking the Edit... button, delete styles with the Remove button, and access styles contained in other PageMaker files by clicking the Copy... button. The scrolling "Style" listing contains the same style sheet names that were available in the Styles palette.

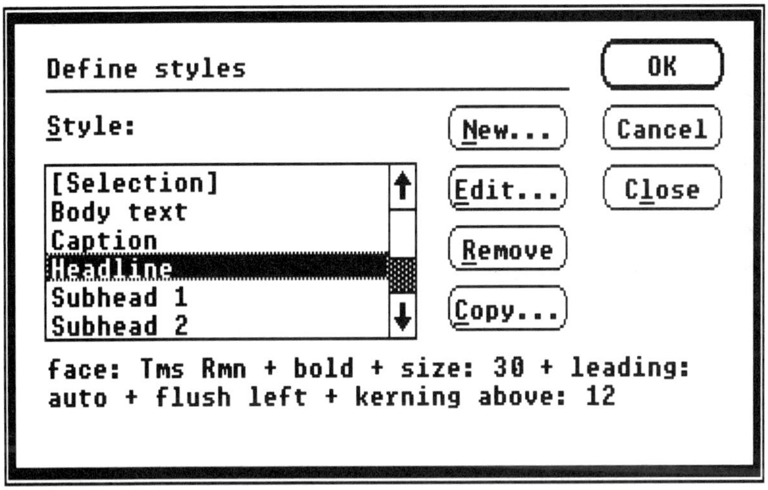

Figure 14.05: *The Define styles dialog box, displaying type specs for the "Headline" style.*

13 Click on the "Headline" style to select it. Notice that the specifications of the "Headline" style appear beneath the "Style" list. We see that, currently, the "Headline" style sheet includes the type face Times bold, and that the type size is 30-point, the leading is Auto, and so on. This specification listing allows us to quickly determine the attributes of any style sheet that we select from the scrolling style listing.

14 Click on the Edit... button, displaying the Edit style dialog box. This dialog box allows us to change the name of a style sheet, or modify its attributes using the dialog boxes, accessible via the Type...,Para..., Tabs..., and Color... buttons.

15 First, we should change the name of the "Headline" style so that it more accurately reflects its purpose. Enter the name "Catalog Flag" into the "Name" option, replacing "Headline."

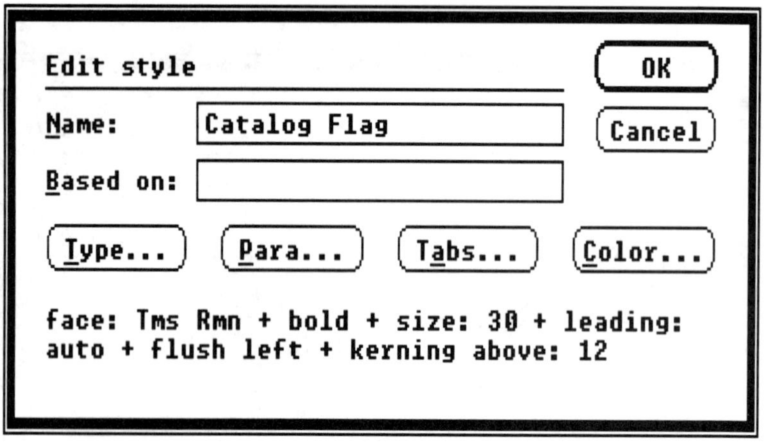

Figure 14.06: *The Edit style dialog box, containing our new style name, "Catalog Flag."*

16 Now click on the Type... button to change the type specs of the current style sheet. The Type specifications dialog will appear, which you may recognize from previous sample projects. Using the process outlined in Chapter 6, *Creating a Simple Newsletter*, change the type specs to 46/40 Bookman bold. Then click OK to return to the Edit style dialog box.

17 The only paragraph specification that we need to alter is the alignment. So click on the Para... button to go to the familiar Paragraph specifications dialog box, and then select

"Center" from the "Alignment" options. Since this is the last specification we want to alter, click the OK button three times. The first click returns you to the EDIT STYLE dialog, the second closes the EDIT STYLE dialog, and the third closes the DEFINE STYLES dialog and returns you to the publication window.

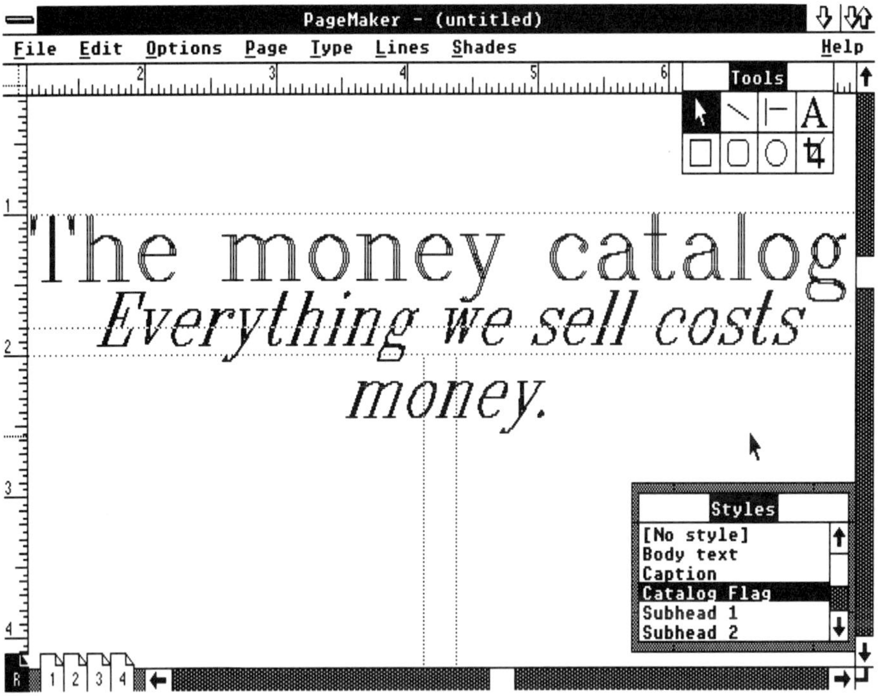

Figure 14.07: *The publication window as it appears after completing alterations to the "Catalog Flag" style sheet.*

Notice that despite the fact that our flag text is no longer selected, it has been changed to our recent specifications. Once a paragraph has been tagged to a certain style sheet, it will continue to reflect any changes made to the style specs. Also notice that the Styles palette no longer contains a "Headline" option. It has been replaced by "Catalog Flag."

Our next operation is to create a new style that we will apply to the second line of text in our flag. In creating a new style, you have one of two options. You may specify an entirely new style, determining type and paragraph specifications from scratch. Or you may create a new style based on an existing style, allowing you to build on prevailing specifications. We will avail ourselves of this second method.

18 Again choose the DEFINE STYLES... command from the TYPE menu. When the DEFINE STYLES dialog box appears, select the "Catalog Flag" style from the scrolling list and click on the NEW... button. This brings up the EDIT STYLE dialog box. The "Name" option is empty, since this is a new style and so far has no name. However, the "Based on" option now contains the "Catalog Flag" style. Note that the name "Catalog Flag" is the only specification listed in the lower portion of the dialog.

19 Click on the TYPE... button, change the type specs to 24/Auto Bookman italic, and click OK. Now notice the specifications listing at the bottom of the EDIT STYLE dialog. The type style bold has been subtracted from our "Catalog Flag" style, and italic has been added. Our changes to the type size and leading are also noted.

20 Recalling our flag text, we decide that the centered alignment will be suitable for this style as well, so there is no need to alter the paragraph specifications for this style. Thus, our last step is to name the style. Enter "Flag motto" into the "Name" option box, and click OK.

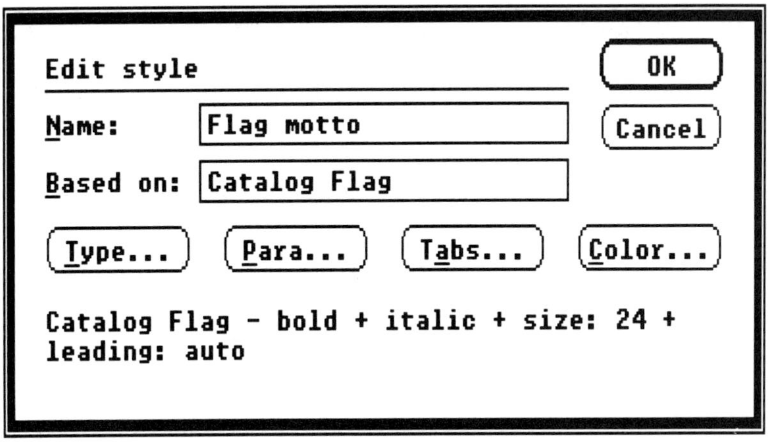

Figure 14.08: *The Edit style dialog when creating a new style sheet based on the "Catalog Flag" style.*

You may notice that your screen display has been unchanged by the creation of our new style. This is because we haven't yet applied the style to any text, and the style name is too far along in alphabetical order to be currently displayed in the Styles palette. We will now apply the style to some text.

21 Select the text tool and click only once anywhere in the second line of flag text. Then scroll down the Styles palette until the "Flag motto" style appears, and select that style. Notice that despite the fact that no text was actually selected, the entire second line of text changes to 24-point Bookman italic. This is because style sheets affect entire paragraphs, from one line return to the next. Therefore, by applying this style sheet while the insertion point was set within the paragraph, the entire paragraph has been affected.

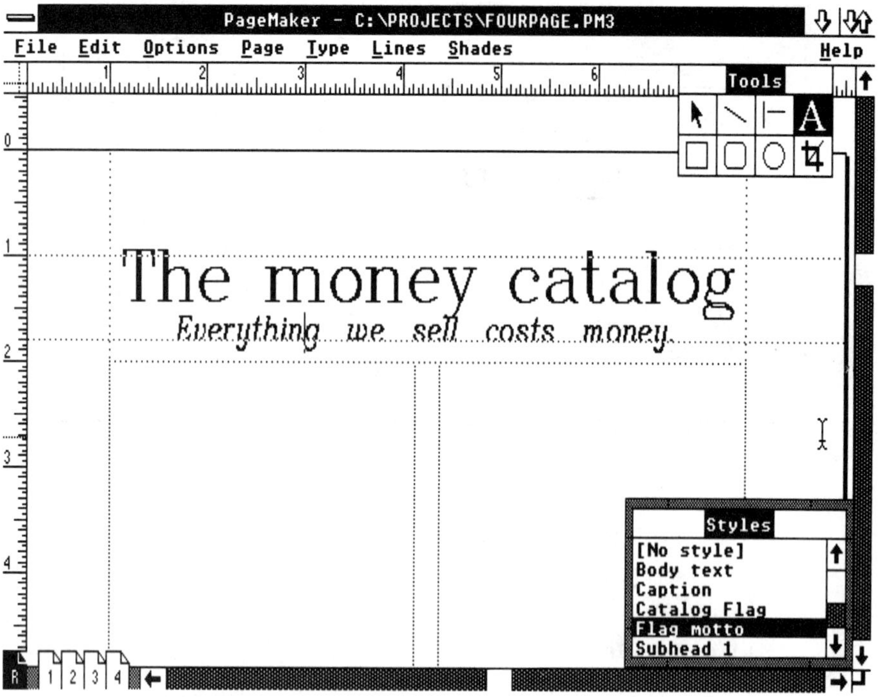

Figure 14.09: *The "Flag motto" style sheet applied to the second line of flag text.*

Creating the folio

Our flag and motto line are now complete. The next master page item to create is the folio, or page number text.

22 Scroll down to the bottom of the page. Then drag two guides from the horizontal ruler, to the 10.3- and 10.5-inch markers on the vertical rulers, respectively.

23 Select the text tool and drag from the top left ruler guide intersection to the bottom right ruler guide intersection. Type "February, 1989 issue → Page **Ø**." Here we have two more special character notations. The → symbol indicates that you should press the TAB key. This will create a gap between the date and the page number. The **Ø** symbol represents PageMaker's special page number character, CTRL-SHIFT-3. On the master page, this character will appear as a simple zero, but on any other page, it will reflect the current page number, from 1 to 9999.

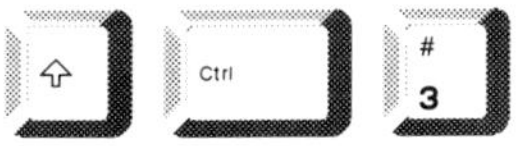

Your folio text probably looks pretty strange right now. Since we created the "Flag motto" style sheet while no text was selected, its type specifications have become our defaults. Among other things, this means that your folio text is centered. And tabs don't work very well when inserted within centered text. We will next demonstrate how to change the alignment and tab settings so that the date is flush left and the page number is flush right.

24 With the text tool, triple-click anywhere on your folio text to select the entire paragraph. Then scroll up the Styles palette until you reach the top, and select the "*No style*" option. This "untags" our text, so that it is no longer affected by a style sheet. Notice that there is no immediate change to our folio text, since it retains the specifications ascribed to the "Flag motto" style sheet.

25 Press CTRL-T to access the TYPE SPECIFICATIONS dialog box. Since we are accessing this dialog directly, without going through the EDIT STYLE dialog, our type spec changes will not affect a style sheet. Change the settings in this dialog to 12/Auto Bookman light (plain) and click OK.

26 Now choose the INDENTS/TABS... command from the TYPE menu, or press CTRL-I, bringing up the INDENTS/TABS dialog box. This dialog allows you to alter the location of tabbed and indented text, in much the same way that you would move tabs on a typewriter. You may select from the following four varieties of tabs:

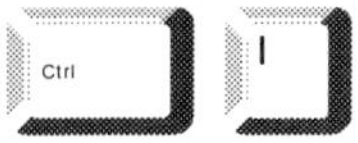

- **Left**, the traditional tab, where the first letter of text after the TAB character is flush left with the tab setting.

- **Right**, where a section of text between one TAB and another, or the TAB and a line return, is flush right with the tab setting.

- **Center**, where a section of text between one TAB and another, or the TAB and a line return, is centered at a specific point.

- **Decimal**, where the decimal point in a tabbed number, such as $45.95, is aligned at a specific location.

PageMaker also allows you to select from a series of **tab leaders**. Tab leaders determine what kinds of characters, if any, occupy the space between text specified by a TAB.

- **None**, the space between text is empty.
- **Dot leader**, specifies a row of dots, or periods, preceding tabbed text.
- **Dash leader**, specifies a row of dashes, or hyphens, preceding tabbed text.
- **Underline leader**, a solid underline occupies the length of a TAB.
- **Character leader**, allows you to enter the character of your choice, which will be repeated for the duration of a TAB.

You determine the location of a tab by selecting a tab type and a tab leader, and then clicking in the area just above the ruler near the bottom of the dialog. A tab instantly appears at the point where you click. The ruler allows you to measure the location of the tab from the beginning of your text. Also, you may drag an existing tab to relocate it.

27 Click on the CLEAR button in order to dispose of all existing tabs. The tabs shown in the area above the ruler at the bottom of the dialog box will then disappear. Using the scroll bar provided with the ruler, scroll rightward until the triangular column width indicator appears. Next, select the "Right" tab type option and click above the ruler at the 5.5-inch marker. The right tab symbol will appear where you click, accompanied by a number under the CLEAR button, displaying the exact location of the tab.

28 Drag the right tab symbol rightward, all the way to the end of the column. (If you accidentally miss the existing tab and create a new one, drag the unwanted tab directly downward outside the dialog to dispense with it). When you finish your drag, the number under the CLEAR button should read "6.5." Then click the OK button.

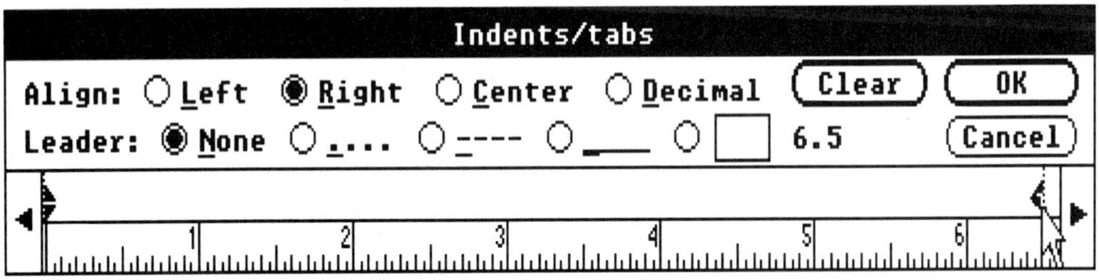

Figure 14.10: *The Indents/Tabs dialog box, containing our folio tab specifications.*

29 Don't worry if your page number is not flush right, as in our tab specifications. As we mentioned earlier, tabs do not work correctly when a paragraph is centered. Generally, tabs work best when text is flush left, so press CTRL-L, or choose the ALIGN LEFT command from the TYPE menu.

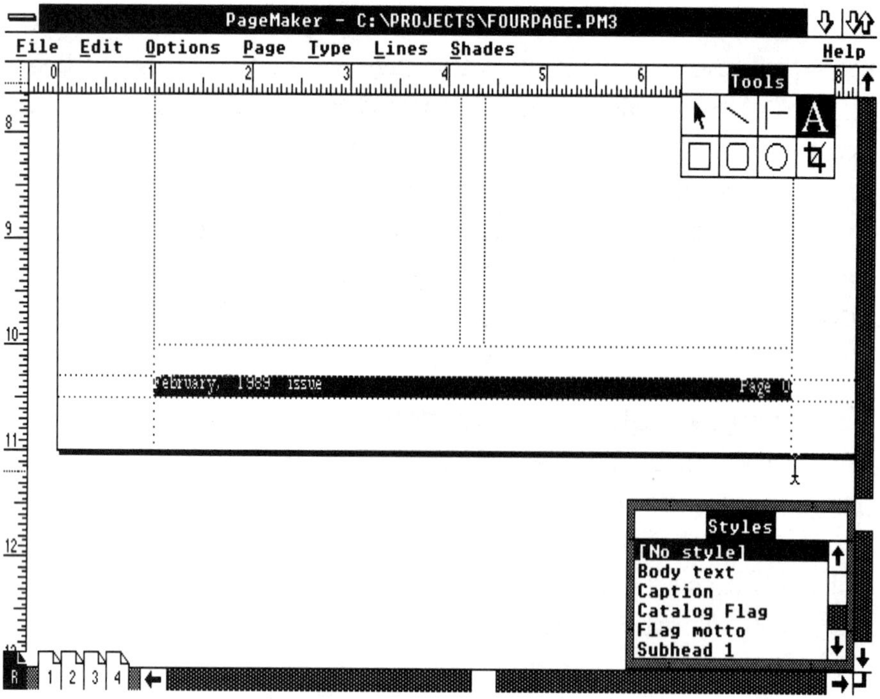

Figure 14.11: *The master page folio, containing flush left date and flush right page number character.*

30 Notice now, despite our promise that tabs work with flush left text, that the page number is about one-quarter inch from being flush with the right ruler guide. This is a peculiarity specific to PageMaker's automatic page numbering feature. When text containing a page number is flush left, regardless of its tabbing, the application provides enough space to the right of the page number character for three extra digits, allowing for the possibility of a page numbering

1000 or higher. To override this provision, press CTRL-R, or choose the "Align right" option from the TYPE menu. By combining alignment and tabs, you have now created a folio with a flush left date and a flush right page number, all in a single text block.

31 This is a good time to save your document. Press CTRL-S or choose the SAVE command from the FILE menu. Enter the name "Four-page catalog" or some other appropriate name into the SAVE PUBLICATION AS dialog box, and click OK.

Placing and formatting body copy

Now that we have finished creating master page items and ruler guides, we will move on to the actual page. Our first operation will be to place a long text file using PageMaker's autoflow feature.

32 Click on the page 1 icon at the bottom of your screen display. Once you arrive at page 1, choose the LOCK GUIDES command from the OPTIONS menu. This will prevent any of the column guides or ruler guides that we created on the master page from being accidentally moved.

14 Advanced Catalog

Autoflowing a long text file

33 Press CTRL-D, or choose the PLACE... command from the FILE menu, select a four-page or longer text file, or the LOREM.TXT text file, and click OK. When we have placed text in past sample projects, we have gotten the manual text flow cursor, which we have clicked or dragged to place a

single column of text. This time, however, we are presented with the autoflow cursor. This is because we chose the AUTOFLOW command from the OPTIONS menu before we created our file.

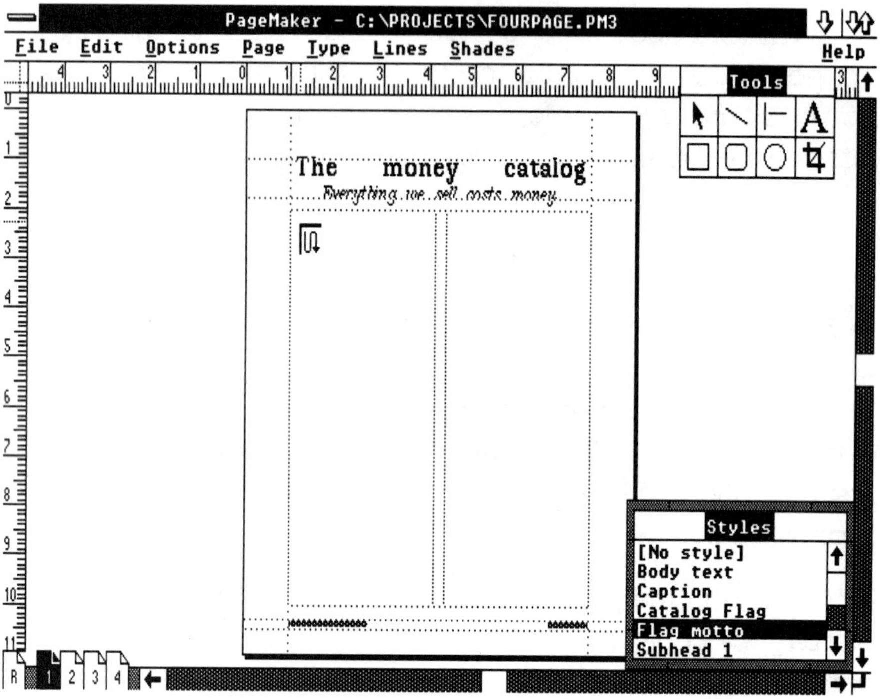

Figure 14.12: *The autoflow cursor, ready to begin pouring our long word-processing file.*

34 Position your autoflow cursor at the top of the first column. Then click. Depending on the speed of your computer, the text may pour very quickly. Once it finishes pouring the first column, it pours the second. Then it flips to the second page, pours those columns, flips to the third page and pours those columns, flips to the fourth page, and so on. If you don't stop it, PageMaker will continue to pour the article, creating pages in order to keep pouring. It's sort of like the *Sorcerer's Apprentice* scene in the movie *Fantasia*—Mickey Mouse brings his broom to life, but is later unable to stop it, instead causing it to reproduce hundreds of times over. Fortunately, there is a way to terminate PageMaker's automatic page creation, by simply clicking on the arrow tool icon in the toolbox. As soon as you select the arrow tool, PageMaker will finish pouring the current column, and then stop. If you chose a plain text file, such as the LOREM.TXT file, the text will be formatted according to the default values of Palatino 24/Auto, centered. We will be reformatting this text shortly.

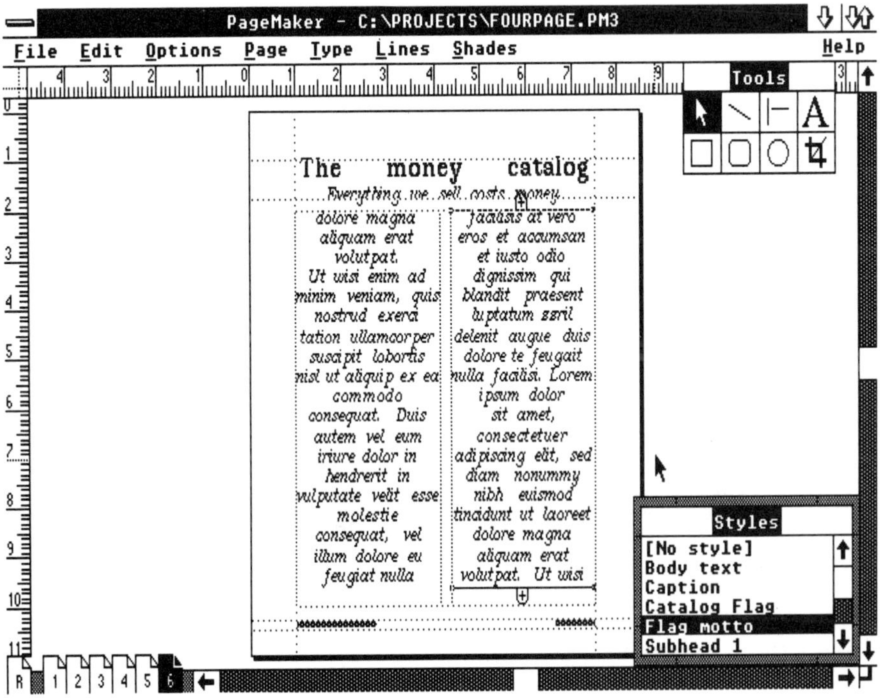

Figure 14.13: *PageMaker reaches page 6 before we select the arrow tool to put an end to its automatic text pouring and page creation cycle.*

As you can see in Figure 14.13, PageMaker arrived at page 6 before we finally got around to stopping it. Your file may have even more pages. But this is not a problem, since PageMaker allows you to delete pages just as easily as you created them.

Editing the body copy style sheet

35 To format our new text file, we will use a style sheet, just like we did on the master page. Select the text tool, and click anywhere in the text on page 1. Then press CTRL-A to select the entire file and click on the "Body text" style in the Styles palette. "Body text" is another of PageMaker's preset style sheets, which will change our text to 12/Auto Times Roman. This does not match our Bookman motif, however, so the style will need to be edited.

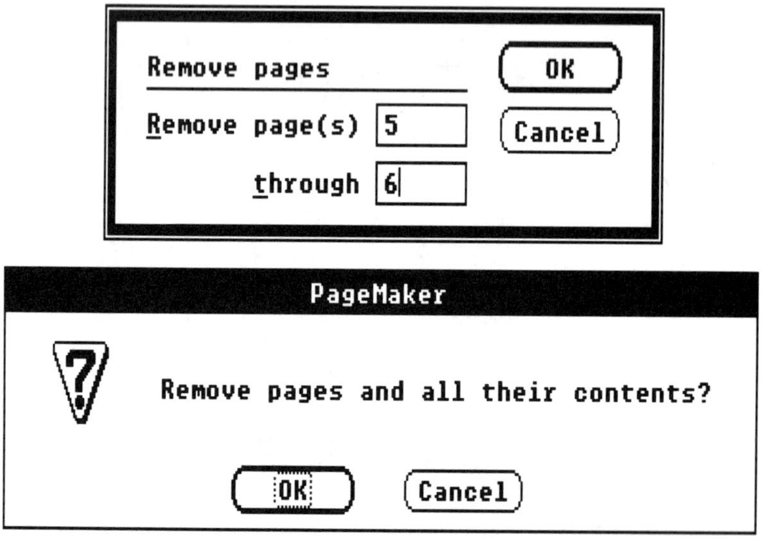

Figure 14.14: *The Remove pages dialog box, containing our specifications, followed by the subsequent Alert box.*

36 Press the CTRL key, and click on the "Body text" option in the Style palette. By CTRL-clicking on a style sheet, we can display the EDIT STYLE dialog box without having to choose the DEFINE STYLES... command. Once the EDIT STYLE dialog appears, click on the TYPE... button, and change the type specs to 12/ Auto Bookman light (plain) and click OK. Then click on the PARA... button to display the PARAGRAPH SPECIFICATIONS dialog. Select the "Justify" option, then input 0.25 for the "First" option and 0.065 for the "After" option. Next click the OK button twice to return to the publication window.

Deleting pages

37 To get rid of any extra pages that PageMaker created in your file, choose the REMOVE PAGES... command from the PAGE menu. This brings up the REMOVE PAGES dialog box. The "through" value is currently selected, containing the number of the current page. In our case, this number is 6. Leave this value unaltered, and press TAB to select the "Remove page(s)" value. Enter 5 for this option—we want to delete all pages after page 4, and the first page after page 4 is page 5. Then click OK. An Alert box will then display, asking you if you really want to "Delete page and all items on it?" If you are sure of your specifications, click on the OK button. (Pressing the RETURN key will cancel the operation, since it is the CANCEL button that has a heavy outline.)

38 After confirming the removal of all pages after and including page 5, you will find yourself at page 4. Click on the page 1 icon, since we have not finished working on this page. Then press CTRL-S to update your file on disk.

Now your text is changed to justified 12/Auto Bookman light, and our manipulation of the body copy is complete.

Adding ad spaces and graphics

This publication is supposed to be a catalog, but it certainly has a large quantity of text. But before we are finished, we will create spaces for advertisements and add graphic embellishments and a price listing.

Sometimes when you create a document, you want to first position your graphics, and then pour your text around them. But in PageMaker, it usually works best to first pour your text, as we have done, and then add the graphics.

Repositioning existing text around a graphic

In these next few steps, we won't actually be creating ads, since this is a fairly easy procedure—similar to the coupon we created in Chapter 11, *Creating an Intermediate Flyer*—and it would be too time-consuming in the context of this sample project. Instead, we will simply create boxes that will act as markers, indicating where the ads can be later pasted into place after the file is printed, or imported electronically into our PageMaker file.

Throughout the remainder of this chapter, we will be instructing you on how to move your cursor using a coordinate system. In this coordinate system, "H:0.0" = the 0-inch marker on the horizontal ruler, "V:0.0" = the 0-inch marker on the vertical ruler. All other coordinates are measured from this point. For example, H:5.6 is equal to 5 6/10 inch.

39 Click the secondary mouse button near the bottom of page 1. Then select the rectangle tool and drag from H:1.0, V:7.0 to H:7.5, V:10.0 to indicate the size of our ad space.

Your rectangle should be the width of your margins, with a 2-point line weight and transparent interior, as shown in Figure 14.15.

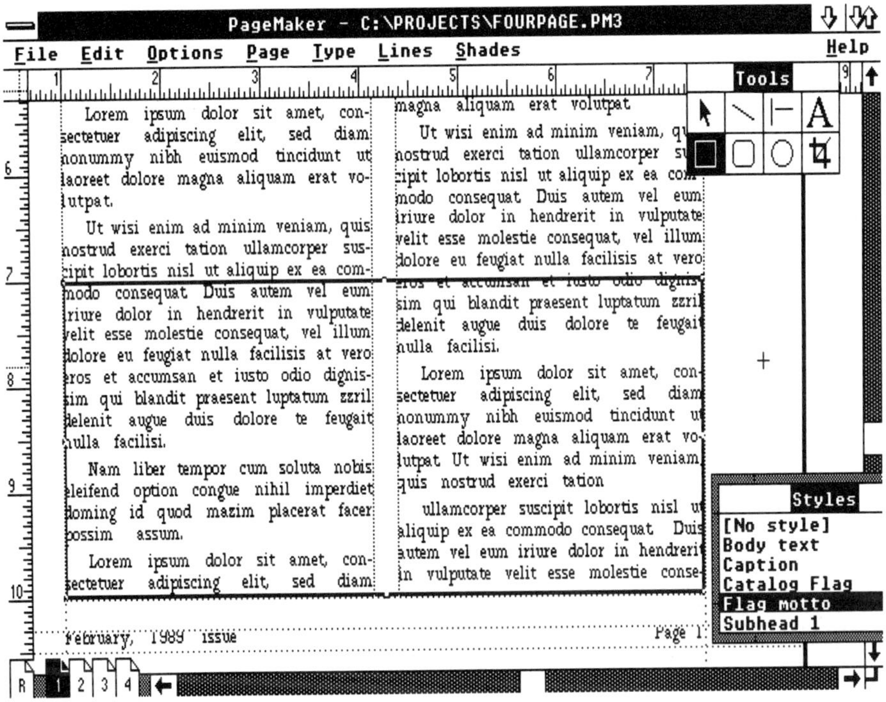

Figure 14.15: *The large rectangle that will represent our ad space currently overlaps text.*

40 As you can see, our large rectangle overlaps about a third of the text on this page. This must be remedied by altering the length of each of the two text columns. Select the arrow tool and click on the first column to select it. Then drag the lower handlebar upward to approximately V:6.9, so that there is about 1/10 inch between the end of the text and the rectangle. The text that is displaced by your shortening of this column will automatically wrap into the next column, and so on. Next, click on the right column to select it and drag its lower handlebar upward to V:6.9 or thereabout.

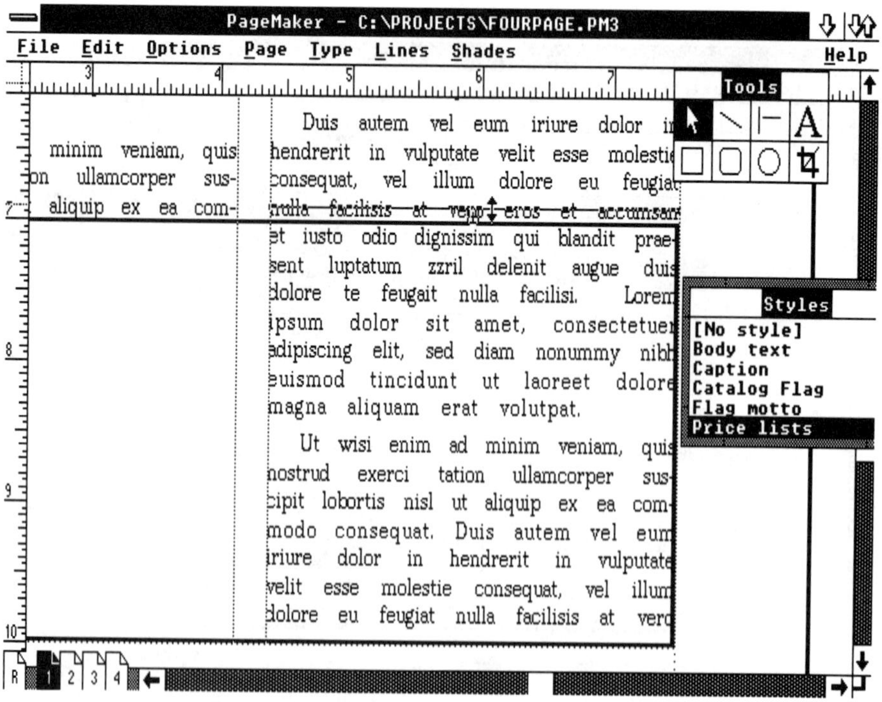

Figure 14.16: *The lower handlebars of each of our two columns of text have been lifted so that they no longer overlap the rectangle.*

41 Now we will draw an X the size of our rectangle, indicating that it is not a real graphic, but only a spaceholder. Select the diagonal-line tool and drag from H:1.0, V:7.0 to H:7.5, V:10.0, the same coordinates we used to draw the rectangle. This creates a diagonal line from the upper left corner to bottom right corner of the rectangle, the first stroke of our X. Now, while the line remains selected, choose HAIRLINE from the LINES menu, reducing the weight of the line. For the second stroke of the X, draw from H:1.0, V:10.0 to H:7.5, V:7.0 with the diagonal-line tool, joining the other two corners of the rectangle. Also change this line to a hairline.

42 This completes page 1. Press CTRL-W to zoom out to the "Fit-in-window" view size. Then press CTRL-S to update your file on disk.

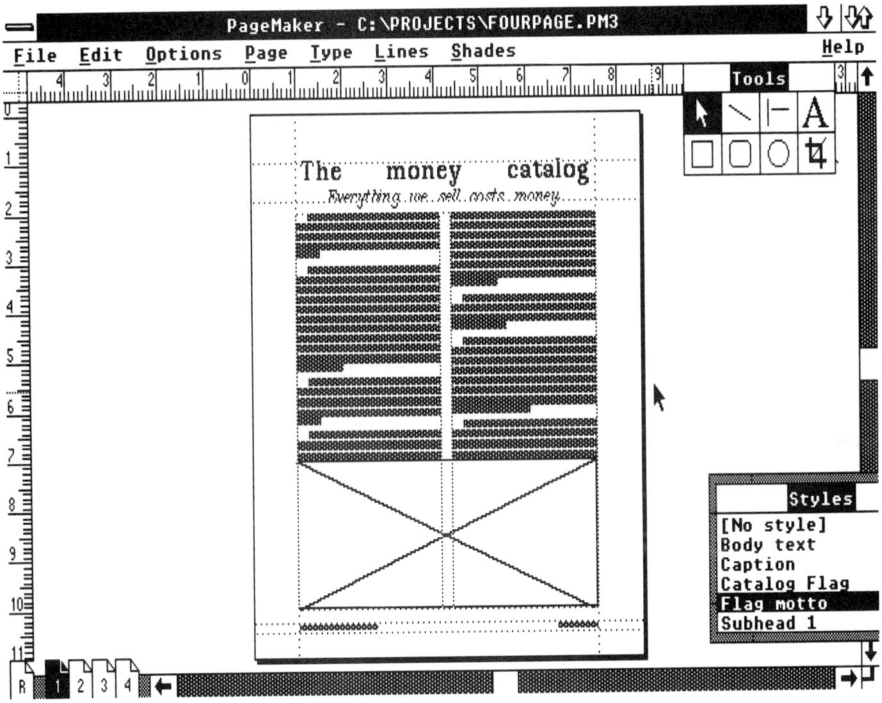

Figure 14.17: *The completed page 1, with autoflowed text and advertisement spaceholder.*

Wrapping text around a rectangular object

Suppose that we would like to create a space for another advertisement, this time on page 2. Rather than positioning this ad at the bottom of the page, we want it to stand out more prominently, attracting attention in a distinctive manner. To accomplish this, we will position a smaller vertical ad in the very middle of page 2, wrapping both columns of text around the rectangle. If we had to do this by hand, it would be a difficult procedure, requiring that we break our story into a number of additional columns, each with varying widths. PageMaker, however, provides an automatic text wrapping feature, which we will now demonstrate.

43 Click on the page 2 icon at the bottom of your screen display to turn to the second page. Upon arrival, select the rectangle tool and drag from H:3.0, V:3.5 to H5.5, V:8.5, thus creating a tall rectangle with a 2-point line weight in the middle of your page.

44 Click the secondary mouse button in the middle of your rectangle, zooming in to "Actual" size. If necessary, press the ALT key and drag to move your screen image, using the grabber hand so that the rectangle is centered in your publication window.

45 Select the diagonal line tool and create an X that extends the height and width of your rectangle, dragging first from H:3.0, V:3.5 to H5.5, V:8.5 and then from H:3.0, V:8.5 to H5.5, V:3.5. Next, select the arrow tool, click on one of the diagonal lines to select it, then SHIFT-click on the second line to select it as well. Choose HAIRLINE from the LINES menu to decrease the weight of both selected lines (see Figure 14.18).

46 Once again, our rectangle is obscured by text. We will remedy this by taking advantage of PageMaker's versatile and easy-to-use text wrapping feature. Select the rectangle by clicking on its 2-point outline with your arrow tool. Choose the TEXT WRAP... command from the OPTIONS menu to bring up the TEXT WRAP dialog box.

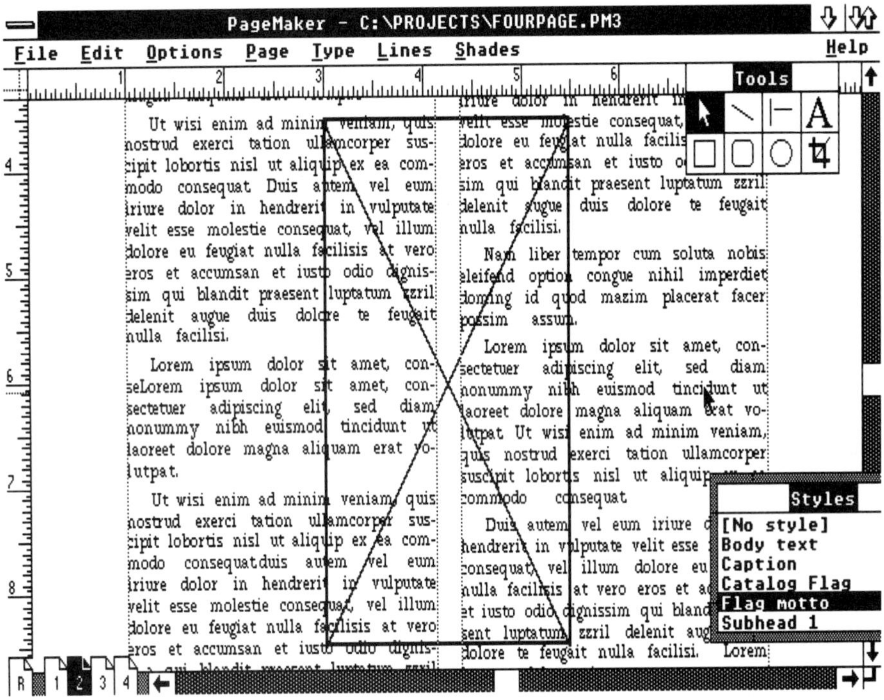

Figure 14.18: *The page 2 ad spaceholder, covered by text.*

The TEXT WRAP dialog contains three "Wrap option" icons and three "Text flow" options. Each option is used to determine the visual manner in which overlapping text is forced to wrap around a selected graphic element. The first "Wrap option" icon, which is currently selected, indicates that text merely overlaps a graphic, as we saw in Figure 14.18. The second icon specifies text to wrap rectangularly around a graphic. The third icon, which is dimmed, is the custom wrap option, allowing you to wrap text around complex graphic. We will demonstrate this feature on page 3.

The "Text flow" icons determine where text is allowed to pour in reference to a graphic. The first option allows for no text below the selected graphic; the second allows for text above and below the graphic, but none to the left or right side; and the third allows text to wrap a graphic on all four sides.

The "Standoff in inches" options determine the dimensions of the **graphic boundary**. As we will see, the TEXT WRAP... command creates a rectangular dotted line around the selected graphic. This graphic boundary forms a border of white space around an image, through which text is not allowed to penetrate. The "Left," "Right," "Top," and "Bottom" values are measured—in our case, in decimal inches—outward from the selected graphic element.

47 Select the second "Wrap option" icon. This causes the second "Text flow" icon to become automatically selected. However, since we want text on the left and right sides of our rectangle, select the third "Text flow" icon instead.

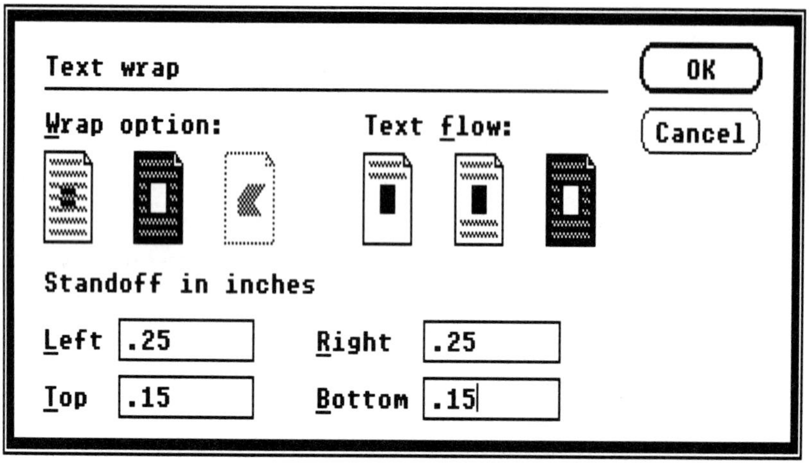

Figure 14.19: *The Text wrap dialog box, containing our specifications.*

48 Enter 0.25 for the "Left" and "Right" options and 0.15 for the "Top" and "Bottom" options. Then click OK.

49 That's all there is to it. PageMaker has now automatically created a graphic boundary around your rectangle according to your specifications. To get a better view of the graphic boundary and the manner in which your text has wrapped around the spaceholder, press CTRL-W to zoom out to "Fit-in-window" size, as shown in Figure 14.20. Then press CTRL-S to update your file on disk.

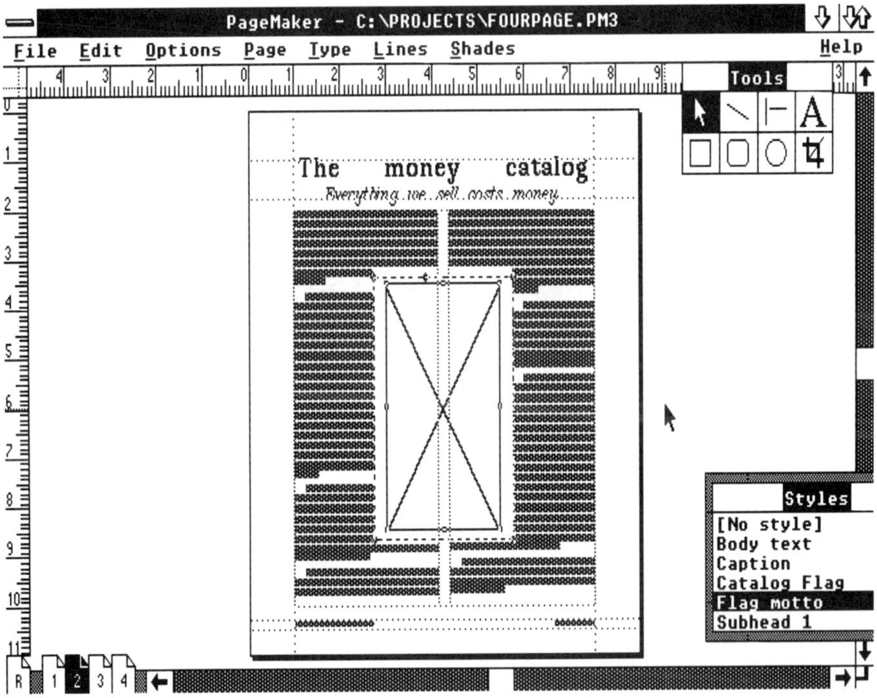

Figure 14.20: *The ad spaceholder with graphic boundary, causing text to flow around it in a rectangular manner.*

Incidentally, don't worry when your graphic boundary disappears upon saving your file. Text wrap boundaries only appear when a graphic is selected; the saving operation deselects all elements in your publication. If you want to see the boundary again, merely reselect the rectangle.

Wrapping text around a complex graphic

Our final demonstration of wrapping text around a graphic requires that we import a graphic from the paint environment. Any original graphic or clip-art will do, as long as it was created in PC PAINTBRUSH, WINDOWS PAINT, or some other paint-format software.

50 Turn to the third page by clicking on the page 3 icon at the bottom of your screen display. If the text fills only part of the page, and there is a plus (+) in the bottom handlebar of the last text block, click on the handlebar with the arrow tool and drag it to the bottom of the page. Press CTRL-D, select your paint-format graphic, and click OK. If your graphic is saved in the proper format, a paintbrush icon will appear. If your graphic placement icon does not show a paintbrush, select the arrow tool to cancel the place icon and choose the PLACE... command to find an appropriate graphic.

51 Click with your paintbrush cursor in the upper left area of your page. When the paint graphic appears, enlarge or reduce the graphic by SHIFT-dragging one of its corner handles, as described in the previous sample project, so that the graphic is roughly similar in size to the rectangle on page 2. Then center the graphic vertically and horizontally on your page by dragging it with the arrow tool.

52 Click the secondary mouse button in the center of the graphic to zoom in, and center the graphic using the grabber hand (accessed by pressing the ALT key and dragging).

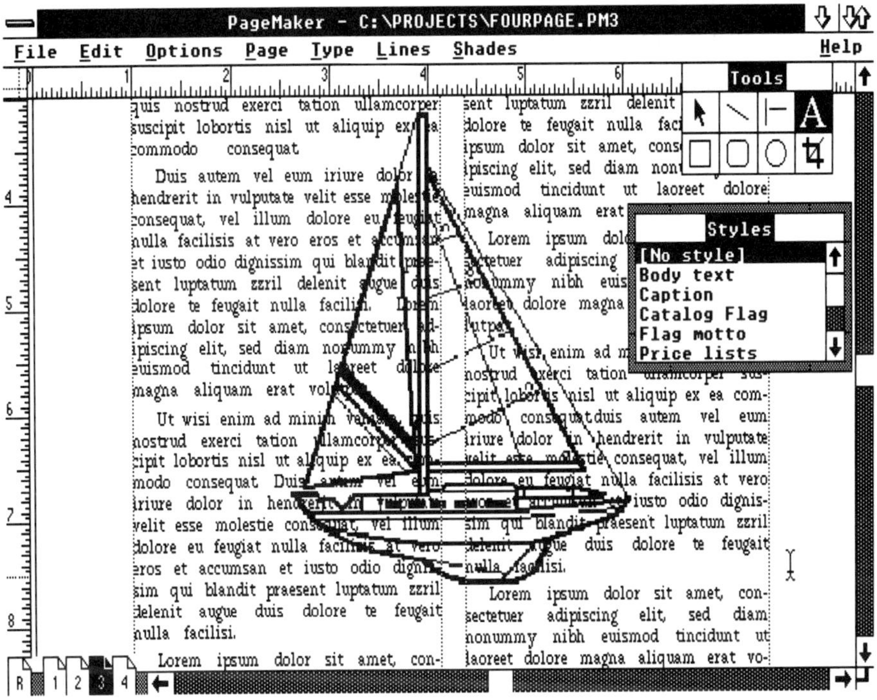

Figure 14.21: *Our paint graphic is the image of a sailboat, positioned in the middle of page 3, with text over it.*

53 Once again, there is text over our graphic. While the graphic is still selected, choose the TEXT WRAP... command from the OPTIONS menu, producing the TEXT WRAP dialog box.

As we mentioned earlier, we imported a complex graphic because we intend to wrap our text irregularly around this image. So rather than creating a standard rectangular graphic boundary, we want our boundary to imitate the outline of the graphic itself. It stands to reason that we should select the third "Wrap option" icon. Unfortunately, this option is dimmed. In PageMaker, you must always create a rectangular graphic boundary first, and then manipulate that boundary in the publication window. We will demonstrate how this works in the next few steps.

54 Select the second "Wrap option" and the third "Text flow" option. Then enter 0.15 for each of the distance values, and click OK. A rectangular graphic boundary now surrounds your image.

In the next few steps, we will describe how we alter the boundary around our sailboat graphic. Since your graphic is undoubtedly different than ours, we suggest that you read the next few steps before adapting the techniques to your graphic requirements.

We will also be referring to our boat graphic by its parts. For the record: the *bow* is the front end of the boat, the *stern* is the back end, and the *keel* is the large fin underneath the boat.

To wrap text irregularly around a graphic, you must manipulate the rectangular graphic boundary. Currently, the boundary has four handles, one at each corner. Each of these corners may be moved independently by dragging at them. Pressing the SHIFT key while dragging constrains movement horizontally or vertically. You may also drag at the boundary **segments**, the dotted lines between handles, stretching or reducing the text wrap limitations. This allows for limited irregular text wrapping, but the only way to really imitate the outline of a graphic is to add handles to the boundary, which is accomplished by clicking on a segment with the arrow tool.

55 We first wish to create a new boundary handle at the bow of our boat. We do this by clicking at a point nearest the bow on the left boundary segment. This new handle will act as a hinge. We SHIFT-drag the upper left corner handle horizontally inward until the affected segment is parallel to the left edge of the boat's sail, as shown in Figure 14.22.

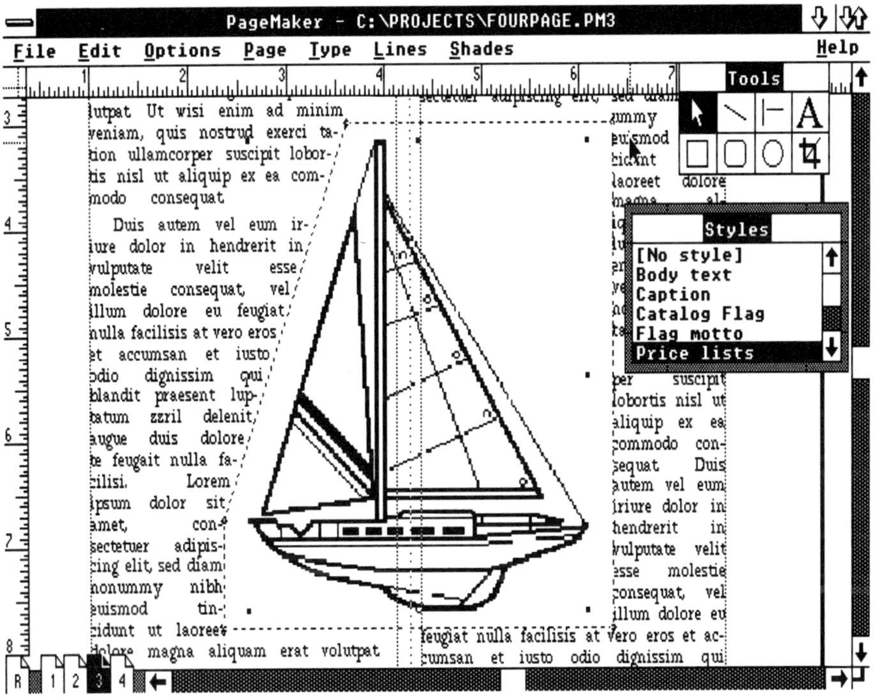

Figure 14.22: *We create a fifth boundary segment, and drag it parallel to one of the sails.*

56 A sixth handle is created by clicking near the stern. We then SHIFT-drag the upper right corner handle leftward until this affected segment is parallel to the right side of our sail.

57 Two more handles are created by clicking on the right vertical segment, a bit under the stern, and on the bottom segment, to the right of the keel. Both of these handles act as hinges, so that two segments are affected when we drag the lower right corner handle upward and inward to imitate the intersection of the keel and the underside of the boat.

58 Finally, we click on the left vertical segment under the bow and then on the bottom segment to the left of the keel. Then we drag the bottom left corner handle upward and inward. Figure 14.23 shows the final appearance of our graphic boundary. For this figure, we have zoomed in to "200%" size, and temporarily hidden the toolbox, Styles palette, rulers, and scroll bars to get a better view.

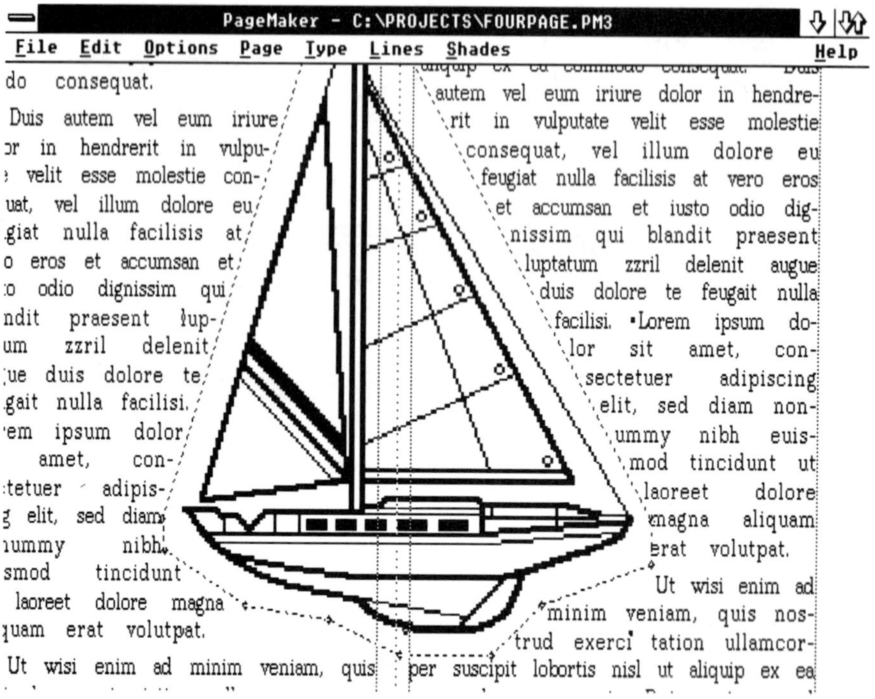

Figure 14.23: *The sailboat at 200% view size, with completed irregular graphic boundary.*

Now try this technique on your own graphic. Locate handles at points where you want to create hinges, representing corners in the general outline of your graphic. If you create one too many handles, you can delete it by dragging it on top of another handle.

This ends our demonstration of text wrapping techniques. Our next steps will describe PageMaker's image control features. We will begin our demonstration on our existing paint graphic, and then import a gray-scale TIFF image on page 4.

Applying graphic special effects

Graphics saved in the paint and TIFF formats are composed of a predetermined number of tiny dots, or **pixels**. This is different than drawings saved in the PICT or EPS format, where graphics are typically defined as mathematical objects. For more detailed information about PageMaker graphic theory, see Chapter 10, *Using Graphics in PageMaker*.

Graphics that are defined as the combined result of thousands to hundreds of thousands of tiny pixels, such as paint and TIFF graphics, can be subjected to **image control** in PageMaker. This means that PageMaker is capable of changing the lightness or darkness of each of these pixels.

All paint graphics and many TIFF images are composed of only two gray levels. This means that each and every pixel that makes up an image is either black or white. Photographs scanned using a gray-scale scanner can produce as many as 16 gray levels, or even more. A single pixel in such an image might be light gray, or medium gray, or dark gray, or very dark gray, and so on, or, of course, black or white.

Our paint graphic on page 3 naturally has only black and white pixels. In the next few steps, we will alter the black pixels to a lighter shade of gray, and leave the white pixels white.

Controlling a black and white graphic

59 Your paint graphic should be selected. Choose the IMAGE CONTROL... command from the OPTIONS menu, bringing up the IMAGE CONTROL dialog box.

The first group of options in the IMAGE CONTROL dialog box control the manner in which an image is displayed in PageMaker. You may set the function, angle, and frequency of your graphic using the "Screened" options. The "Screen" options determine whether gray values in the selected graphic are displayed as a series of small dots or parallel lines. The "Angle" option determines the direction in which the dots or lines are arranged. And the "Lines/in" option specifies the number of dots or lines in an inch. Typically, this option should be set to 60 when printing to a laser printer and to 90 or 120 if printing to a typesetter. For more information about these options, see Chapter 10, *Using Graphics in PageMaker*.

The "Lightness" option brightens a graphic. The "Contrast" option controls the amount of difference between the lightest and the darkest sections of a graphic. These options are controlled by the scroll bars alongside them.

60 Select the leftmost screen consisting of dots rather than lines. Then press the TAB key and enter 60 for the "Lines/in" option.

61 We want to lighten the darkness of our black pixels and leave our white pixels white. This means that we should press on the right "Lightness" arrow until the number in the "Lightness" option box reads "25%." This means that what was 100% black in the graphic will now be 75% gray. Next, click on the OK button. This will apply your changes to the selected graphic.

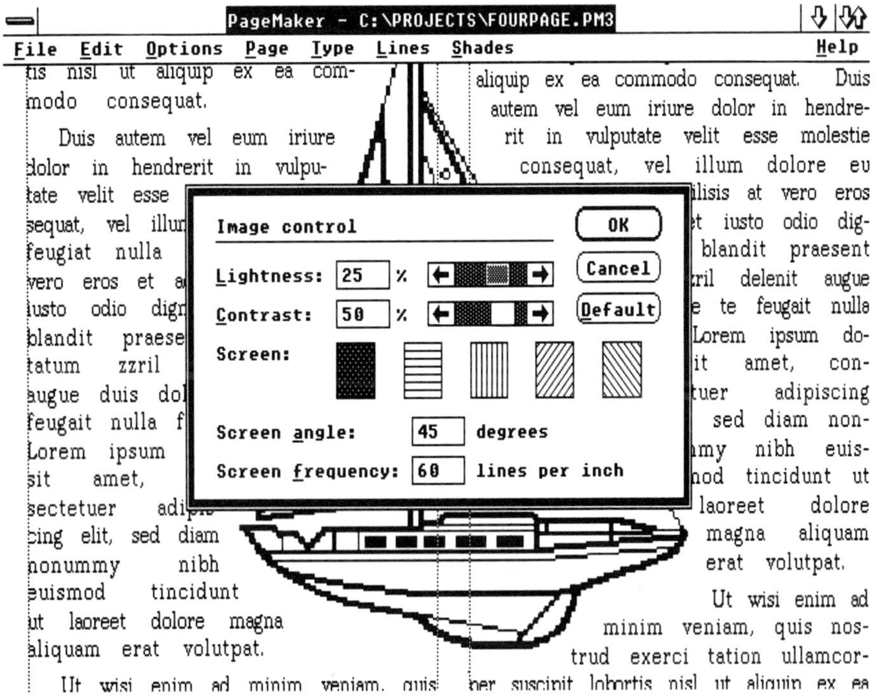

Figure 14.24: *Increasing the lightness of our paint graphic changes the black pixels to a shade of gray.*

62 Notice that the white portions of your graphic, which used to be transparent, are now opaque, covering up some of your text. Choose the SEND TO BACK command on the EDIT menu, or press CTRL-B, to put the graphic in back of the text so that the text is no longer hidden.

63 Press CTRL-W to view the entire page. Press CTRL-S to update your file on disk.

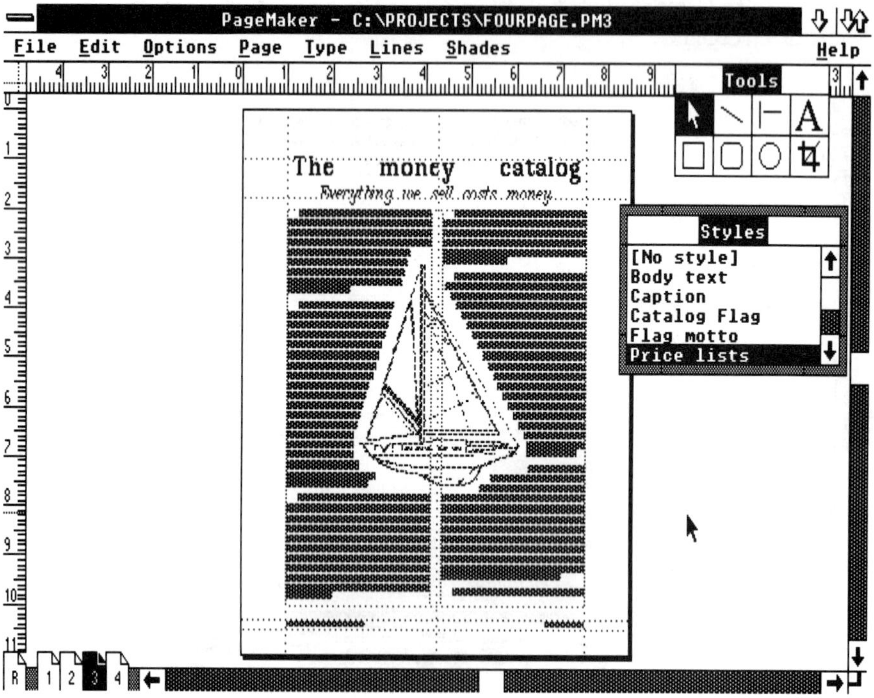

Figure 14.25: *The completed page 3, with irregular text wrapping and grayed paint image.*

Removing and inserting pages

64 Click on the page 4 icon to turn to the fourth page. We already have more than enough text, since this is a catalog, so let's use this page to add a price listing. The easiest way to perform this kind of drastic change to a page is to simply remove it and create a new page.

65 Choose the REMOVE PAGES... command from the OPTIONS menu. The REMOVE PAGES dialog box will already contain the correct page numbers to be removed, from page 4 to page 4. So click the OK button. When the Alert box comes up, click the OK button.

66 After page 4 is removed, you will find yourself at page 3. We now want to insert a *new* page 4 into our catalog, so choose the INSERT PAGES... command from the OPTIONS menu. The INSERT PAGES dialog box allows you to insert any number of pages before or after the current page(s). The "Insert" option currently contains a 1, which is the number of pages we want to insert. The "After" option is selected, which will add the new page after the current page, as we prefer. Since all the options are already correctly set, click OK.

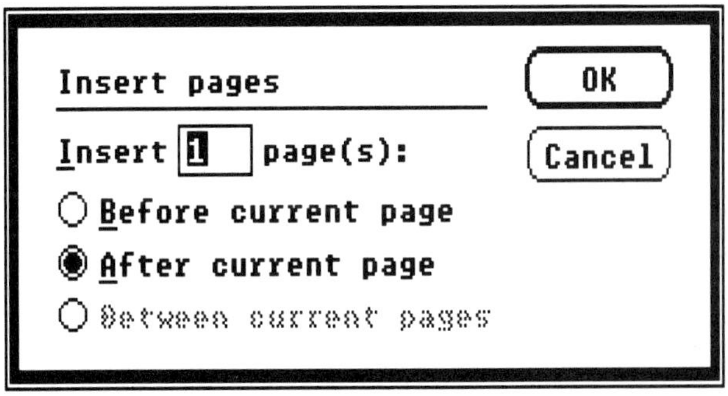

Figure 14.26: *The Insert pages dialog box, containing our specifications.*

Controlling a gray-scale graphic

Once again, we are on page 4. The page is free of any text or graphic elements.

During the next few steps, we will import and apply image control settings to a gray-scale scan saved in the TIFF format. For our example, we will be using the PHOTO.TIFF document saved on the GETTING STARTED disk, included with your application.

67 Press CTRL-D, select the PHOTO.TIF scan, and click OK. Click with your TIFF-type placement cursor at the top of the page. After the image is placed, drag it into position using the arrow tool.

Figure 14.27: *Our imported gray-scale photographic scan.*

68 If necessary, reduce the image proportionally by SHIFT-dragging at one of the corner handles so that the image does not extend below the 6.75-inch mark on the vertical ruler. Later, we will be creating a price listing below this point, so for now this area must be left empty.

69 Choose the IMAGE CONTROL command from the OPTIONS menu to bring up the IMAGE CONTROL dialog box. Select the lines icon from the "Screen" options and enter 90 for the "Lines/in" value. This turns your scan into a line-screen image, and also prepares it to be output to a typesetter if you later choose to do so.

Figure 14.28: *The manipulated gray-scale photographic scan, surrounded by a double-line border.*

70 Select the rectangle tool and draw a box that exactly traces the perimeter of your scan. Then choose the double-line weight from the LINES menu.

71 Press CTRL-S to update your file on disk.

Preparing a price list

This ends our discussion of graphic manipulations. Our next and near-final series of steps is devoted to the creation of a short price list, a necessary part of any catalog.

72 First, we will create a new style sheet, based on the existing "Body text" style. Click on the arrow tool icon to deselect all elements in the publication window. Then select the "Body text" style from the Styles palette. This style is now the default setting for this file.

Creating a new style sheet with tabs

73 Now, CTRL-click on the "No style" option in the Styles palette. This will bring up the EDIT STYLE dialog box, with an empty "Name" option and the "Body text" style listed for the "Based on" option. By CTRL-clicking on the "No style" option, you can create a new style based on the style that was previously selected.

74 Click on the TABS... button, to bring up the INDENTS/TABS dialog box. Then click the CLEAR button to delete all existing tabs. We will now insert two new tabs. Select the "Left" option and click above the ruler at around ¾ inch. If necessary, drag this tab until the number under the CLEAR button is 0.75. Create a second left tab at 2.5.

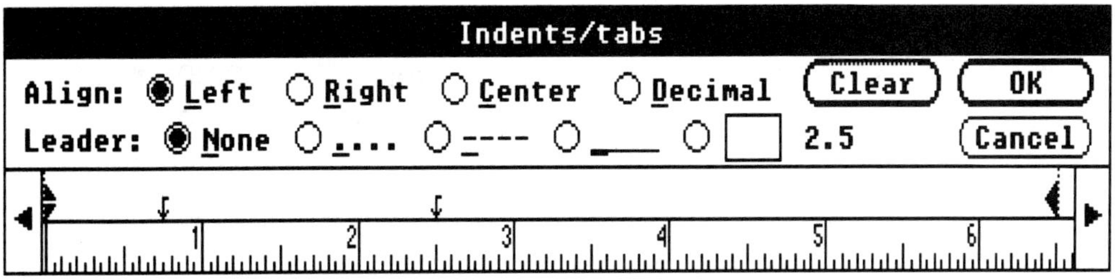

Figure 14.29: *The Indents/Tabs dialog box, containing our specifications for the "Price lists" style sheet.*

75 Notice the indent markers at the beginning of the ruler. The top half of the triangle is moved inward slightly, indicating a first-line indent. Drag this top marker back to zero, eliminating the first-line indent, and click OK.

76 Enter "Price lists" for the style sheet name. Then click OK.

Before we create our price list, we need to create a ruler guide to help us position the first line of text. So drag a guide down from the horizontal ruler to V:7.0. (If you incorrectly position the guide, you will not be able to move it because the LOCK GUIDES command is active. Choose the LOCK GUIDES command from the OPTIONS menu to deactivate it, move your ruler guide, and then reactivate the LOCK GUIDES command.)

78 Scroll down the Styles palette and select the "Price lists" option. This is now the default style sheet. Then select the text tool and click just below our ruler guide. Input the following text:

Number →	Item →	Price ¶
04024 →	LCD clock radio →	139.95 ¶
04025 →	Stereo clock radio →	229.95 ¶
07220 →	Gold-plated watch →	79.95 ¶
07231 →	w/ moon phases →	99.95 ¶

10188 →	Knife sharpener →	69.95 ¶
43899 →	35-func calculator →	24.95 ¶
44899 →	2k data calculator →	34.95 ¶
57002 →	5-speed fan →	49.95 ¶
57305 →	Portable heater →	179.95 ¶
57309 →	Portable AC unit →	249.95 ¶

79 This fills out the length of the first column. Since the content of our text is not important, our second column will be an exact duplicate of the first. Press CTRL-A to select every word in the current text block. Then press CTRL-INSERT to copy the selected text. Press the right arrow (→) key to move to the last character of type in the current text block and press SHIFT-INSERT to paste the copied text.

80 The text is now copied and pasted, but it has yet to be poured into a second column. Select the arrow tool. Then select the price list text block and click on the lower handlebar tab. Your cursor changes to the autoflow icon. Move your cursor to just below the ruler guide in the second column. Then press the CTRL key. Notice how your autoflow cursor changes to a manual flow cursor. The CTRL key will always toggle the autoflow cursor to the manual flow cursor, and vice versa. While the CTRL key is still pressed, click with the manual flow cursor to pour the second column of text. (Incidentally, if your second column text pours a little strangely, select the text tool, click in the second column, press CTRL-A to select all of the text, and reselect the "Price lists" style sheet. This should solve the problem.)

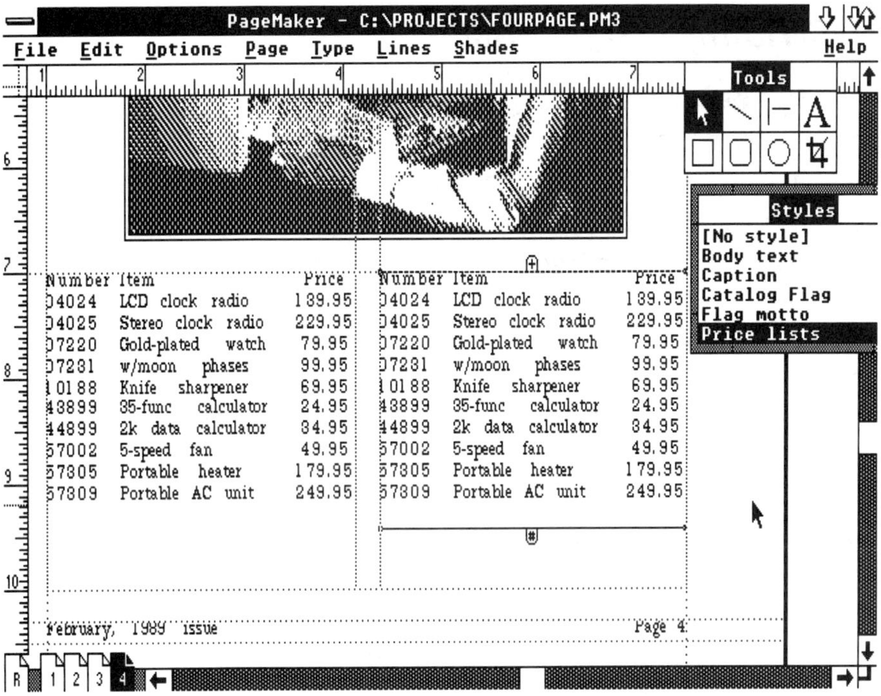

Figure 14.30: *Our two columns of price listings.*

81 Notice that the numbers in our text are aligned rather strangely. The first numbers in each row are flush with each other, so that tens of dollars in one row may line up with hundreds of dollars in another. To fix this, CTRL-click on the "Price lists" style name in the Styles palette. When the EDIT STYLE dialog box appears, click on the TABS... button. The INDENTS/TABS dialog box displays our two left tabs above the ruler. Drag downward on the right tab until your cursor is outside the dialog box. Then release. This dispenses with the inappropriate tab. Now select the "Decimal" option, and create a decimal tab at 2.75. Then click the OK button twice.

Overriding a style sheet

The decimals in the price values now line up, as is most commonly seen in a price list. The only problem left is to visually differentiate the list headings, "Number, Item, Price," from the list itself. We will do this by directly assigning new type specs to the list headings, overriding their style sheet specifications.

82 Select the text tool. Triple-click on the top line of type in the first column. Then press F6 to bold the type. A bold style helps to differentiate the heading from the list items, but the heading needs a little more emphasis. Press CTRL-M to bring up the PARAGRAPH SPECIFICATIONS dialog box, enter 0.15 for the "After" value, and click OK. Now we will rearrange the tabs so the "Price" head is centered above the dollar listings. Press CTRL-I to access the INDENTS/TABS dialog box, drag the decimal tab down to delete it, select the "Left" option, and create a new tab at 2.5. Now drag the first tab from 0.75 to 1.25 inches. This will center the "Item" heading over its column. Click OK.

Notice the Styles palette. The "Price lists" option is followed by a plus sign, indicating that there are certain differences between the selected text and its style sheet. These differences will be retained until you again click on the "Price lists" style sheet while this line of type is selected.

83 Triple-click on the first line of type in the second column and repeat Step 82.

84 Select the perpendicular-line tool. Drag from H:1.0, V:7.25 horizontally to H:7.5, V:7.25. This creates a horizontal line separating our lists heads from the list items. Then press CTRL-S to update your file on disk.

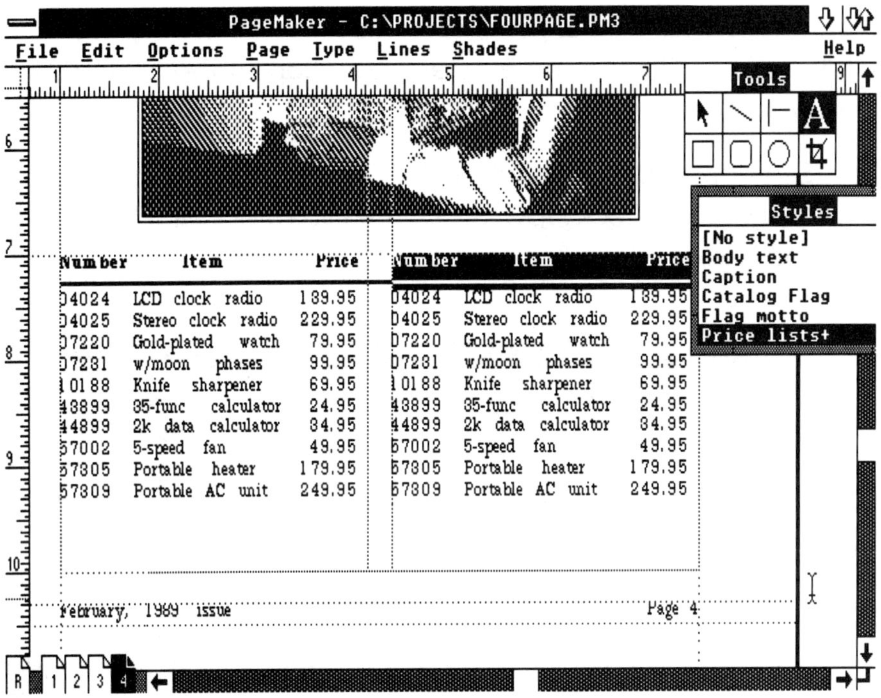

Figure 14.31: *The listing text, complete with distinguishable headings.*

Last-minute clean-up

One important fact about any electronically composed page is that nothing is permanent. If you don't like something, it can be easily changed. We will now take advantage of this fact to modify our catalog.

85 Press CTRL-W to view all of page 4. Notice how close the flag text from the master page is to the scanned photograph. Some white space between the two elements would improve the appearance of this page dramatically. To create this white space, click on the master page icon at the bottom of your screen display.

86 Select the arrow tool and click on the flag text to select it. Drag the text block upward so the top ruler guide aligns with the baseline of the first line of type.

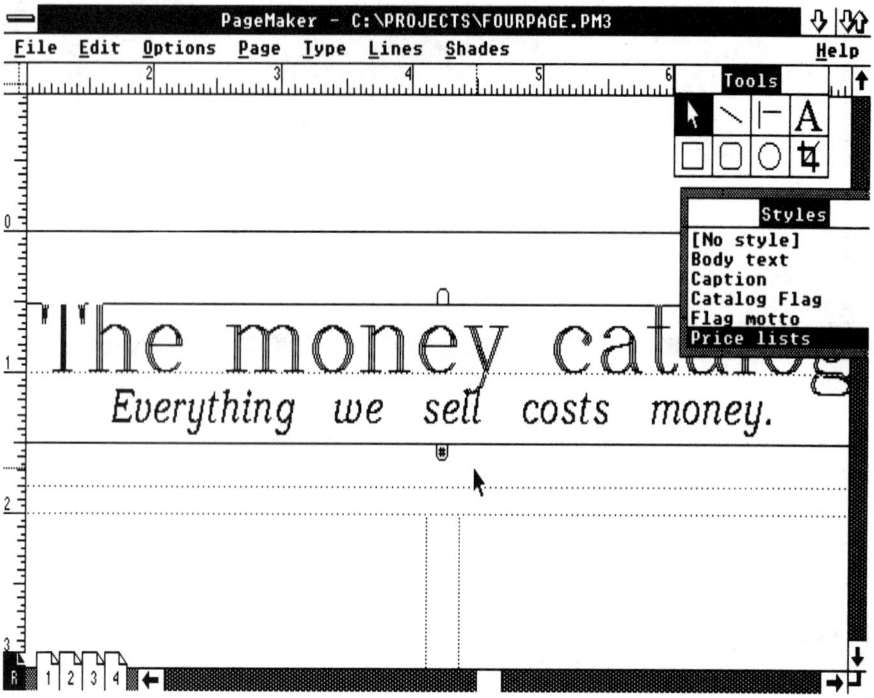

Figure 14.32: *The flag text moved upward to a location that visually complements the page elements.*

87 Now click on the page 4 icon to see what a difference a little effort can make. If you are satisfied, press CTRL-S to update your file on disk.

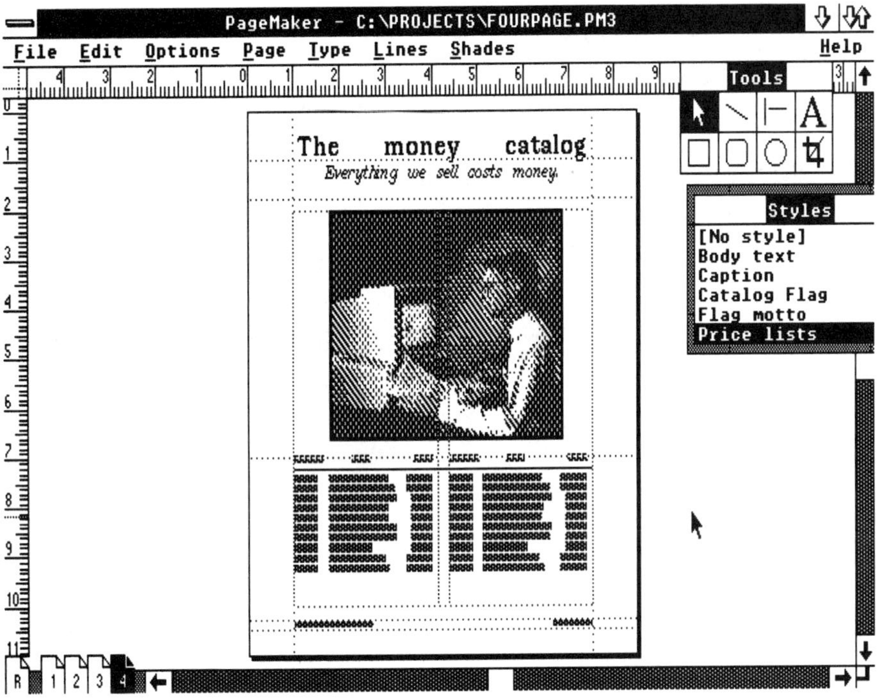

Figure 14.33: *The completed page 4, after moving the flag text.*

Printing the four-page catalog

88 Your catalog is now complete. The only step remaining is to print the finished document. Make sure your printer is turned on and selected in the PRINTER SETUP... dialog box. Then press CTRL-P to access the PRINT TO dialog box. Indicate one copy, and print from page 1 to 4 as described at the end of our first sample project (see Chapter 6, *Creating a Simple Newsletter*). When your flyer is finished printing, examine the pages of your catalog, paying special attention to the results of our text wrapping and image control experiments. Make sure they meet your expectations. If you see any problems, make the necessary changes to your file.

Successfully completing this chapter demonstrates an understanding of the most advanced functions and operations offered by PageMaker. We hope that this project has helped you to better understand the topics covered throughout this book and has provided you with a more developed working knowledge of the PageMaker.

Glossary

Alert dialog box. *A dialog box that warns you of the consequence of a command, and allows you to cancel or confirm it.*

Angle. *The angle formed between the the lines of the halftone grid and the horizontal, where 0 degrees indicates that the horizontal lines of the halftone grid are parallel to the horizontal edges of the page. Used to create special effects with TIFF or paint-type graphics using the* IMAGE CONTROL *command.*

Application defaults. *The settings used in all publications unless a different value or option is chosen. For example, the default type size is 12 points unless it is changed. See Publication defaults.*

Clipboard. *The imaginary board in memory where text and graphics are cut or copied to and pasted from. The clipboard can only hold one selection at a time. If a second selection is copied or cut, it will replace the first selection on the clipboard.*

Color model. *A method of specifying colors using combinations of three or four primary colors. You may use one of three methods in PageMaker: Hue, lightness, saturation (HLS), Cyan, Magenta, Yellow, Black (CMYK), or Red, Green, Blue (RGB).*

Corrupt*. A file or application is corrupted when part of the file has been erased or distorted. This is usually caused by a defective drive, a power surge, or static electricity.*

Crop*. To crop a graphic image is to electronically cut out parts of the graphic so that only a portion of the original shows on the page.*

Default*. A value or option that PageMaker uses unless it is changed. For example, the default type size in new publications is 12 points.*

Dialog box*. a box that appears on the screen when PageMaker needs information. It may contain any combination of radio buttons, text boxes, option boxes, list boxes, and buttons.*

Discretionary hyphen*. A manually inserted hyphen that appears only when it is needed, "disappearing" when it is not needed. Discretionary hyphens are inserted by pressing command -.*

Downloadable fonts*. Laser fonts that are not built into a printer, but which can be loaded into its memory during the printing process. Downloadable fonts can be transferred to the printer manually or automatically.*

Drag-placing*. A graphic or text block is drag-placed by pointing the mouse tool at the object, holding the mouse button down, moving the mouse until the graphic is correctly positioned, then releasing the mouse button.*

Draw-type graphic*. A graphic that is defined by equations describing distance, angle, curvature, etc., which means it can be scaled, rotated, and sheared without sacrificing quality. Opposed to a paint-type graphic.*

EPS*. (Encapsulated PostScript). A kind of draw-type graphic file created using the PostScript language, which allows a tremendous variety of graphic effects without sacrificing quality. A drawing program such as Adobe Illustrator creates PostScript files.*

Export filter*. A translation program built into PageMaker that converts text formatted in PageMaker into a text file so it can be edited in a particular word processor. PageMaker contains filters for most word processors on the Macintosh.*

Fixed space. *An amount of space inserted between characters that does not change when the text is justified.*

Frequency. *The number of halftone cells per square inch of a graphic. The higher the frequency, the finer the detail of the graphic, but the fewer levels of grey available, because fewer machine pixels can fit in the halftone cells.*

Function. *The arrangement of machine pixels in a halftone cell. In a halftone, different arrangements and numbers of machine pixels are used to imitate different levels of grey and to create special effects.*

Graphic boundary segment. *One of at least four dotted straight lines that surrounds a graphic and defines the graphic boundary.*

Graphic boundary. *The dotted line surrounding a graphic that defines how the text can flow around a graphic. The graphic boundary consists of any number of graphic boundary segments which can be moved to fit any irregularly shaped graphic.*

Halftone cell. *a square in the halftone grid containing a number of machine pixels. The halftone cells are used to imitate shades of grey using patterns of very small black dots.*

Halftone grid. *An invisible grid comprised of many halftone cells that overlays a photograph or scanned image in order to convert it to a halftone.*

Halftone. *A representation of a photograph or graphic containing many shades of grey, that is created by converting the greys into different patterns of very small black dots, so the photo can be reproduced in black and white.*

Handle. *The small rectangles surrounding a selected graphic object, text block, or line, and the small solid diamonds in the graphic boundary surrounding a selected graphic. Click the mouse pointer on a handle to change the shape, length, or size of the selected element.*

Handlebars. *The horizontal bars containing tabs at the top and bottom of a text block that appear when it is selected using the arrow tool. Used when resizing or threading text blocks.*

Image control. *The* IMAGE CONTROL... *command can be used to change the brightness and contrast of a scanned image or paint-type graphic, and to create special effects using halftones.*

Import filter. *A translation program built into PageMaker that converts the commands used by a particular word processor to PageMaker commands, so that the indentations, bold and italicized text, centering and justification are preserved. PageMaker also comes with import filters for many graphics programs, so spreadsheets, paint and draw-type graphics, scanned images, and more can be displayed on the page.*

Kerning. *Adjusting the distance between adjacent characters by a tiny amount to avoid*

***Kerning** pairs. A pair of letters that must be kerned to avoid noticeable white spaces. Common kerning pairs are the capital W and A, and capital A and V.*

Machine pixel. *The smallest point a laser printer is capable of printing. The size of the dot depends on the resolution of the printer. A Linotronic imagesetter, for instance, can print 1270 dots in one linear inch.*

Mapping. *See grey-level mapping.*

Grey-level mapping. *An option in the* IMAGE CONTROL... *command used to change the grey levels in a graphic. For instance, the 10% grey level in a scanned image can be changed to 90% grey, or all the white in a graphic can be turned to black and vice versa. Used mainly for special effects.*

Paint-type graphics. *Also called a bit-mapped graphics, these graphics consist of dots at a fixed resolution. They cannot be manipulated as easily as draw-type graphics, but some effects can only be created in this type of file. Common paint-type graphics programs are MacPaint and FullPaint.*

Palette. *A box that can be displayed on the screen containing several options, either frequently used tools, colors, or text styles.*

Pasteboard. *The electronic surface on which the pages in PageMaker's publication window lie, and where text and graphic objects can be temporarily kept.*

Pica. A typographical unit of linear measurement. Six picas approximately equal one inch.

Pixel. The smallest dot that can appear on a monitor, which consists of a rectangular grid of pixels. The higher the resolution of your monitor, the more pixels it can display per inch. A Macintosh SE screen has a pixel density of 72 per vertical inch.

Point. A typographical unit of measurement exactly equal to one twelfth of a pica.

PostScript. A page description language created by Adobe Systems Inc. used by many high resolution laser printers and imagesetters, including the Apple LaserWriter series.

Printer font. A file that is loaded into the RAM memory of printer, which tells the printer precisely how to print all the characters in a type family.

Publication defaults. The settings used in a particular publication unless a different value or option is chosen. Publication defaults apply to a particular publication, and do not carry over to other publications.

Publication. A document created in PageMaker, which may consist of one page or six hundred pages.

Pull-down menu. The list of options that appears you point the mouse arrow at one of the menu titles at the top of the screen and press the mouse button.

RAM. Random Access Memory. A form of temporary memory in a printer or computer where programs and files are kept. Information can be moved around in RAM very quickly, but the information is lost when the power is turned off.

ROM. Read Only Memory. A form of permanent memory that is as fast as RAM, but cannot be changed, and remains even when the power is turned off.. It is often used in laser printers, to store printer fonts so they are always available; for example, the typestyle Palatino is always available on the Apple LaserWriter Plus because it is stored in the printer's ROM memory.

Screen font. *An electronic file used to represent a group of characters on-screen. Screen fonts are loaded with the Font/DA Mover or with utilities like SuitCase and Font Juggler. Screen fonts are usually available in families, containing a set of screen fonts for each type style available.*

Select. *Text blocks, graphic objects, or text itself is selected before some action is applied to it. Objects show that they are selected by displaying handles around their borders, text shows that it is selected by displaying in reverse video (white letters on black background).*

Story. *A single text document threading through multiple text blocks is called a story. Stories can be imported or created in PageMaker.*

Style sheets. *Attributes from the Type specifications dialog, Paragraph specifications dialog, Indents/Tabs dialog and Define colors dialog can be combined onto a single style sheet which can then be quickly applied to any paragraph in a PageMaker publication. Style sheet attributes can be edited, which instantly update all paragraphs to which they have been applied.*

Tabs. *1) An alignment point set in the horizontal ruler, which can force text to align, left, right, centered, or on a decimal point. 2) A small protrusion in a handlebar of a text block, which is used to drag the location of the handlebar. Tabs sometimes contain symbols which indicate whether or not more text exists beyond the current text block.*

Tag. *(Style sheet tags) Used in wordprocessing files to link text paragraphs to defined style sheets. PageMaker can read tags when importing text files, applying style sheet formats, or write tags to exported text files.*

Text block. *An object containing text. Text blocks contain all or part of a text story. When selected, handlebars appear above and below a text block.*

Text-entry cursor. *The I-beam shaped cursor that appears when the text tool is selected from the toolbox. Clicking this text tool sets the insertion point, at which text can be entered. This can also be used to select existing text or to create a new text block.*

Threaded Text. *A story which is contained in more than one text block.*

TIFF. *Tagged Image File Format, a graphic file format developed by Aldus Corporation to hold scanned images and other bit-mapped graphics.*

View sizes. *One of the seven levels of magnification at which the current page(s) of your publication can be displayed. The larger the level of magnification, the less of the page is visible at any one time.*

Window. *A movable and sizable area of the on-screen display which contains some specific information or program element.*

Index

Index

Index

Index

Index

Acknowledgements

The authors would like to thank each of the following people for their assistance and support: Kathi Townes, Aldus PC Technical Support, Bill Gladstone, Susan Glinert, and everyone at Publishing Resources Inc.: Susan Janow, Scott Harmon, Eric Patzer, Tom Midgely, and Brian Griswold. Special thanks (4) to: R.D., S.R., J.G., A.E., and J.M.

Lastly, we would like to recognize the assistance of Juan Thompson in the area of PC technical research and support.

TradeMarks

About the Authors

Craig Danuloff and Deke McClelland provide training and consulting services through Publishing Resources Inc. Their previous work includes; *Desktop Publishing Type & Graphics, Mastering Aldus FreeHand,* and *Mastering Adobe Illustrator 88.*

PUBLISHING RESOURCES INCORPORATED

711 Walnut Street, Suite 200
Boulder, Colorado 80302
303/ 442-8221

Publishing Resources Inc. is a member of the Aldus Authorized Training Program, offering classroom and on-site training in Aldus PageMaker and Aldus FreeHand.